Baseball Magic and Mayhem
in St. Louis

Baseball Magic and Mayhem in St. Louis

The 1926 Cardinals, World Series Champions

Kevin J. Abing

McFarland & Company, Inc., Publishers
Jefferson, North Carolina

ISBN (print) 978-1-4766-9838-0
ISBN (ebook) 978-1-4766-5824-7

LIBRARY OF CONGRESS CATALOGING DATA ARE AVAILABLE

Library of Congress Control Number 2025053352

© 2026 Kevin J. Abing. All rights reserved

No part of this book may be reproduced or transmitted in any form or by any means, electronic or mechanical, including photocopying or recording, or by any information storage and retrieval system, without permission in writing from the publisher.

Front cover image: Photo postcard of the 1926 St. Louis Cardinals (Process Photo Studios)

Printed in the United States of America

*McFarland & Company, Inc., Publishers
Box 611, Jefferson, North Carolina 28640
www.mcfarlandpub.com*

To my dad, Francis,
who passed on his love for the Cardinals,
and to my mom, Mary,
who tolerated, if not indulged, *my* love for the Cardinals

Acknowledgments

Writing this book, by and large, was a solitary undertaking, but several librarians and archivists cheerfully offered their help along the way. Cassidy Lent with the National Baseball Hall of Fame and Museum in Cooperstown provided digital copies of newspaper clippings and articles during the craziness of the Covid-19 pandemic, and her colleague Claudette Scrafford helped track down photos. Charles Brown guided me through manuscript and photo collections at the St. Louis Mercantile Library. Ami Null, Dennis Northcott, and Lauren Sallwasser with the Missouri Historical Society as well as Michael Hancock at the National Archives and Adele Heagney with the St. Louis Public Library patiently answered my numerous questions.

Above all, I want to thank my wife, Laura. Though she is a Milwaukee Brewers fan, her love, encouragement, and excellent editorial skills helped bring this St. Louis Cardinals story to life.

Table of Contents

Acknowledgments	vi
Preface	1
Introduction: The Rise and Fall of a St. Louis Baseball Empire	3
CHAPTER 1. Something New, Something Old	7
CHAPTER 2. The Brain Trust	19
CHAPTER 3. The Cast of Characters	33
CHAPTER 4. Laying Down the Law in Texas: Spring Training, February 21–April 12	50
CHAPTER 5. Cool Bats, Cold Weather: April 13–May 2	59
CHAPTER 6. Highs, Lows, and Courtroom Woes, May 2–May 26	69
CHAPTER 7. "Billy the Kid" and "Ol' Pete" to the Rescue, May 27–June 28	82
CHAPTER 8. Trouble in the Mound City, June 30–July 25	97
CHAPTER 9. The Race Heats Up, July 27–September 2	109
CHAPTER 10. The "Home" Stretch, September 3–September 30	127
CHAPTER 11. Reaching the Mountaintop, October 1–14	146
CHAPTER 12. A Messy Divorce, October–December 1926	168
Epilogue: The Brain Trust Revisited	176
Chapter Notes	181
Bibliography	203
Index	209

Preface

I grew up on our family farm near Platteville, Wisconsin, located in the "driftless area" in the southwest corner of the state. Except for a misguided few, most in my family are diehard St. Louis Cardinals fans—a tiny island of Cardinal red amidst a sea of Brewers and Cubs blue. My grandfather and dad lived on a farm near the hamlet of Potosi, Wisconsin, nestled along the banks of the Mississippi River, and they rooted for the Cardinals primarily because they could listen to them on the radio, St. Louis being the National League's westernmost team at the time. They also admired the aggressive, no-holds-barred brand of baseball the Cardinals played in the 1930s and beyond. When I was a kid, my dad regaled us with stories of Dizzy Dean, Pepper Martin, Frankie Frisch, and others of the famed "Gas House Gang" along with the heroes of the 1940s championship teams—Enos Slaughter, Red Schoendienst, Terry Moore, Marty Marion, and, of course, Stan "the Man" Musial.

Dreams of one day playing second base for the Cardinals filled my head as I, my brother, and our neighbor, Bruce, spent countless hours playing ball in pastures and hay fields. Living in the middle of nowhere, we made do as best we could with just the three of us. One of us pitched, one hit, and the other covered the rest of the field. We then rotated after the hitter made three "outs." Don't ask what constituted an out; the rules changed from one pasture or field to another. It was, in essence, a glorified batting practice. And, truth be told, we probably spent more time looking for baseballs hit into tall grass, hay, or cornfields than actually playing baseball.

Those dreams surged when I tried out for my high school's junior varsity team and stepped on a real baseball field for the first time, one where I didn't need to worry about slipping in cow manure. But the dream quickly crashed and burned when I discovered I couldn't hit a curveball. Hell, who am I kidding? I couldn't hit, *period*! The splinters I collected in my ass from sitting on the bench were tiny stakes driven into the heart of any hope of ever making it to the big leagues.

I'm over the disappointment … now … but my devotion to Cardinals baseball carried on undiminished as I pursued other career paths. Finally, I've reached the stage of my life when I want to combine two great loves (both secondary to my wife, Laura, of course!): history and the St. Louis Cardinals.

For much of the early twentieth century, the Cardinals flailed along as regular occupants of the bottom half of the National League standings. But all that changed in 1926. Led by owner Sam Breadon, general manager Branch Rickey, and player-manager Rogers Hornsby—three of baseball's most influential and enigmatic personalities—the Cardinals survived a furious pennant chase and then brought home a World Series title to a championship-starved city and its long-suffering fans. This book tells the story of that team within the context of Prohibition-era America in general and St. Louis in particular. Many gifted writers have penned histories of the Cardinals franchise, though only one, Paul Doutrich's exceptional *The Cardinals and the Yankees, 1926*, focuses on that specific season.[1] But I want to dive deeper to flesh out the ups, downs, bumps, bruises, twists, and turns the players endured during the grind of that eventful summer.

The blueprint that vaulted the Cardinals to the top of the baseball world in 1926 ushered in a period of sustained success. The Cards won eight National League pennants and five world championships between 1927 and 1946. St. Louis fans braved some lean years in the 1950s and 1970s; however, the Cardinals have been, for the most part, pennant contenders. Still, there is nothing quite like the first glorious taste of championship baseball, and the approaching centennial of the 1926 title is the perfect time to relive that magical turning point in Cardinals history. My grandfather and dad passed away years ago, but I hope, as they sit in their heavenly bleacher seats, they enjoy being regaled with this story of their beloved Redbirds.

Introduction: The Rise and Fall of a St. Louis Baseball Empire

It's no secret St. Louis has always been baseball mad. The origins of the sport in the Mound City are hazy, though most historians credit Jeremiah Fruin as the "father" of baseball in St. Louis. He grew up in Brooklyn, New York, and played baseball with the Charter Oak Club before relocating to St. Louis and making a living as a local contractor. He brought baseball across the Mississippi, introducing the game in the 1850s. It caught on quickly among young boys of the town, but organized clubs weren't formed until 1860 when the Cyclone, Morning Star, Empire and Commercial clubs were established. Those early teams played games on ball fields located along the riverfront east of Broadway and north of North Market Street, at the old fairgrounds, at the "Gamble Lawn Grounds" near the old Rock Springs, and at the former military parade grounds at Lafayette Park. The *Daily Missouri Republican* commented in March 1861 that the "game of base ball now so popular in this as in Eastern cities was ushered in yesterday afternoon by the Cyclone Base Ball Club on their old grounds in Lafayette Park." They played a team made up of players from the other clubs and "a jolly time was had," especially when a player charging to catch a fly ball stepped into a hole which altered his movements into the "lofty tumbling of a gymnast." But the paper happily noted the pockmarked playing field was "soon to be remedied, as the clubs have petitioned the Common Council for the privilege of leveling the same at their own expense."[1]

Civic boosters aimed for a higher level of baseball. In the fall of 1874, a group of wealthy citizens formed a stock company and raised $20,000 to organize a professional baseball team, christened the Brown Stockings, or Browns for short. Their plan was to join the National Association of Professional Baseball Players for the 1875 season. The stock company then procured "twelve experts in the national game," primarily from the Brooklyn Atlantics. In April 1875, veteran Atlantics outfielder John C. Chapman explained to a reporter that he and his Brooklyn teammates bolted the East Coast for St. Louis because the city was "bound to be the greatest place on the continent for base ball this season." It was a matter of civic pride to the "very rich and nice people" who formed the company because they wanted "their city ably represented in base ball." St. Louis townsfolk, he added, "are all agog with base ball excitement. Five thousand people witnessed our practice game last week." But the primary reason for the switch was no doubt the "big inducements" the stock company offered.[2]

The stock company's sizable investment proved to be a success. During its inaugural season, the Browns became the league's top gate attraction, drawing an average of 2,300 fans to games at Grand Avenue Park (later renamed Sportsman's Park), where a diamond had been laid out in 1866. But the National Association folded after the 1875 season, succumbing to a floundering economy, dishonest and drunken players, erratic scheduling, and poorly financed small market teams. The Browns were among the more profitable clubs to join the newly formed National League in 1876. The team finished second with a 45–19 record, but the following year, gambling scandals tainted the Browns and the entire league's reputation. Disillusioned St. Louis fans stayed away in droves, and team owners dissolved the organization.[3]

To fill this gap in the city's sporting scene, sportswriters Alfred H. Spink and his brother, William, created a makeshift semi-pro team and resurrected the Brown Stockings (and interchangeable Browns) name. Though the Browns cruised to one victory after another, St. Louis baseball fans reacted unenthusiastically. Many still harbored a grudge against the game, and the new iteration of the Browns played before sparse crowds during the 1879 and 1880 seasons.

At this juncture, an unlikely savior resuscitated professional baseball in St. Louis. Chris Von der Ahe was born in Germany in 1848—though he claimed he was born in 1851, perhaps a ruse to avoid compulsory military service—and immigrated to the United States as a teenager. Like many of his Teutonic brethren, Von der Ahe made his way to the Midwest. He settled in St. Louis and began his working career as a grocery clerk. By 1874, he had accumulated enough wealth to purchase the spacious Golden Lion Saloon, just one block from Grand Avenue Park. Ned Cuthbert, Browns player-manager and occasional bartender, convinced Von der Ahe there was a direct correlation between baseball games and increased beer consumption at his saloon. Chris needed little prodding from Cuthbert to capitalize on that link and secure concession rights at Grand Avenue Park. But this venture was endangered when the ballpark owner threatened to dismantle the run-down stadium. To protect his interests, Von der Ahe plunged into a bold but economically risky venture to help finance desperately needed renovations of the newly renamed Sportsman's Park.[4]

To some, Von der Ahe cut a comic figure as an owner. His grasp of baseball's finer points was shaky, and his thick German accent and mangling of the English language amused rivals and friends alike. He was flamboyant, self-absorbed, and an inveterate womanizer. He also possessed a volcanic temper. Author Edward Achorn likened him to a combination of George Steinbrenner, Charlie Finley, and Bill Veeck with a "splash" of Yogi Berra.[5] Chris reveled in being "der poss bresident," but he was no fool. He shrewdly perceived that baseball and a day at the ballpark could be entertaining. The refurbished Sportsman's Park would be the cornerstone of a baseball renaissance on the city's west end, luring large crowds with cheap ticket prices, Sunday baseball, and plenty of beer for sale. His scheme worked. Working-class fans loved the antics he staged, and crowds once again thronged to the ballpark in 1881. The Browns' success piqued the interest of other independent ball clubs, and Von der Ahe and eight fellow owners thumbed their noses at the established National League, whose owners appealed to a respectable middle- and upper-class fan base. They charged an outlandish 50 cents for tickets and frowned upon Sunday baseball and selling beer at games. Von der Ahe and his fellow rebels formed their own professional league, the American Association, which appealed to the laboring masses looking for a brief respite from their daily drudgery.[6]

The new league opened for the 1882 season and prospered immediately in comparison to the staid National League. Thanks to 25-cent seats, scheduled Sunday games, and free-flowing beer, the average attendance at American Association games outpaced National League games by 30 percent. The Browns finished next to last that first season, but it did not take long for Von der Ahe to assemble a baseball dynasty. Under the leadership of first baseman and manager Charles Comiskey, the Brown Stockings finished in second place in 1883, one game behind the pennant-winning Philadelphia Athletics. St. Louis then reeled off four consecutive pennants from 1885 to 1888 and championship wins against the National League in 1885 and 1886.[7]

The team's fortunes faded thereafter, coinciding with the collapse of the American Association in 1891. Internal strife prompted Cincinnati and Brooklyn to jump to the National League; other franchises went bankrupt; and both the National League and the new Players' League siphoned off several star players. The Browns were especially hard hit, losing seven players, including Comiskey. When the American Association folded, St. Louis and three other teams joined the National League in 1892, but the Browns continued to stumble in the standings. Von der Ahe, plagued by excessive drinking and scandalous love affairs, became so irrational that league owners stripped him of the franchise, which was purchased by brothers Frank and Stanley Robison. The new owners changed team uniforms to include bright red socks for the 1899 season with the forlorn hope the switch might improve the team's luck. But the newly dubbed Cardinals fared no better. For the next two and a half decades, St. Louis baseball fans suffered through a distinct "era of failure." The Cardinals and the American League counterpart Browns (a new franchise that moved from Milwaukee after the 1901 season and named to remind fans of the Von der Ahe dynasty) were mired in mediocrity with occasional glimpses of inspired play. One author deemed the Browns the "most storied and least able teams of all time." Another called the St. Louis clubs "arguably the two worst teams in the history of the game since 1901."[8]

Things changed, for the Cardinals, at least, in 1926. Prior to that season, the team slowly but surely assembled the building blocks that propelled St. Louis to the top of the heap in the National League. Seasoned veterans like Rogers Hornsby, Jess Haines, and Bill Sherdel provided a steady presence. Hungry young ballplayers such as Jim Bottomley, Les Bell, Tommy Thevenow, Chick Hafey, and Taylor Douthit earned their stripes climbing through multiple levels of Branch Rickey's farm system and then blossomed in the major leagues. And shrewd trades for Bob O'Farrell, Billy Southworth, and legendary pitcher Grover Cleveland Alexander sparked the surge that put St. Louis over the top.

The Cardinals' triumphant journey did not occur in a vacuum. Sweeping changes engulfed American society in the 1920s, and those changes presented opportunities and obstacles for the Cardinals as the team labored through the baseball schedule. To tell the story fully and place the season within a wider context, the first chapter describes the currents of change swirling throughout the country, in St. Louis, and within Major League Baseball. Succeeding chapters begin with brief vignettes of the people, places, and events that shaped life in St. Louis.

Those subsequent chapters tell the story of that season of magic and mayhem. Chapter Two is dedicated to the triumvirate who put the pieces of the championship team together. Owner Sam Breadon, general manager Branch Rickey, and player-manager Rogers Hornsby provided brilliant and inspired leadership on the way to the World Series title, but their combustible personalities tore the relationship apart only months later. The next chapter peers into the life stories of the interesting cast of characters who composed the team. The rest of the book traces the Cardinals' trek from spring training through the World Series and beyond. Cardinal fans were understandably exhilarated as their diamond heroes erased years of disappointment, but the shocking developments after the World Series punctured and deflated their euphoria. Their angst, however, soon disappeared as the Cardinals emerged as a perennial powerhouse.

With that, the stage is set to tell the story of the 1926 St. Louis Cardinals. It's time to play ball!

Chapter 1

Something New, Something Old

The National Scene

American society has always been subject to the precarious push of modernization and the comfortable pull of tradition. Eventually, those who cling, either by circumstances or personal inclination, to the "good 'ol days" give way to change's steady forward march but not without determined resistance. At times, the pace and depth of change becomes so intense that the stark contrast between modernists and traditionalists gives the impression of two separate, incompatible societies vying with one another for supremacy. We are experiencing this phenomenon in the twenty-first century, with its dizzying technological changes and strident culture wars. The 1960s was another such period, and the tension between progress and tradition was equally evident in America during the 1920s.

The American people emerged from World War I disillusioned by the conflict's senseless carnage. They lost their optimistic faith in human progress and tired of the crusading reforms of the Progressive Era.[1] What they wanted, according to President Warren Harding, was a "return to normalcy," but millions wanted something different to replace outdated traditions and morals. They redirected their focus to their own personal fulfillment and acquisition of the good things in life.[2]

They had an increased amount of time and money with which to conduct their soul-searching. Technological advances enabled businesses to churn out more consumer goods than ever, lowering the cost of living and raising the standard of living to make the U.S. the most prosperous country in the world. Installment buying, or buying on credit, made expensive durable consumer goods available even to families of limited means. Consequently, Americans embarked on a voracious spending spree. By the mid-1920s, 11 million U.S. households had a phonograph, 17.5 million had a telephone, and 10 million had a car. The automobile profoundly changed the way Americans lived more than any other innovation. It linked rural America to the outside world, reducing the isolation of villages and farms, and changed the morals of young people. The new "science" of advertising fueled the public's appetite for more by hinting about the unfortunate consequences of not owning a particular item. With the backing of the federal government and the widespread approval of the American public, business, in essence, became the new national religion.[3]

Labor-saving appliances not only gave many unprecedented amounts of leisure time but also helped create subcultures among the young and women who rebelled against the strictures of traditional society. More young people than ever attended high school and drew increased attention from advertisers, emerging for the first time as influencers of American society. Women likewise capitalized on evolving societal boundaries to enjoy a more liberated lifestyle. More worked outside the home than ever before, and they challenged Victorian norms by wearing flimsier dresses with rising hemlines, sporting shorter bobbed haircuts, drinking and/or smoking in public, and adopting a more open attitude toward sex. These so-called "Flappers" became the iconic symbol of the decade.[4]

Americans had numerous recreational outlets to occupy their growing leisure time. Going to the movies was the most popular form of entertainment during the "Roaring 20s." The movie industry and its mass-produced films became an economic giant and an influential purveyor of American culture. Box office revenues soared from $301 million in 1921 to $720 million in 1929, more than four times the receipts of all spectator sports and live theatre combined.[5] Listening to the radio was the second most popular leisure activity. By 1926, five million homes in the U.S. had radios and 21 million more had ordered sets. The variety of entertainment provided by the new medium "appeared to collapse time and space." Distance became irrelevant, and the gap between urban and rural cultures narrowed because both audiences listened to the same news, sporting events, and music. By "bringing the world into the home," radio helped create a nationalized mass culture.[6]

Despite radio's clamoring for the public's attention, reading—magazines and especially newspapers—was widespread. The exploding popularity of tabloids transformed the way news was presented, emphasizing sex, crime, sports, and celebrity gossip. Many newspapers mimicked the style to compete. The histrionic stream of information, or "ballyhoo," from newspapers, magazines, radio, advertising, and publicity agents created a culture of celebrity. Frenzied fans could not get enough stories about movie star Rudolph Valentino, aviator Charles Lindbergh, or a slew of sports stars, such as Red Grange, Bill Tilden, Jack Dempsey, and Babe Ruth, the king of "ballyhoo." The "roar" of the 1920s reflected American society's seemingly headlong embrace of excess and counter-culturalism. The "drive for higher and longer, for faster or, simply, for more became a national preoccupation."[7]

But not for everyone. The excesses of the age alarmed cultural conservatives from small towns and rural areas in the Midwest and South. To them, the country's moral decay was evident in the greed and amorality of America's urban mass consumer society, rising divorce rates, increased crime, and the popularity of sensual jazz music, which led to suggestive new dances like the Charleston and the shimmy.[8]

They believed the bewildering social forces emanating from urban America caused individuals to question traditional morals or grasp at "new sources of moral and ethical guidance." Sociologists attributed this alienation to modern society where people lost their "cultural moorings as they jostled for living space and employment, often in dehumanizing conditions." Religious worship or community activity could not alleviate their frustration. In response to this crisis of faith, some modernists attempted to adapt religion to connect with 1920s sensibilities, but this religious flexibility elicited bitter condemnation from fundamentalists who adhered to literal interpretations of the Bible. Evangelists and gifted "showmen" such as Aimee Semple McPherson and former baseball player Billy Sunday enthralled millions of Americans yearning for continuity amidst the radical changes engulfing the country. Sunday, especially, with his hyperphysical preaching style, gave voice to the ever more strident and vengeful attitude toward the forces undermining American culture. Modernists and conservative religious leaders clashed across the South and Midwest, climaxing with the Scopes "Monkey Trial" of 1925 which gripped the attention of the entire nation.[9]

Part of the religious concerns among White, Anglo-Saxon Protestants stemmed from the huge influx of Eastern European immigrants, the vast majority of whom were Roman Catholic or Jewish. U.S. "natives" feared the culture and lifestyle of these newcomers threatened traditional American society and fanned suspicion that they would insidiously introduce the virus of international communism to undermine the country's political stability. Heightened fear sparked a nativist backlash and resulted in immigration quotas aimed specifically at unwelcome foreign elements. At a more grassroots level, the determination to root out perceived threats to WASP's social status gave rise to a resurgent Ku Klux Klan.[10] Prohibition was yet another attempt to enforce old-time morality in the U.S., but it was a losing battle from the beginning. The federal government lost $500 million dollars annually in liquor tax revenue and spent millions to enforce nationwide temperance through the Volstead Act. But the government hired only 1,500 federal agents to police the activities of 100 million people in a country that had 3.5 million square miles of territory and 18,700 miles of coastline and borders.

In one sense, Prohibition was a success; Americans did drink less. However, Prohibition's hoped-for moral transformation never materialized because the American public's thirst for a drink was insatiable. The "dry" law essentially made criminals of millions of U.S. citizens, who brewed beer or distilled spirits in their homes, and it fostered the growth of organized crime, which raked in billions of dollars and used those profits to bribe less than zealous and poorly paid Prohibition agents. Bootleggers fanatically protected their share of the pie, inevitably sparking violent turf wars among rival factions. The national murder rate climbed by nearly a third after Prohibition started. The hypocrisy, criminality, corruption, mayhem, and murder during the "noble experiment" continued until it mercifully perished in 1933.[11]

From the Banks of the Mississippi

St. Louis of the 1920s experienced the same push-pull effects of the nation's modern vs. traditional struggle. Though a hustling commercial and industrial center and the seventh largest city in the U.S. with an estimated 840,000 residents in 1926, St. Louis was in many respects still a patchwork of smaller, insular conservative ethnic communities.[12] Since its founding in 1764, a mixture of French, Spanish, New England Yankees, and American Southerners bestowed a cultural mix that was part frontier, part Southern, and part bustling urban center upon the community. The area's abundant natural resources—plenty of timber, numerous springs, stone outcroppings, easy access to the river, and a gently sloping plateau ensconced beyond a rocky bluff well above the Mississippi's flood waters, along with its location 18 miles below the confluence of the Missouri and Mississippi rivers—guaranteed the city would thrive as a point of transit and trade.[13]

As settlement in the region increased, buoyed by the tremendous influx of German and Irish immigrants in the 1830s and 1840s, the St. Louis economy evolved into a commercial hub and later into an industrial center. The Germans were looking for a better life for their families or fleeing political persecution after failed revolutions in their homeland in 1848. Though they clung to their native language, read German-language newspapers, attended private German schools, and participated in numerous German societies, or *vereins*, they melded relatively easily into the American economic and political systems. Several became prominent business leaders, especially within the brewing industry.

The Irish who migrated to St. Louis largely occupied the other end of the socioeconomic spectrum. The devastating potato famine of the 1840s pushed thousands off the Emerald Isle. Those who made it to St. Louis established sizable enclaves called Tipperary and Kerry Patch. The latter, a notoriously violent and dilapidated area of ramshackle wooden housing on the city's near north side, was a "constantly shifting district, ebbing and flowing with northwestern in-and-out migrants."[14]

St. Louis' ethnic mix was bolstered in the late 19th and early 20th centuries when thousands of Italian immigrants from Lombard arrived. They clustered in the "Little Italy" neighborhood surrounding Columbus Square at Tenth and Carr streets and in an area in southwest St. Louis just beyond Kingshighway, which the locals dubbed "Dago Hill." After 1900, Italians from Sicily poured into both neighborhoods. A gang of roughs known as the Green Ones (a.k.a. Green Onions) started extorting money from "Little Italy" businesses and resorted to murder if the merchants didn't pay. When the criminal activity and violence became too much, many law-abiding Italians fled to "the Hill." By the mid–1920s, more than 5,000 first and second-generation Italians resided there; most were young men who worked in local brickyards, clay mines, and foundries. Once on the Hill, most residents spent their entire lives in the tightly knit neighborhood, sustained by the vibrant social network of churches, schools, local businesses, and mutual aid societies.[15]

St. Louis' sizable Black population also clustered in constricted areas, though not by choice. Prior to World War I, African Americans comprised six percent of the city's population, and de facto segregation maintained the distance between the races. Black children played in separate park playgrounds and attended separate schools. Blacks sat in segregated areas in theaters and at Sportsman's Park and were excluded from White hotels, restaurants, and barber shops. St. Louis voters took things a step further in 1916 when they approved a segregation ordinance that prohibited a person of one race from moving to a block in which 75 percent of the residents were of another race. Court injunctions and a Supreme Court decision declaring such ordinances unconstitutional prevented it from being implemented, but discriminatory sales practices by the St. Louis Real Estate Exchange and restrictive deed covenants by organized White homeowner associations continued to confine Blacks to fringe or decaying areas. In 1922, White residents of the 4500 block of Cote Brilliante Avenue established a covenant that restricted the sale or renting of properties on the block to African Americans. However, in September 1925, Agnes Tegethoff rented the premises at 4517–4519 Cote Brilliante to a Black family. Tegethoff's neighbors objected and filed suit to enforce the covenant. In July 1926, Judge John W. Calhoun, though sympathizing with the tenants' plight, issued a court order that the Black family must vacate in 30 days. According to the *Globe-Democrat*, nine more suits to oust African American families from the block were pending.[16]

The racial separation did not deter thousands of African Americans from relocating to St. Louis, lured by abundant factory jobs during World War I. The number of Black residents soared to 70,000 by 1920. Most of the new arrivals settled in the Ville and Mill Creek neighborhoods on the north side. Denied access to services at many local businesses, African Americans developed their own religious, social, educational, and business institutions within their hemmed-in areas. A lively blues and jazz musical scene emerged, most notably at venues such as the Rosebud Café or Booker T. Washington Theater where Cab Calloway, Eubie Blake, and Bessie Smith made names for themselves. Though segregation proscribed Black musicians from playing with White musicians in public places, they mingled together after hours in local nightclubs.[17]

By the 1920s, St. Louis remained a "spatially divided place." While the central business corridor continued to prosper, city elites preferred life on the affluent west end. Most of the city's ethnic populations continued to be crammed into the areas to the north and south, especially near the river, what author Eric Sandweiss called poor "fenced off corners."[18]

The changes sweeping the nation during the 1920s slowly but surely infiltrated the city, including those fenced off corners. The frenetic Progressive-era civic improvement activity slowed during the post–World War I hangover. Property owners, especially in heavily German areas, resisted widespread city improvements, fearing they would bear the brunt of increased taxes. Historian James Neal Primm noted this conservative stance "amounted to civic neglect."[19] But St. Louis residents eventually embraced the Roaring Twenties' hectic change of pace, approving an $87 million bond issue in 1923 for city improvements. Flush with the infusion of cash, city leaders embarked on a furious drive to give the city a facelift. The street lighting system was electrified and synchronized. City engineers transformed the "aromatic"

River des Pères into an underground sewer. Olive and Market streets were widened to spur development downtown, and Gravois Avenue and Natural Bridge Avenue on the south and north sides respectively were straightened and widened. A flurry of construction projects—Memorial Plaza, Kiel Auditorium, Civil Courts Building, Masonic Temple, and Scottish Rite Cathedral—transformed the city. In 1926 alone, St. Louis added ten new office buildings, 76 factories/workshops, 39 theaters/amusement places, seven churches, six hotels, three banks, 19 schools, 40 warehouses, and three hospitals.[20]

St. Louis' manufacturing and commercial enterprises likewise benefited during the boom period. Long known as "Shoe City," St. Louis churned out more than 53 million pairs of shoes in 1924. In 1926, the value of its shoe output topped $250 million. Industry leaders estimated one in every five people in the U.S. wore shoes manufactured in St. Louis. Some 4,000 light and heavy industrial manufacturers also buoyed the Mound City economy. It was a national leader in hardware, woodworking, and electrical manufacturing and boasted nine auto parts manufacturers. The city produced manufactured goods worth more than $1 billion in 1926, ushering in "the greatest prosperity in many a year."[21]

An unwanted consequence of the city's industrial expansion was the ever-present smoke caused by Illinois soft coal used by factories, trains, and local residences. In 1924, a smoke detector installed at Shaw's Garden determined that each St. Louis resident inhaled 15 tablespoons of soot every five days, and emissions killed trees in Forest Park. In June 1926, the *St. Louis Star* urged the city to "kill the smoke demon." Besides being a disgrace to a progressive community, the smoke stoked annual costs of $15,500,000 for higher hospital and doctor bills, cleaning and dry-cleaning needs, and electrical use to counter the sooty darkness. The *Star* thought the exorbitant figure to be "well calculated to shake St. Louisans out of their lethargy of indifference, of placid acceptance of smoke as part of the price of city life." But the situation had not improved by year's end. On December 13, the *Post-Dispatch* quipped, "Presumably the sun rose, but whether it did nobody knows."[22]

The ever-present haze may have cast a pall over the city, but it did not deter St. Louis residents' head-long rush to embrace the Roaring Twenties' cultural and technological changes. Auto ownership in St. Louis exploded. During the first six months of 1926, the number of vehicle owners tallied 138,607, easily surpassing the total licenses issued in all of 1925. More than 300 periodicals and newspapers accelerated the city's cultural homogenizing process, informing readers about the country's latest fashion trends, celebrity gossip, sporting news, and crime sprees. Seven radio stations, most notably KMOX, WIL, and KSD, added their voices to the burgeoning consumer culture. Even sports, especially baseball, became a "handmaiden for Americanization," loosening the iron grip youth gangs had on nearly every Italian American boy. Ballplayers like Tony Lazzeri and Joe DiMaggio were heroes to kids such as the Hill's most famous products, Yogi Berra and Joe Garagiola.

Neighborhood teams helped many Italian kids adapt to mainstream American society while preserving their community and ethnic subculture.[23]

Prohibition, of all the cultural "innovations" of the 1920s, encountered the most severe resistance among the city's ethnic subcultures as consuming alcohol was the "backbone of family traditions and get-togethers." St. Louis' numerous breweries and distilleries happily met the pre–1920s demand and poured out ample supplies of beer, wine, and stronger spirits to the city's Italian, Irish, and German drinkers. By 1915, beer brewing was the Mound City's fourth most important industry. Counting production value, tax revenue, salaries, and affiliated businesses, beer brewing was a $140 million industry. But Prohibition tried to wring the industry dry. It shuttered 14 of St. Louis' 21 breweries and rendered some 40,000 brewery-related jobs unnecessary. The value of production declined from $26 million in 1914 to $4.8 million by 1929.[24]

Some breweries soldiered on as best they could. The behemoth Anheuser-Busch Brewery once occupied 70 city blocks and had 150 buildings. Owner August A. "Gussie" Busch vowed to keep the company operating, much to the relief of its 7,000 employees. He sold one-half of the company's unneeded icehouses, warehouses, and other holdings, borrowed extensively from friends and banks, and sold most of the animals kept at his home, Grant's Farm. Though the company lost millions from 1919 to 1921, it survived by creatively diversifying its product lines. It converted its wagon shop into a manufacturing plant for rail cars and truck bodies. It made refrigeration cabinets, ice cream, a malt-based soft drink called Bevo, corn sugar, corn oil, livestock feed, a nonalcoholic beer, and a product called Malt-Nutrine for nursing mothers. Anheuser-Busch's most profitable endeavors were the production of Budweiser Barley Malt Syrup, introduced in 1921, and Budweiser Yeast. The latter was unveiled in 1926 when the brewery installed a plant in one of its idle buildings, capable of producing ten tons of yeast daily. It wasn't difficult to pinpoint the reason for their popularity. Both were key ingredients for the illegal, but flourishing, home-brew trade. Years later, Gussie admitted, "We ended up as the biggest bootlegging supply house in the United States."[25]

Truly, St. Louisans flouted Prohibition laws. Italian immigrants viewed saloons as social refuges and hated the Puritanical bent of the 18th Amendment. The rest of the city felt the same way. As Gary Ross Mormino wrote in *Immigrants on the Hill*, rural Missourians, who consistently supported the "drys," must have considered St. Louis and Kansas City, which "staunchly opted wet," as a modern-day Sodom and Gomorrah. It didn't help that St. Louis flaunted the fact that 2,152 of the state's 3,504 saloons were in the city. Despite "dry" efforts to clamp down on drinking, there was no shortage of places where a man or woman could quench their thirst. While many of the city's saloons remained open as soft drink parlors, half defied the law and continued to sell liquor. Thousands distilled their own spirits or made "home brew" in cellars and garages, and some 14,000 "beer flats" dotted the city's landscape. Bootlegging became extremely profitable, supplying alcohol to the city's approximately

1,000 speakeasies. Someone asked a policeman where a person could find some liquid refreshment, and the officer responded that "the coal dealers in the next block was the only place in St. Louis where he can't get a drink!"

Alcohol consumption actually declined by at least one-half during Prohibition, perhaps due to the high cost of illegal liquor or because a good deal of moonshine liquor was adulterated and even poisonous. Several St. Louis residents died drinking the hard stuff, especially wood alcohol. But someone, somewhere, picked up the slack. Arrests for drunkenness nearly tripled between 1920 (1,861 arrests) and 1925 (5,092 arrests), and the number of alcoholics treated at City Hospital surged 74 percent from 1914 to 1919 to 1920–1925.[26]

The obscene profits made from bootlegging naturally attracted the attention of organized crime. Gangs were present in St. Louis prior to Prohibition, but their activities were generally restricted to robbery, extortion, etc. After the 18th Amendment criminalized alcohol production, many residents became bootleggers, producing wine, moonshine, and other beverages for their own consumption. Organized street gangs quickly infiltrated the lucrative, but often dangerous, traffic of illegal liquor. Capitalizing on connections with well-oiled crime syndicates in Chicago and Detroit, St. Louis mobsters ingratiated themselves as part of the city's economic, social, and political fabric. No less than six gangs took part in bootlegging operations once Prohibition started, but four "families" emerged as the leading power brokers in St. Louis. Two Irish American organizations, Egan's Rats and the "Jellyroll" Hogan gang, rose to the top initially. The intense competition for supremacy sparked vicious gang wars in the early 1920s. The Sicilian Green Onion gang had terrorized Little Italy merchants for years, but they diversified their operations to include bootlegging and protection money. Almost immediately, they engaged in a murderous battle with the archrival Cuckoo gang, a struggle that lasted into the early 1930s. The intensified violence caused a dramatic spike in St. Louis' murder rate, increasing seven-fold between 1912 and 1927. In 1923 alone, police attributed 25 unsolved murders to disputes among criminals, and some 60 killings resulted from the Green Onion–Cuckoo gang fray.[27]

Federal agents and local police were unable to do much to stem the deteriorating situation. St. Louis residents neither supported Prohibition laws nor the people enforcing them. The less than avid backing caused high turnover among disillusioned federal agents already overwhelmed by seemingly impossible expectations. The danger on the city's streets—46 policemen were killed in the line of duty during the decade—surely did not help morale. It's small wonder that several of those supposed to police things often succumbed to temptation and accepted bribes to look the other way.[28]

The National Pastime

To paraphrase an old adage, entertainment imitates life, and as one of the most popular forms of entertainment in the 1920s, baseball mirrored the trends and turmoil that defined the decade. As Mitchell Nathanson wrote in *A People's History of Baseball*, the game "symbolically and conceptually speaking is America." Being the national pastime, it has borne "significant emblematic weight" throughout its history because it's been used "to inform us as to our national values and beliefs, to promote and reaffirm what it means to be an American, to define the essence of our country." But it also "permits us to see our collective selves at something less than our best." Thus, its shortcomings "in a way, defined us, represented us, and told us who we are."[29]

At the dawn of the Prohibition era, Americans were a people in search of more—more fun, excitement, and money. Unfortunately, their collective greed often corrupted that search. Baseball was no different. From its earliest days, baseball and gambling were intertwined. Betting occasionally became so intrusive that gamblers and players conspired to fix games. Some players, like gifted first baseman Hal Chase, notoriously and openly courted bribes. Yet owners, despite public declarations about keeping the game pure, rarely confronted the elephant in the room. The news that several members of the Chicago White Sox threw the 1919 World Series against the Cincinnati Reds forced the owners to finally act. Facing the possibility of declining attendance by angry, disillusioned fans, owners turned to federal judge Kenesaw Mountain Landis to become Major League Baseball's first commissioner.

If the owners hoped to somehow control Landis, they badly miscalculated. His over-the-top, glory-seeking behavior in court generated a great deal of publicity, yet his questionable legal decisions were often overturned by superior courts. But several factors worked in his favor as he became the new baseball czar. He was an avid baseball fan determined to protect the integrity of the game as he viewed it, and the owners appreciated the way he delayed a decision in the defunct Federal League's anti-trust lawsuit against the American and National Leagues until the rival league folded and the problem simply went away. Moreover, he *looked* like a judge. He was short and slight of build, but his shock of wild gray hair, his "craggy visage and scowl ... virtually oozed moral rectitude."[30] The owners gave him unfettered power to police the game, and he wasted little time exercising that power. He banned eight White Sox players for life for their part in the "Black Sox Scandal" and embarked on an extended—though inconsistent—crusade to stamp out gambling's corrosive effect on the game.[31]

Landis' stern hand helped restore the public's faith in the game, perhaps because he represented, like President Harding, a return to "normalcy." Once the stench of scandal dissipated, baseball, like the country at large, experienced a boom period or "Golden Age" during the 1920s. With increased leisure time, millions of fans flocked to major league parks seeking an escape from life's more serious problems. Average club attendance increased 50 percent from the previous decade, spurred by the accelerated growth of cities and small towns and the proliferation of automobiles, which made it easier for people in the suburbs and rural areas to attend games.

The dramatic expansion of radio ownership spread the "gospel" of baseball nationwide, giving people who had few opportunities to attend games the next best thing—a sense of immediacy following their teams and heroes that newspapers lacked. Most major league owners and sportswriters were openly hostile or cautiously suspicious of broadcasting baseball games. Owners feared it would hurt attendance if fans could listen to games for free from the comfort of their homes, while sportswriters suspected it would undermine their position as the most important source of baseball information. In 1924, the Chicago Cubs were the first to allow regular broadcasts and showed that radio made the sport available to an audience well beyond the home team's city. It took years, however, for club owners to fully appreciate the new medium's financial possibilities. Nevertheless, it was clear radio had become big business, and the synergy between it and baseball could not be ignored for long.

All these developments generated substantial profits for major league owners, though the wealth was not evenly distributed. The Yankees easily outpaced all other clubs in that regard. Nor did the players, baseball's "working class," uniformly enjoy the fruits of their labors with boosts in salaries. The owners possessed every advantage to control labor costs and imposed a two-tiered wage system. Babe Ruth, Rogers Hornsby, and other big stars secured lucrative contracts because they drew fans to the ballpark. But most players' wages failed to keep pace with the industry's profits.[32]

The sport also reflected urban-rural tensions in the U.S. Its links to the country's past gave it a "compelling power" among American sports fans.[33] Promoters idealized the game's rural origins and imbued it with cherished American values, in the process elevating the game to the lofty status of a "civil religion." It was a democratic game that could be played anywhere by anyone. It offered opportunities to those who worked hard and had the talent, no matter their background. The game molded good character, emphasizing honesty, good sportsmanship, and clean living, and its intense competition reflected Americans' belief in "rugged individualism" and "free competitive order." Players succeeded with initiative, hustle, and a fighting spirit.

But this rosy portrayal clashed with the realities of increasing urbanism, immigration, and self-indulgence. Nevertheless, sportswriters of the 1920s tried to preserve baseball's rural connections. They often pointed to the rural backgrounds of many of the game's best players, where they learned the value of hard work and self-reliance. They played for the love of the game and were uncorrupted by city vices. On the other hand, "city boys" (or their moral equivalent "college boys") tended to "live big, go to the best restaurants, drive sports cars, stay at the best hotels, and visit the race-track." What's more, the large immigrant populations residing in cities were an "alien" element that did not conform to the "Anglo-Saxon idea of sport" which emphasized fair play and not solely the lure of money.[34]

The very nature of baseball underwent its own "modern" vs "traditional" culture war. Prior to the 1920s, legendary pitchers such as Christy Mathewson, Walter Johnson, and Grover Cleveland Alexander ruled the day. Managers resorted to a scientific "inside" game of scratching out one run at a time through bunts, stolen bases, squeeze plays, or hit and run plays. Most hitters choked up on the bat to strategically place hits. Home runs occupied a minimal role in baseball strategy. Usually, only one baseball was used throughout a contest, and by the later innings, the ball was little more than a mushy orb that didn't fly very far. What's more, pitchers could throw spitballs or doctor baseballs with files, nails, etc. Late in games, hitters had a hard time seeing, much less hitting, dirty baseballs stained with tobacco juice.

Drastic changes, however, were afoot. The excitement fans craved meant discarding the low-scoring affairs of the Deadball Era for offensive barrages punctuated by home runs aplenty. Club owners were more than happy to give the public what they wanted and effected rule changes that fundamentally altered the way the game was played during the slugging 1920s. First, the owners resolved baseball's own "wet" vs. "dry" issue when they outlawed use of the spitball.[35] But in this case the roles were reversed. The "wets" were remnants of the Deadball Era, while the "dry's" represented forward-looking modernists who aimed to make the game more hitter friendly. Secondly, the league instructed umpires to remove any scuffed or smudged baseball from games and replace it with a new, clean ball, which presented hitters with a much more inviting target. Beleaguered pitchers groused even more that the ball seemed much livelier, but that belief was debatable. There were no changes in ball specifications between 1910 and 1926, when a cushioned-cork ball was introduced.

Lastly, batting styles changed. Hitters moved their hands closer to the knob of the bat and swung at pitches as hard as they could. Surprisingly, this "bombs away" mindset did not result in an expected surge of strikeouts. The hero (or villain if you were a pitcher) who ushered in this free-swinging mentality was the larger-than-life figure of Babe Ruth. He emerged from a rough upbringing in Baltimore to become one of the Deadball Era's top pitchers with the Boston Red Sox. His days on the mound, however, dwindled when his prodigious hitting power prompted a full-time move to the outfield. The Babe set a new major league record when he slammed 29 home runs in 1919.

Baseball history changed in 1920 when Red Sox owner and theater impresario Harry Frazee sold Ruth to the New York Yankees to pay theater-related debts. Ruth's arrival in New York inaugurated a baseball dynasty, while frustrated Boston fans suffered through numerous "cursed" seasons. Babe obliterated his 1919 record, launching 54 long balls during the 1920 season. His slugging exploits catapulted him to a level of celebrity that only aviation hero Charles Lindbergh approached. He became the game's greatest gate attraction, and his kindness, charisma, love of kids, and his voracious appetites for food, drink, and women personified the excesses of the 1920s and added to his legend. His success inspired everyone in the major leagues to adopt his "swing from the heels" approach, and the results were nothing short of remarkable. In 1917, all 16 major league teams combined to hit 338 home runs. By 1925, that figure soared to 1,167. The home run onslaught did not precipitate a decline in batting averages. A .300 batting average was commonplace, and the decade boasted eight .400 hitters, whereas there were only four from 1901 to 1920. "Inside" baseball strategies were relegated to afterthoughts.[36] As John P. Rossi wrote in *Baseball and American Culture: A History*, "baseball as we understand it today was born in the decade of the Roaring Twenties."[37]

The Yankees were not the only dynasty born during this frenetic period. The St. Louis Cardinals, after decades of frustration, finally put the pieces together in 1926 to take first place in the National League and then trump the mighty Yankees in the World Series. Three strong-willed individuals blended their talents and suppressed, albeit temporarily, their oversized egos to direct the team's transformation.

CHAPTER 2

The Brain Trust

Befitting the "larger than life" culture of the 1920s, Victor Miller burst onto St. Louis' political scene "like a bombshell." The Joplin, Missouri, native attended the University of Missouri and earned a law degree from the Washington University School of Law in 1912. He practiced law in St. Louis for several years before Governor Arthur Hyde appointed him president of the St. Louis Police Board in 1921. The ambitious 32-year-old vowed to clean up the city's rampant crime and numerous bootleg joints and carried out his duties with swagger and a loaded police revolver. His overzealous campaign and bombastic rhetoric made plenty of enemies along the way. In June 1921, he arrested several prominent politicians in a St. Louis hotel room for playing poker. Later that year, he claimed in a speech that 70 percent of the city's criminals were ex-servicemen, a remark that drew scathing rebukes from veterans' groups. He also angered the city's firemen, calling them the "world's best pinochle players" when comparing their work to that of police officers. The final straw was Miller's charge that Soldan High School was the home of "vice clubs" among promiscuous boys and girls. Outraged civic groups and parents protested his sullying the character of the city's youth so vehemently that Governor Hyde dismissed Miller as president in April 1922. The Post-Dispatch *characterized Miller's record as "an orgy of official lawlessness, of irresponsible words and acts."*

But Miller's political career was far from over. In 1924, he ran as a Republican candidate for governor. Though losing in the primary, he did surprisingly well in St. Louis, prompting a run for mayor the following year. He narrowly defeated his Democratic challenger and commenced two turmoil-filled terms. Charges of widespread cronyism and fraud dogged his administration, capped off by the revelation that A.M. Ryckoff had overcharged the city more than $150,000 while completing a street lighting project. During the 1929 primary, Miller's closest advisors noticed his health and mental capacity were declining. His condition was so bad that, after he won the election, his campaign strategists demanded Miller appoint Jules Field as his secretary. Thereafter, Field handled most of the executive duties while department heads administered day-to-day activities. In 1932, Miller announced he would not run for a third term. Prior to the March 1933 primary, Miller and his wife left St. Louis for New York. There he *was judged incompetent to manage his affairs, and his wife was named his legal guardian. Victor Miller's rise and fall was, according to the* Globe-Democrat, *a "meteor streaking across [St. Louis'] political skies."*[1]

The triumvirate that led the 1926 Cardinals—a tough-talking, hard-drinking, self-made millionaire; a pious, tight-fisted, brilliant baseball innovator; and a supremely gifted, supremely arrogant superstar player-manager—weren't as colorful or controversial as Victor Miller, but they were a mercurial brain trust in their own right. The three ringleaders shared some overlapping characteristics, but more divergent personalities could not be found. They respected each other's abilities, but on a personal level, their relationships were, at best, strained. Nevertheless, the stars aligned during that magical summer of 1926, allowing everything to click on the way to a World Series championship.

The Self-Made Millionaire

Cardinals owner Sam Breadon. His trade of star player-manager Rogers Hornsby made him a despised figure among St. Louis fans (Missouri Historical Society, St. Louis).

Though not as flashy a team owner as Chris Von der Ahe, Sam Breadon shared several traits with the earlier "der poss bresident." The way each spoke was instantly noticeable—Von der Ahe's Germanic, broken English and Breadon's unmistakable New York accent, something he never lost even after four decades in St. Louis. He would say, "The Cah-dinals finished foist." Both were astute businessmen, and the success of the Cardinals under Breadon certainly rivaled that of Von der Ahe's Browns. In the 27 years Breadon owned the Cardinals, the team won nine National League pennants and six World Series championships. Despite the team's rise to the top, Sam's role during the 1926 season was largely overshadowed by the two other members of the St. Louis triumvirate. Breadon didn't seem to mind. The *Sporting News* described him as a "conservative, soft speaking business man" who preferred to talk about the team rather than himself.[2]

Sam was born on July 26, 1876, in New York City, one of eight children of Irish immigrants William and Jane Breadon. The family lived in the Ninth Ward of old Greenwich Village. "Nothing fancy," Sam recalled, "a tough neighborhood. You had to be able to handle yourself, or you did not do so well." His rough-and-tumble youth taught him never to run away from a fight, a lesson that served him well. The family struggled to make ends meet, and their finances became even more precarious after Sam's father died when Sam was young, so he dropped out of school at age 15 to help support the family. He worked for a time as a bank clerk on Wall Street for $125 per month, but that sedate life wasn't for Sam.

In 1902, against his mother's wishes, he took a leap of faith and moved west to join two friends who had opened an auto dealership/garage in St. Louis. Sam earned $75 a month working as a grease monkey, learning the automobile business from the ground up. Through the grease and grime, Breadon saw the industry's potential, which fueled ambitions to open his own auto shop. Within a year, the garage owners heard rumors about Sam's plan and fired him on the spot. Near destitute, he borrowed money to continue supporting his mother while he eked out a living on 15 cents a day. Ever resourceful, Sam convinced a company in 1903 to consign him 30 cases of popcorn. He hired boys to sell the treat on a percentage basis at the dedication parade for the World's Fair held in St. Louis the following year. His scheme cleared a profit of $35, so Sam treated himself to a steak dinner and a new set of clothes. He persuaded Marion Lambert, owner of the pharmaceutical company that manufactured and marketed Listerine mouthwash, to become a partner in a new automobile dealership. Lambert was impressed with Sam's work ethic and honesty, and he was more than willing to provide financial backing to get the dealership rolling. The venture flourished from the start, and it wasn't long before Sam became the sole owner. He acquired a dealership and sold Pierce-Arrow automobiles, making millions along the way.[3]

The auto wheeler-dealer was also a sports fan. He played basketball and football and boxed when he was young. He became a devoted follower of the Cardinals, despite their on-field struggles. With the team on the verge of bankruptcy, Breadon, at a friend's urging, joined 1,200 investors in 1917 who purchased the club for $375,000 to keep it in St. Louis. Sam's initial investment was rather meager—only four shares for $200—but he gradually consolidated his control of the Cardinals. He acquired $2,000 in stock and loaned the team $18,000 to prevent it from defaulting on a payment to former owner Helene Britton. In recognition of his contributions, the board of directors elected him team president in January 1920. By 1922, he was the majority stockholder.[4]

In addition to Breadon's new role, another development made 1920 a milestone in Cardinals history. One of Sam's first moves was to relocate the team from the ramshackle firetrap known as Cardinal Park (formerly Robison Field or League Park), situated near Fairground Park at Vandeventer and Natural Bridge avenues. The club's home since 1892, it was the last major league park with wooden stands. The *St. Louis Globe-Democrat* estimated it would cost some $400,000 to $500,000 to reconstruct the stands to comply with building codes. The park's sorry state gave Breadon nightmares that the stands would either burn to the ground or collapse and kill spectators. It was a blessing in disguise that the Cardinals drew sparse crowds at the time. Given the team's anemic financial situation, it was a no-brainer for Breadon to sell the old ballpark and surrounding land for $275,000 and negotiate a deal with Browns owner, Phil Ball, to become a tenant at Sportsman's Park. Breadon considered this one of the two most important decisions he made as Cardinals owner.[5]

The Baseball Innovator

The man Breadon replaced as team president—Branch Rickey—was one of the most influential figures in St. Louis Cardinal and Major League Baseball history. Rickey revolutionized the game twice. Most notably, he signed Jackie Robinson to break Major League Baseball's color barrier in 1947. His second innovation, perfecting and expanding the Cardinal farm system, has not received the level of public acclaim as the Robinson signing because it was more of an organizational move, yet it profoundly changed the way major league clubs operated. It would be hard to imagine the modern game without it. Rickey also made St. Louis Cardinal sartorial history after he was inspired by some decorative cutouts of cardinals at a Men's Fellowship Club meeting in February 1921. He had prototypes made and the iconic "birds on the bat" logo has graced Cardinal uniforms since 1922.[6]

Wesley Branch Rickey, according to historian Harold Seymour, was born to a "poor and pious Ohio farm family." His parents were devout Christians and imbued Branch with a lifelong appreciation for the strength and serenity of religious principles and an aversion to swearing or drinking alcohol. Branch enjoyed an exceedingly close relationship with his strong-willed, nurturing mother, Emily. She instilled an unwavering confidence and sense of self-worth that emboldened him to take risks throughout his life. From her, he learned the value of hard work and the importance of education. Branch especially prized the latter for he was determined to use his intellectual gifts to reap more earthly rewards than his industrious but financially strapped parents. He taught at the local grade school without a high school diploma, earning enough money to enroll at Ohio Wesleyan College in 1901. In addition to his coursework, he starred on the football team and emerged as the starting catcher on the baseball team. During the summer of 1902, he played baseball with a semi-pro team from Portsmouth, earning $25 per week, a welcome boost to his precarious financial situation. That pay-for-play action, however, cost him his amateur status and ended his eligibility to play collegiate sports.

Despite the setback, fortune smiled on Branch because the college baseball team needed a new coach, and he eagerly took the job. After graduating in 1904, he played minor league ball in Dallas and reached the major leagues as a catcher when the Cincinnati Reds purchased his contract late in the season. But his career was nearly derailed before it started. Out of respect for his mother's wishes and her religious conviction, Branch refused to play baseball on Sundays. Neither the young catcher's familial nor religious devotion impressed Reds manager Joe Kelley, and he released Rickey before he appeared in a single game. During the offseason, Branch taught and coached at Allegheny College in Meadville, Pennsylvania, for two years before returning to Ohio Wesleyan as athletic director, where he coached football, basketball, and baseball.[7]

During the summers, Branch resumed his professional baseball career. The Chicago White Sox purchased his contract for the 1905 season but traded him before he appeared in any games to the cellar-dwelling St. Louis Browns. He made his major league debut on June 16 against the Philadelphia Athletics. He had the bad luck of facing one of the dominant pitchers of the decade in the eccentric but tremendously talented future Hall of Famer Rube Waddell. Branch went 0 for 3 against the fireballing southpaw with two strikeouts. The rest of the Browns fared no better in the 10–1 loss. That one contest was the extent of Rickey's season for he left the team to care for his ill mother in Ohio. Once she recovered, Branch returned to St. Louis, only to be sent to the Dallas Giants of the Texas League to get more playing time. He batted a respectable .296 at Dallas, earning another uninspiring shot with the Browns in 1906.

The following season, he played with the New York Highlanders (renamed the Yankees in 1915), but an injured throwing arm essentially ended his playing days. The starting Yankee catcher was hurt, and manager Clark Griffith asked Rickey to catch a game against the Washington Senators, despite his ailing arm. Early in the contest, Branch tried to throw out a Senator baserunner attempting to steal. The throw was caught—not by the second baseman or shortstop—but by outfielder Willie Keeler who was playing in shallow *rightfield*. "That's how erratic my arm was," Branch related years later. He did not attempt another throw for the rest of the game, and the Senators stole a grand total of 13 bases—a standing Major League Baseball record. The apparent demise of his baseball career and a bout with tuberculosis prompted Rickey to explore a less physically strenuous career, so he studied law at the University of Michigan, graduating in 1911. But he couldn't give up baseball entirely and landed the job to coach the university's baseball team. Discovering he had a shrewd eye for evaluating the potential of his players, he recommended several to Browns owner Robert Hedges.[8]

Rickey's judgment impressed Hedges enough that he brought Branch on board as the Browns' second vice-president and secretary in 1913. Later that year, Hedges appointed Rickey to lead the team on the field as well. Rickey's managerial style was a drastic departure from the hunch-based, seat-of-your-pants mentality that dominated baseball at the time. True to his academic training, Branch viewed baseball as a science and used cold logic to make decisions. Foreshadowing the sabermetric explosion later in the century, he recognized the value of specialized and systematic numerical analysis as a tool to guide training regimens, player evaluation, strategy development, and organizational structure. Years later as general manager of the Dodgers, he developed the formula for calculating today's ubiquitous on-base and slugging averages. To apply these principles to his new managerial duties, Branch set up classrooms with blackboards and charts and gave the players lessons in baseball theory every morning during spring training. He introduced new training techniques with sliding pits and batting cages, but it did little to improve the Browns' play. The team finished fifth in the standings in 1914 and sixth in 1915.[9]

Obviously needing an open pipeline of major league talent, Rickey and Hedges knew they didn't have the financial resources to outbid New York or Chicago clubs for prospects, so they decided to utilize a farm system for acquiring players. They tried to purchase one or more minor league teams, but the National Association—Major League Baseball's governing body at the time—nixed the scheme.[10] After Phil Ball purchased the Browns in 1916, Rickey's relationship with the new owner quickly soured. Ball resented Rickey's "professorial demeanor" and support of temperance. Fortunately for Branch, his time in this personal baseball purgatory did not last long.

In 1917, a group of investors acquired the Cardinals to prevent the team from moving out of St. Louis. Rickey was offered the job of team president after several sportswriters and baseball insiders recommended him as the best candidate to right the floundering franchise. Branch had no qualms about jumping to the cross-town rival Cardinals. After making the move, he tried to build a young fan

General manager Branch Rickey was one of the most influential individuals in Major League Baseball history (Missouri Historical Society, St. Louis).

base by expanding the owners' idea of the "Knothole Gang." The group was made up of needy kids who received free admission into the ballpark. Rickey got the team's stock purchasers—wealthy people whose children didn't need free passes—to subsidize the plan. The Knothole Gang eventually included more than 10,000 rabid Cardinals fans.[11]

Rickey also tried to resurrect the farm system because the Cardinals operated under the same financial black cloud as the Browns, but World War I rudely interrupted. Desiring to do his bit for his country, Rickey entered military service at age 37. He was commissioned a major and spent a little over four months with the 1st Gas Regiment of the Chemical Warfare Service, instructing troops about the dangers of mustard gas. After the war ended, Rickey returned to the Cardinals only to find the team's finances had struck rock bottom, further stalling the farm system. Rickey's attention was diverted by his elevation to on-field manager in 1919 in addition to duties as team president. When Sam Breadon assumed the front office role, Rickey was demoted to vice president/general manager but kept his on-field managerial role. His pride wounded; Rickey considered resigning. He stayed after the board offered him the majority of the remaining Cardinals stock.

Branch and the new president formed an unlikely but effective duo. Breadon was a product of the teeming urban chaos of New York and a grade school dropout. The son of Irish immigrants, his politics leaned toward the Democratic Party. His fastidious habits complemented his reserved personality, but he enjoyed the occasional drink (or several) and singing in a barbershop quartet. To Sam, a handshake was as good as a signed contract for he was a man of his word. The garrulous Rickey, on the other hand, was as "rumpled as an unmade bed." He hailed from the more bucolic setting of a Midwestern farm, and he prized education. A diehard Republican and devout Christian, Branch never uttered anything worse than "Judas Priest." Breadon, in contrast, often resorted to colorful (a.k.a. profane) language. He often referred to Rickey as that "goddamned Sunday school teacher." Though Rickey chewed cigars, he was a teetotaler. Paradoxically, despite his Bible quoting, Branch rarely let moral scruples get in the way of bending the rules in his dogged pursuit of profit. As journalist/author Jimmy Breslin wrote, Rickey was "neither a savior nor a Samaritan. He was a baseball man, and nowhere in his religious training did he take a vow of poverty." Breadon, unlike Phil Ball, overlooked Rickey's "faults" and appreciated his administrative abilities, his frugality, and especially his ability to evaluate baseball talent.[12]

Breadon's pragmatic sale of Robison Field provided the capital needed to get the farm system off the ground, and Breadon essentially gave Branch a free hand to run the show. Rickey did not invent the farm system, but he perfected it, reflecting the corporate organizational structure and emphasis on "product" standardization and mass production within the 1920s business world. His rational system of player development achieved a vertical integration that allowed raw, young talent to percolate up through a chain of Cardinal-owned or controlled minor league clubs as they became major league-ready. To bypass the exorbitant prices upper-level minor league teams charged for promising ballplayers, Rickey resorted to large-scale tryouts to identify talent as cheaply as possible. He sifted through numerous would-be ballplayers to uncover some diamonds in the rough, such as Ray Blades, Jim Bottomley, and a local St. Louis product, Clarence "Heine" Mueller.

Commissioner Kenesaw Mountain Landis hated the "chain store" scheme. He believed it hindered the movement of players up to the major leagues and that parent clubs would strangle locally owned minor league teams. Thus, he engaged in a years-long but ultimately futile battle with Rickey to undo the system. St. Louis first bought a one-half interest in the Fort Smith, Arkansas, club in 1919 and eventually added Houston of the Texas League and Syracuse of the American Association. At the system's peak in 1940, the Cardinals controlled 32 minor league teams. Initially, many major league insiders dismissed the idea as unworkable, contending that baseball teams couldn't afford the expense of running a farm system. But as the Cardinals churned out one prospect after another, the system became self-sustaining. Rickey sold surplus prospects to other major league teams, which helped finance the "chain store." It also feathered Rickey's personal finances as he received ten percent of the sale price for any player contract. Eventually, every team in both leagues followed suit.[13]

Rickey was better at spotting and developing talent than managing it. He thrived as a teacher of baseball theory and fundamentals, but his chalkboard sessions may have been too intellectual for players who had little formal schooling.[14] Once Rickey took over, the Cardinals made progress, rising from seventh place in 1919 to third place finishes in 1921 and 1922. But the team slid to fifth place the following year and then to sixth in 1924. Breadon decided the problem was Rickey's management and was determined to fire him. To lead the Redbirds, Breadon turned to the team's star second baseman, Rogers Hornsby.

The Superstar Player-Manager

Rogers Hornsby was one of the more peculiar figures in baseball history. His skill with a bat was remarkable. No less an authority than Ty Cobb called Hornsby the best hitter he had ever seen, and Hall of Famer George Sisler of the St. Louis Browns said Rogers had a better sense of the strike zone than anyone else in baseball.[15] He was easily the most feared hitter in the National League during the 1920s and ranks among the greatest right-handed hitters of all time. He won seven National League batting titles, and his .358 lifetime batting average is third behind Cobb's .366 and the .365 of the Negro League's Oscar Charleston.[16] From 1921 through 1925, Hornsby enjoyed a batting spree that few major leaguers could match. He won the batting title every year during that five-year span along with two triple crowns. He pummeled pitchers with a .402 batting average, 29 home runs, and 119 RBIs. His fielding at second base was adequate (popups gave him fits), but he was exceptional at turning double plays. He also was blessed with good foot speed, flying around the bases to turn hits into doubles or triples.[17]

Hornsby's greatness as a player obscured personal eccentricities and failings. Over the years, various authors have described his personality as cold, gruff, aloof, acerbic, contentious, distant, caustic, uncivil, belligerent, and other unflattering terms.[18] He was considered bluntly honest to a fault. As Rogers wrote in his autobiographical account, *My War with Baseball*, "I've never taken back anything I ever said and I've never failed to say exactly—and I mean exactly—what I was thinking." And he said it to anyone, "from the owner to the bat boy." His honesty was paired with a complete lack of tact, and he seemed to go out of his way to antagonize everyone. Bill James, a founding father of sabermetrics, declared he'd vote Hornsby the "biggest horse's ass in baseball history." It was not surprising, as Charles Alexander wrote in his biography of Hornsby, that his life was "full of conflict, complications, and frustration. Hornsby's is the story of a determined, difficult man who, for all his fabled frankness, wouldn't acknowledge his own conspicuous shortcomings." Sportswriters, however, found his straight-shooting honesty great for business. Baseball was Hornsby's life, and he followed a fanatical regimen to optimize his talents. He did not read or go to movies for fear they would weaken his batting eye. He did not smoke, drink, or play cards. He was largely a mystery to his teammates. On road trips, he never roomed with anyone. If he wasn't at the ballpark, he was in the hotel lobby, watching people come and go.[19]

Besides baseball, Hornsby's only other interest was gambling on horse races, and he applied the same single-minded focus to wagering on the ponies that he did to baseball. Unfortunately for him, he lost more often than he won, squandering most of the money he earned. It is said that he bet nearly half a million dollars during his career. Hornsby was completely up front about his addiction. It was, he said, his only enjoyment outside baseball, and what he did with his money was nobody's business but his own. His gambling caused a good deal of unease among Breadon, Rickey, and especially Commissioner Landis. Coming off the Black Sox scandal a few years earlier, Landis identified gambling as the root of baseball's troubles, and he ordered Hornsby to stop. Hornsby refused, arguing that betting on the horses was legal and no worse than baseball owners playing the stock market.[20]

Rogers Hornsby was born April 27, 1896, near the tiny west Texas village of Winters. His father died when Rogers was only two years old, and his mother, Mary, relocated the family to her parents' farm near Austin. During the winter of 1902–03, Mary and the family moved to Fort Worth to work in meatpacking plants. Rogers attended the local elementary school and played baseball with his brothers and neighborhood kids. Years later, he claimed he "loved to play baseball better than eat." His mother encouraged his baseball ambitions, even sewing uniforms for an informal team Rogers organized. He exhibited a natural affinity for the game, and by the time he was 15 years old, he was good enough to play in a city league with grown men. He played baseball and football at Fort Worth's North Side High School before dropping out after two years. Either he had had enough of school, or he needed to find work to support his mother and sister, but he secured a job running office errands for the Swift and Company stockyards.

By the time Rogers was 17, he had grown to nearly six feet tall, though he tipped the scales at only 135 pounds. He played third base for the plant's baseball team with older co-workers before moving on to play with a team in Denison, where he caught the eye of Cardinals scout Bob Connery. When the team's season ended, Connery arranged for the purchase of Hornsby's contract for $500. On September 3, 1915, the scrawny, error-prone shortstop boarded a train to join the Cardinals at Cincinnati. Hornsby told esteemed sportswriter Roy Stockton of the *St. Louis Post-Dispatch* that he failed to make a good impression on manager Miller Huggins. After seeing the Texan swing the bat, Huggins determined the rookie was too skinny and too weak to hit with much power, so he tried to change Hornsby's batting style. Rogers stood in the back corner of the batter's box and held the bat at the knob, but Huggins wanted him to crouch and choke up on the bat. When the season ended, Huggins told Rogers that the team was going to farm him out. The hayseed thought Huggins meant that he needed to work on his uncle's farm, so he spent the offseason there. "There is no work to do on a plantation in the winter," he told Stockton, "I just hunted and tramped around enough to get up a good appetite and keep my muscles hard and never missed a meal." He ate a lot of steak and chicken and drank all the milk he could. When he reported to spring training, he had bulked up to 175 pounds and could hit with more power.[21]

Player-manager Rogers Hornsby piloted the Cardinals to their first World Series title, but his toxic feud with owner Sam Breadon and general manager Branch Rickey led to his shocking departure (St. Louis Cardinals Hall of Fame and Museum).

Rogers' fanatical zeal for baseball and his unfaltering belief that he was always right inevitably led to clashes with teammates. He simply could not tolerate players who did not play with the same passion he did, and his withering and brutal criticisms of those players often made the star the most despised man on the team. Hornsby, however, did not always practice what he preached. He had a poor showing during the war-shortened 1918 season. His average dropped from .327 in 1917 to .281, and his performance in every other offensive category declined as well. His draft status and mother's illness certainly weighed upon him, but a strained relationship with teammates factored in as well. In July, Cardinals president Branch Rickey admitted to the *Post-Dispatch* that the Texan was not on speaking terms with his teammates. Some Cardinals accused Hornsby of having a "swelled head" and playing only for himself. Rickey echoed that sentiment. Hornsby "is one of the greatest ballplayers I have ever known. But he also has a peculiar character, various traits which are hard to understand, cannot be understood…. He is egotistical. He likes to believe he is the greatest player in the game. Moreover, he must be made to believe it if his club is to realize to the maximum of his ability." In an August game, he failed to slide and was tagged out at home plate. When a teammate questioned Hornsby about not sliding, he allegedly replied, "I'm too good a ball player to be sliding to the plate for a tail-end team." He derided his comrades as "stool pigeons."[22]

Hornsby also clashed with management. Salary disputes with Cardinal ownership, even after his rookie season, became an annual event. His dislike of manager Jack Hendricks, a graduate of Northwestern University, whom he considered a "college boy" and a "boob manager," was the most probable reason for Rogers' poor 1918 season. Hornsby apparently, had a peculiar aversion to college-educated men. According to Roy Stockton, Hornsby "can't mention a college without a few decorative adjectives. If a man comes from a university, he's dumb and the higher the university the greater the degree of dumbness in Hornsby's estimation."[23] Once the season ended, he vowed never to play for St. Louis again if Hendricks continued as manager. Not wanting to alienate the team's star player, Rickey fired Hendricks and took over as manager himself for the 1919 season.[24] One can only imagine what Hornsby's initial reaction was to his new boss. The ill-educated Hornsby undoubtedly chafed at Rickey's professorial "college boy" demeanor and prolonged theoretical strategy sessions. He contemptuously called Rickey "'the Ohio Weeze-leyan' so-and-so" behind his back. Nevertheless, the two maintained an uneasy peace, and the Cardinals' fortunes improved with third place finishes in 1921 and 1922. Hornsby's hitting prowess earned him the nickname "The Rajah," a nod to the craze for all things Arabian after the 1921 release of the Rudolph Valentino movie, *The Sheik*. As the National League's best player, Rogers apparently deserved a moniker to equal Babe Ruth's "Sultan of Swat" in the American League.[25]

Despite the Rajah's presence, the Cards took a decided step backward during the 1923 season. Though he won the National League batting title again, Hornsby had a difficult year. Injuries limited him to 107 games, and he was no doubt distracted by his messy divorce and mother's illness. Again, claims that Hornsby was "dogging it" flared up. Things finally boiled over after a tough double header on August 23 against the Giants in New York. St. Louis lost the first game 8–7. The Cardinals scored three runs in the top of the ninth inning to tie the game, but Irish Meusel hit a one-out home run in the bottom of the ninth for the Giants' win. Hornsby failed to collect any hits during the contest and was no doubt in a foul mood, especially after an incident that occurred in the top of the ninth. He was perched on third base when Rickey gave the batter the take sign with a 3–1 count. The star second baseman made his disgust with Rickey's order abundantly clear. The Cards' manager yelled at Hornsby to, "Stay in the ball game!" and, according to Harry Pierce of the *St. Louis Star*, muttered something about Hornsby trying to run the team. A "reliable source" told Pierce that some teammates informed Hornsby about Rickey's disparaging remark, which stoked the Texan's hair-trigger temper.

St. Louis gained a split, defeating the Giants in the nightcap 7–4. Hornsby collected three singles and drove in two runs, but that did little to assuage his surliness. After the second game concluded, a fuming Hornsby told the manager that he wanted his name removed from a list of players who would participate in a barnstorming tour Rickey had organized. Pierce's source said Rickey "remonstrated in a very forceful manner," and Hornsby responded with a right hook to Rickey's face. Several teammates stepped in to break up the fight. As soon as news of the confrontation leaked, rumors circulated that the Cubs and Giants had reached out to the Cardinals about a possible deal for the disgruntled second baseman.[26]

Rickey insisted Hornsby would not be traded and brushed off the whole encounter as a petty squabble that every team faces. He intimated someone who wanted to "make a mountain out of a molehill" leaked the story to the press. Rickey told sportswriter Martin Haley of the *Globe-Democrat* that neither he, nor Hornsby, nor anyone else connected to the Cardinals had talked. "Who did?" he cryptically asked Haley, "I know; do you? What were his reasons? I know that, too; don't you?" Though Rickey never divulged the suspect's name, Haley wrote, "In baseball circles it is known that the someone is a party who would like to see Rickey ousted from the management of the club." Breadon likewise dismissed all trade rumors as bunk. Rickey and Hornsby, he added, "had their little difference, but it is history now."[27]

The feud was anything but history and carried on into late September. Hornsby was out of action for nearly two weeks because of a skin infection. Before a September 26 game against the Brooklyn Dodgers, the team doctor told Rickey that Hornsby was healthy enough to suit up. When Rickey asked his second baseman to play, Hornsby refused to even put on a uniform or sit on the bench. Tempers flared in the clubhouse. Hornsby unleashed an expletive-laden invective and landed a punch to Rickey's jaw, precipitating a wild exchange of blows. The melee ended only after other players pulled the combatants apart. Hornsby's blatant disregard for team rules made what happened next inevitable. Sam Breadon declared Rogers was a keystone of the club, but he could not condone such disrespectful behavior. He fined Hornsby $500 and suspended him for the rest of the season. He added that the Cardinals had absolutely no plans to trade Hornsby despite his insubordination, though Breadon must have been sorely tempted. John McGraw, manager of the New York

Giants, had long desired to acquire Hornsby to rival Babe Ruth as a gate attraction. McGraw made several offers ranging anywhere from $100,000 to $300,000 for Hornsby, but Breadon and Rickey refused every overture.[28]

An unrepentant Hornsby pointed a conspiratorial finger at Cardinal management, claiming the team suspended him to facilitate his departure by presenting him to the public as a temperamental star who played by his own rules to undermine club morale. He denied he had any plans to take over Rickey's managerial reins and had always given his best effort and followed the manager's instructions to the letter. Rickey lashed back with a statement to correct Hornsby's public charges. "I have been in charge of baseball teams," he wrote, "in one capacity or another, for twenty years, the last ten years in major league baseball. During that time only one player has ever spoken disrespectfully to me. I am not a 'fighting manager.' However, I am not sorry I resented the vile and unspeakable language used by Hornsby in New York." Hornsby repeated his vow not to play as long as Rickey continued as manager, but the two patched up their rift prior to the 1924 season.[29]

The reconciliation did not improve the team's win-loss record. The Cardinals tumbled to sixth place with a disappointing 65–89 finish, despite Hornsby pacing all of major league baseball with a blistering .424 batting average. The team's poor showing only heightened Breadon's misgivings about Rickey's managerial abilities. In fact, he twice asked Hornsby during spring training if he'd like to manage the team. He declined both times. But it was clear Breadon was looking to make a change.

During the 1925 season, the Cardinals were wallowing in last place in late May with a 13–25 record when Breadon finally removed Rickey as field manager and tabbed Hornsby as his replacement. It was, Breadon later admitted to the *Sporting News*, the "'toughest assignment' he had ever made for himself."[30] He valued Rickey as an employee, but he did not let sentiment prevent him from doing what he thought best for the team. He convinced Rickey to stay on as vice president, which allowed him to focus on scouting and developing talent through the farm system. Rickey was angry about losing his on-field role, and in a petulant snit, he put a substantial block of his Cardinals stock up for sale. Hornsby again declined the offer to manage, but Breadon was adamant, shouting "I won't have any f------ Sunday School teacher running my team!" Hornsby relented only after Breadon agreed to help him purchase Rickey's stock. The deal gave Hornsby a 12.5 percent interest in the team.[31]

Roy Stockton believed the elevation to manager changed Hornsby. Previously he was known as a remarkable ball player "who loved baseball, but except for his batting prowess and his skill on the diamond, there was not much color to this Hornsby person." But the promotion changed Hornsby into a "dynamic leader; a chief for whom his warriors would go to any limit to win."[32] Rogers made it clear that he was the absolute boss. He recalled that he told the team he "didn't want to see any pitcher throw his glove in the air in disgust if he happened to be taken out of the game." If anybody did that, he "might have to throw up their fists in the club house."

Hornsby also simplified the game for the players who were numbed by Rickey's cerebral approach. One player recalled Rickey "had more signals than a freight yard. Some of the boys thought they had to raise their hands to go to first base." To sports scribe John B. Sheridan, this "business of trying to play all nine positions from the bench is enough to turn a baseball club into an insane asylum." Rickey's squads, Sheridan continued, were "always poor fielding teams—scared, hunted, harassed by too much paternalistic direction." Freed from Rickey's burdensome directions, the Cardinals responded immediately to Hornsby's simplified style, winning 15 of the first 19 games under their new manager. "All he ever asked of anybody," said third baseman Les Bell years later, "was that they give him all they had out on the field." Bell and the others no doubt cheered Hornsby's first command: "Throw that damned blackboard outta the clubhouse. This ain't a football team."[33]

Other changes included reining in the seemingly constant shuttling of young prospects like Bell, "Chick" Hafey, and Taylor Douthit between St. Louis and the minor leagues. And player-manager Hornsby insisted upon installing Tommy Thevenow, a slight and light-hitting prospect with the Cards' Syracuse franchise in the International League, as the starting shortstop. Given an extended chance to prove themselves as big leaguers, Bell, Hafey, Douthit, and Thevenow all stuck with the ball club and rewarded Hornsby's faith in them. The Redbirds rallied to finish the season in fourth place, inspiring hope for the 1926 season.[34]

Chapter 3

The Cast of Characters

While the Cardinals inspired hope for the 1926 season, Prohibition wreaked havoc on St. Louis' legal brewing businesses and social stability. All too often, the constitutional mandate backed by the Volstead Act of 1919 also had dire personal consequences. In early February 1926, for example, police found the body of Paul Birritteri drowned in a whiskey vat located beneath the wood floor of a shed at the rear of his home at 5343 Odell Avenue. While investigating a clog in the line running from the vat to a still in the basement, Birritteri was overcome by the fumes and fell through a hole in the floor and into the expansive 22-foot-long × 16-foot-wide × 8-foot-deep construct. After police removed Birritteri's body, his wife and four children suffered the indignity and financial loss of having officers smash the still and leave a guard with the vat of mash awaiting its destruction.[1]

Support for the Volstead Act in St. Louis was lukewarm at best, and incidents like this and the violence arising from gangs battling to control the city's bootlegging added fuel to the fire of public opposition. In April 1926, U.S. Senator Walter Edge of New Jersey asked Health Commissioner Max Starkloff to comment on the status of Prohibition in St. Louis. Starkloff's blunt assessment: "There is no such thing as prohibition in St. Louis." To formalize that situation, the city's Board of Aldermen overwhelmingly approved a resolution calling for the repeal or modification of dry laws, which they deemed a "festering sore" and acts of "tyranny and oppression." Alderman Samuel Wimer declared, "The people have risen up in arms against the hypocrisy of the prohibition law. We should not be forced to run through the back doors of 'speak easys' instead of walking through the front doors like gentlemen."[2] Much to gentlemanly dismay, the country faced another seven years of the "noble experiment."

St. Louis baseball fans were starving for their own "noble experiment." The Brown Stockings of the American Association hoisted a championship banner in the Mound City in 1888, but, since then, professional baseball in St. Louis was mired in decades of mediocrity. Periodic glimpses of inspired play raised the hopes of fans only to be cruelly crushed as St. Louis teams once more sank into the second division, or bottom half of the standings.[3]

But things *felt* different going into the 1926 season. Sportsman's Park, the home field shared by the Browns and Cardinals, was undergoing a $500,000 facelift. Double-decked grandstands extended along the foul lines and increased the seating capacity from 18,000 to 32,500. Martin Haley of the *St. Louis Globe-Democrat* penned that perhaps the new ballpark would "prove the charm necessary to bring the town out of its baseball lethargy." It was a fact, he added, that new parks were "synonymous with victory in the immediate past." He pointed to the Yankees winning the World Series in 1923 in the new Yankee Stadium and to the Giants and Senators, who won pennants in 1924 in the refurbished Polo Grounds and Griffith Stadium, respectively.[4]

The Cardinals' strong finish in 1925 under Rogers Hornsby's managerial leadership also energized fans' dreams of a National League pennant. "Many years have elapsed," claimed the *Post-Dispatch*'s Roy Stockton, "since St. Louis had a baseball manager as enthusiastic about his team's chances as is Rogers Hornsby of the Cardinals this season."[5] Hornsby reinforced those expectations while preparing for his first spring training as field boss. In January, he told the *Sporting News* that the pitching staff was "going to make or break us. In other departments we look strong enough so that if the pitchers come through we will be in the running all the way."[6]

On the Mound

Eighteen candidates for that pitching staff reported to camp, which Hornsby planned to whittle down to 11. Jesse "Pop" Haines was one of the staff's veteran holdovers. He was born in July 1893 in Clayton, Ohio, a small town near Dayton, before his father moved the family to a farm five miles away in Phillipsburg. Jesse quit school after the eighth grade to drill wells with his brother, but baseball was Pop's real passion. He pitched with several local semi-pro teams before being invited to pitch one game for the Dayton Veterans of the Class B Central League in 1913. From 1914 until 1920, he bounced around, playing with no less than eight minor league teams. He pitched one game for the Cincinnati Reds in 1918 and delivered a promising performance; however, he was released shortly thereafter. Haines considered quitting baseball but latched onto a semi-pro team before once again playing in the minor leagues. He pitched well enough to pique the interest of several major league clubs; Branch Rickey borrowed $10,000 from local banks—an enormous sum for the cash-starved team—to secure Haines' services. Thanks to the pipeline from the St. Louis farm system, Haines was the last player Rickey purchased.

The 26-year-old rookie debuted for the Cardinals on April 17, 1920, and went on to pitch 18 seasons for St. Louis. When Jesse retired at age 44, he was the Cardinals' all-time leader in wins, complete games, and total innings, and he was elected to baseball's Hall of Fame in 1970. Pop started out as a fastball-curveball pitcher, but his fastball began losing steam, so he developed a knuckleball in 1923, which helped him win 20 games for the first time. Haines' pitch didn't flutter like most knuckleballs. He grasped it with the first knuckles of his index and middle fingers, enabling him to throw harder and with more control. Unfortunately, his initial success and feel for the pitch eluded him during the 1924 and 1925 seasons. When spring training for 1926 rolled around, many questioned if Jesse was at the end of his rope. Hornsby wasn't one of them. Like his manager, Haines did not smoke or drink and was wholly devoted to the game. But what Hornsby most admired was Pop's competitive fire. He hated losing and often called out teammates for careless errors, mental lapses, or halfhearted efforts. Despite the pitcher's pedestrian results in 1925, Hornsby was determined to give him a chance at redemption.[7]

Hard-throwing, hard-partying Charles Flint "Shad" Rhem was another returning pitcher with something to prove. Flint hailed from Rhems, South Carolina, a tiny hamlet some 30 miles from the Atlantic coast named for an ancestor who settled there in 1846. He attended Clemson University from 1920 to 1924 to study engineering, yet he apparently did not graduate. Baseball was not part of his college plans even though he had played since he was nine. Fortunately for Clemson, the baseball coach persuaded Flint to join the team. Rhem dominated college hitters with his fastball, averaging 15 strikeouts per game. He signed with the Cardinals for the 1924 season and was assigned to the Fort Smith (Arkansas) Twins of the Class C Western Association. He tallied 22 wins and led the league in strikeouts with 282, earning a September call-up to St. Louis. Going into 1925, great things were expected of the burly twirler with the thick southern drawl and blazing fastball. He was a training camp sensation and won his first five regular season games on the mound; he struggled badly thereafter, however. Shad finished with eight wins and 13 losses and was battered to the tune of a 4.92 ERA. Sportswriters attributed his trouble to "illness," most likely a quaint euphemism referring to his penchant for drink and the night life. Long-time St. Louis sportswriter Bob Broeg lamented that Rhem "loved to celebrate every victory by bending his elbow. Come to think of it, after every defeat then and thereafter too."[8]

Flint placed the blame squarely on Branch Rickey. In a 1926 interview with Thomas Holmes of the *Brooklyn Daily Eagle*, Rhem said, "I don't mind telling you that Branch Rickey cramped my style, and that I think 'master minding' from the bench is the plain unvarnished bunk." Their pitching philosophies often clashed, but Rhem followed Rickey's orders despite his "firm conviction that [Rickey] was wrong." Flint ended up "throwing something in which I had no confidence." When he faltered after his hot start, Rickey began pulling the pitcher as soon as he got into hot water. "I blame that, more than anything else," Rhem charged, "for the fact that I dropped eight straight games." To Rhem, "yanking a pitcher merely because you haven't confidence in him is the surest way of all to wreck a young pitcher's morale."[9]

Despite Rhem's lackluster showing in the latter part of the 1925 season, Cardinal brass hoped he could curtail his nighttime debauchery and harness his obviously gifted right arm. But Flint did not endear himself to management by holding out at the start of spring training in 1926. General manager Branch Rickey said the club offered the hurler a substantial increase despite his poor record the previous year, but Flint wanted more "and the Cardinals are prepared to let him drift out of baseball if he insists." The *Post-Dispatch* predicted Rhem would sign "or else pursue the calm and placid life of a grocery clerk in the family mercantile in Rhems, S.C." The calm, placid life was not for Flint, and he signed his contract on February 25.[10]

Flint's comrade on the pitching mound Willie (Bill) Sherdel, the acknowledged staff ace, also staged a brief contract holdout, which he ended the day after Rhem. The diminutive southpaw (Sherdel stood 5 feet 8 inches and most likely weighed less than 150 pounds) had two pitch speeds: slow and slower. But he kept hitters off balance with a masterful change-up and a quick-pitch delivery that was later outlawed. "Wee Willie" was born on August 15, 1896, in Midway, Pennsylvania, and grew up in nearby Hanover. Baseball was Sherdel's lifelong passion, and he earned a reputation as a hard-throwing southpaw on local sandlot teams. In fall 1914, Bill entered the preparatory department at Gettysburg College; academic life, however, was not in the cards for Sherdel. He left school and signed with the Hanover Hornets of the Class D Blue Ridge League in 1915. Bill enjoyed a good deal of success his first two years and then moved up to the Milwaukee Brewers of the American Association. He found his fastball was not very effective against more seasoned hitters, so he took his lumps on the mound while perfecting a change-up and slow curve. Despite a poor record in Milwaukee, Branch Rickey saw enough in Sherdel to dispatch a scout to sign him in July 1917. He debuted in St. Louis in April 1918 and struggled, though he eventually turned things around. He finished with a 6–12 record but sported a solid 2.71 ERA in 182 innings. He blossomed in 1922, winning 17 games, though he struggled mightily during the next two seasons. As a result, Branch Rickey demoted him to a spot starter and reliever. Bill's prospects brightened in 1925 after Hornsby assumed control of the team. He won 15 and lost 6 and completed 17 of his 21 starts. Hornsby looked to Sherdel to anchor the pitching staff in 1926.[11]

Flint Rhem's pitching helped keep the club afloat during its early season struggles. But his penchant for the night life hampered his effectiveness later that summer (St. Louis Mercantile Library at the University of Missouri-St. Louis).

Fellow lefty John Walter "Duster" Mails hoped to land a starting spot after he fashioned a 7–7 record with the Cardinals the previous year. Mails was one of baseball's more colorful free spirits of the 1920s. He first appeared in the majors with the Brooklyn Dodgers in 1915 but then spent the next few years toiling in the minor leagues before making a big splash with the Cleveland Indians during the hotly contested 1920 pennant race. He won seven games without a loss to help the Indians clinch the pennant and subsequently pitched spectacular ball during the World Series. Duster followed that up with a 14-win campaign in 1921; however, the Indians released him in 1922 after his ERA ballooned to 5.28. He returned to his native California and pitched with the Oakland Oaks of the Pacific Coast League in 1923 and 1924.

Mails never lacked for confidence in his abilities and routinely referred to himself as "The Great Mails." He endeared himself to Oakland fans with his brash persona, especially after winning 23 games in 1923 and 24 in 1924. One particularly dramatic episode cemented his place in West Coast baseball lore. In a late-season game against the Portland Beavers, Mails clung to a narrow lead into the last inning, but Duster ran into some trouble. Runners were on base, and the opposition's star hitter, Jim Poole, was at bat and worked the count full. According to sportswriter Bozeman Bulger of the *New York World*, the crowd, "sensing the drama of the situation, grew deathly quiet as Mails started to wind up." Suddenly, he stopped, held up his hand for continued quiet, and made a public declaration to Poole and the entire crowd. "We have come to a serious moment," he said. "Either we do or we don't. The pennant will be decided on the next ball I pitch or the one that you hit.[12] After I turn loose this old pill, Mr. Poole, one of us will be a hero and the other will be a bum. There is no alternative." After a short pause, Mails added, "And, Mr. Poole, The Great Mails can not be a bum!" He backed up his bravado with a blistering pitch to strike Poole out and win the game.[13] The normally taciturn Hornsby probably gritted his teeth at some of Mails' eccentric antics but tolerated them as long as Duster backed up his big talk.

Art Reinhart, yet another left-hander, aimed to parley his 1925 success into a spot on the 1926 mound crew. Reinhart was born on May 29, 1899, in the hamlet of Ackley, Iowa. He was another of several Cardinals who attended college. Reinhart studied at the University of Iowa and starred as a pitcher on the baseball team, throwing four no-hitters during the 1918 season. He was a sturdy six feet tall and 175 pounds, and his exploits on the mound attracted interest from several major league clubs. Cardinal scout Charlie Barrett, however, beat out the Tigers and Indians for Reinhart's services. Art faced one major league batter in 1919 before being shipped to Houston of the Texas League, where he fashioned a 13–15 record with a sparkling 2.14 ERA. For several consecutive years, the Cardinals invited Reinhart to spring training, but he couldn't crack the St. Louis roster. He bounced around the minors, logging time with Milwaukee, Seattle, and Los Angeles before landing with the Syracuse Stars, a Cardinal farm team in the International League, in 1922.

Reinhart thrived under the tutelage of manager Frank "Shag" Shaughnessy, a long-time minor league outfielder who made brief appearances in the major leagues with the Washington Senators in 1905 and Philadelphia Athletics in 1908. Art put together two solid seasons with Syracuse, winning 19 and 17 games in 1923 and 1924, respectively. But he and the team floundered in 1925, leading to Shaughnessy's dismissal. The manager's misfortune proved to be a lucky break for Reinhart. Shaughnessy joined the Cardinals as a scout for exactly one week before he took another managerial job, but it was enough time to inform Rogers Hornsby that Reinhart could help the Redbirds despite Art's modest production at Syracuse. "Bring Reinhart in now and he'll win 60 per cent of his ball games in the National League," he told Hornsby, "I don't think he will win more than 40 per cent if he stays in the International, but he'll thrive up there where the umpires will give him strikes when he pitches over the corners." The Cardinal skipper took Shaughnessy at his word and added Reinhart to the roster in June. The southpaw lived up to Shaughnessy's prediction as he won 11 games against five losses and was among the league leaders with a 3.05 ERA. His breakthrough was key to the Cardinals' rise to fourth place, and Reinhart seemed to be a lock for the 1926 staff.[14]

Still another portsider vying for a spot in the rotation was a young fireballer named Bill Hallahan. He was born in Binghamton, New York, on August 4, 1902. Unlike several other Cardinal pitchers, Bill was not university material. He failed several grades in school and quit after the eighth grade. Baseball was his one and only passion. He played on the local sandlots and with semi-pro teams for several years, earning a reputation as one of the hardest throwers in the area. Velocity was not a problem for Bill, but he was never quite sure where his pitches were going to go, and he became known as "Wild Bill" Hallahan. Nevertheless, professional scouts took notice. Bill got his first chance at professional baseball after the 1923 season when he signed with the Syracuse Stars, part of the Cardinal farm system.

Branch Rickey got his first look at Hallahan during spring training in 1924 and saw the good and bad in the young hurler. "He's so wild," Rickey decided, "he can hardly hit the backstop, but there's a pitcher who someday will pitch and win a World Series game." Wild Bill more than lived up to his nickname, walking 112 in 149 innings during the 1924 season. His wildness drove managers crazy, and he was shuttled from Syracuse to Fort Smith to Kalamazoo, Michigan. But Bill shined during spring training in 1925. He pitched no-hit ball for seven innings against the San Francisco Seals of the Pacific Coast League and ended up with a two-hit shutout. He made the Cardinal squad coming out of spring training, but two ineffective performances prompted Rickey to option Bill to Syracuse. He struggled after his demotion, winning eight while losing 15 and walking 114 in 178 innings throughout the 1925 season. Hallahan hoped his third spring training with St. Louis would be the charm to temper his lack of control.[15]

The final left-handed candidate for a pitching spot was Eddie Dyer, a Louisiana native whose father moved the family to Houston after his lumber and general store business failed. In high school, Eddie starred in football and baseball and earned an athletic scholarship to Rice Institute (now Rice University), where he was named All-Southwestern Conference halfback in football. Dyer also played outfield and pitched for the baseball team. He performed well enough to receive a $2,500 bonus from Branch Rickey to sign with the Cardinals. In 1922 and 1923, he bounced between the minors and St. Louis; however, he made a splash in his first major league start in late September 1923, when he pitched a 3–0 shutout against the Chicago Cubs. Dyer stuck with the Cardinals in 1924 and 1925, compiling a modest pitching record. He hoped 1926 would be a new start.[16]

The Cardinals shored up the pitching staff with three right-handed acquisitions during the offseason, including Walter Huntzinger. A native of Pottsville, Pennsylvania, Huntzinger starred as the lead pitcher of the University of Pennsylvania nine and joined the New York Giants immediately after graduating in 1923. Manager John McGraw didn't use Huntzinger in high-leverage situations, relegating him to mop-up duty. Walter finally made an impact in 1925, pitching in 26 games in relief and winning five against only one loss. He showed enough that the Cardinals purchased his contract on January 5, 1926.

Right-hander Sylvester (Syl) Johnson, a 25-year-old from Portland, Oregon, was another new addition. At eight years old, he was a regular player on the local sandlots. He started out as a catcher, but after a fastball hit him in the mouth, loosening some teeth and knocking him out cold, he decided it would be safer to be on the pitcher's mound. He dropped out of high school and worked with his father in a paper mill, but baseball remained uppermost in Syl's mind. When not working, he pitched with minor league teams in Portland and Vancouver. In 1921, poor offensive support and a spate of bad luck resulted in a deceptively dismal record of 12 wins and 26 losses, despite a 3.82 ERA. Johnson's side-armed fastball garnered interest from a Detroit Tigers scout, and the Tigers purchased Syl's contract prior to the 1922 season. Unfortunately, misfortune continued to dog him. During an exhibition game, a line drive shattered the bones joining his wrist and hand. If that weren't enough, Johnson spent more time on the bench after part of his tonsils were removed. Yet he posted a 7–3 record and earned an invitation to return to the Tigers in 1923. He rewarded the team's faith by compiling a 12–7 record and 3.98 ERA. The next year, he suffered through a miserable campaign, going 5–4 with a bloated 4.93 ERA. His bad luck continued in 1925. In May, Bibb Falk of the White Sox smacked a pitch that hit Syl in the left eye and fractured eight bones. Johnson recuperated in Chicago for three weeks before being shipped back to the minors in California, where he turned in a dismal 3–17 record. Cardinal scout Charlie Barrett still saw something in Syl, convincing Breadon, Rickey, and Hornsby to give the righty another chance in the big leagues.[17]

Victor (Vic) Keen, a cast-off obtained from the Chicago Cubs, was the third offseason, right-handed acquisition. Keen's father was a Methodist minister, so it was little surprise that Vic developed into a mild-mannered, devout young man. He starred as the mainstay of the University of Maryland pitching staff and received contract offers from 15 of the 16 major league clubs before signing with the Cubs. Dubbed "Parson" by *Chicago Tribune* beat writer Irving Vaughn, Vic won 12 games in 1923 and 15 in 1924. He featured a fastball that had "plenty of smoke on it" despite his slight build at 5 feet 10 inches tall and 165 pounds. Keen also had a serviceable curveball and a good change up. But a sore arm spelled disaster during the 1925 season. He won only two games while losing six, and his ERA ballooned to 6.26 as the Cubs tumbled to last place. In December 1925, the Cardinals raised eyebrows when they traded shortstop Jimmy Cooney to Chicago for Keen. New coach Bill Killefer was a strong believer in Keen and urged the Cardinals to make the swap. Killefer managed Keen in Chicago and knew what he could do when healthy. "One thing is certain," Hornsby asserted in his typically blunt manner when the deal was announced, "we did not give away for Keen a player who will be missed as a Cardinal regular." He acknowledged the trade should help both clubs because Chicago needed a shortstop, and he was confident Keen would bounce back in a St. Louis uniform.[18]

Compared to the Parson, Herman Bell, a 28-year-old right-hander from Iowa, followed an unconventional path to professional baseball. He enlisted in the Army during World War I, after which he worked on a ranch in Colorado for three years. He did not play any ball during that time, but the baseball itch was too strong. He broke in with Sioux Falls of the Dakota League in 1922. After the league disbanded in 1923, Bell played semi-pro baseball in St. Louis where Cardinal scout Charlie Barrett spotted and signed him. He made the team in 1924, putting together a pedestrian 3–8 record with a 4.92 ERA. However, he did enjoy one bright shining moment that season. On July 20, he started and won both games of a doubleheader versus the Boston Braves. In the opener, he had a perfect game through 7⅓ innings before settling for a two-hit, 6–1 win. Branch Rickey was so impressed with how easily Bell breezed through the Boston lineup that he let him start the second game, which he won 2–1, giving up only four hits. That brief heroic effort did not clinch a permanent spot on the team, however. Herman spent all of 1925 with Milwaukee of the American Association before earning an invitation to the Cardinal camp in 1926. For some unexplained reason, Bell did not arrive for spring training until March 11, the last player to report. James Gould of the *St. Louis Star* joked there "was some suspicion here that Herman had mistaken the year he was to have reported for training." Hornsby was undoubtedly more than miffed by the actions of someone who had to battle to make the roster.[19]

The Rajah displayed more patience with Allen Sothoron, a right-hander who was one of 17 pitchers allowed to continue throwing a spitball after it was outlawed in 1920. He grew up in a small town in western Ohio and played baseball for Juniata College in Huntingdon, Pennsylvania. He began his professional career in 1912 as an outfielder but switched to the mound in 1913. Sothoron pitched a handful of games with the St. Louis Browns in 1914 and 1915 before spending the entire 1916 season with the Portland Beavers of the Pacific Coast League, where he enjoyed a banner campaign. The righty pitched an incredible 397 innings and led the league with 30 wins. That performance earned another shot at the majors in 1917, and he took advantage of the opportunity. Allen strung together three solid seasons with the lackluster Browns—winning 20 games in 1919—before tumbling to an 8–15 record and 4.70 ERA in 1920. The following year, he was shuttled from the Browns to the Red Sox and then to Cleveland, where he pitched well. Another bad year in 1922 found him spending the 1923 season in the minor leagues. He caught on with the Cardinals in 1924 and won ten games that season and the next, though by the 1926 spring camp, it appeared the 36-year-old was nearing the end of the line. Hornsby likely viewed Sothoron as an unofficial pitching coach for the younger staff members.[20]

Behind the Plate

As for the other half of the battery, catching duties were in the capable hands of Bob O'Farrell, another gift from the Chicago Cubs. O'Farrell played high school and semi-pro baseball in his hometown of Waukegan, Illinois. He turned to catching because no one else wanted the job. He got his big-league break when the Waukegan nine hosted an exhibition game with the Chicago Cubs in 1915. O'Farrell caught the eye of Cubs player-manager Roger Bresnahan, who offered Bob a contract on the spot; O'Farrell made his debut with the Cubs in September that same year. He was sent down to the minors in 1916 but rejoined the Cubs for good in 1918, backing up starter Bill Killefer. Injuries curtailed Killefer's season in 1920, and O'Farrell stepped into the starting lineup. He earned praise for his defensive work—leading the league in putouts and assists—and hit over .300 during the 1922 and 1923 seasons. Bob was recognized as one of the best catchers in the majors; however, his time in Chicago essentially ended in June 1924, when he suffered a concussion and fractured skull from a foul tip that hit his catcher's mask. He did not play for the remainder of the year, opening the door for future Hall of Famer Gabby Hartnett. The Cubs traded O'Farrell to the Cardinals in May 1925, one week before Hornsby was named manager. Hornsby inserted Bob into a starting role, and he provided a steady hand as the Cardinals surged up the standings into fourth place.[21]

With O'Farrell entrenched behind the plate, the battle for a backup role fell to both Firman "Bill" Warwick, who had bounced around the minors for several years before getting a brief promotion to the Cardinals in 1925, and Henry "Ernie" Vick. Warwick was born in Philadelphia in 1897 and attended the University of Pennsylvania, where he became a star catcher for the university baseball team. Local followers compared Warwick's slugging exploits to Babe Ruth. Bill also took a turn at football, even though he had never played the game before and was "given special instruction" by head coach Bob Folwell. Once his university days were finished, Bill played with several independent clubs in 1920 and 1921 before signing with the Pittsburgh Pirates in July to begin his professional career. He made only one plate appearance during the 1921 season before spending the next four years in the minor leagues. In

1925, he hit .306 and clouted 20 home runs with San Antonio of the Texas League, which prompted the Cardinals to purchase his contract as a late season call-up. In 13 games with St. Louis, Warwick hit .293 with two triples and a home run in 47 plate appearances. It was hoped he could provide a potent bat off the bench for the Cardinals in 1926.[22]

Ernie Vick was born in Ohio and attended the University of Michigan, where he not only studied medicine but also starred on the baseball diamond and football field. In fact, the 5'9", 185-pound Vick played center and was named to Walter Camp's All-American team in 1921. Branch Rickey capitalized on connections with his alma mater and persuaded the Wolverine backstop to throw his fortune in with the Cardinals. Vick spent most of the 1922 season with Syracuse and then was optioned to Houston of the Texas League for the entire 1923 season. A strong spring camp in 1924 helped Ernie make the Cardinal roster, but he played sparingly, so Branch Rickey sent him to Louisville of the American Association to get some regular work. Vick's season was cut short on September 12 when a pitch broke his jaw. He made the Cardinals again in 1925 and, again, played little as his batting average plummeted to .188. Hornsby hoped either of the two inexperienced backstops could develop into a viable option to spell O'Farrell occasionally, but the Cardinal manager looked all season long for a veteran presence to back up his starting catcher.[23]

Around the Bases

Unlike the catching position, Hornsby believed relatively few changes were needed among the position players—no doubt reflecting the team's strong 1925 finish. The infield was set. Hornsby, of course, anchored things at second base. Jim Bottomley, one of the first and best products of Branch Rickey's farm system, manned first base. He was born in Oglesby, Illinois, to a coal mining and farming family. Jim quit high school at age 16 to work and contribute to the family finances. In addition to various jobs, he played baseball with several semi-pro teams until a local policeman tipped off Branch Rickey about the smooth-fielding, hard-hitting first baseman. Rickey had Cardinal scout Charlie Barrett contact Bottomley, who responded on September 10, 1919, with a letter scribbled on tablet paper. He informed Barrett he "would like to have a tryout in some league." Noting he hit and threw left-handed and played first base, he rated his fielding as very good and his hitting as good. He had "never played with or against any major or minor league team, but have played with and against some fast amateur teams."[24] Barrett invited Jim to St. Louis for a tryout where he impressed the Cardinals enough that he immediately signed a contract for $150 per month.

Bottomley moved quickly through the minors. He arrived in St. Louis late in the 1922 season and hit .325 in 37 games. He had a confident, almost cocky swagger about him, and he wore his cap at a rakish angle over his left eye. With his ever-present smile and genial disposition (hence the nickname "Sunny" Jim), he quickly became a fan favorite, especially among female fans. He never lost his modest congeniality nor his affinity for the simple rural life. Upon his retirement as an active player with the St. Louis Browns in 1936, the team orchestrated a "day" in his honor. When asked what he'd like as a retirement gift, Jim asked for a Jersey cow because, "They're the best milkers." During Bottomley's rookie season in 1923, he promptly established himself as one of the National League's leading run producers. He drove in 94 runs and finished second in the batting race, hitting a lofty .371 to Hornsby's .384. Jim set a major league record by driving in 12 runs in a 1924 game against Brooklyn, and he would drive in more than 111 runs for six consecutive seasons. He would go on to win the National League MVP award in 1928 and was posthumously voted into baseball's Hall of Fame in 1974.[25]

Tommy Thevenow, a lean 23-year-old from Madison, Indiana, manned the shortstop position. Like several teammates, Thevenow emerged from a rural, small-town setting and got his start playing with the local nines. He moved on from Madison to play with a semi-pro team in Centralia, Illinois, and then signed with the Joplin, Missouri, Miners of the Class C Western Association for the 1923 season. "Silent" Tommy had a stoic nature, saying very little as he went about his business with little fanfare. His hitting was nothing to write home about, but his glovework was phenomenal. He had terrific range at short and possessed a strong arm that could throw accurately from various angles. His fielding during a pregame practice so impressed Branch Rickey, who was in Joplin to scout a player on the opposing team, that he purchased Thevenow's contract for $4,000. "This incident," wrote L.H. Addington of the *Sporting News*, was "just another tribute to Rickey's ability for spotting young talent on the hoof. He had never seen or heard of Thevenow until that afternoon in Joplin, but it took just one wink of his wise old eye to know his man." Tommy was promoted to the Double-A Syracuse Stars in 1924. He led International League shortstops in assists and batted a respectable .270.

Thevenow made the Cardinal roster coming out of spring training in 1925, but after batting a dismal .182 ten games into the season, Rickey sent him back to Syracuse. This move "somewhat peeved" Hornsby when he took over as manager. He was sure Thevenow's fielding would be of great value to the club, and he wanted to recall the Hoosier and install him as the regular shortstop. The negotiated agreement with Syracuse blocked that plan. According to a newspaper account, Thevenow had to remain the entire season with Syracuse unless a satisfactory substitute was provided, and "Hornsby did not have one at that time." Former Stars manager "Shag" Shaughnessy assuaged Hornsby's anger, convincing him that, after another year of steady work at Syracuse, Thevenow would be ready to "step into the St. Louis shortstop berth next spring, never to be replaced unless because of injury or old age." Hornsby wasn't willing to wait until next season. He recalled Thevenow in mid–August, plugged him into the lineup, and let him play. His fielding continued to turn heads, and his hitting improved. He finished the season with a .269 batting average.

During spring training, Hornsby sung Thevenow's praises to anyone who would listen. The Rajah claimed Thevenow was already the third best shortstop in the National League—behind Glenn Wright of the Pirates and Dave Bancroft of the Boston Braves—and predicted Tommy would become one of the best fielding shortstops in the National League within two years. His batting was a work in progress, but Hornsby considered him a tough out in clutch situations and was confident he could teach Thevenow a lot about "the art of batting."[26]

To Thevenow's right, Lester (Les) Bell was slated to handle third base. Bell was born in Harrisburg, Pennsylvania, in 1901. He cut his teeth playing on local sandlots and with Technical High School before playing shortstop in the semi-pro West End Twilight League in 1920. A local newspaper spouted that Bell had "all the ear-marks of a future major league star." Les was leading the West End League in batting at .482 when he signed a contract with the Detroit Tigers in July 1921 and was assigned to the Bristol [Tennessee] State Liners of the Appalachian League. Amid financial woes, the club released Bell and other players who lived outside Bristol. He returned to Pennsylvania and finished the season with the West End Club.

The following year, Les played for the Lansing, Michigan, club in the Central League and hit .329. The Cardinals purchased Bell's contract in August 1922 and farmed him out to Syracuse and then to Houston for the 1923 season. Cardinal scout Charlie Barrett told St. Louis sportswriters in early September, "I got a young feller comin' in here to play short some o' these days that will make the fans open their eyes. He's a great boy, can hit, field and throw, and he'll be this club's shortstop next year. I'm right on this feller; he's no counterfeit." Bell got a chance to prove himself during a late-season call-up in 1923. He debuted on September 17 against the Philadelphia Phillies, going one for four with two errors in the Cardinals' 6–5 win. Bell's play over the remainder of the season impressed Branch Rickey as well as the team's superstar second baseman. Hornsby claimed in early October that Les was the "best player on the team at the present time." Bell battered National League pitchers with a .373 average in 15 games, though his fielding was somewhat ragged.

During spring training in 1924, Rickey moved Bell from shortstop to third base, but when the season started, Les found himself back at short. The results weren't good. In 17 games, he hit a humdrum .246 and made nine errors. Vowing to find a more capable shortstop, Branch Rickey optioned Bell to the Milwaukee Brewers in exchange for Jimmy Cooney. Bell took out his frustration on American Association pitchers and pummeled them to the tune of 230 hits, 53 doubles, 18 home runs, and a league-leading .365 average. To no one's surprise, the Cardinals recalled Bell and penciled him in as the team's starting third baseman for the 1925 season. His fielding woes continued with 36 errors, but he emerged as an effective run producer, knocking in 88 runs. Hornsby made it his personal mission to boost Bell's confidence for the 1926 campaign.[27]

Two players were in line for utility infield roles. George "Specs" Toporcer was the first infielder to wear glasses and refuted the widespread assumption that someone who did so could not hit and field in the big leagues. George was born in New York on February 9, 1899, and grew up living above his father's modest shoemaking shop on Manhattan's Upper East Side. George loved to play baseball, but his school's team often bypassed him because of his thick glasses and rail-thin build. No doubt motivated by the embarrassment, George honed his baseball skills on New York sandlots, even after his father passed away in 1913, and George quit school to help run the family shop. His athletic ability improved enough that Toporcer earned a spot with Syracuse in 1920 and then made the Cardinals in 1921 after a strong spring training. Over the next several years, he provided solid hitting while earning a reputation as a "jack-of-all trades" infielder.[28]

One of Rogers Hornsby's most important managerial moves was to install Tommy Thevenow as the starting shortstop. His tremendous glove work and clutch hitting were crucial to the Cardinals' success (St. Louis Mercantile Library at the University of Missouri-St. Louis).

D'Arcy "Jake" Flowers provided additional infield insurance. He grew up in Cambridge on Maryland's eastern shore, where his father worked as a waterman on Chesapeake Bay and his mother was a self-employed dressmaker. He played shortstop for Washington College in Chesterton and his hometown Cambridge Canners of the Eastern Shore League. His bat—he led the league in home runs with 14 in 1922—and speed and range at shortstop caught the eye of a Cardinal scout. The Cardinals purchased his contract in 1923, and he made his National League debut later that season against the Reds on September 7. Jake struggled at the plate against major league pitching, hitting only .094, so he opened the 1924 season with Fort Smith of the Class C Western Association. There he thrived, hitting .318 with 22 home runs, but the Cardinals optioned him to Oakland in August, and he finished his season in the Pacific Coast League. Jake had surgery during the offseason to repair an injured index finger, which he suffered while at Fort Smith. That injury likely cost Flowers the chance to earn the shortstop job with the Cardinals in 1925. He was sent back to Oakland and, again, had a fine year despite missing the first 25 games of the season after his injured finger became infected and missing time after a broken ankle in late September. Jake had recovered fully by spring training in 1926 and was ready to compete for a roster spot.[29]

Roaming the Wide-open Spaces

The outfield proved to be more of a mystery. Hornsby planned to carry five outfielders, and only leftfielder Ray Blades seemed assured of a starting job. Ray first caught the attention of Branch Rickey in 1919 after the semi-pro Mount Vernon, Illinois, team on which Blades played second base defeated the Cardinals in an exhibition game. His professional career began with Memphis of the Southern Association in 1920. He then moved on to the Houston Buffaloes of the Texas League for the 1921 and 1922 seasons. He was leading the Texas League in hitting at .330 when the Cardinals called him up on August 18, 1922. Blades played 37 games with St. Louis and fared well, ending the season with a .300 batting average. Tragic circumstances and his erratic fielding at second and third base prompted a position change for 1923. The Cardinals' budding star leftfielder Austin McHenry died in November 1922 of a brain tumor at the age of 27. His untimely demise left a gaping hole in the lineup. With Hornsby firmly entrenched at second base, Rickey tabbed Blades to step into the outfield breach. Ray worked hard to master the nuances of outfield play and became one of the better defenders in the National League.[30]

Charles "Chick" Hafey appeared to have the inside track for rightfield. A native of Berkeley, California, he was one of eight children born to James and Anna Hafey. While pitching for a local winter team, Chick was scouted by University of California professor and part-time Cardinals' scout Charles Chapman. Chick's pitching days ended during his first spring training in Bradenton, Florida. Branch Rickey watched him crush baseballs into a grove of trees deep in leftfield and immediately switched Chick to the outfield. During the 1924 season, he hit .360 for the Houston Buffaloes and earned a promotion to St. Louis in August. He slumped in 1925, hitting a lowly .219 by the end of June and was sent to Syracuse in the International League. A month later, he was back in St. Louis after Ray Blades suffered a leg injury. Chick started hitting and never stopped, finishing the season with a .302 average. He never played another minor league game again. Several contemporaries insisted few major leaguers hit the ball harder than Hafey, despite being plagued with vision problems throughout his career. He had a chronic sinus condition that required several operations, so Hafey took to wearing glasses for the 1929 season—the first outfielder to do so. In the field, he was blessed with great range and one of the National League's most powerful throwing arms. Famed New York Giants manager John McGraw once said of Hafey, "With two good eyes, he'd be the best player in the game."[31]

Something other than vision was the problem for Heine Mueller, who was competing for the starting job in centerfield. A native of the south side of St. Louis, he naturally was a fan favorite. The 1926 season was his seventh with the Cardinals. He typically performed well in spring training but fizzled during the regular season and was benched or sent back to the minors. He had all the physical tools to become a star. He could hit, run, field, and throw, and the brash outfielder wasn't shy about touting his athletic prowess. He compared his hitting ability to Babe Ruth and claimed he was faster than Ty Cobb. His problem, however, was between his ears. As described by longtime sportswriter Fred Lieb, Mueller "frequently forgot his instructions from the bench to the plate."

His free-spirited antics prompted teammates to lovingly nickname him "Rockhead." His baserunning, especially, left something to be desired. He had the bad habit of running with his head down, "paying little attention to where he was going just so he got there fast." William McGoogan of the *Post-Dispatch* recalled an incident in a 1923 game against Pittsburgh in which Mueller raced from first to third on a pop foul to the catcher with only one out, a blunder that resulted in his demotion to the minors even though he was hitting above .400 at the time. Thomas Holmes of the *Brooklyn Daily Eagle* related a story in which Mueller hit a home run with Rogers Hornsby perched on first base. Hornsby saw immediately that the ball was leaving the park and leisurely jogged on his way to second base. Mueller, however, "put his head down and tore around as fast as he could and passed the astonished Hornsby as though Rog was standing still." Mueller was called out for passing the baserunner in front of him, and his clout over the fence became a single with no one scoring. His clownish tactics made good copy for the newspapers and amused teammates and foes alike but failed to win any ball games.[32] To gain Hornsby's trust and earn more playing time, he adopted a more serious mindset about his profession.

Perhaps Mueller's new attitude was also spurred by the competition for the centerfield job from a fleet-footed hotshot rookie named Taylor Douthit. Douthit grew up in Oakland, California, and earned a degree in agriculture from the University of California in Berkeley. A late bloomer, he didn't play baseball at his high school until his senior year, but he led the team to a state championship. At Cal, Taylor played on the varsity team for three years and hit over .400 his senior season. Once again, Professor Chapman provided an enormous assist to the Cardinals when he convinced Branch Rickey to offer Douthit a contract. Ten days after graduating in spring 1923, Taylor was wearing a Redbird uniform. He spent most of the season at Fort Smith and earned a September call-up with the Cardinals. In 1924, he roamed the outfield for St. Joseph of the Class A Western League, though he played 53 games with the Cardinals. In 1925, he started the season in St. Louis but was farmed out to the American Association Milwaukee Brewers in late June. In 92 games at Milwaukee, Douthit led the league in hitting with a .372 average, having tallied 25 doubles, ten triples and ten home runs. He showed off both his speed by stealing 26 bases and his arm, tallying 16 assists. Taylor's performance earned another September call-up with

St. Louis. Hornsby recognized the young outfielder's talent and remarked during the offseason that he was looking to Douthit to man centerfield in 1926.³³

Roscoe "Wattie" Holm was set to battle for the final reserve outfield spot. Holm was born in Peterson, Iowa, and attended Lake Forest Academy preparatory school near Chicago, where he starred on the baseball, football, and track squads. He enrolled at the University of Iowa to play baseball and football and to study dentistry. After his freshman year, he played with a professional team during the summer. In the fall, he was set to play quarterback on the gridiron; however, the Big Ten informed him he lost his eligibility by being paid to play baseball. Holm told a reporter,

Fleet-footed rookie centerfielder Taylor Douthit emerged as an important contributor with the bat, on the field, and on the basepaths (St. Louis Cardinals Hall of Fame and Museum).

"They took everything but my books on dentistry away from me, and I gave those away a short time afterward. I left school the next spring when I got a chance to try with the Cardinals." Branch Rickey assigned Holm to Syracuse, where he split time at shortstop and in the outfield and batted .313. He earned an invitation to the Cardinals spring training camp in 1924. Rickey tried to make him a catcher but abruptly switched him to the outfield. Wattie proved to be a solid backup, hitting .294 with ten doubles, four triples, and 23 RBIs, but he slumped badly in 1925. His batting average plunged to .207, and Rickey demoted him to Syracuse. Holm was determined to redeem himself in 1926.³⁴

Ten-year veteran Jack Smith was another outfield candidate, though he apparently did not fit into Hornsby's plans, despite being one of the few left-handed batters on the roster. Smith became a regular with the Cardinals in 1916. A fleet baserunner, his hitting suffered until the introduction of the lively ball in 1920. His average jumped from .223 in 1919 to .332 the following year, and he proceeded to hit over .300 through the 1923 season. His work at the plate declined thereafter, and his troubles against southpaw pitchers relegated him to the bench whenever a lefty was on the mound. Smith disliked his platoon situation and made no secret that he wanted to be traded. Hornsby was more than happy to oblige and made it clear the outfielder could be obtained in exchange for a catcher.

With the cast of characters essentially set, Hornsby eagerly looked forward to the task of molding the squad into a competitive force in the National League.

Chapter 4

Laying Down the Law in Texas: Spring Training, February 21–April 12

The Cardinals and Browns weren't the only professional baseball teams preparing for the upcoming season. Like the Cardinals, the St. Louis Stars of the Negro National League, which lost to the Kansas City Monarchs in the 1925 championship series, were looking to challenge for a title in 1926. The Stars assembled a formidable offensive team, capitalizing on the advantageous dimensions of Stars Park, their home base since 1922. Situated at Market and Compton streets, the ballpark shared its left field wall with a streetcar barn. The 35-foot wall was only 269 feet from home plate and made right-handed sluggers like third baseman Dewey Creacy, leftfielder Wilson Redus, catcher Mitchell Murray, Hall of Fame shortstop Willie Wells, and Hall of Fame first baseman George "Mule" Suttles salivate. Coming over from the Birmingham Barons, the burly Suttles and his menacing 50-ounce bat found the left field porch particularly inviting. Setting the table for this offensive machine was none other than fleet centerfielder James "Cool Papa" Bell, the third Hall of Famer from the 1926 team.[1]

The Stars commenced spring training in St. Louis on March 29, though cold weather forced the team to practice indoors at the local YMCA. Spring camp ended on an equally dismal note as the Stars lost three of four exhibition games against the reigning champion Monarchs at Stars Park. The regular season started even worse. The Stars opened the season in Kansas City and lost five straight to the Monarchs, though St. Louis rebounded to finish 61–35–2, six games behind the Monarchs.[2]

The team was an offensive juggernaut, leading the Negro National League in batting average (.329), home runs (116), runs (711), doubles (178), triples (74), and stolen bases (155). Mule Suttles had a season for the ages, leading the league with a .425 average, 32 home runs, 130 RBIs, 19 triples, a .472 on base percentage, an .877 slugging average, and an OPS of 1.349. Dewey Creacy chipped in with a .340 average and finished second in the league with 23 home runs and 107 RBIs. Willie Wells slashed pitchers for an average of .373, and Cool Papa Bell sparked the attack with a .334 average and led the league with 36 stolen bases and 107 runs scored. A slipshod mound crew, however, sabotaged the St. Louis sluggers. Logan Hensley won 18 games with a 4.16 ERA, but opponents battered *the pitching staff to the tune of a 5.24 ERA.*[3] *Though the Stars fell short in 1926, they paralleled the Cardinals by claiming league titles in 1928, 1930, and 1931.*

With title aspirations of his own, Rogers Hornsby concocted a spring training plan that deviated drastically from his predecessor. Admittedly a "trifle old-fashioned," Hornsby wanted to follow "camp policies that were regarded as safe and sound before Florida and the wave of exhibition games broke into the scheme of things." In other words, he jettisoned nearly all Branch Rickey's training practices. Hornsby believed a prolonged, tiresome conditioning grind was not effective, so he scaled back workouts from Rickey's two-a-day sessions to one practice from 10:00 a.m. to 2:00 p.m. Stopping for lunch after a morning practice and regrouping for an afternoon workout was too disruptive. "As a rule," he said, the "luncheon lapse has taken [the players] off their minds and they are tired and sluggish." He further claimed too much practice was worse than not enough "for if the men are driven too hard they become stale long before the season opens, or they balk at the work and this may bring discipline into contempt. Keeping players fit mentally is just as important a part of training as the physical end of it."

Despite foregoing lunch during practice, the Cardinal manager firmly believed a proper diet was an important part of the "physical end of it." Ever since he arrived in the big leagues, Hornsby had been a fan of eating a lot of steak to build up his strength and was going to have his team follow a similar regimen with plenty of beef, greens and other vegetables on the menu. When the squad was on the road, Hornsby planned to switch to the "American Plan" in which players ate at the hotels where the team stayed rather than using the "European Plan," which allowed players to eat wherever they wanted. The Rajah was convinced the Cardinals' road woes in 1925 stemmed in part from players pocketing their $3.50 meal allotment and not eating as they should.[4]

Hornsby also thought it unnecessary to face a lot of big league pitching during spring training. If the players were in good condition and got plenty of batting practice, he reasoned, they would be fine. As a result, he ignored recent training locales in Florida or California and set up camp in his native Texas at San Antonio. Nearly all the Cardinals' exhibition games were against minor league teams, including the San Antonio Bears, Fort Worth Panthers, and Houston Buffaloes of the Texas League as well as teams from Waco, Tulsa, Oklahoma City, Des Moines, Springfield, and Shreveport. Even the University of Texas baseball team was on the schedule.[5] Hornsby's desire to establish a winning culture influenced his thinking, even if it was against lesser competition. "Let them get the winning habit now," he said during camp, "and they will carry it with them through the season."[6]

Aware the Cardinals' mound crew was the team's biggest question mark, Hornsby hired Bill Killefer, former catcher and manager of the Chicago Cubs, to coach the staff. Killefer was widely respected as a pitching guru who coaxed the best from his players, and Hornsby had great confidence in Killefer's "ability to produce winning pitchers out of our material."[7] Hornsby wanted to make sure that material was in good shape going into the regular season and had pitchers and catchers report on February 21 to Hot Wells (a.k.a. Terrell Wells), a sulfur bath resort just outside San Antonio. This had been a popular "boiling out" place for players when Texas was the primary training spot for major league baseball, and Hornsby thought the resort worth another try.

An undoubtedly blurry-eyed group of Redbird pitchers and catchers arrived in San Antonio on Sunday night, February 21. During the exhausting 26-hour train trip from St. Louis, they played cards to while away the time. Texas state law, however, forbid card playing on Sunday, "so the window shades were pulled down while passing through towns." When the team arrived, a brass band and contingent of city officials and other dignitaries greeted the players, no doubt to welcome home their native son, Hornsby. Then members of the city Fire Department, Police Department, and Chamber of Commerce provided automobiles to haul Cardinal players to the new Terrell Hotel, some five miles from San Antonio. With the team ensconced at the hotel, Hornsby laid down only a few training rules. "They are big league ball players and are of sufficient age to know what is good for them," he said. He requested that the men retire by 11:00 each evening and decreed that only pitchers were permitted to play golf. Hornsby's obsession with hitting no doubt sparked his fear that golf would adversely affect the swings of position players who would lead the team's offensive attack.[8] During the first week, Hornsby did not completely discard Rickey's old training regimen. He scheduled two workouts per day. After the second session, players indulged in the spa's mineral baths to relax muscles and help get rid of excess weight gained during the offseason.

On March 1, the full team assembled for spring camp. Hornsby left no doubt about his expectations for the team. "We are going some place in the National League pennant race this year," he told the players, "and we have no room on our club for second-division ball players." He warned them not to go around telling everyone they were going to win the pennant, but....

> *we are going to win just the same. If there's anybody here who doesn't believe we are going to win, there's a train leaving for the north tonight and our secretary, Clarence Lloyd, will have a ticket for him. I'll trade away any one who doesn't think we are going to win. If there's a man here who thinks we are a second division ball club, well, I just don't want him around.*

Hornsby could in no way be considered an accomplished psychologist, but he made it unmistakably clear he thought the Cardinals were good enough to make some noise in the pennant race. He again told the players that curfew was 11:00 p.m. and only pitchers were permitted to play golf. He also said gambling was allowed, provided "a reasonable limit [was] observed," an odd rule given Hornsby's profligate gambling habit.[9]

"Here's my policy," Hornsby told sportswriter William McGoogan, "and it doesn't take long to say. They do or they don't for me. If they do, all right. If they don't, we'll get somebody that does." He wouldn't play favorites nor interfere with a player's "liberty or pursuit of happiness, but if they won't play good baseball they can do their pursuing in the bush leagues." The Cards skipper claimed he wouldn't need any "detectives or snitches" because he would know, like some curmudgeonly Santa Claus, who was naughty and who was nice.[10]

The first full day of practice got off to an ominous yet comedic start. Heine Mueller "had to get in the way of a foul ball" and was knocked flat on his back. Concerned but largely unsympathetic teammates gathered around him and one quipped, "He's all right; it hit him on the head." The blow may have knocked some sense into Mueller. For the remainder of training camp, he seemed to be all business.[11]

The Cardinals managed to avoid further accidents over the next few days and kicked off the exhibition season against Waco on March 6. Hornsby slammed a home run in his first at-bat and added another long ball in the 8–3 victory. Despite the promising start and Hornsby's optimism, the Cardinals literally operated under a black cloud as training camp progressed. Bad weather—cold temperatures, chill winds, and persistent rain—hounded the team. Given the damp atmospheric conditions, it was a good thing the Cardinals altered their home white uniforms, removing the familiar birds on the bat logo because the colors tended to run all over the front of the jersey. A small, old English style "St L" monogram was embroidered on the left sleeve.[12] Rain forced the cancellation of games on March 10 and 11. The following day, the Cardinals managed to play split-squad games against the Houston Buffaloes and San Antonio Bears. The game in San Antonio was "played under conditions more suited to ice hockey than baseball." Temperatures hovered around freezing, and a cold, raw wind blew in from the north. Less than 600 fans braved the frigid conditions to watch the Cardinals win 12–3. Rookie outfielder Taylor Douthit collected four hits, while Thevenow and Hornsby each had three.[13]

The cold and rain continued to plague the team and upended Hornsby's training regimen. The Cardinals had split-squad games scheduled against San Antonio and Houston on March 19. The San Antonio contest, however, was cancelled. The weather in Houston was not any better. Regardless, Hornsby was determined to get in some work and the game went on. The Cards were down 4–2 at the end of seven innings when the steady rain gave way to a heavy downpour. The umpires halted the game, and the ground crew pulled up the bases and rolled out tarpaulins to cover the batter's box and pitcher's mound. Hornsby, however, protested so vehemently that the umpires relented, and the game resumed in the deluge. St. Louis scored six runs in the top of the ninth inning to pull away in a 9–4 victory. Nevertheless, the game demonstrated that the numerous off days affected the team, which had only two hits through the first seven innings against a Class A pitcher.

The March 20 contest was also washed out, the fifth cancellation in the past ten days. Making the situation worse, the team couldn't practice on seven of those days. Long-time residents told *Globe-Democrat* sportswriter Martin Haley it was the worst March weather in 45 years. Mother Nature caused so many idle days, Hornsby worried his pitchers' conditioning would suffer. He had good reason. Hallahan and Sherdel came down with bad colds and several others complained about sore arms.[14] The inaction affected the collective batting eye of the team as well. On March 22, the Cardinals eked out a 1–0 win over San Antonio. They managed only four hits, and the run scored on a San Antonio error. Not only were hits scarce, but only a handful of batted balls managed to get out of the infield. While the offense was nonexistent, the combined pitching of Flint Rhem and Victor Keen was sensational.[15]

That same day, a split squad travelled to New Braunfels, Texas, a small town of 7,000 inhabitants northeast of San Antonio, for an exhibition game against the Des Moines Demons, 1925 champs of the Western League. Beyond being the county seat of Comal County, New Braunfels' claim to fame was that it was the only city in Texas founded by German Royalty, when Prince Carl of Solms-Braunfels purchased 1,200 acres in 1845. It also was the site of a daring daytime bank robbery by the notorious Newton Boys gang in 1922.[16] The Cardinals' arrival was a much more festive occasion for the townspeople because it marked the first ever visit by a major league team. Schools and businesses closed and nearly 1,000 people journeyed to the county fairgrounds to watch the game. A band enlivened the occasion, aided by Duster Mails who climbed into the stands in his uniform to lead the band, exchanging hats with the conductor. The Cardinals broke out of a batting slump and thrilled the crowd by pounding out 12 hits in the 9–3 victory. Fans saw former New York Giant Walter Huntzinger pitch six stellar innings of shutout ball and Hornsby slug a mammoth grand slam. The blow sailed far over the right fielder's head but did not clear the fence, "for the barrier in the Fairgrounds [was] about a half mile from home plate."[17]

Hornsby's forces had rounded into shape by the end of March. On the 25th, Bill Sherdel hurled a complete game, 3–1 victory over San Antonio. Thevenow continued his good spring with some nice defensive work and hot hitting, raising his average to .350. Three days later, the offense came alive. The team "drowned three Fort Worth pitchers under a deluge of 21 hits" in a 16–7 rout. Blades, Mueller, Bottomley, and Hafey all had three hits apiece.[18]

The Cardinals played their first and, as it turned out, only game against major league competition on March 29. The Chicago White Sox met the Redbirds in Dallas in miserable weather. Cold and heavy mist shortened the game to seven innings, which the Cards won 2–0. Bill Hallahan pitched all seven innings, giving up only two hits, though he lived up to his nickname by walking five batters. Catcher Bob O'Farrell smacked two doubles and drove in both runs for St. Louis. Hornsby was pleased with the team's enthusiastic play and boasted, "We looked like the great ball club that we are." The second game of the series was cancelled after the rain changed to snow overnight.[19]

The Redbirds won their 19th straight game on April 3, defeating the Dallas Steers by a 3–1 score. Rhem hurled his second complete game in eight days and used his "blazing speed and dazzling curve" to hold Dallas to only two hits during the first seven frames. The St. Louis offense, however, again sputtered. The team managed only six hits, three by Hornsby. The lack of hitting did not worry the Cardinal manager too much. He mused that the Cards would play for one run at a time because the ball was dead. "It's deader than a dud," he asserted, "and for that reason I'm trying to concentrate on an attack which will get us a run in the close ball games." "Of course," he added, "we'll go after a bushel of runs whenever we get the opposing pitcher where we want him. I think I have a smart club on attack as well as a powerful one, so we're not fretting any because they slowed up the ball on us."[20]

The Cardinals wrapped up their training season in Texas on Easter Sunday with a 6–4 victory over Dallas. A crowd of 4,000 enjoyed beautiful weather as did Duster Mails, who pitched a complete game. He held Dallas in check until the ninth inning when the Steers pushed three runs across. Not to worry, the Great Mails announced to the crowd because he "was just breezing along." He gave up only six hits, but he also walked six and committed two errors. Two sensational plays by shortstop Tommy Thevenow saved Mails from further damage.[21] The team traveled to Louisiana, on April 5 to play the Shreveport Sports of the Texas League. After 20 consecutive wins, St. Louis suffered its first loss as Shreveport thumped the Redbirds 13–7 "before a howling crowd of 1000 pop-eyed fanatics." Walter Huntzinger started and held the Sports to one run in the first four innings. He took a 6–1 lead into the fifth but completely fell apart. Shreveport pounded Huntzinger for six runs on eight hits in the fifth and sixth innings. All told, Huntzinger gave up 15 of the sport's 19 hits and became the first Cardinal pitcher during the spring to be removed "under fire" from a game. Adding injury to insult, Syl Johnson suffered from a case of food poisoning.[22]

As the regular season approached, Cardinal fans received some divine affirmation. On April 5, former big-league player and famed evangelist Billy Sunday visited St. Louis and preached to a packed crowd of 2,700 at Moolah Temple. During his 1¼-hour exhortation, Sunday chided people for relying on wealth, power, and fame as sources of satisfaction. Only a Christian faith in Jesus Christ, he warned, could do that. The crowd may have been disappointed his talk lacked the "rich slang" or "circus tactics" for which he was known, but they were no doubt pleased when he told the audience, "If the Lord would hear my prayers in the matter of the baseball pennant race I'd pray that St. Louis would get a pennant. No, two pennants."[23]

The Cardinals concluded spring training by winning 16–2 over the Class C Springfield [Missouri] Midgets of the Western Association. Chick Hafey continued his hot hitting with four hits and showcased his rifle arm by throwing out two baserunners. The squad brimmed with confidence as it made its way to St. Louis. It was a young team. Fifteen players on the 25-man roster were products of Rickey's farm system, a testament to his ability to find and develop raw baseball talent. Despite the Cards' youth, they certainly achieved Hornsby's goal of establishing a winning culture, coming out on top in 22 of 23 exhibition games.[24]

William McGoogan pondered what had transformed the team, which finished fourth in 1925. "Much of the Cardinals' troubles last year," he insisted, "were blamed on a bad start caused by poor condition ... dissatisfaction with the manager, lack of a capable shortstop and ineffective pitching." But heading into 1926, the club was in good physical condition despite the persistent bad weather, and the players seemed to have no problems with Hornsby as manager. He understood the players' perspective and enjoyed their respect and admiration for the most part. Thevenow seemed more than capable of filling the hole at shortstop, and catching was in good hands with O'Farrell behind the plate. The outfield was set with Blades in left, Hafey in right, and Mueller beating out Douthit in center. The team's pitching was still a question mark, but McGoogan considered Keen and Johnson upgrades, with solid starters in Haines and Sherdel, and Rhem had pitched well and seemed primed for a good season. The offense, despite several barren periods, seemed poised to assault National League pitching. Chick Hafey hit .444 with nine doubles, three home runs, and two triples. O'Farrell slugged four doubles and three home runs while hitting a lusty .432. Even Thevenow got into the act, batting a lively .347 with five doubles and two triples.[25]

With spring training behind them, the Cardinals and Browns resumed the annual intra-city rivalry series at Sportsman's Park on April 12–13. The *Sporting News* claimed fans would be impressed by the newly renovated stadium with its double-decked stands that encircled the field and new concrete stands replacing the old wooden bleachers. A covered pavilion now stretched from the rightfield foul line to the centerfield bleachers. It was "truly metropolitan in every respect" and was a "monument to baseball which should make the fans of the Mound City feel very proud, though they have not had a pennant winner to shout about since the dark ages. Who knows but what this is the year?"[26] Hornsby, Bottomley, and the other Cardinal power hitters must have been decidedly less enthusiastic about the revamped ballpark. The playing field was larger with the rightfield fence moved back from 300 to 320 feet away from home plate. The concrete wall in leftfield, formerly 350 feet, was pushed back five feet, though dead centerfield was moved in slightly to 430 feet from home plate. The 12-foot wall along the bleachers and pavilion also made home runs less likely.[27]

Browns owner Phil Ball and his National League counterpart Sam Breadon eagerly anticipated record crowds for the "new" stadium's unveiling. In addition to the updated facility, the fans of both teams were energized about their favorite team's prospects. Both staged strong pushes to finish in the first division in 1925, and both enjoyed a good deal of success in spring training. However, much to the chagrin of Ball and Breadon, miserable weather followed the Cards to St. Louis. A disappointing crowd of only 22,632 fans braved the conditions to watch the Browns defeat the Cardinals 4–2. The Browns mustered only three hits, aided by five Cardinal errors. Lester Bell had a tough game at third base, and fans in the crowd loudly voiced their displeasure with his play. Hornsby thrilled the crowd with a home run in the fourth inning, but he failed to come through in the clutch, fouling out with the bases loaded to end the game. The real fireworks occurred late in the battle in the upper deck on

4. Laying Down the Law in Texas: Spring Training, February 21–April 12   57

Sportsman's Park after its $500,000 makeover prior to the 1926 season (St. Louis Mercantile Library at the University of Missouri-St. Louis).

the third base side. A Cardinal fan and a Browns rooter got into a "fistic sideshow" that threatened to spread into a free-for-all. Sportswriter Roy Stockton commented it "was one of the best 'battle royals' ever put on here, it being at least 10 minutes before a policeman reached the milling group. Several black eyes were noticed as the crowd filed out after the game."[28]

Another farcical distraction was the presence of a "poor, inoffensive" resin bag on the pitcher's mound. Pitchers had used resin for years to get a better grip on the ball, but it was one of the "foreign substances" banned after the 1919 season, though hurlers continued using it surreptitiously. As they staggered under the offensive onslaught of the early 1920s, National League owners tossed pitchers a bone in 1925 by advising league president John Heydler to talk with American League president Ban Johnson about letting umpires place a resin bag behind the mound so pitchers could dry their hands. During the winter meetings, baseball's joint rules committee agreed to the proposition. In February, however, American League owners voted not to approve the rule, claiming it might "open the way to [the] return of freak pitching now under ban." This decision prompted Commissioner Landis to order both leagues to have the bag available. But Ban Johnson, engaged in a perpetual power struggle with Landis, ordered junior circuit owners not to allow their hurlers use of the bag. During the St. Louis city series, Browns pitchers conspicuously ignored the bag, while Cardinal pitchers made liberal use of it. *St. Louis Star* sportswriter James Gould thought the controversy "has provided already and will continue to provide many a laugh to the fans this season." But there really was nothing to laugh about. Resin did not give pitchers any real advantage, and the fans quickly lost interest.[29]

Rain postponed Sunday's game, costing both teams a substantial payday. Only 6,000 fans braved the cold on Monday to watch the Browns again defeat the Cardinals, this time by a score of 3–2. Chick Hafey's home run and Les Bell's RBI single helped the Cardinals forge a 2–2 tie in the seventh inning. The Browns struck back in their half of the frame. Oscar Melillo drew a walk off Duster Mails, one of seven he issued during the game, and raced to third on star first baseman George Sisler's single. With one out, Melillo and Sisler executed a perfect double steal. Sisler broke for second, and Mails took the bait. He was about to make the throw to nab Sisler when he suddenly remembered Melillo, who was streaking for home. He whirled around but his throw was too late to prevent the winning run from scoring. Mails' inattention capped another shoddy defensive display by the Cardinals. They had five errors, with Les Bell contributing two.[30]

Despite the Cardinals' less-than-stellar play against the Browns, optimism was sky high as the team looked forward to the opening day contest against the world champion Pittsburgh Pirates. Pittsburgh was one of two teams Hornsby feared going into the season along with the New York Giants. Sportswriter Martin Haley believed the Cardinals' roster was "one of the greatest collections of youthful talent that St. Louis baseball ever has enjoyed." This club was "filled to the brim with possibilities" and "bubbling over with the enthusiasm of adolescence and possessing ability enough to make a torrid bid for first honors." New York sportswriter John Foster agreed. "The Cardinals," he argued, "have the rollicking energy of a lot of kids… [and] have no knowledge as to when they are beaten and are fighting mad enough to dispute the final score—almost."[31]

Chapter 5

Cool Bats, Cold Weather: April 13–May 2

The Cardinals opened their season on April 13, but another momentous opening occurred two days later. On the morning of April 15, the inaugural flight of the Chicago—St. Louis airmail route run by the Robertson Aircraft Organization arrived at Lambert Field, then little more than a 170-acre clearing with no runways. The pilot, a tall, gangly, handsome flyer by the name of Charles Lindbergh, had left Chicago at 6:00 a.m. and arrived in St. Louis at 9:08 a.m. with some 12,000 letters. That afternoon, a crowd of 2,000 spectators gathered for a dedication ceremony and to watch Lindbergh take off on the return flight to Chicago. Several speakers lauded the event as an epoch in St. Louis' aeronautic history. Efforts to make the city an aviation hub achieved little until Robertson Aircraft secured the airmail contract with the federal government. Major Albert Lambert predicted planes would connect St. Louis with cities in South America within two years. After the speeches, Lambert's daughter, Myrtle, then christened the maroon De Haviland bi-plane with strewn flowers on the lower silver-painted wings. At 4:00 o'clock, Lindbergh climbed into the cockpit and took off to pick up a batch of 15,000 letters at Springfield, Illinois, before flying on to Chicago.

Flyers considered this mail route particularly dangerous because of the changeable weather. Pilots relied on visual contact with the ground for navigation, and storms or fog essentially had them flying blind. In September, Lindbergh parachuted 5,000 feet through darkness and dense fog from his plane as the engine sputtered on the last drops of gasoline. He abandoned his plane again in November when driving snow blinded him. He had the dubious honor of being the first four-time member of the "Caterpillar Club," composed of flyers forced to jump from their planes to save their lives. The dangers faced on this mail route were nothing compared to those Lindbergh faced the following year on his solo trans–Atlantic flight, a feat that earned him international acclaim.[1]

Back on the ground, a disappointing crowd of only 17,000 Cardinal fans braved the cold weather on opening day, April 13. While their teeth chattered, fans enjoyed the pre-game pageantry of a marching band, saw Mayor Victor Miller throw out the first pitch, and watched Rogers Hornsby receive a floral horseshoe, basket of flowers, and silver trophy for being voted the league's most popular player in a nationwide contest conducted by a Cleveland news-gathering agency. When the festivities concluded, the crowd settled down to watch the Cardinals test their mettle against the defending world champion Pittsburgh Pirates.

The Pirates featured one of the most menacing lineups in the league. Three future Hall of Famers—Max Carey, Kiki Cuyler, and Paul Waner—patrolled the outfield. Another Hall of Famer, Pie Traynor, manned third base, while Glenn Wright ranked among the best all-around shortstops in the game. Unlike the Redbirds, the Pirates were somewhat bruised and battered coming out of spring training. Traynor was playing on a gimpy leg, second baseman Eddie Moore twisted an ankle that was eventually diagnosed as a broken bone in his foot, and a protracted respiratory illness knocked lead-off hitter extraordinaire Max Carey out of action. Carey's absence was particularly damaging. Herman Wecke of the *Post-Dispatch* argued the Pirates without Carey "function just about as badly as a Ford without an engine."

The Cards jumped on Pirates starter Vic Aldridge immediately, scoring a run in the first on Hornsby's RBI single. Jim Bottomley's home run in the fifth stretched the lead to 6–0. Flint Rhem's superb pitching through the first five innings made the lead seem insurmountable, but the St. Louis offense faltered, while the Pirates chipped away, aided by shoddy St. Louis fielding. Les Bell botched a double-play ball in the sixth, and Bottomley followed with a muffed grounder that scored two Pirate runs. In the seventh, Bell fumbled Clyde Barnhart's easy roller. Then Heine Mueller and Chick Hafey let a flyball fall safely for a double, allowing Barnhart to reach third and score on a sacrifice fly. The Pirates staged a two-run rally in the ninth, aided again by subpar Cardinal defense. With one out, Pittsburgh first baseman George Grantham hit a popup toward short. Les Bell called Tommy Thevenow away only to let the ball fall safely for a hit. The Pirates eventually scored two runs on Eddie Moore's bases-loaded single to narrow the deficit to one run. With men on second and third and one out, Rhem bore down and got Carson Bigbee to pop up to Bottomley. Glenn Wright came to bat and hit a vicious line drive that Mueller caught after a hard sprint to save the game.[2]

The good health the Cards enjoyed during the spring did not last long in the regular season. The frigid weather for game two, according to James Gould of the *St. Louis Star*, was "unfit for publication." Only 2,800 fans showed up to watch the Pirates swamp St. Louis, 10–3. The Cardinals were down 1–0 with one out in the third inning when a line drive by Pirate catcher Earl Smith slammed into starter Jess Haines' right foot. The ball bounded clear across the first base foul line while Haines writhed in pain on the ground. Four individuals, including Pirates manager Bill McKechnie and Smith, carried Haines off the field to the clubhouse. Later, he was taken to St. John's Hospital and received good news that he did not sustain any broken bones, but he most likely would miss at least two weeks with a severe contusion. After Haines' departure, three wild and ineffective relievers took the mound. The

Pirates seized control in the fifth inning, scoring four runs aided by Chick Hafey's failed shoestring catch with the bases loaded. For good measure, Pittsburgh added five more runs in the eighth inning.[3]

The next day, Hornsby told reporters, "Throw out that game yesterday. It was one of those affairs that come in the life of every ball club—just one of those things. We'll be back in there today, fighting harder than ever." The Cards backed up their manager's words by defeating Pittsburgh 2–0 in front of 4,000 fans. St. Louis managed only six hits off curveball specialist John Morrison, but Hornsby accounted for three of them and drove in both runs. The star was former Cub Vic Keen. He scattered five hits in the complete game shutout and survived a scary moment in the sixth. Reminiscent of the day before, Glenn Wright of the Pirates smoked a line drive which hit Keen in the ankle. Hornsby's stomach must have churned as he watched another of his pitchers lying prostrate on the ground. After receiving medical treatment for five minutes, however, Keen rose to his feet and finished the game. The victory was especially gratifying for Keen after his poor 1925 season. When Hafey snared Clyde Barnhart's fly ball to end the game, Keen "stood in the center of the diamond and did a war dance" and gave catcher Bob O'Farrell a hug for guiding him through the hard-hitting Pittsburgh lineup. After Cardinal pitchers were flattened by line drives in successive games, the *Post-Dispatch* reported the St. Louis mound staff complained that the mesh screen behind home plate, which stretched to the top of the grandstand, made it nearly impossible to see hard liners coming back through the box.[4]

St. Louis wrapped up the series with a dramatic 3–2 victory. Syl Johnson took the mound and pitched well, giving up only four hits before being lifted for a pinch hitter in the eighth inning. St. Louis trailed 2–1 going into the ninth, and things looked grim because Pirate starter Tom Sheehan had limited Cardinal batters to only five hits over the first eight innings. Chick Hafey led off the Cardinals ninth and struck out. Les Bell then laced a single down the leftfield line. The next batter, Bob O'Farrell, hit a potential double-play grounder to second baseman Eddie Moore, who fumbled the ball and could only get a force at second. Hornsby sent Specs Toporcer to pinch run for the lumbering O'Farrell and Jake Flowers to bat for Thevenow. Flowers came through with a single that sent Toporcer racing to third base. Hornsby dipped into his reserves once more and sent Wattie Holm to pinch hit for relief pitcher Allen Sothoron. Sheehan quickly got two strikes on Holm. He took the next pitch, which umpire Cy Pfirman called a ball. The Pirates, however, argued the pitch was a strike and should end the game in their favor, but Pfirman stood by his decision. Holm worked his way out of the hole and drew a walk to load the bases. By this time, Sheehan was clearly frustrated and rattled, and he hit Ray Blades in the lower back to push Toporcer across with the tying run. Heine Mueller stepped to the plate and slapped a clean single to center to win the game.[5]

Taking three out of four games from the champion Pirates boosted the Redbirds' confidence tremendously. Despite losing one of his top starters, Hornsby was pleased with the solid pitching from newcomers Keen and Johnson, and he was confident the sputtering offense would soon right itself. Furthermore, the come-from-behind victory in the series finale showcased the team's fighting spirit.

The Chicago Cubs rolled into town on April 17 for a four-game series. Not much was expected from the Cubs in 1926. They finished in the National League cellar the year before and were breaking in a new manager, Joe McCarthy, a very successful minor league skipper who had never played or managed in the big leagues. The Cubs did have some building blocks, however. The pitching staff was young but had promising workhorses in Charlie Root, Sheriff Blake, Guy Bush, and Percy Jones. First baseman Charlie Grimm and second baseman Sparky Adams were solid ballplayers, and talented catcher Gabby Hartnett was in the early stages of a Hall of Fame career. The Cubs' most significant acquisition was outfielder Hack Wilson. Once property of the New York Giants, Wilson was an ideal fit for Chicago and the excesses of the 1920s. At first glance, he did not give the appearance of a major league ballplayer. He stood five feet, six inches and weighed a stout 200 pounds. His barrel chest and blacksmith arms testified to his enormous power, but his muscle-bound thighs and calves perched on tiny size 5½ feet made him look, as one wag said, like he was "built along the lines of a beer keg, and not unfamiliar with its contents." Fans loved him and his exuberant, pugnacious personality. It didn't hurt that he emerged as one of the National League's most feared sluggers in the last half of the 1920s.[6]

In the opener, Willie Sherdel continued the Cardinals' stellar pitching, going the distance in a 3–2 win. Flame-throwing Cubs pitcher Tony Kaufman held Hornsby's team to two singles and two doubles, but the Cardinals managed to score two runs without virtue of a hit. Fan favorite Heine Mueller was one of the game's heroes. He stole home in the first inning and doubled in the eighth, eventually scoring the winning run on Bottomley's infield single. The Cubs lost a chance to take the lead in their half of the eighth when Hafey retrieved Wilson's double off the rightfield wall and fired a terrific throw to nab a runner at home plate. They threatened again in the ninth when former Cardinal, Howard Freigau, led off with a double. But Sherdel pounced on an attempted sacrifice by Charlie Grimm and threw out Freigau at third base. Bottomley made a nice running catch of a foul ball, and then Sherdel picked off pinch runner Cliff Heathcote to seal the victory. The game was marred by a bean ball duel between Sherdel and Kaufman. Things came to a head in the fifth inning after Kaufman just missed nailing Sherdel with a pitch. The Cardinal hurler decided he had had enough and flung his bat at Kaufman. Both benches cleared and surrounded the feuding pitchers, but cooler heads fortunately prevailed.[7]

Cardinal bats came alive in game two, despite "bone-brittling" temperatures. St. Louis pounded two Chicago pitchers for 15 hits in a 10–5 triumph. The home team took a 3–0 lead in the first on Jim Bottomley's towering home run that bounced off the rightfield pavilion roof onto Grand Boulevard. The Cubs came back with four runs in the second inning, largely due to some "dumb" Cardinal baseball, but Flint Rhem settled down thereafter. He gave up only two hits in the last seven frames and retired the last 13 Cubs in a row. The Cards took control, scoring five runs in the third, aided by Bob O'Farrell's RBI double and a two-run single from Mueller.[8]

At this early point in the season, St. Louis' outfield picture got a little less crowded when Hornsby finally unloaded Jack Smith. Despite being teammates for ten years, Smith never really fit into Hornsby's plans. A deal for a veteran catcher to backup O'Farrell never materialized, so the team announced that Smith had been sold to the Boston Braves.[9]

The Cubs snapped the home team's four-game winning streak with a tough 5–4 victory in 14 innings. Walter Huntzinger pitched all 14 innings for St. Louis. He was one out away from a win in the ninth, when Howard Freigau doubled home Hack Wilson to knot the score at three. This and other early season National League games, wrote Herman Wecke of the *Post-Dispatch*, gave proof that the "rabbit" had been taken out of the baseball. "No more are clubs going after bunches of runs," he asserted, "It's one tally at a time. The sacrifice and the stolen base, baseball antiques, are being used in order to advance base runners." And it was the Cardinals' inability to bunt and advance runners that cost them the game. In the tenth inning, Huntzinger led off with a single. Ray Blades twice failed to bunt the pitcher over and then struck out with Huntzinger thrown out at second attempting to steal. Hornsby followed with a single that would have scored the baserunner had Blades been able to bunt successfully. In the 12th, Huntzinger failed to sacrifice Tommy Thevenow, who would have scored on Blades' double. But with one out, Thevenow was doubled off third on Heine Mueller's low line drive to second baseman Sparky Adams. Then in the 13th inning, Hornsby led off with a single, but Bottomley could not move him over, popping out to the third baseman. Chicago, on the other hand, won after Hack Wilson walked, was bunted to second, and scored on St. Louis native Charlie Grimm's single to center.[10]

The homestand ended in disappointing fashion when the Cubs blanked the Redbirds 7–0. Veteran southpaw Wilbur Cooper held the Cardinals to four singles and a Hornsby double, while Arthur Reinhart surrendered one dozen hits, including a "healthy" home run to Hack Wilson. The offense, expected to be the team's strength, mustered a lackluster .244 average so far, and Cardinal hitters were striking out at an alarming rate. They whiffed 43 times in the first seven games, with Hornsby and Hafey setting the pace with six punchouts apiece.

The team boarded a train for Pittsburgh, the first stop on an 11-game road trip, stopping in Terre Haute, Indiana, on April 21 for an exhibition game. The *Globe-Democrat* noted that Sam Breadon and the Cardinals did not believe in open dates even though manager Rogers Hornsby did not care for these sideshow contests. That difference of opinion would explode into an ugly confrontation later in the season.[11]

The world champion Pirates limped home for their first homestand, losers of six of their first eight games and tied for last place. The Buccaneers' hitting, like St. Louis' bats, struggled and manager Bill McKechnie decided to bench touted rookie Paul Waner and put Clyde Barnhart in his place to jumpstart the offense.[12] More than 30,000 excited fans filed into cavernous Forbes Field to watch the clash. The pattern of urban streets in the Midwest and Northeast resulted in city blocks that had longer north-south than east-west dimensions; consequently, ballparks constructed during the Deadball Era had longer leftfield foul lines than those in rightfield. In the case of Forbes Field, the leftfield foul line stretched 360 feet from home plate while the rightfield line was a scant 300 feet—a gift Pirate owner Barney Dreyfus gave Pittsburgh's lefthanded hitters in 1925. The area behind home plate stretched 110 feet to the backstop, the farthest in the National League. The most visible feature was the flagpole located 462 feet in left-centerfield. There the fans watched as Pirate players and various dignitaries hoisted the American flag and National League pennant as part of the pre-game festivities.

The game itself disappointed the Pittsburgh crowd. The Pirates took a 3–1 lead against Victor Keen in the second inning, but the Cardinals clawed back with single tallies in the third and fourth innings to tie the game. Fans became more glum when star third baseman Pie Traynor left the game after getting spiked by Chick Hafey in the third inning. Traynor joined the Pirates' walking wounded, including shortstop Glenn Wright, who had a cut and bruised hand, and Max Carey, who still was not fully recovered from his illness. The score remained knotted until the top of the tenth when Chick Hafey launched a home run over the leftfield fence with one man on base. Keen shut down the Pirates in the bottom half of the inning to end his second consecutive impressive start.[13]

Syl Johnson took the mound for St. Louis in the second game of the series, hoping to duplicate his fine performance in his previous turn against Pittsburgh. However, he got off to a rough start in the bottom of the first. Max Carey took his spot as the leadoff hitter and promptly singled and took second when Mueller booted the ball. With two out, Thevenow fumbled Barnhart's grounder. Pie Traynor took advantage of the miscue. He roped a line drive to centerfield. Mueller tried to make a shoestring catch, but the ball got by him and rolled to the fence in right-center. Traynor, ignoring his injured toe and lame right ankle, circled the bases for a three-run, inside-the-park home run. The Cardinals closed within one when they scored two in the sixth on a Hornsby triple, Bottomley double, and Hafey single, but Pirate hurler Vic Aldridge made the lead stand up in the 3–2 victory. Johnson took the hard-luck loss though all three runs he surrendered were unearned.[14]

A heavy downpour delayed the start of the series finale on Saturday, April 24. While he waited for play to begin, a frustrated Rogers Hornsby declared, "if we ever hit our regular batting stride some good pitcher is going to suffer." The Cardinals hit their batting stride, at least on this day, and made Pirate ace Ray Kremer suffer. They knocked Kremer out of the game in the first inning by scoring four runs on two-run doubles by Bottomley and O'Farrell and cruised to a 9–3 thrashing of Pittsburgh. The Cardinals banged out 13 hits, including Hornsby's first home run of the season, an inside-the-park smash that "danced around the center field flag pole." He added a double and a single for a perfect 3-for-3 day. Pitcher Flint Rhem contributed three hits himself to the attack while he pitched a four-hit complete game for his third straight victory. "It was almost pathetic," lamented Pittsburgh sportswriter Charles J. Doyle, "to watch the Pirates as they stood at the plate before Rhem."[15] As the Redbirds boarded a train for Cincinnati, they were no doubt thrilled that they were perched in second place, only one game behind the Giants.

The Reds fielded a dangerous club. They boasted one of the league's best pitching staffs with Pete Donohue, former Yankee Carl Mays, the towering and ultra-durable lefty Eppa Rixey, Cuba native Adolfo Luque (whose skin was light enough to allow him to play in the majors), and promising rookie Red Lucas. The regular lineup was stout defensively and dotted with several tough hitters in future Hall of Fame centerfielder Edd Roush, veteran first baseman Wally Pipp who came over from the Yankees after being replaced by Lou Gehrig, right fielder Curt Walker, pitcher-turned-outfielder Rube Bressler, and catcher Eugene "Bubbles" Hargrave. The Reds led the National League in team batting in 1926 with a .290 average and placed three hitters in the top ten but did not exhibit much power, hitting only 35 home runs during the season.

Their ballpark, Redland Field (renamed Crosley Field in 1934), was very pitcher-friendly. Wedged into a city block, it was a somewhat utilitarian structure that blended well with the brick warehouses and factories in Cincinnati's Queensgate neighborhood. Like most ballparks that opened during the Deadball Era, the field itself contained acres of greenspace for outfielders to roam. The foul lines extended 360 feet from home plate, and straightaway centerfield measured an expansive 420 feet. It took nine years before the Reds' Pat Duncan hit the first fair ball over Redland's fences on June 2, 1921. One of the park's quirkier features was a flagpole that towered 82 feet above the playing surface in left-centerfield. Any ball that hit the pole and bounced back onto the field was in play. Its signature feature was the terrace, a 15-degree incline in front of the leftfield wall, causing many an outfielder unfamiliar with the terrain to sprawl face-first on the ground chasing a fly ball over his head.[16]

The Cards and Reds squared off on an arctic Sunday afternoon in front of a sparse crowd of some 6,000 fans. Bill Sherdel took the mound for St. Louis, and Cincinnati handed the ball to young righthander Red Lucas. Sherdel pitched well, surrendering only two hits and one run in the first six innings, but the wheels came off in the seventh. The Reds plated three runs and pulled away for a 4–0 victory. Jess Haines' scoreless inning of relief in the eighth, his first appearance in two weeks, was the game's only bright spot for the Cardinals. The weather had not improved the next day, and a paltry gathering of some 2,000 souls filed into the ballpark. Again, the Cardinal bats were as cold as the temperature, and the Reds scraped by 3–2 in ten innings. St. Louis jumped out to a 2–0 lead in the first inning on hits by Mueller, Hornsby, and Hafey, but Reds starter Pete Donohue settled down and limited St. Louis to only four hits through the next nine innings. While Walter Huntzinger pitched another fine game, he gave up a run in the eighth and the tying run in the ninth due to some lousy fielding. With two outs, Thevenow booted a sharp groundball by Reds first baseman Walter Christensen. Then shortstop Frank Emmer picked an opportune time to get his first hit of the season, a broken bat looper over Thevenow that tied the game. The Reds won it in the tenth, aided by Taylor Douthit's mishandling of Babe Pinelli's line drive. Douthit had a very rough day filling in for Ray Blades, who hurt his knee during pre-game practice. The fleet rookie committed two errors and struck out three times.[17]

The April 27 game was rained out, so the Cards sent Vic Keen to pitch the last game of the series against Eppa Rixey, who was making his first start of the season for the Reds. Once again, the weather was miserable. It was so cold that Herman Wecke of the *Post-Dispatch* estimated roughly 400 people were in the stands when the game began. St. Louis won in the ninth, on a dramatic and controversial two-run home run by Bob O'Farrell. The Cardinal catcher smashed a hard liner that went through a gap in the low fence cordoning off temporary stands in rightfield. Reds outfielder Christian Walker jumped over the fence to field the ball, but the umpires ruled the hit was a home run since the ball left the field of play, just as if it had gone over the fence. The *Cincinnati Enquirer* asked what were "those silly seats doing out on fair grounds in right field? They are utterly useless and a menace to the fielders, as well as likely to lose a game at any time." This time the "silly seats" helped Keen win his third straight game.[18]

The exciting win buoyed the team's spirits as they headed to Chicago, but the Cubs' hospitality in the confines of Wrigley Field was less than friendly. Sloppy fielding by the Cardinals put them at the short end of a 6–5 score in the first game. Syl Johnson got the start against rookie righthander Charlie Root for the Cubs. Johnson had a rough go of it in the blustery conditions, giving up home runs to Joe Munson and Hack Wilson. After Wilson's clout, Hornsby lifted Johnson in the fifth inning with St. Louis down 4–2. Jim Bottomley drove one out of the yard in the sixth to shave the lead to one, and the Cardinals took the lead 5–4 in the seventh. Cubs second baseman Sparky Adams booted an easy ground ball with two outs, and Rogers Hornsby promptly drilled a shot off the rightfield wall for a two-run double. The Cardinals returned the favor in the Cubs half of the seventh. Lefty Walter Mails was on the mound for the first time that season, and Thevenow fumbled Adams' grounder to start the inning. Adams was bunted over to second and scored on Wilson's two-out single to center. St. Louis' charity continued in the eighth inning. Former Cardinal Jimmy Cooney led off with a single. On an attempted sacrifice bunt, Mails tried to nip Cooney at second base, but his throw was wild. Hornsby yanked Duster from the game in favor of Jess Haines. Sparky Adams redeemed himself by poking the game-winning single to centerfield.[19]

Hornsby tabbed veteran spitballer Allen Sothoron to start game two. At the start, fans enjoyed balmy weather; however, at the end of the second inning, the wind shifted abruptly to the north, and the temperature dropped 28 degrees in 14 minutes, turning the game into what *Chicago Tribune* sportswriter Irving Vaughan called a "windy, wild and weird battle." The Cardinals jumped on Cub starter Sheriff Blake for two runs in the first inning and two more in the second on Ray Blades' home run. The Cubs roared back with four runs in their half of the fourth, knocking Sothoron out of the game. St. Louis regained the lead with two tallies in the sixth. The wind aided O'Farrell's lead-off triple, and he scored on Thevenow's single. An error and Blades' wind-blown single plated the Cardinal shortstop to put St. Louis ahead by one. The Cardinals tacked on three more runs in the seventh, helped by relief pitcher Art Reinhart's two-run single. Down by four going into the eighth, the Cubs pushed two runs across on Gabby Hartnett's double. In the ninth, the game seemed to be over; the Cubs had no one on base with two outs. But Chicago registered back-to-back singles, and then the wind intervened in the Cubs' favor. Hack Wilson hit a fly ball behind second base, which the wind blew back over the infield where it fell for an RBI single. Howard Freigau followed with an infield single to knot the score. Chicago won it in the 11th inning. Relief pitcher Percy Jones hit a double to deep left, and then the menacing Hack Wilson came to bat. Hornsby signaled to Reinhart to intentionally walk the Cardinals' nemesis. Reinhart pitched two balls but then carelessly put the next pitch close enough for Wilson to lash a game-winning single. The southpaw lost more than the game. Before the Cardinals reached the clubhouse, an irritated Hornsby fined Reinhart $50 for not following instructions.[20]

Redbird hitters battered Cub pitching on May 1, scoring eight runs on 14 hits, including Les Bell's home run, Jim Bottomley's inside-the-park round tripper, and Bob O'Farrell's three-run blast. The Cardinals could have added more, but Heine Mueller's baserunning blunder in the third inning cost the team additional runs. He was on first base when Hornsby bunted down the third base line. The ball got through Chicago's third baseman Howard Friegau and rolled into short leftfield. Third base was left uncovered, and Cardinal Coach Bill Killefer frantically waved Mueller to advance. For some inexplicable reason, the normally hard-charging outfielder slammed on the brakes and remained at second. Bottomley forced Mueller at third, and then Chick Hafey hit a vicious line drive that turned into a double play. If Mueller had gone to third, the Cubs most likely would have drawn in the infield, and Hafey's scorcher would have been a base hit.[21]

St. Louis enjoyed a two-run lead going into the eighth inning when the Cubs threatened with two men on base and two outs. Sparky Adams hit a routine groundball to Thevenow, who hesitated while making the throw to first, allowing Adams to reach base safely. That opened the floodgates. Cliff Heathcote singled home two runs, which knocked Rhem out of the game. Victor Keen relieved and promptly gave up a three-run home run to leftfielder Joe Munson. When the inning ended, the Cubs plated five runs. The 11–8 loss dropped the Cards under the .500 mark for the first time in the season.

The series finale saw another frustrating late-inning St. Louis loss in front of an overflow crowd of 36,000. Bill Sherdel took the mound for the Redbirds, while the venerable Grover Cleveland Alexander started for Chicago. One of the greatest pitchers in baseball history, "Ol' Pete" had become a shadow of his former self by 1926, due to unchecked alcoholism, epileptic seizures, and shell shock suffered during World War I. With his pinpoint control and veteran guile, he could still be effective, but on this day the Cardinals scored four runs off Alexander through five innings. The Cubs, however, scratched across single runs in the second, fifth, and seventh innings and took the lead with two runs in the eighth. Hack Wilson, who homered earlier, doubled in the tying run and scored on Charlie Grimm's hard smash off Sherdel's bare hand. St. Louis retook the lead in the ninth, but the Cubs snatched the win in the bottom of the ninth. Gabby Hartnett led off with a double. Alexander bunted to Bottomley, who made a wild heave to get the pinch runner at third, allowing the winning run to score.[22]

St. Louis finished the road trip in sixth place with a disheartening 8–10 win-loss record, two games behind the surprising Brooklyn Dodgers. Struggles away from home, a trend that had plagued the Cardinals for years, dulled the exhilaration of the opening series with the Pirates. The offense continued to flail along with a .254 batting average, though Hornsby was among the league leaders with a .397 mark. The pitching, on the other hand, proved to be stingier than expected. Rhem and Keen had three victories each while newcomers Syl Johnson and Walter Huntzinger put together effective outings. The Redbirds certainly looked forward to returning to Sportsman's Park for a long homestand, but their misery was not over.

Chapter 6

Highs, Lows, and Courtroom Woes, May 2–May 26

St. Louis' civic improvement frenzy, sparked by the $87 million bond issue of 1923, was still going strong in May 1926. A new $2.5 million Jewish hospital at Kingshighway and Forest Park Boulevard opened in mid–May. Board president Aaron Waldheim declared the seven-story, H-shaped structure of red Harvard brick and Bedford stone was without doubt "the most complete and fully equipped hospital and surgical institution in the world." On May 19, city officials broke ground for the new $4 million civic courthouse that would grace Memorial Plaza on the block bordered by Chestnut, Market, Eleventh, and Twelfth streets. When completed in 1930, the edifice, at 380 feet, was the tallest building in the city. To show off their civic pride, city leaders announced St. Louis would stage a 16-day exposition in September at Forest Park to celebrate the country's sesquicentennial and showcase the city's industrial progress. The Globe-Democrat *editorialized it would be the "greatest exposition that St. Louis has had since the World's Fair of 1904."*[1]

That optimistic feeling took a back seat to an explosive revelation emanating from the courtroom of Circuit Court Judge George E. Mix. On May 5, the trial of William Allen Rutherford, a lieutenant in the army reserve and member of a wealthy Pine Bluff, Arkansas, family, was set to begin. Rutherford had been indicted on a charge of second-degree murder for the October 10, 1925, shooting of Jack Tucker, a 19-year-old African American bellboy at the Majestic Hotel because he refused to procure Rutherford some female companionship. Rutherford brandished his service revolver, which discharged—accidentally, he contended—and shot the bellboy, who died two days later. On the day of the trial, prosecutors announced Rutherford agreed to plead guilty to a manslaughter charge and pay a fine of only $500.

The not-so-subtle stench of corruption ignited a public firestorm. A Post-Dispatch *editorial protested, "Why prate about responsibility for the prevalence of crime when such scandalous proceedings as those of the Rutherford case result in a mockery of justice?"*[2] *Attorney General North T. Gentry launched a grand jury investigation and secured a new indictment against Rutherford as well as indictments against Circuit Attorney Howard Sidener and Samuel Bender, attorney for Jack Tucker's mother, for fraud and compounding a felony by accepting a large sum of money not to prosecute the Rutherford case. In addition, John Rutherford, William's brother, was charged with bribery. The legal wrangling dominated newspaper headlines throughout the summer. In the end, state prosecutors failed to compel either of the Rutherford brothers to return from Arkansas, and the cases against Bender and Sidener fell apart.*[3]

Once the dust settled in late September, the Post-Dispatch *raged, "After all the uproar about the wanton murder of a bellboy being fixed for $500, it is disgraceful that this pitiful fine remains and will always remain the whole punishment visited upon the murderer for this brutal crime." The newspaper was "thoroughly ashamed … nothing can be done with public officials who would consent to such an outrage" and laid the blame for "this ill-smelling affair" upon the Republican Party which had long controlled St. Louis and the courts. "Their margin of power," the editors lamented, "is so great that they make the price of life what they like. St. Louis needs a political housecleaning worse than any other American city. Its Augean stable needs to be cleansed of all the filth and foulness which has accumulated in 20 years."*[4]

The Cardinals would become embroiled in a legal squabble later in May, but early in the month, the team was still licking its wounds from the drubbing they suffered at the hands of the Cubs. When the demoralized club left Chicago on May 2, Hornsby and his crew were just grateful to return to St. Louis. Sportsman's Park, however, provided no relief. The Reds came into town and added to Redbird woes with a 9–6 victory. The Cardinals touched Reds pitcher Eppa Rixey for five runs in five innings on a two-run triple by Jim Bottomley and a run-scoring double from Hafey. Vic Keen, seeking his fourth straight win, took a 5–3 lead into the sixth inning when he "lost all sense of direction." With two outs, he walked three straight men, the last forcing in a run. Then came a triple steal, with Sammy Bohne stealing home to tie the game. Second baseman Hughie Critz followed with a two-run single. Carl Mays relieved Rixey and surrendered a run in the bottom of the sixth then shut down the Cardinals over the final three frames.[5]

Perhaps the frustration of the losing streak prompted the Cardinals to demote "The Great" Duster Mails to Syracuse of the International League. Hornsby was no doubt tired of the pitcher's free-spirited antics, and his wild throw which cost a game during the series in Chicago was enough for Hornsby to "put his foot down emphatically on one of those happy-go-lucky wandering minstrels who find their way into professional baseball every now and then." The California native was less than thrilled about pitching in the East, and when he complained, the Cardinal manager unleashed a verbal thrashing, telling the eccentric lefty that he would get into condition either for St. Louis or Syracuse and forget about the West Coast. Sportswriter Roy Stockton said the situation reflected "the injustice of the baseball system." Mails was happy pitching in California, but the Cardinals lured him back to the major leagues. But rather than letting him go back to California the Cardinals wanted him "to go to prison in Syracuse."

Mails finally relented, but he steamed over what he called a raw deal. "I worked like a truck horse in the South for seven weeks without pay getting into condition," he complained and asked, "What good did it do? The season has been running for three weeks now and I've been worked in one inning, just long enough to be charged with the loss of a game. I've been used in batting practice only once in three weeks. It looks as if I've been ticketed for some time. However, I've had many ups and downs, and I guess I can stand this one." But Duster was determined to have his way. Shortly after arriving in Syracuse, according to Leo Doyle of the *Baltimore Evening Sun*, Mails "made it just miserable enough for the management of the Syracuse ball club" that he got his wish and was sent to the San Francisco Seals. Duster played professionally for nine more years but never threw another pitch in the major leagues.[6]

Even after five consecutive losses, Hornsby's confidence in his youthful charges was unshaken. The Cardinals' record stood at 8–11, four games behind the surprising Brooklyn Dodgers. "There's our only comfort," Hornsby told a reporter and added, "Of course games won now count as much as games won in the stretch, but it does take some of the sting out of the misfortune to see strong neighbors having their troubles also." The Pirates and Giants, he argued, will rebound and the Cubs "can't stand the pace they're setting ... and will crack soon."[7]

The Redbirds finally broke the losing streak on May 4, edging the Reds 3–2, and it was an unlikely hero who saved the day. Hornsby usually gave his starting pitchers plenty of latitude to work out of jams, but on this day, he pulled Walter Huntzinger in the third inning with no outs. The Reds had pushed one run across in the second inning and another in the third on three straight singles. Perhaps Hornsby feared the game would quickly get out of hand, so he brought in seldom-used Herman Bell, who proceeded to shut down the Reds for the rest of the game. Bell even contributed an RBI single in the fifth inning before Les Bell laced a two-run single in the bottom of the eighth to secure the win.[8]

The Cards' misfortune returned the next day in a 6–1 loss. Cincinnati starter Red Lucas won his fourth game in five decisions, holding the anemic St. Louis offense to five hits, two by relief pitcher Allen Sothoron. On the other side of the diamond, Syl Johnson's bad luck continued. In the second inning, Wally Pipp smashed a line drive that hit Johnson in the right foot, breaking one of his toes. He managed to get out of the inning without further damage to himself or the scoreboard. In the third frame, however, the Reds jumped on Johnson, who was in obvious pain, for four runs on three doubles and a triple. "What a jinxed nomad is this side-wheeling right-hander," wrote Martin Haley of the *Globe-Democrat*. Hornsby mercifully removed the snake-bitten pitcher and brought in Sothoron "to protect Phil Ball's nice new bleacher and pavilion walls." Hornsby failed to protect himself when he collided with catcher Val Picinich at second base. The impact hurled the Rajah to the ground, and he rolled over several times. After several minutes of rest, he was able to resume play.[9]

The Brooklyn Dodgers—or Robins as they were known in honor of manager Wilbert Robinson—followed the Reds for their first appearance in St. Louis on May 6. The Dodgers finished in last place the season before, and most baseball insiders felt the entertaining and inept "Daffiness Boys" posed no threat to the upper division. Robinson overhauled the roster during the offseason to rebuild the team. Except for sweet-swinging rookie slugger Floyd "Babe" Herman, Robinson populated the team with hard-drinking veterans, such as shortstop Rabbit Maranville, who were well past their prime. Maranville was part of an exclusive Dodgers crew that called itself the "Four-for-Oh" club, referencing the hitless game club members more than likely experienced after a night out on the town. They were often heard chanting to one another, "All for one and four-for-oh!"[10]

At this early juncture, however, Brooklyn stunned the baseball world perched atop the National League standings. They arrived riding a three-game winning streak and taking nine of their last ten games. Amazingly, they achieved this lofty status without a single win from star pitcher Dazzy Vance. Vance was one of the decade's dominant pitchers with a blazing fastball and a curve that Reds outfielder Rube Bressler compared to "an apple rolling off a crooked table." In 1924, he fashioned a 28–6 win-loss record, leading the league with 262 strikeouts and a 2.16 earned run average. Sportswriters named Vance the National League's most valuable player, much to the dismay of St. Louis fans who felt Hornsby's triple crown trumped the Dodger pitcher's work. Thus far in 1926, however, Vance had pitched poorly and failed to win a game. A "bevy of boils" was blamed for the future Hall of Famer's floundering performance. Nevertheless, Brooklyn sportswriters, egos inflated by the Dodgers' unexpected success, engaged in a bit of trash talk. Thomas Holmes of the *Brooklyn Daily Eagle* commented favorably on the revamped Sportsman's Park, but "the Cardinals were still the same old Cardinals—in seventh place and slipping southward fast."[11]

The Cardinals' prospects were further dimmed when Hornsby took himself out of the lineup because of the wrenched back he suffered the day before, a problem that plagued him for the rest of the season. In addition, the Rajah juggled the batting order to try to produce an offensive spark. He benched struggling Ray Blades and Chick Hafey and inserted Wattie Holm in leftfield and Taylor Douthit in center. Heine Mueller shifted to rightfield. The hoped-for spark lasted one inning. It was enough, however, to scratch out a 3–1 win over the Dodgers and Vance. In the Redbirds' half of the first inning, Douthit slapped a double down the leftfield line. Specs Toporcer—who took Hornsby's place at second base—walked, and then Holm hit a towering triple to the flagpole, driving in two runs. Les Bell followed with an RBI single to knock Vance out of the game. It did not matter that St. Louis failed to score for the rest of the contest because Flint Rhem pitched brilliantly. In nine innings, he gave up only five hits and had the Dodger hitters "backing and jumping around the plate, baffled, puzzled and nonplussed by the slants and dips and curves." Some stellar defense aided the cause. In the sixth inning, Rhem had retired 12 Dodgers in a row before giving up a double to first baseman Babe Herman. Center fielder Gus Felix hit a bouncer that went through Rhem's legs and seemed destined for center field, but Tommy Thevenow made a remarkable stop some 20 feet behind second and pegged a strong throw to Bottomley to nip Felix at first. The Dodgers' third base coach, thinking Felix had a sure hit, had waved Herman home, but Bottomley whipped the ball to O'Farrell in time to make the putout.[12]

That was the only St. Louis victory in the series as Cardinal hitters continued their collective doldrums. In game two, veteran hurler Burleigh Grimes held the Redbirds to five hits in a 7–1 loss. Grimes' spitball had St. Louis consistently hitting the ball on the ground. Shortstop Rabbit Maranville had two putouts and six assists while Grimes had eight assists himself. Dodger bats, on the other hand, pounded St. Louis' diminutive lefty Bill Sherdel for seven runs in 4⅓ innings. The only St. Louis highlight was Jess Haines' work in relief of Sherdel. Pops gave up only one hit in 3⅔ shutout innings.[13]

Hornsby was back in the lineup for game three, but it did not help as the Dodgers downed St. Louis 5–3. Babe Herman hit a tie-breaking, two-run homer off Art Reinhart in the seventh inning to clinch the game. Another injury and another baserunning blunder by Heine Mueller added to the Redbird troubles. Leftfielder Wattie Holm crashed into the concrete wall in the fifth inning while trying to stab Chick Fewster's long drive. He had to leave the game, and team doctor Robert Hyland said contusions on Holm's knee and elbow would sideline him for a week to ten days. Mueller's gaffe was not physically painful, though it did cost a potential run. He singled with one out in the bottom of the first and raced to third on Hornsby's base hit. The Redbird manager took off for second base on a delayed steal, but Heine strayed too far off third, perhaps thinking it was a double steal and was tagged out in a run down.

The Cardinal offense continued to slumber in the series finale. Some 12,000 fans witnessed a pitching duel between Bob McGraw of Brooklyn and Bill Hallahan of St. Louis. Hallahan, in fact, held the Dodgers hitless for the first four innings, but he gave up a run in the fifth and then a two-run double to Gus Felix in the eighth. Jim Bottomley accounted for the only Cardinal tally with a prodigious home run that Richard Vidmer of the *New York Times* wrote "may have landed anywhere this side of the Canadian border."[14]

The Cardinals dropped into seventh place with a lackluster 10–15 record, while the Dodgers maintained their hold on first. This was, however, Brooklyn's high-water mark for the season. They went on to take two of three from the Cubs but tumbled thereafter and reclaimed their title as the clown princes of the National League. That reputation was cinched in an August 15 game during which three Dodger baserunners ended up on third base at the same time, a situation author Glenn Stout described to be "in contradiction of not only the laws of physics but the laws of baseball." The blunder sparked a plethora of jokes, such as "Man to cab driver: 'The Dodgers have three men on base.' Cab driver: 'Which base?'" At season's end, the Dodgers were comfortably ensconced in sixth place.[15]

Despite the less-than-stellar on-field exploits, interest among St. Louis fans still flourished. The Board of Aldermen voted on May 7 to hold their meetings on Friday morning at 11:00 so that its members could attend afternoon Cardinals and Browns games. One alderman objected because the move would conflict with his legal business, but board colleague A.H. Niederluecke pontificated, "Gentlemen, when it comes to a conflict between business and pleasure, you know pleasure is always first."

Ever-progressive Cardinal owner Sam Breadon resolved to tap into the exploding popularity of radio to expand the fan base even more. In response to numerous requests from fans, Breadon and Browns owner Phil Ball announced on May 11 that they had reached an agreement with station KMOX to broadcast inning-by-inning updates for games played at Sportsman's Park. Work crews hoped to have the necessary lines installed in time for staff announcer Melvin Dix to call the first game of the Cardinals–Giants series that day.

Not everyone was happy with this development. Sportswriter James J. Gould of the *St. Louis Star* thought the "radio plan" was unlikely to succeed. "It is quite a question, in the first place," he argued, "whether a play-by-play radio story would add vast numbers to the army of patrons at the park, and, in the second place, only a newspaper account can bring the scene properly before a fan who hasn't seen the game." Revealing his obvious newspaper bias, Gould concluded baseball "is no bedtime story; it must be seen to be appreciated and lacking this, the nearest thing to the actual action is to read about it. Radio is a distinct success in its place and there seems no good reason why it should step out of that place." He must have been pleased when KMOX abandoned the project after a few weeks because it was too expensive. Radio and KMOX, however, soon became inseparable from Cardinal baseball.[16]

The New York Giants arrived in St. Louis with a disappointing fourth-place record, a bitter pill for mercurial manager John McGraw to swallow. The New Yorkers had won four consecutive National League pennants from 1921 to 1924 and finished second to the Pirates in 1925. They were expected to contend for the National League flag again in 1926, but the season turned out to be a particularly difficult one for McGraw, personally and professionally. Sinusitis plagued him throughout the spring. In addition, first baseman Bill Terry's holdout and the loss of slugger Hack Wilson to the Cubs because of a routine paperwork mix-up made McGraw more peevish than usual.[17]

The results of the first two games of the series didn't improve McGraw's mood. A Ladies Day crowd of some 4,500 watched Vic Keen win his fourth of the season, a complete-game 5–4 victory. Heine Mueller tripled in the fourth and scored on Les Bell's sacrifice fly. Bell added a solo home run, while Ray Blades, back in the lineup after Holm's injury, swatted a two-run shot in the fifth. Blades added to his heroics with a leaping catch at the leftfield wall to rob Giants shortstop Travis Jackson with two runners on base. The following day, the Cardinals and Flint Rhem handed the

Giants their fifth straight loss, 6–5. St. Louis got off to a quick start in the first when Bottomley drove a Hugh McQuillen pitch out of the ballpark onto Grand Boulevard. Rhem added a two-run single in the second, prompting McGraw to remove McQuillen with no one out. The St. Louis righty shut out the Giants through the first five innings before giving up a two-run home run to outfielder Billy Southworth, a drive that hugged the rightfield foul line before landing fair by one foot. St. Louis recouped those two runs in the seventh before Rhem tired in the eighth. Southworth singled home two more runs to pull the Giants within one. With runners on first and second and no outs, Hornsby brought in Jess Haines to relieve Rhem. Pops halted the rally and retired the Giants in order in the ninth to secure the win.[18]

McGraw decided drastic changes had to be made. The Giants released third baseman Heine Groh and sold pitcher Art Nehf to the Reds. The remaining players, according to sportswriter Harry Cross of the *New York Times*, were on "pins and needles since Manager McGraw started to scatter his players in all directions last night, and the players didn't know but that they would be supplanted by a trainload of new talent." McGraw's wakeup call had the desired effect. On May 12, Jimmy Ring stifled the Cardinals in a 2–1 victory. Bill Sherdel was the hard-luck loser. He pitched eight solid innings but gave up back-to-back home runs to Billy Southworth and Irish Meusel in the third. The Giants closed out the series by trouncing the Redbirds 12–1. Four St. Louis pitchers surrendered 18 hits, including five doubles, a bases-loaded triple, and home runs by Southworth and Meusel again. Adding to the "horrors of the day," wrote James Gould of the *St. Louis Star*, the "fielding of the St. Louisans bordered on the impossibly bad." The two-and-a-half-hour farce, he concluded, was "one of the most tiresome exhibitions of the 1926 season." The Giants' elation was tempered by an injury to shortstop Travis Jackson, who twisted his knee sliding into home on the front end of a double steal.[19]

Thus far, the homestand had been disastrous. The Cardinals lost seven of 11, and the anticipated potent offense managed a meager .218 batting average. Not even Hornsby was spared from the team-wide slump. He had not driven in a run since May 3.[20] The only glimmer of hope was that the bottom-feeding Boston Braves were next on the schedule. The Braves lost 100 games in each of the 1922 through 1924 seasons, though the team improved to 70–83 in 1925 under player-manager Dave Bancroft. Reality returned in 1926. Boston stumbled out of the gate and was floundering in last place when they came to St. Louis for a four-game series.

The Braves proved to be the cure for what ailed the Cardinals. In game one, St. Louis routed Boston 12–7 as Vic Keen won his fifth game, though he did not pitch well. He benefited from seven Boston errors, a Mueller home run, triples from Les Bell, O'Farrell, and Bottomley, and doubles from Hornsby and Bottomley. On May 16, the Cardinals exploded for 16 hits and 13 runs in a 13–2 laugher. Flint Rhem pitched a complete game for his sixth win, and he even contributed a home run and three RBIs to the cause. St. Louis banged out 16 more hits to win game three, 8–5. Mueller and Bottomley slugged home runs, and pitcher Bill Sherdel added three hits to the offensive onslaught. He also shut out the Braves for the first six innings before getting nicked for five runs in the seventh and eighth frames. A sparkling, backhanded stop by third baseman Les Bell on a smash by Boston shortstop Dave Bancroft saved Sherdel from further damage.[21]

Rain on May 18 turned the field into a "sea of mud" and forced the cancellation of the final contest of the series with Boston, the first rainout at Sportsman's Park of the season. Cardinal hitters, now that their bats had reawakened, were probably disappointed, but the team didn't complain too much. It was only their second day off in the past three weeks.[22]

Another regular occupant of the second division, the Philadelphia Phillies, followed the Braves into St. Louis. Despite the team's lowly status, the Phillies were a fighting crew, reflecting the combative nature of their manager, Art Fletcher. Away from the baseball diamond, Fletcher was a soft-spoken, gentlemanly church goer, but on the field, he took on the persona of his mentor, John McGraw, and became a "fiend." The pitching staff, to put it charitably, was fiendishly bad. However, the lineup, featuring aging but still dangerous lefthanded slugger Cy Williams, gave opponents fits. National League managers feared the dead pull hitter so much that they employed a novel shift to try to neutralize his fearsome drives. The leftfielder moved to centerfield, while the centerfielder shaded into rightfield. On the infield, the first baseman moved back into short rightfield along the foul line. The second baseman stepped back into short right center, the shortstop positioned himself behind second base, and the third baseman moved in to take care of any surprise bunt attempts.[23]

Williams and his teammates gave St. Louis fits in game one of the series when the Phillies topped the Cardinals, 6–2. Though Jess Haines had pitched in relief several times, this was his first starting assignment since being hit by a line drive in April. The results were mixed. He pitched a complete game, though he gave up 11 hits and six runs. Meanwhile, Hal Carlson held St. Louis scoreless for the first eight innings before surrendering two inconsequential runs in the ninth. Carlson did more damage on the basepaths. In the third inning, he laced a drive down the rightfield line and raced to second trying to stretch it into a double. On his slide, he spiked Hornsby on the instep of his left foot. The Cardinal manager was too hobbled to continue, and Specs Toporcer took his place. Hornsby, however, was back in the lineup the next day. He told Martin Haley of the *Globe-Democrat* that his wrenched back was the more bothersome injury, causing sharp pains every time he swung a bat, made a throw, or moved quickly on a fielding play. He continued to play because he was "set on having his club at the .500 mark when the long trip around the Atlantic seaboard starts at the close of this month."[24]

St. Louis took a step toward that goal by taking game two from Philadelphia 4–1. The Cardinals maximized their offense, scoring four runs on only four hits, including Les Bell's two-run blast in the second inning. It was enough for Vic Keen, who pitched superbly for his sixth win in seven decisions. After retiring George

Harper to end the game, he once again rushed to Bob O'Farrell and gave him a bear hug in appreciation for his catcher's patience.

On Friday, May 21, the Cardinals swamped the Phillies 12–4. Flint Rhem had a shaky start, giving up a three-run blast to George Harper in the first frame but held the Phillies hitless after the third to earn his seventh win against only one loss. St. Louis tied the game with three runs in the third and exploded for seven runs in the seventh. With two outs and the bases loaded, Bob O'Farrell chased all three runners home with a double down the leftfield line. Thevenow followed with an RBI single, and Ray Blades added a two-run triple. O'Farrell legged out his own triple in the eighth to drive in another run.[25]

Saturday, May 22, was a special day. Mayor Victor Miller declared it "Rogers Hornsby Day" in celebration of the Rajah receiving the most valuable player award for the 1925 season. An hour before the 3:00 p.m. game, drum corps and various civic clubs staged a parade from the fairgrounds to Sportsman's Park. Commissioner Kenesaw Mountain Landis, National League president John Heydler, Cardinal owner Sam Breadon, and members of both teams marched to the flagpole in centerfield to raise the colors. Players then formed a circle at home plate, where sportswriter James Gould, president of the Baseball Writers Association, presented Hornsby with a bronze medal and $1,000 in $5 gold coins. Hornsby allowed each teammate to take one coin from the bag. Perhaps inspired by their manager's largesse, the Cardinals celebrated further by achieving Hornsby's .500 goal with a 9–2 triumph over Philadelphia before 11,000 fans. Bill Sherdel pitched his best game of the season. He used his "baffling" slow ball and a little extra zest on his fastball to pitch seven shutout innings, giving up only three hits. Ray Blades took advantage of a stiff wind to rightfield to launch a three-run home run in the seventh, and Taylor Douthit followed with his first round-tripper of the season. The Phillies were determined not to let the wind provide the only assistance and committed four errors in the last two innings, allowing St. Louis to score three unearned runs.[26]

The stay at .500 was short. On Sunday, Hal Carlson again tamed the Cardinals by a 7–5 score. Hornsby, trying to find a reliable starter beyond Rhem, Keen, and Sherdel, sent Walter Huntzinger to the mound, but he did not last long. He gave up four runs, walking two and surrendering two home runs before Hornsby pulled him after only 1⅔ innings. Art Reinhart proved equally ineffective, walking four more Philadelphia batters.[27]

The Cincinnati Reds rolled into St. Louis on Monday, May 24, to begin a string of seven consecutive contests. The first three would conclude the Cardinal homestand before shifting to Cincinnati for a four-game series. The red-hot Reds had vaulted into first place, winning 16 of 21 games in May, and their inspired play helped them jump out to a 6–0 lead after five innings before a Ladies Day crowd of 5,500. Starter Allen Sothoron failed to retire a single Cincinnati batter. After giving up two singles and a double to score a run, Hornsby yanked Sothoron in favor of Bill Hallahan. Without much time to warm up, Hallahan walked Rube Bressler to fill the bases. A Bottomley error allowed another run to score, and then Wild Bill plunked Hughie Critz with a pitch to force in another. A sacrifice fly pushed the fourth Cincinnati run across before Hallahan walked another to again load the bases. Reds pitcher Eppa Rixey stepped to the plate and hit a grounder back to Hallahan. He tossed to O'Farrell to force the lead runner, and the Cardinal catcher pegged a throw to Jim Bottomley at first. Sunny Jim must have been daydreaming because he was a few feet off the bag when he took the throw, but umpire Peter McLaughlin called Rixey out at first. Manager Jack Hendricks and the entire Reds team bolted from the dugout and protested bitterly for several minutes. McLaughlin refused to reverse his decision, halting the Cincinnati assault.

The outcome seemed bleak for the Cardinals after the Reds added two more in the third inning. Rixey, the tall, lanky southpaw, cruised through the first five innings without allowing a baserunner. He struck out O'Farrell to lead off the sixth before Thevenow reached on an error. Pinch hitter Ernie Vick singled to break up the no-hitter. Blades followed with a walk to load the bases, and Taylor Douthit beat out a slow roller to first to drive in the first run. Hornsby lofted a towering sacrifice fly to the flagpole in center to drive in Vick. Rixey's mastery of the Cards was over. Mueller led off the seventh with a single and advanced to third on centerfielder Edd Roush's error. Les Bell then blasted the team's longest home run of the season to shave Cincinnati's lead to two runs. Jack Hendricks had seen enough and brought in the veteran submarine-style pitcher Carl Mays, who set the Cardinals down without further damage. The eighth inning was a completely different story. Douthit led off with a single. Hornsby and Bottomley walked, and Heine Mueller cleared the bases with a triple. Specs Toporcer hit a pinch-hit triple to score another

Slugging first baseman Jim Bottomley was a leading run producer through much of the 1920s (St. Louis Cardinals Hall of Fame and Museum).

run, and Blades doubled Toporcer home, prompting Mays' removal. Douthit capped the seven-run explosion with an RBI single. *Cincinnati Enquirer* sportswriter Jack Ryder called it the "saddest defeat of the season." Rixey and Mays, he wrote, "gave the most finished and effective exhibition of the dastardly art of blowing a certain victory into a humiliating defeat just about ever seen today."[28]

The following day, St. Louis enjoyed partly cloudy skies with balmy temperatures climbing into the upper 80s. Jim Bottomley's day was also partly cloudy as he found himself in Circuit Judge Robert W. Hall's courtroom. He and the Cardinals were defendants in a civil lawsuit brought by Irwin Hayes, a 27-year-old chauffeur. On June 2, 1925, Irwin attended his first-ever major league game at Sportsman's Park to watch the Cardinals battle the Reds. In the eighth inning, the Cardinals trailed by one run and Bottomley came to bat. Hayes perched in the top row of the rightfield bleachers, waved his hands and shouted, "Smack it this way, Jim." The always congenial Bottomley obliged. He lofted a long drive that hit Hayes squarely on the nose, fracturing it in seven places. Hayes claimed the Cardinals were negligent for not having a screen to protect the bleachers and sued for $7,500 in damages.

The stilted legal repartee that took place during the trial generated a good deal of laughter from the baseball fans who crowded into the courtroom. Conrad Paeben, Hayes' attorney, questioned Bottomley's motives on the stand.

> "Did you strike the ball that was thrown at you?"
> "The records say I did."
> "You created a situation known as a home run?"
> "It turned out to be a home run."
> "What did you do?"
> "I ran around the bases and made a home run."
> "Was it your intention to create a home run?"
> "Well, yes, if I could. It was my intention to hit the ball."
> "Did you swing your whole 180 pounds against that ball with your bat as hard as you could?"
> "I guess I used it all."
> "Did you know where it was going to land when you walloped it?"
> "No, I did not."

Cardinals attorney Sam McChesney cross-examined Bottomley and asked, "You can't place the ball, can you?" "No" was Sunny Jim's terse response. Bottomley was anxious to get to that day's game against the Reds and, despite Paeben's objection, was allowed to leave the courthouse and rush to the ballpark.

Paeben then examined general manager Branch Rickey about the bleacher seating. Sportsman's Park had 2,000 screened bleacher seats, and 1,200 were unoccupied that day. Hayes had plenty of options to sit in a protected area but chose to sit in an unscreened seat. Paeben asked, "Wouldn't the patrons be protected from baseballs if you had a roof over the bleachers?" Rickey replied, "They wouldn't be bleachers then." He admitted that a roof would block some balls but not all.[29]

Bottomley arrived at Sportsman's Park too late to start the game, though his absence wasn't missed. His replacement, Jake Flowers, hit a home run that did not strike a paying customer but did drive in three St. Louis runs in the 9–7 victory. The Reds' tabbed Adolpho Luque, a native of Cuba and the seventh from his homeland to reach the major leagues, to take the mound. Luque's (pronounced Loo-Kay) light skin and blue eyes helped him avoid Major League Baseball's color barrier, opening the door for a 20-year pitching career. Though he had the distinction of being the first Latin pitcher to start and win a World Series game, he was a tough-luck hurler for much of his career, with the exception of the 1923 season when he led the National League with 27 wins and a 1.93 earned run average. On this day, however, his tough luck continued. The 35-year-old was uncharacteristically wild, walking four in 3⅓ innings, while Cardinal hitters battered him for six hits and nine runs, five earned. Taylor Douthit and Ray Blades continued their hot hitting, and Hornsby contributed four RBI's. Vic Keen teetered on the brink of disaster throughout the game. He allowed 12 hits, including three home runs, and seven runs but wriggled out of trouble to win his seventh game in eight decisions.[30]

May 26 got off to a rocky start for the Cardinals and the Reds. The jury in the suit against the Redbirds decided in favor of Irwin Hayes after deliberating for 75 minutes. The verdict was a surprise as professional baseball clubs nearly always won similar cases on the basis that fans knew and assumed the risks for their personal safety when seated in an unprotected area. However, the jury in Hayes' case—only two of whom had ever played baseball the *Globe-Democrat* pointed out—found the Cardinals liable for the broken nose caused by Bottomley's home run and ordered the club to pay Hayes $3,500. Team attorneys immediately filed a motion for a new trial because the verdict went against the weight of evidence. In October, a judge granted the motion, and in January 1928, a jury rejected Hayes' suit for $15,000 in damages.[31]

As for the Reds, with the team on a three-game losing streak for the first time in the season, manager Jack Hendricks held a morning meeting to voice his displeasure with the pitching staff's poor work. Hendrick's reading the riot act did no good. St. Louis swept the series with an 8–5 win. Flint Rhem took the mound and gave up three runs in the first inning. In the second frame, he walked Reds pitcher Red Lucas and third baseman Chuck Dressen and seemed destined for an early shower. His luck, however, turned when Curt Walker sent a sizzling line drive toward rightfield. Hornsby leaped high to snare the ball, then flipped it to Thevenow at second base, who relayed it to Bottomley at first to complete the triple play. Reprieved, Rhem settled down and pitched well until he was lifted for a pinch hitter in the seventh. Lucas sailed through six shutout innings before Bob O'Farrell connected for a solo home run in the seventh. Then in the eighth inning, the Cards erupted for seven runs. Heine Mueller's three-run clout and Les Bell's single knocked Lucas out of the game, and St. Louis continued its onslaught against reliever Jake May.[32]

The Cardinals boarded a train for an extended road trip, no doubt feeling much better about their situation than they did at the start of the month. The team had just swept the league-leading Reds and improved their record to 21–19, four games behind Cincinnati. Rogers Hornsby had cause for concern, however. Flint Rhem and Vic Keen had fashioned a sparkling 14–2 combined record, but the rest of the pitching staff had been wildly inconsistent. If St. Louis was to make a serious push for the pennant, several other pitchers would have to pick up the slack. The offense likewise had been erratic. The team ranked sixth in the league with a .265 batting average. On the other hand, St. Louis was third in the league in runs scored and had the top three home run hitters in the league in Jim Bottomley with seven (though his batting average was a pedestrian .255), Les Bell who had six, and Ray Blades with five. Given the team's well-known struggles on the road, everyone knew the upcoming series with the Reds, Cubs, Phillies, Giants, Dodgers, and Braves would go a long way toward proving whether the Cardinals were contenders or pretenders.

Chapter 7

"Billy the Kid" and "Ol' Pete" to the Rescue, May 27–June 28

St. Louis experienced several architectural highs and Prohibition lows to kick off the summer. A throng of 75,000 onlookers from all over the U.S. and Canada attended the June 13 dedication of the new $3 million Concordia Theological Seminary at DeMun and San Bonita avenues. The 71-acre campus was, according to the St. Louis Star, the largest Protestant theological school in the world and the "greatest monument ever erected to Lutheranism." Not to be outdone, two weeks later some 10,000 Catholic worshipers jammed inside to witness the consecration of the $3.5 million St. Louis Cathedral at Lindell Boulevard and Newstead Avenue. Another 6,000 crowded outside on the cathedral grounds and throughout the neighborhood to listen to loudspeakers as Papal legate Cardinal Bonzano celebrated the pontifical Mass, with Cardinal Hayes of New York delivering the homily. Four cardinals, 15 archbishops, 120 bishops, 60 monsignori, and 1,000 priests added to the solemnity of the ceremony.

On the secular side, F.D. Nims, president of the Southwestern Bell Telephone Company, raised the U.S. flag to signal completion of the exterior of the new Bell Telephone Building on Olive Street. The massive 31-story Art Deco structure was, at the time, the tallest building in St. Louis and could be seen from the bluffs on the Illinois side of the Mississippi River.[1]

In contrast to these spiritual and architectural heights, Prohibition agents literally and figuratively plumbed the depths of the world of illegal liquor in St. Louis. The literal part involved a June 25 raid on a garage in the 2600 block of Morgan Street. Deputy Administrator James Dillon, who had just returned to duty after suffering a serious gunshot wound to his neck during another raid nearly three weeks earlier, and a passel of federal agents and city detectives searched the premises for an hour before they located a manhole cover buried underneath two feet of ashes. They descended nearly 40 feet down a passageway into an expansive and long-forgotten section of Uhrig's Cave. There they found a well-equipped bootlegging operation, consisting of a 15-foot platform capping two 24,000-gallon mash vats and two 200-gallon stills. Electric lighting had been installed and an exhaust fan atop the platform carried off poisonous fumes. Agents discovered 27 five-gallon cans of alcohol, "which examination *disclosed to be of excellent quality." Unable to haul the stills through the passageway, the police used hatchets to destroy the entire operation.*

Uhrig's Cave, once part of the old Uhrig Brewery, started at Jefferson Avenue and Washington Boulevard and stretched for blocks. In the late 19th century, the area had been converted into an entertainment venue where top-flight musical acts and dramatic theater were staged. With cold beer and good food, Uhrig's Cave became one of the city's most popular gathering spots.[2]

The figurative depths involved the murder of Walter Burgoyne, a 22-year-old boxer known as Buddy McHale in the ring. Burgoyne and the police were on a first-name basis as the pugilist had been arrested 49 times on various charges. He and a friend were at William Costello's saloon at Jefferson and Cass avenues on the night of June 13. The two demanded whisky but Costello said he had none left. After a heated verbal exchange, Burgoyne and his companion departed. When Costello ambled out of the bar at 1:00 a.m., Burgoyne and his friend pulled Costello from his car and beat him. Costello managed to free himself, ran back into the saloon, and retrieved a pistol. When he emerged from the bar, Burgoyne fled. Costello fired and shot Burgoyne in the abdomen. Police arrived and took the wounded boxer to the hospital, though, in "accord with gang ethics," he refused to divulge the name of his assailant. But before he died, he told his father that Costello was his killer.[3]

The Cardinals experienced their own highs and lows. The momentum St. Louis had generated during the homestand was lost immediately during the road trip when the Reds swept the Cardinals in a May 27 doubleheader. In game one, the Cardinals jumped to a 1–0 lead on Pete Donohue in the second inning when Les Bell hit a home run to leftfield, the first fair ball of the season to sail over the fence at Redland Field. The Reds struck back in their half of the inning. Bubbles Hargrave tripled home a run off Bill Sherdel and scored on a sacrifice fly. Donohue's error in the third led to an unearned run that knotted the score. The game remained tied until the Reds pushed two runs across in the bottom of the eighth. St. Louis scored a run in the ninth on another Donohue error and had the tying run on third base and no outs, but the Cards failed to score as Sherdel and Blades struck out and Douthit flied out to end the game.

The second game was equally frustrating for St. Louis. Syl Johnson squared off against Carl Mays. The Reds took a 1–0 lead in the third. St. Louis had a chance to tie the game in the fourth frame, but umpire Peter McLaughlin called Heine Mueller out at the plate as he tried to score on Thevenow's grounder to Wally Pipp. Mueller took the call lying down, literally. He disagreed so vehemently that he lay on top of home plate and "heaved great clouds of dust in the general direction of the arbiter, whose dignity could not stand the strain." To no one's surprise, Mueller was tossed from the game. St. Louis pulled even in the sixth on a Bottomley triple and RBI single from Chick Hafey. Cincinnati, however, took the lead in its half of the sixth after O'Farrell dropped a foul ball off Edd Roush's bat. Given a second chance, Roush promptly doubled and scored on second baseman Hughie Critz's single. Johnson again suffered from tough luck. He pitched well, giving up one earned run in six innings, yet his record fell to 0–3. On the plus side, he managed to avoid any physical harm.[4]

Unfortunately for St. Louis, the pitching staff's performance the following day was abysmal. Bill Hallahan, Jess Haines, and Eddie Dyer combined to surrender 11 hits, 13 walks, and 12 runs in the Reds' 12–4 rout. The *Globe-Democrat* claimed the "exhibition of utterly untamed pitching" deserved a "place in the Smithsonian Institution or the Chamber of Horrors at the Eden Musée Wax Works." Hallahan started and walked eight in 5⅓ innings. Haines played only a bit role. He faced two batters in the sixth and gave up hits to both before he was pulled for Dyer, who in 2⅔ innings of relief gave up three hits, walked five and was charged with seven runs in the seventh inning. Hughie Critz, Cincinnati's diminutive second baseman and hardly a feared slugger, walked five times in the contest.[5] The Reds completed the four-game sweep with a 3–1 victory on May 29. Jack Hendricks tabbed former Cardinal southpaw Jake May to make his first start of the season, and he rewarded the Reds' manager with a complete game, five-hitter. Though he pitched well, Vic Keen suffered his second loss of the season.[6]

The Cards moved on to Chicago for a five-game series against the second-place Cubs. Flint Rhem took the mound and halted the losing streak by pitching a complete 5–2 win over Joe McCarthy's crew. St. Louis nicked lefty Wilbur Cooper for 12 hits. Hornsby had three of the safeties, including a two-run home run in the first inning. It was only his second four-bagger of the season. The Redbirds finished the month by splitting a double header on a rainy afternoon in front of a raucous crowd of 35,000—an overflow of some 4,000 fans were on the field behind ropes. St. Louis took the first game 5–3 behind a solid effort from pitcher Herman Bell. Cardinal batters raked Cubs starter Guy Bush for 13 hits with Bob O'Farrell leading the barrage with four hits and two RBIs. Taylor Douthit added three base hits, and Les Bell and Jim Bottomley had two apiece.

Syl Johnson took the mound against Cubs lefty Percy Jones in the second game. St. Louis jumped out to a lead in the second on a Bottomley home run. The Cubs' threat in the third fell short when Douthit raced to deep center to take a home run away from slugger Hack Wilson. After making the catch, Douthit spilled over the rope separating the crowd from the field of play. Chicago tied the game at three apiece in the sixth inning. The score remained knotted going into the eighth when umpires halted the game because of rain. However, both teams and the crowd howled in protest, and the umpires let the game continue. St. Louis took the lead with two runs in the eighth off Charlie Root, but the Cubs stormed back against Bill Hallahan. He gave up back-to-back hits before "Wild" Bill walked Gabby Hartnett to load the bases as well as the next two batters to tie the game. Hornsby had seen enough and brought in Walter Huntzinger, who was just as ineffective. He walked

7. "Billy the Kid" and "Ol' Pete" to the Rescue, May 27–June 28

in another run and then gave up a two-run single to Charlie Grimm. The Cardinals battled back with two runs in the top of the ninth and had the bases loaded with one out. Pinch hitter Jake Flowers flied out to leftfielder Mandy Brooks, who threw out Les Bell trying to score from third base to end the 8–7 Cubs victory.[7]

A brisk breeze blowing out toward the bleachers portended a slugfest for the June 1 game, and the Cardinals and Cubs did not disappoint. An RBI single from Hornsby followed by a Bottomley home run spotted St. Louis a three-run lead in the first. The Cubs got one back in their half of the frame when Cliff Heathcote slammed a Bill Sherdel offering into the rightfield seats. The Cards led 4–2 going into the bottom of the third until Cubs catcher Gabby Hartnett slugged a grand slam to put Chicago in front 6–4. The Redbirds tallied one run in the fourth, but Chicago recouped that run when Heathcote hit his second circuit clout, ending Sherdel's day on the mound. Allen Sothoron relieved and evaded further scoring until the sixth. St. Louis had scored three in the top of the inning to take an 8–7 lead. The Cubs climbed back on top when Sothoron gave up a two-run homer to Mandy Brooks. The see-saw contest continued when the Cards plated a run to tie the game in the seventh, only to have the Cubs push the winning tally across in the bottom of the inning for the 10–9 win.[8]

The series concluded with another offensive barrage. The Cubs rang up three runs in the first off Vic Keen on doubles by Sparky Adams and Cliff Heathcote and a two-run blast by Hack Wilson that left the ballpark and landed on Sheffield Avenue. A rattled Keen walked the next batter, and then first baseman Charlie Grimm hit a vicious drive that Keen tried to field with his pitching hand. The ball caromed to Tommy Thevenow in time to start a double play, but the smash dislocated one of Keen's fingers and the former Cub hurler's day was over. It was expected he would be out of action for ten days. The Cardinals picked up the slack and exploded with six runs in the top of the second, featuring a two-run double by Douthit and a three-run clout by Hornsby. Eddie Dyer took Keen's place on the mound, allowing the Cubs to climb within one run in the third before he was lifted for Jess Haines. Pops pitched 6⅔ effective innings of relief, though he did surrender the tying run in the sixth. The Cardinals, however, delivered a 14–6 win for Haines as they came back with two runs in the seventh and five more in the eighth.

As the Redbirds left Chicago for Philadelphia—after a stop for an exhibition game in Akron, Ohio, on June 3—their elation was tempered by the loss of Keen and the absence of Chick Hafey. Vision problems had been a persistent issue for the outfielder. Years later, he pointed to a game in 1926 in which he was twice hit with pitches. Team doctor Robert Hyland tested Chick's eyesight by placing a card over one eye and then the other. However, official statistics indicate Hafey was hit by two pitches during the entire 1926 season, and they occurred in separate games in mid–April. Though Hafey's memory of the details may have been faulty, his recollection of the test result was not: "With the right, I could see clearly, but with the left I couldn't make out my name over my locker." He continued to play with his ailment, but during the series in Chicago, Hafey complained of blurred vision caused by a buildup of pus under one of his eyelids. Hornsby had him see a specialist in Chicago, who told Hafey the condition would require regular medical care. Hornsby sent Hafey back to St. Louis to be examined by Doctor Hyland.[9]

The rest of the team arrived at Baker Bowl in Philadelphia to take on the Phillies, who were in a tight race with the Boston Braves for last place. Baker Bowl, so named in 1923 in honor of Phillies owner William F. Baker, was completed in 1895, replacing the original stadium that burned to the ground the year before. It had the distinction of being the first "modern" steel, brick, and concrete stadium. Situated on a city block between Lehigh and Huntington avenues and Broad and North 15th streets, the ballpark had a well-deserved reputation as a "band box." Left and centerfields were a "normal" 341 and 408 feet respectively; however, right center was 300 feet from home plate, and the rightfield line extended a scant 280 feet. To reduce the number of cheap home runs, the Phillies placed a screen above the rightfield wall to reach a height of 60 feet. Locals often referred to the stadium as "the hump" because a hill in centerfield—some ten feet higher than the area around home plate—covered a railroad tunnel that passed beneath. Train reverberations occasionally surprised unsuspecting outfielders. One major leaguer from the 1920s and 1930s called Baker Bowl "an atrocity as far as baseball was concerned."[10]

The weather in Philadelphia was an atrocity as well. Cold and a steady drizzle washed out game one of the series. The weather had not improved on June 5, but the teams forged on and played a double header before a paltry crowd of less than 3,000, one of the smallest Saturday crowds in the ballpark's history. Flint Rhem started the first game and pitched a spectacular six-hit shutout for his ninth win. Hornsby aided the cause with a two-run home run in the first inning, and Rhem chipped in with a run-scoring single in the second. The Cardinals took game two by a 7–4 score. The Phillies had a 2–0 lead when the Redbirds loaded the bases with two outs in the third inning. Wattie Holm, who had been platooning with Heine Mueller whenever a lefty was on the mound, hit a routine grounder directly at second baseman Barney Friberg, but the ball took a bad hop, hit Friberg in the nose, and then bounded into short centerfield. By the time shortstop Heine Sand retrieved the ball, all three Cardinal baserunners had scored. St. Louis tallied four more runs in the fourth inning, and Herman Bell coasted to the complete game victory. Holm continued his hot hitting with four hits and four RBIs. The sweep pushed St. Louis back into fourth place, while the Phillies dropped to the bottom of the standings.[11]

Philadelphia was one of two cities that did not allow Sunday baseball, so the Cardinals were idle at the major league level. Owner Sam Breadon was not about to squander the money-making opportunity presented by the open date and scheduled an exhibition game against the York White Roses of the New York-Pennsylvania League. The Cards won 6–2 and drew more fans than had witnessed the game in Philadelphia the day before. The team returned to the rainy City of Brotherly Love only to have the June 7 game cancelled. In fact, rain postponed the entire slate of

National League contests that day. The final game of the series on June 8 was also shut down after a deluge flooded Baker Bowl. The postponed games would be made up when St. Louis returned to Philadelphia in late July. In the meantime, the Cardinals moved on to face John McGraw's Giants at the venerable Polo Grounds in New York.[12]

The 1926 version of the Polo Grounds was the stadium's fifth iteration. It was situated in a former meadow in the north Harlem area of Manhattan, flanked by the imposing Coogan's Bluff on the west and the Harlem River to the east. The geographic constraints gave the Polo Grounds its distinctive horseshoe or bathtub shape with "ridiculously short distances down the foul lines (279 feet along leftfield and 258 feet in rightfield) and equally ridiculously long distances to the power alleys and centerfield (483 feet from home plate)." The alcove in centerfield wedged between two grandstand sections was another distinctive feature. A building set back from the bleacher fences housed home and visitor clubhouses as well as administrative offices. The entire distant alcove area—even the stairways leading to the separate clubhouses—was in play.[13]

Like the Cardinals, the Giants were struggling to avoid the second division. At the start of the series, New York was in fifth place and sported a .500 record. St. Louis knocked the New Yorkers down another notch in the standings with a 4–2 win in the first game. Only 10,000 fans filtered into the cavernous 55,000-seat park to watch Bill Sherdel outduel Jimmy Ring. Sherdel pitched a complete game and received support from Hornsby's two-run single and run-scoring hits from Mueller and Blades. The Redbirds topped the Giants again on June 10 for their fifth straight win. Flint Rhem shut down the Giants to win his tenth decision. Harry Cross of the *New York Times* claimed Rhem "seems to be able to do anything to a baseball except make it entirely disappear." He benefited from stellar outfield play by Douthit and Mueller and from a Douthit home run and "concealed" RBI triple by Heine Mueller, which landed behind third base and "disappeared around the corner of the stand and hid in a corner!"

The Cardinals and Vic Keen completed the sweep with a 10–2 rout on June 11. Knuckleball pitcher "Fat Freddie" Fitzsimmons held the Cardinals scoreless through five frames and took a 1–0 lead into the sixth. St. Louis tied the contest when Blades doubled and scored on a wild pitch. Another errant pitch in the seventh allowed St. Louis to pull ahead 2–1. Fitzsimmons was lifted for a pinch hitter, and McGraw sent in Chick Davies to pitch. The Cardinals greeted him rather rudely and poured four runs across in the eighth and another four in the ninth. Shoddy Giants defense prompted sportswriter Harry Cross to complain that it "would have been a bad day to send the Giants out to catch a train. They never would have made it." "The only explanation," wrote Will Murphy of the *New York Daily News*, was that "Mr. McGraw's Giants were eager to show the general public just how rotten they could be when they put their minds to it."[14]

The mood in the opposing clubhouses could not have been more different. The

Post-Dispatch reported McGraw was "ready to trade any player on his team" in a desperate effort to strengthen his floundering club before the June 15 trade deadline.[15] Rogers Hornsby and the Cardinals, on the other hand, were jubilant. They recovered from the disastrous stop in Cincinnati to win their last six games due to a string of strong pitching performances, steady defense, and timely, if not robust, slugging. The streak lifted the Cardinals to third place, only three games behind the Reds. It took a rainout on June 12 to temporarily cool off the red-hot Redbirds before they took their act to Brooklyn.

Ebbets Field, home of the Dodgers, opened in 1913, one of several new stadiums built between 1909 and 1915. Located in an area with the less-than-magical names of "Pigtown," "Goatville," "Tin-Can Alley," and "Crow Hill," Ebbets Field was a magical baseball palace. Its modest seating capacity of 28,000 in 1926 facilitated an intimate, personal connection between fans and Dodger players. It was, according to author Peter Golenbock, "a suitable place for falling in love with the game." Its architectural features added to its charm. A massive rotunda—80 feet across and 27 feet high—dominated the area inside the main gate. Italian marble columns, a tile floor depicting baseball stitches, and a large chandelier with baseball bat fixtures suspending glass baseball globes made going to the ballpark a memorable experience. Like other stadiums built at the time, the constraints of urban neighborhoods gave Ebbets Field asymmetrical dimensions. The leftfield line stretched some 419 feet, while the right-field line was a mere 301 feet from home plate. In between, center and right-centerfield expanded to 450 and 500+ feet respectively. In rightfield, a 19-foot wire screen topped a 19-foot concrete wall that was "bent in the middle," with the bottom half sloping outward, a feature that made for some interesting ricochets of fly balls.[16]

The Dodgers were not awed by the Cardinals' recent success and took the first game of the series 8–5 on June 14. Herman Bell started and turned in a forgettable performance. He lasted only 1⅓ innings and was torched for seven hits and five runs. Bob McGraw of the Dodgers earned the victory though he gave up five runs on 11 Cardinal hits. He was spared from further damage when Ray Blades lined into a triple play that squelched a promising inning for St. Louis.[17]

Heine Mueller did not do much with the bat, going 0–4, but he did make a nice throw from rightfield to cut down a Brooklyn runner at second base. It turned out to be his last game as a member of the St. Louis Cardinals. That night, St. Louis traded Mueller to the Giants for veteran outfielder Billy Southworth. According to Hornsby, John McGraw approached him during their recent series and proposed a straight Southworth for Mueller swap. Hornsby contacted Sam Breadon, who wired back his approval. The move surprised many, given the Cardinals' hot streak and the fact that Mueller was a hometown product and six years younger than Southworth. But Hornsby was in a win-now mode and believed Southworth would provide a steadier level of play than the colorful Mueller. Hornsby acknowledged Heine's physical abilities, but admitted he had "the habit of making bad plays that are disastrous in a good many instances."[18]

7. "Billy the Kid" and "Ol' Pete" to the Rescue, May 27–June 28

"Billy the Kid" Southworth was a Nebraska native, who made his major league debut with Cleveland in 1913. He bounced back and forth between the minor and major leagues before he finally established himself with the Pirates in 1918. He was traded to the Boston Braves in 1921 and compiled three solid seasons, batting over .300 each year. John McGraw admired Billy's ability and swung a deal for Southworth after the 1923 season. It turned out to be an expensive deal for the Giants. It cost them Casey Stengel, shortstop Dave Bancroft, and Bill Cunningham. Southworth never cared for playing for the dictatorial McGraw, especially after the Giants' manager shifted Billy from rightfield, where Ross Youngs was a fixture, to centerfield.

Outfielder Billy Southworth's acquisition from the Giants provided an enormous spark during the Cardinals' frenetic pennant chase (St. Louis Mercantile Library at the University of Missouri-St. Louis).

Uncomfortable patrolling the Polo Grounds' wide-open space, Southworth slumped to a .256 batting average in 1924. He rebounded with a .292 mark in 1925 and busted out of the gate in the 1926 season, leading the league in hitting for the first month. He cooled off considerably, prompting McGraw to sit him on the bench. McGraw admired Heine Mueller's speed, and when the Giants' manager offered Southworth, the Cardinals quickly agreed to the bargain.[19]

Billy was in the St. Louis lineup on June 15, playing rightfield and batting fifth. His debut was unspectacular: one hit in four at bats with two strikeouts against Dazzy Vance; nevertheless, the Cardinals triumphed 5–0. Bill Sherdel pitched his best game of the season with a complete game, five-hit shutout. Jim Bottomley supplied the offensive fireworks with his tenth home run—a two-run blast in the sixth—and an RBI single. The win pushed the hard-charging Redbirds into third place, only 1½ games behind the Reds.[20]

Inclement weather washed out the rubber game of the series, and the Cardinals moved on to Boston, celebrating Bunker Hill Day with a double header at Braves Field. That venue was the last of the "modern" stadiums, opening in 1915, and its spacious dimensions—the largest in the major leagues—reflected the emphasis on the inside game of the Deadball Era. The foul lines measured 402 feet in left and 365 feet in right. The deepest corner of centerfield was a mammoth 550 feet away. It was nearly impossible to hit a ball over the fence, even after the introduction of the lively ball in 1920. Through the 1927 season, 219 of the 235 home runs at Braves Field (93 percent) were inside-the-park jobs. The first home run over the leftfield wall did not occur until 1925.[21]

A crowd of nearly 25,000 hopped off the trolley that stopped at the departure station within the stadium walls to witness the Braves–Cardinals double header. In the first game, Flint Rhem pitched another gem to improve his record to 11–1. The Cards won 4–2, and the Braves could only muster six hits off the South Carolina native. The Redbird hurler did, however, suffer a scare in the bottom of the ninth when a line drive off the bat of centerfielder Eddie Brown hit Rhem in the stomach and knocked him to the ground. While lying there, he managed to toss the ball to first to beat the runner. Jim Bottomley again swung the big bat, driving in three runs with a triple and single. Vic Keen took his turn on the mound in the second game and, despite some bouts of wildness, came away with a 6–2 victory, his ninth of the season.[22] With the sweep, St. Louis leapfrogged Pittsburgh into second place, only ½ game behind the Reds.

Yet another rainout on June 18 forced yet another double header on Saturday, and the Braves were subjected to yet another sweep at the hands of the Cardinals. Prior to the start of the game, Hornsby told James O'Leary of the *Boston Globe* that he was satisfied with the team's place in the standings and had no desire to be in first at that point. "We have some comparatively young players," he said, "and there is no use in putting any extra strain on them so early in the race." But the team seemed determined to maintain its upward surge despite the manager's concern. Jess Haines got a rare start in game one and seized the opportunity. He rediscovered the "mystery" of the knuckleball that had eluded him for the previous few years and baffled the Braves to earn a 4–0 victory. Herman Bell started game two and rebounded from his disastrous turn in Brooklyn. St. Louis bunched three runs in the third inning on a Hornsby single and Bottomley double, while Bell pitched seven shutout innings before giving up single runs in the eighth and ninth. It was Bell's third victory in four starts on the road trip. The streaking Cardinals had won 11 of their last 12 games, though they did not pick up any ground in the pennant race because Cincinnati also swept a double header in Philadelphia.[23]

Having taken care of Boston, the Cardinals embarked on a whirlwind schedule in which they would be travelling three nights in a row. Brooklyn was the first stop for a single game on Sunday. Hornsby tabbed Bill Sherdel to start, and for the second time within a week, he pitched a shutout. Third baseman Jerry Standaert had both of Brooklyn's hits, otherwise, Sherdel would have pitched a perfect game. Thomas Holmes of the *Brooklyn Daily Eagle* surmised that the Dodgers "reached the conclusion that the only way to beat Billy Sherdel is to cripple him." Cardinal hitters lashed out 15 hits in the 9–0 victory. Billy Southworth and Les Bell contributed three hits apiece, and Hornsby added a double and home run to the attack.[24]

Monday, June 21, was supposed to be an open date, but instead the Cardinals were booked to play a single game in Pittsburgh. During the Cardinals' previous visit to the Steel City, Pirates owner Barney Dreyfus suggested that the game scheduled for September 8 be moved to June because, after an extended absence from their home field, the June slot would be a more lucrative gate attraction. The resurgent Pirates had climbed back into the race and were eager to knock the red-hot Cardinals down a peg. They did just that, winning a 13–11 slugfest. Both starters—Flint Rhem for St. Louis and Lee Meadows for Pittsburgh—didn't last long. The Cardinals jumped in front in the first when Hornsby doubled home a run, but the Pirates came right back with three runs on George Grantham's bases-loaded triple. The Cards knocked Meadows out in the second inning, putting up four runs. The Pirates returned the favor with four runs in the third, sending Rhem to the showers after giving up one run and leaving two men on base with no one out. Syl Johnson relieved and gave up two runs on an RBI single and sacrifice fly. Hornsby apparently sensed Johnson didn't have his good stuff because he pulled him and brought in Art Reinhart to finish the inning. The game seesawed with both teams scoring two runs in each of the fourth and fifth innings. The Pirates bolstered their lead with two runs in the seventh off Walter Huntzinger. The Cardinals battled back with single runs in the eighth and ninth. Hornsby came to bat with two outs and runners on second and third base. Pirates ace Ray Kremer got the Rajah to lift a harmless fly ball to centerfielder Max Carey to end a game Charles Doyle of the *Pittsburgh Post-Gazette* called "weird, wild, woolly, and at times nothing short of insane."[25]

The Redbirds' strong showing on the road trip, spurred by excellent pitching and stout hitting, whipped up pennant fever among the Cardinal faithful. A band and contingent of several hundred fans greeted the team when it arrived at Union Station at 8:45 a.m. on June 22. They showed their support again in the afternoon before the Cardinals took the field against Pittsburgh. They staged a parade from Grand Boulevard and Olive Street all the way to Sportsman's Park. A large Tuesday afternoon crowd of 16,000 got to view a pitcher's duel. Vic Keen took the mound for St. Louis while Lee Meadows, whom the Cardinals pummeled the day before, pitched for Pittsburgh. Meadows exacted his revenge with a 3–1 triumph. He scattered six Cardinal hits and ended Rogers Hornsby's 17-game hitting streak enroute to his eighth win against zero defeats. Keen pitched well but gave up two solo home runs to shortstop Glenn Wright, a triple to Max Carey, and a run-scoring single by Paul Waner.[26]

The loss dropped the Redbirds to third place, 2½ games behind the Reds. The setback proved to be a blessing in disguise. By virtue of the team's place in the standings, the Cardinals were able to claim pitcher Grover Cleveland Alexander on waivers from the Cubs rather than the Reds and Pirates, who also submitted claims. The cost to acquire the future Hall of Famer was the $4,000 waiver price. Roy Stockton of the *Post-Dispatch* was ecstatic about the move: "This must be the Cardinals' year. Everything is breaking for them. Even in defeat they profit ... the Cardinals' chances of winning the pennant, already considered very bright, will be more roseate than ever."[27]

The Cubs' parting with the veteran hurler apparently shocked Chicago fans and sportswriters alike. One month earlier, Cubs fans celebrated Grover Cleveland Alexander Day by presenting Ol' Pete with a brand-new Lincoln automobile. Baseball insiders, though, shouldn't have been too surprised because it was well known that Alexander and manager Joe McCarthy had been feuding since spring training. McCarthy was more of a disciplinarian than previous Cub managers, and he treated stars and benchwarmers equally. If you produced, you played. McCarthy's methods didn't sit well with the laid-back Alexander, who said he "wasn't going to be ordered around by a bush league manager." As the season progressed, Ol' Pete's drinking got worse, and McCarthy became convinced he was a bad influence on the younger players. Things came to a head in early June in Philadelphia. Alexander had stayed behind as the team left for the East coast, and when he finally rejoined his teammates, he was in no condition to pitch. McCarthy had had enough. He unleashed a verbal tirade against the wayward Cub and refused to admit him to the club's dressing room. He suspended Alexander indefinitely on June 15 and ordered him to return to Chicago. "This isn't the first time by any means," McCarthy told a *Chicago Tribune* reporter. "This is the sixth time it has happened in the last nine or ten days.... I absolutely refuse to allow him to disrupt our ball club and will not have him around in that condition." Alexander returned to Chicago ostensibly to get back into shape, but the Cubs released him a week later. McCarthy reasoned that the Cubs finished last in

Discarded by the Cubs and scooped up by St. Louis off waivers, pitcher Grover Cleveland Alexander steadied the Cardinal mound crew. His exploits during the World Series were the stuff of legend (St. Louis Mercantile Library at the University of Missouri-St. Louis).

1925 with Alex and if they were to finish last again in 1926, "I'd rather it was without him."[28]

Obviously, the transaction came with some risk for the Cardinals. There are different versions of who pushed to claim Alexander. Branch Rickey wasn't among the advocates. He was out of town tending to farm system work when Alexander's name showed up on the waiver wire, and even if he had been available, it's debatable he would be interested in an aging pitcher who had a well-known battle with the bottle. Yet others believed Ol' Pete still had something left in his right arm. Coach Bill Killefer had managed and played with Alexander for years and seemed to know how to get the best from his former battery mate. For his part, Hornsby and Alexander had been friends and greatly respected each other's talent. Perhaps Sam Breadon made the call on his own, but he hedged his bet by making it a condition that Alexander's wife, Aimee, travel with the team on the road to try to keep him in good enough shape to pitch.[29]

No matter the reason, Alexander was fortunate to find a more comfortable environment than he experienced in Chicago. Killefer called Alexander the night the announcement was made. "I'm in condition and ready to pitch right now," Pete told his former teammate, "I hope that I can do something to help you boys win a pennant." When he reported to St. Louis the next day, Hornsby told him, "Glad to have you on the team. Think you can help us. Just follow the curfew like the other guys." Alexander was more than pleased to be part of the Redbirds. The *Sporting News* reported how he boasted that St. Louis "looks like a pennant team. I'm not going to say anything about myself, but don't let anybody tell you that this arm hasn't a few more good ones left in it. I'm tickled to be with the team and Hornsby and Killefer. All Rog has to do is nod his head and I'll jump through a hoop for him." To make room for the newest arrival, the Cardinals waived Walter Huntzinger, who was claimed by the Cubs.[30]

The excitement generated by Alexander's arrival must have inspired the Cardinals. They rebounded to capture a 6–2 victory over the Pirates. With Pittsburgh leading 1–0 in the fourth inning, St. Louis loaded the bases with two outs. Light-hitting Tommy Thevenow came to bat and came through in the clutch—an increasingly frequent result as the season progressed—with a line single to leftfield, scoring two runs. Despite having to work around six walks, Jess Haines held the 2–1 lead until the seventh frame when the Cards salted away the victory. Haines started the rally with a base hit. Walks to Ray Blades and Taylor Douthit set the stage for Rogers Hornsby before 8,000 fans, who were on their feet screaming. The Rajah did not disappoint. He picked the perfect time to hit his first home run of the season at Sportsman's Park, crushing Don Songer's pitch into the leftfield bleachers for a grand slam. The next day, Pirates manager Bill McKechnie lauded the confidence Hornsby had instilled in his team: "I thought we had them on the run with our two victories. But the way they fought back yesterday and beat us proves to me that it is the club that must be feared."[31]

The final game of the series ended in an anticlimactic 3–3 tie. Both teams agreed prior to the game to stop play at 4:45 so the Pirates could catch a train to Pittsburgh. The Bucs tallied single runs in the first, second, and sixth innings off Flint Rhem to lead 3–0 going into the eighth. Up to that point, Ray Kremer had given up only four hits. Specs Toporcer pinch hit for Rhem to lead off the eighth, and he rapped a solid single to rightfield. Ray Blades fought off a pitch and dumped a Texas League single into right, sending Toporcer to third base. With one out, Hornsby hit a long sacrifice fly that pinned Paul Waner to the rightfield wall. Jim Bottomley followed with a double off the wall in right center to score Blades, and Billy Southworth, who had been struggling since joining St. Louis, doubled to right to tie the game. When the contest was halted after nine innings, a good many of the 8,000 fans in attendance filtered out of the ballpark grumbling about the unsatisfying conclusion.[32]

The Chicago Cubs followed Pittsburgh into town. The game on Friday, June 25, was rained out and would be played as part of a Sunday double header, but Cardinals management ratcheted up the fans' excitement with the announcement that Grover Cleveland Alexander would make his Cardinals debut against his former team on Sunday. On Saturday, Hornsby sent Bill Sherdel to the mound. Sherdel had pitched 21 consecutive scoreless innings going into the game, but the Cubs quickly ended that streak, scoring three runs in the first inning on Charlie Grimm's bases-clearing triple. Sherdel settled down but gave up a run in the fourth and then was pulled in the sixth after he relinquished three straight singles, which scored a run. Syl Johnson limited further damage to a Gabby Hartnett sacrifice fly. The 11,000 fans in the stands were discouraged and disgruntled by the Cardinals' inability to cut into Chicago's lead. They certainly had plenty of chances. Cubs lefty Percy Jones had allowed five hits and eight walks through the first six innings, though they only managed single runs in the first and sixth innings.

Trailing 6–2, St. Louis' never-say-die mentality was on full display in the seventh inning. The Cardinals finally knocked Jones out of the game after Les Bell doubled, O'Farrell singled, and Tommy Thevenow patiently drew a walk on a borderline full-count pitch. Ray Blades singled one run home. Douthit swung at reliever Charlie Root's first pitch and lofted a single into center, scoring two more runs. McCarthy removed Root and brough in Guy Bush to face the dangerous Rogers Hornsby. He wasted little time, drilling Bush's first pitch into the right center stands for a three-run home run and an 8–6 lead. The crowd and the Cards' dugout erupted. Straw hats sailed onto the field from the stands, and the players were tossing caps, bats, gloves, a catcher's chest protector, and anything else they could lay their hands on into the air. Jess Haines entered the game in relief and gave up a run in the eighth but retired the Cubs in order in the ninth to preserve the dramatic victory, which vaulted the Cardinals back into second place. The story of the game made the front page of the *Globe-Democrat*, an indication that the rampaging Redbirds had captured the city's imagination.[33]

Sunday, June 27, was a perfect day for baseball—fair skies and temperatures in

7. "Billy the Kid" and "Ol' Pete" to the Rescue, May 27–June 28

the low 70s. The excitement building throughout the city was fully manifest. Lines formed at the ticket windows at 8:00 a.m. By noon, the main stadium entrance on Dodier Street had to be roped off. An hour later, the police detailed to manage the crowd had to call in reinforcements. When game one of the double header started at 2:00, a record crowd of more than 37,000 occupied every seat in Sportsman's Park or were packed in the aisles or rear of the lower deck; an estimated 10,000 more were turned away.

If the 39-year-old Alexander had any butterflies before the contest, he didn't show it. Bill Hallahan watched from the dugout as Pete warmed up. The well-seasoned veteran tossed a few pitches to the catcher, stopped to unwrap a piece of chewing gum, gazed at the throng in the stands, and tossed a few more pitches before he went to the bench and put on a red-knit Cardinal sweater. Hallahan turned to a teammate and said, "This is going to be murder. He isn't throwing *anything*!"[34]

Wild Bill's prediction was as inaccurate as some of his pitches. Thundering applause greeted Alexander as he strolled to the mound, while the fans aimed a non-stop stream of verbal abuse at Chicago manager Joe McCarthy as he manned the third base coach's box. Pete and Cub rookie righthander Bob Osborn put up blanks until Billy Southworth slugged a solo home run in the fifth. The Cubs' Charlie Grimm jumped on the one mistake Alexander made and deposited a pitch into the rightfield pavilion to take a 2–1 lead in the seventh inning. It was the last base hit Alexander surrendered. St. Louis promptly tied the score in its half of the seventh when Tommy Thevenow chased Les Bell home with a single. The tension soared when the game went into extra innings. Alexander set the Cubs down in order in the top of the tenth. Southworth drew a walk—one of ten issued by Osborn—to lead off the Cardinals' tenth. Bell bunted Southworth to second, and O'Farrell was walked intentionally to face Thevenow. Tommy hit a roller to third, which Howard Freigau fumbled to fill the bases. None other than Grover Cleveland Alexander came to bat with the opportunity to win his own ball game. The crowd held its breath when Pete hit a long fly ball to left and exhaled when it landed foul. He couldn't complete the fairytale ending and struck out. With the crowd at fever pitch, Ray Blades hit a lazy dribbler to first baseman Charlie Grimm. Grimm fielded the ball and tossed it to Osborn covering first. The rookie, however, did not handle the throw cleanly before Blades touched the bag and Southworth raced home with the winning run. After pitching all ten innings and giving up only four hits, a very satisfied Alexander passed the Chicago dugout and spied Joe McCarthy sitting on the bench, fuming at the tough loss. Pete looked his former manager in the eye, smiled, tipped his cap, and kept walking.[35]

Game two of the twin bill was almost an afterthought. Cubs pitcher Sheriff Blake used a sharp-breaking curveball to strike out ten Cardinal hitters and allow only one base hit in the 5–0 whitewash. Shoddy fielding to the tune of six errors paved the way for three unearned runs by the Cubs. Hornsby especially had a tough day. In addition to going 0–4 at the plate, he committed three errors. The

Post-Dispatch revealed that the Rajah was suffering from an outbreak of boils on his leg, which made it unbearably painful to field his position. The Cards' dismal showing frustrated the huge crowd and set the stage for an embarrassing display of poor sportsmanship at the end of the game. With two outs in the top of the ninth, Sparky Adams hit a pop fly to Hornsby. Umpire Charlie Moran, however, called the batter safe because of catcher's interference by Bill Warwick. The crowd roared its disapproval, and a cascade of seat cushions and pop bottles showered the playing field. Fortunately, no players or umpires were injured, though it took the ground crew some 15 minutes to clear the field so that the game could resume. James M. Gould of the *St. Louis Star* deplored the "near riot" at Sportsman's Park for giving St. Louis a bad name. He recalled that a New York writer once remarked that "St. Louis is one of the finest cities in the country … outside of Sportsman's Park."[36]

The Cardinals' hangover lingered into the next game as Chicago won an 11-3 blowout. Vic Keen was shelled for nine hits and seven runs until he was removed in the fifth with no one out. In that inning, the Cubs sent 13 batters to the plate against Keen and Syl Johnson and scored eight runs on seven singles, a double, one walk, and one hit batsman. The bad luck that followed Johnson struck again. He left the game after being hit in the knee on Sparky Adams' grounder. With the game out of hand, Hornsby took himself out of the game to rest his legs and removed Bob O'Farrell, who suffered a bruised finger on his throwing hand from a pitched ball. St. Louis managed only six hits off Charlie Root with Jim Bottomley accounting for all the Cards' scoring with a bases-loaded double.[37]

The Redbirds were set to board a train to Chicago for a single game, but they made the trip without their team leader. The boils on Hornsby's thighs had hobbled the second baseman enough that Sam Breadon asked team doctor Robert Hyland to persuade the Cards' skipper to undergo an operation to remove an infected carbuncle. Hornsby didn't agree to the procedure until a few minutes before the train left and only after he was told that if he didn't, he would miss an extended period of the pennant chase. Post operation, Dr. Hyland said Rogers was determined to return to action the following Sunday against the Reds. The medical professional was more cautious, asserting "It is possible that he will be fit to return to duty that game. My advice would be to postpone the return to duty a few more days but [Hornsby's] one thought is to get back into uniform to help the team in the pennant fight and he will play as soon as it is physically possible." Prior to his procedure, Hornsby had suffered from boils for two to three weeks, but he played—brilliantly at that—through the pain. It's not clear if the players knew of his ailment, but his inspired performance helped the Cardinals fashion a 15–6 record from June 1 through June 28 and ascend from sixth to second place, 3½ games out of first.[38]

Chapter 8

Trouble in the Mound City, June 30–July 25

Gang activity in St. Louis heated up along with the weather. On July 2, the temperature soared to 98 degrees. That same day, police shot and killed Anthony Selvaggi and wounded Joseph Simon after a high-speed chase into Illinois. Both were members of the Cuckoo Gang and wanted for questioning in connection with the $14,000 robbery of two messengers of the Union-Easton Trust Company on June 22. The shootout was part of a two-week police investigation into Cuckoo Gang activities. The ne'er-do-wells had relocated their headquarters to the east side of the river as a safe haven after their gunmen committed crimes in St. Louis. Police blamed them for at least four murders, a dozen robberies, and scores of hold-ups of whiskey shipments or liquor plants. Though law enforcement could not stop the crime spree, they did all they could to apply persistent pressure upon the illegal liquor trade. Particularly noteworthy was a July 21 raid on the Woermer Pickling Company, located at South 11th Street. Police found a distillery with a daily capacity of 150 gallons of whiskey and a double tier of 91 barrels containing about 20,000 gallons of fermenting mash.[1]

Civic improvements within the Mound City paralleled the battle against crime. In mid-July, demolition crews began tearing down buildings in preparation for widening Olive Street from 60 to 100 feet between Twelfth Boulevard and Channing Avenue. The 20-block stretch once boasted palatial homes of some of St. Louis' business elites, but as the wealthy owners vacated the area for the city's western fringes, many of the homes were converted into boarding houses, which deteriorated badly over the years. Several manufacturing concerns, such as Rosenbrough Monument, Lesser-Goldman Cotton, and Dinks Parrish Laundry had to alter their existing structures to accommodate the new thoroughfare. Though some businessmen grumbled about the project, Dinks Parrish told the Star, *"The street now is worse than an alley, and anything that can be done will improve it."*[2]

The Cardinals were looking to improve health-wise as the depleted crew limped into Chicago on June 29. Above all, the team would be without its field manager and star player for the road trip. In addition, catcher Bob O'Farrell was nursing a bruised finger on his throwing hand and Billy Southworth had hurt his shoulder attempting a diving catch against the Cubs. The team was not ungrateful that the game was rained out as they packed their bags for a four-game set with the Pirates. Still, they were a confident bunch. Bill Killefer was a veteran skipper and more than capable of stepping into the breach as manager, and the platoon tandem of Specs Toporcer and Jake Flowers were skilled substitutes at second base.[3]

Another factor in St. Louis' favor was the Pirates' recent tailspin. They had lost six of their last seven games, and amid rumors of dissension within the ranks, manager Bill McKechnie benched team captain and leadoff man Max Carey. The move did not provide the desired results as the Cardinals bested Pittsburgh, 6–2, behind a complete game from Jess Haines. Ray Blades tagged Lee Meadows for a triple in the first and slugged a solo home run in the third. The Cards clung to a 3–2 lead going into the ninth before Meadows weakened. Two runners were on base via walks when Les Bell came to bat. He worked the count full before he deposited Meadows' next pitch out of the stadium into Schenley Park, one of the longest home runs hit at Forbes Field that season.[4]

On July 1, the Cardinals felt very confident about extending the Pirates' losing streak with ace Flint Rhem on the mound for game two. Rhem gave up two runs in the first but held the Pirates scoreless through the sixth inning. The Cardinals finally broke through against Don Songer in the seventh. With the bases loaded and two out, Les Bell continued his torrid hitting spree by ripping a single to left, scoring two runs and giving St. Louis a 3–2 lead. Rhem, however, couldn't make the lead stand. He gave up five runs, highlighted by a two-run single from Kiki Cuyler and a two-run triple by Pie Traynor. Forty-three-year-old Babe Adams took the mound in the eighth for Pittsburgh and pitched two scoreless innings to end the losing streak and hand Rhem his second loss of the season.[5]

The Cardinals' lack of offensive punch continued the next two days, despite the return of Chick Hafey to the ball club. Pittsburgh topped St. Louis 3–2 in game three. Ray Kremer shut out St. Louis for the first eight innings before surrendering a two-run single to Bob O'Farrell in the ninth. Grover Cleveland Alexander was saddled with a hard-luck loss, despite pitching seven strong innings. Cardinal pitching was not as strong in the series finale. With the score tied 2–2 going into the bottom of the fourth, the Pirates pummeled Herman Bell and Vic Keen for eight runs on seven hits. The third straight loss dropped the Cardinals into third place, four games behind Cincinnati and a half game behind Pittsburgh.[6]

The Redbirds were grateful to return home to start an important five-game series against the first-place Reds. A July 4 crowd of some 18,000 diehards braved the sweltering mid–90s temperatures to cheer on the Cardinals and Rogers Hornsby, who was available to manage the team from the bench. However, he was not yet fit, according to Dr. Hyland, to retake his place in the lineup. Hornsby's presence did nothing to inspire or revive the St. Louis offense as they lost their fourth consecutive game, 7–2. The top four batters in the St. Louis lineup went a combined 1 for 15 against southpaw Jake May. Chick Hafey was one of the few to have some success at the plate with a double and solo home run. His extended layoff from an abscessed upper tooth and an eye ailment did not affect his slugging, though the rust plainly showed in his sluggish play in rightfield. Hafey had plenty of company. The Cardinals committed four errors, and it was a minor miracle that the score was not much worse. The Reds blistered Bill Sherdel and two relievers for 17 hits but left 14 men on base.[7]

Cincinnati and St. Louis squared off in a double header on July 5. The withering heat must have sapped any remaining oomph in the Cardinal bats as pitcher Pete Donohue completely dominated in the Reds' 4–0 triumph in game one. Flint Rhem hurled a credible game—allowing three runs in eight innings—though it was no match for Donohue's performance. Game two pitted Eppa Rixey against Jess Haines. The outlook looked gloomy for the 25,000 fans suffering in the sauna that was Sportsman's Park. Cincinnati jumped out to a 4–0 lead going into the bottom of the fifth when the Cardinals finally broke through to end their week-long batting slump and five-game losing streak. With one out, Chick Hafey singled to deep short and advanced to second on Les Bell's single. Hafey was forced at third on Vick's hard smash, which brought up light-hitting Tommy Thevenow. The Cards shortstop came through with a clutch single to score Bell. Rixey then walked Jess Haines to load the bases for Wattie Holm, whom Hornsby inserted into leftfield for the slumping Ray Blades. Holm doubled off the rightfield wall to score two runs and narrow the Reds' lead to 4–3. St. Louis jumped in front with two runs in the sixth inning off former Giant pitcher Art Nehf. Ernie Vick, giving Bob O'Farrell a rare game off, singled home one run, and Thevenow added a second RBI single.

The lead was short-lived. Edd Roush led off the Reds' half of the seventh and hit Haines first pitch into the pavilion. With one out in the bottom of the eighth, Jim Bottomley drew a walk off righthander Red Lucas. Hornsby sent Billy Southworth to pinch hit for Hafey, and the move paid off handsomely. Southworth lofted a Lucas pitch into the rightfield seats, and the Cardinals claimed the 7–5 win. Haines won his sixth game against one loss, though his pitching was shaky at the start. He set the Reds down in order in the last two innings to preserve the much-needed win, preventing the Cardinals from slipping into a fourth-place tie with Chicago.[8]

Hornsby desperately wanted to be back in the lineup and told reporters during the double header that he would return for the July 6 contest, but Dr. Hyland advised him not to play for a few more days and the manager reluctantly followed orders. Grover Cleveland Alexander shuffled to the mound for the start, and he pitched brilliantly for 8⅓ innings. Martin Haley of the *Globe-Democrat* called Alexander a "smooth-working machine, with perfect control of all his pitching parts." His curveball bit the edges of the plate, high and low. He had surrendered only five hits and had a 2–0 lead when leftfielder Walter Christensen singled, bringing first baseman Wally Pipp to the plate. Ol' Pete tried another curveball, but the pitch didn't break. Pipp jumped on the mistake and drove the ball into the rightfield stands to send the game into extra innings. After a scoreless tenth, the Reds roughed up Alexander for three runs in the eleventh. The Cardinals put two men on in their half of the inning, but Carl Mays induced Southworth to bounce out to Pipp, ending the threat. Mays went the distance, giving up only five hits. Douthit had two and Bottomley had the other three, including a two-run double in the fourth. Despite having lost six of the eight games Hornsby missed, sportswriter Roy Stockton argued there was "no reason for gloom over the showing of the Cardinals." Hornsby was due to return to action in the weekend series against Boston, and Jim Bottomley was showing signs of emerging from his season-long batting funk. Flint Rhem was expected to return to form after some rough outings; Vic Keen, who had been nursing a sore arm, was feeling better, and Jess Haines had strung together several quality starts. The pieces were in place, Stockton surmised, so that "the Cardinals can be expected to start another drive for the pennant."[9]

Stockton's words seemed prophetic. The Cardinals ended the series with an 11–2 thrashing of the Reds on July 7. Jack Ryder of the *Cincinnati Enquirer* called it a "desperate exhibition" in which the Reds "played baseball exactly as it should not be played in every department." Art Reinhart pitched a complete game for his first win of the season, though, according to Stockton, his performance was far from a work of art. Reinhart, he wrote, "was constantly in hot water." One pitch "would hit the dirt and the next would be so high that Bob O'Farrell would have to jump three feet in the air to pull it down. The next would be a yard outside the plate and the next would cut the inside corner by an inch.... At any rate he had the Reds so jumpy at the plate that they could not connect solidly." The Cardinal offense woke up, led by three hits apiece from Taylor Douthit and Specs Toporcer. St. Louis used 15 singles and some porous Cincinnati defense to score six unearned runs in the fifth inning and two more in the eighth. The Reds, Ryder related, were "glad to get out of this super-heated burg for the season." Despite the win, St. Louis dropped to a third-place tie with Brooklyn, thanks to the Dodgers' double-header sweep of the Braves.[10]

After tough series with the Reds and Pirates, St. Louis must have been salivating at the thought of taking on the cellar-dwelling Braves in a five-game set. Rogers Hornsby's return to the lineup against Dr. Hyland's advice—his first action since June 28—raised expectations even further. Bill Sherdel worked his way out of several jams to earn a 2–1 victory, pulling St. Louis within 3½ games of the Reds who suffered a double-header sweep by the Giants. A solo home run from Les Bell and RBI double by Bob O'Farrell furnished all the offense Sherdel needed. Though limping slightly from the carbuncle operation, Hornsby fielded seven chances flawlessly, including a pivotal throw to O'Farrell in the top of the ninth to prevent a Boston runner from scoring.[11]

On July 10, some 7,000 fans witnessed an entirely different game than the pitching duel from the previous day. St. Louis pounded out 16 hits and benefited from eight walks and five Boston errors in an 18–6 laugher. The Cardinals scored four runs in each of the first, sixth, and seventh innings and added three more in the eighth. Hornsby slugged a home run along with two singles; Ray Blades returned to the lineup with a vengeance, slamming a triple and a double; Les Bell drove in five runs with three base hits; Tommy Thevenow had three hits, and Billy Southworth knocked in four runs. Jess Haines coasted to his seventh win, despite giving up 14 hits and six runs himself. The Cardinals pulled one game closer to the Reds, who lost to New York.[12]

The Braves and Cardinals squared off in a twin bill on July 11 in front of a large Sunday crowd of 23,500. In game one, Jim Bottomley slammed a three-run homer in the first inning for a lead the Cards never relinquished. Grover Cleveland Alexander scattered nine hits, enroute to the comfortable 7–2 win, the Cards' tenth straight over the hapless Braves. However, St. Louis was the hapless team in game two, a 19–5 massacre by the Braves. The embarrassment prompted Martin Haley of the *Globe-Democrat* to comment that there was hardly "anything contrary to good baseball that the Cardinals overlooked in their noble efforts to convert the second game into a burlesque performance." Flint Rhem started and lasted but 2⅓ innings, giving up six hits and six runs. Hornsby brought in Herman Bell, who offered no relief at all. He too was roughed up during his 2⅓ inning stint, surrendering three hits and four runs. Finally, Art Reinhart came in and was battered for 14 hits and nine runs in 4⅓ innings. In the eighth inning alone, the Braves sent 12 men to the plate, tallying nine hits and eight runs. Hornsby most likely left the lefty on the mound not wanting to overtax the pitching staff further. To Martin Haley, the three St. Louis pitchers seemed to be "simply tossing the ball to the plate evidently to see how hard and how far the Braves could sock it." The Cardinals' defense resembled a "Keystone Cops" episode: "They committed six errors that we know of, they lost fly balls in the sun, they went after ground balls as if the grounders reeked with leprosy and they relayed throws apparently terrorized by the same fear." The only saving grace was that St. Louis still managed to gain a half-game in the standings as the Reds dropped another contest to the Giants.[13]

The debacle was Rhem's third straight loss, and he had been knocked out of two other starts but managed to avoid being tagged with the defeat. His reversal of form was a mystery to Roy Stockton, who thought the pitcher's health might be the problem. "At least inquiry has disclosed," he wrote, "that several times lately he has appeared to be feeling badly." James Gould of the *St. Louis Star* alluded to another problem: "There have been insinuations that this boy with a brilliant future is not taking the best care of himself. Nowadays, that can mean only one thing." If it were true that Rhem had been "off the reservation," he added, it was incumbent upon Hornsby as manager to discipline the pitcher and teach him "that he has no right to jeopardize the chances of his mates who are giving of their best to the pennant cause." It was likely no coincidence that Rhem's issues corresponded roughly to Grover Cleveland Alexander's arrival in St. Louis. The two quickly became drinking buddies, and while Ol' Pete never missed his turn in the rotation, perhaps Rhem couldn't keep pace. Sportswriter Bob Broeg recounted a story when manager Gabby Street scolded Rhem for drinking. The South Carolinian replied in his thick southern drawl, "Well, Sawge, ah was with Alex, and ah figured he was mo' potent to the club than me, so ah drunk the fastest and the mostest." His drinking was serious enough that the Cardinals included a clause in his 1927 contract that promised a $2,500 bonus if he abstained from alcohol during the season. Rhem made it to midseason before Sam Breadon announced $2,000 was deducted from the pitcher's salary for violating training rules. Rhem admitted he drank, adding that others on the team "were enjoying themselves also."[14]

The pinnacle of Rhem's drinking escapades—an event that reached legendary status in Cardinal lore—occurred during the fierce 1930 pennant chase. Flint failed to show for a late season game against the Brooklyn Dodgers. On September 19, the *Atlanta Constitution* reported Rhem, when confronted by manager Gabby Street the next day, claimed he had been abducted by two thugs and taken to a remote roadhouse to prevent him from pitching. "But that wasn't the worst of it," he told Street. "They forced me to drink glass and glass of hard liquor." This, however, turned out to be more myth than actual legend. Years later, Rhem admitted to being drunk, though he never left the hotel. Street made up the story about the kidnapping.[15]

Apparently Rhem was not the only one in July 1926 to imbibe too much. The *Sporting News* revealed "disquieting reports" that several players were "doing a little fudging on the Eighteenth Amendment" while Hornsby was sidelined. Rumors that a couple of players showed up at the clubhouse "with beautiful hang-overs" reached members of the press, prompting one sportswriter to comment "there is more than a whisper as to the cause of the club's—not Hornsby's—low swat average." A statement "right straight from headquarters" [Branch Rickey?] indicated the Cards' poor hitting "and the ministrations of a friendly bootlegger are closely related—so closely that steps have been taken to break up the friendship." It was said that one accompanied the team "as a sort of steward-in-ordinary." Team brass undoubtedly received revelations of this sort less than enthusiastically as the "barometer has been falling rapidly at Sportsman's Park, with indications of a storm." The team suffered in 1925 when a young pitcher [most likely Rhem] "had his regular settos with the 'red eye,'" and Hornsby, who made few rules to infringe upon his players' personal time, would be quick to act "if transgressions on the common training rules reflect in the condition of his men."[16]

Hornsby never addressed the issue publicly, and it's not known if he did, indeed, raise a storm about the situation, but he decided, since Rhem had such an abbreviated appearance the day before, to give his ace hurler another start on July 12 to close out the series with the Braves. The result was no better than before. Flint gave up four runs in the first inning and was yanked in the second with only one out. St. Louis battled back to tie the game and took a lead on Bottomley's 12th homer in the fifth. Syl Johnson came on in relief in the seventh and gave up two runs on three doubles. Again, the Cards knotted the score on a pinch-hit double by Jake Flowers.

Having burned through four pitchers already, Hornsby brought in Vic Keen, who had been struggling with a sore arm for weeks. He escaped with no scoring in the eighth, but he gave up a two-run home run with two outs in the top of the ninth to take the 8–6 loss. Catcher Bob O'Farrell did everything he could to keep the Cardinals in the game. He had three hits, scored two runs, and threw out four would-be base stealers. Roy Stockton, who one week earlier believed there was no reason for gloom, now sounded the alarm. If Rhem and Keen continued their ineffective hurling, he warned, the Cardinals were in danger of dropping into the second division.[17]

The Dodgers were next on the schedule. They and the Cardinals engaged in another high-scoring affair with St. Louis on top, 12–10. Brooklyn lost, wrote Roy Stockton, "because its pitching was worse than the Cardinals." Bill Sherdel earned his eighth win despite laboring mightily through nine innings. He gave up ten runs and 16 hits, including four doubles and four home runs—three to former teammate Jack Fournier. The Cards' lefty certainly benefited from his comrades blasting 16 hits of their own off three Brooklyn pitchers. Taylor Douthit led the way with four singles while Les Bell added three more. Leading 4–3 going into the bottom of the fifth, St. Louis exploded for seven runs. Douthit had two hits and two stolen bases in the inning, and Sherdel contributed a two-run double.[18]

July 14 was the 12th annual carnival and baseball game to benefit the Tuberculosis Society. Pre-game festivities included concerts by the Mail Carriers' Band, Jefferson Barracks Band, and St. Edward's Drum Corps. Various youth teams ran relay races; 150 runners participated in a 2.9-mile junior marathon from the fairgrounds to the ballpark, and Sherman Park gymnasts performed. Capping the event, Mrs. Paul Adler won a safe driving contest in which three entrants weaved their way "through a hazard of barrels." The game itself dampened the festive atmosphere for the 16,000 fans. The Dodgers topped St. Louis, 5–2, saddling Jess Haines with his first loss since May 19. Two bad innings sabotaged Pops' otherwise solid outing. In the third, Haines walked pitcher Doug McWeeny with two outs. Then Hornsby lost Chick Fewster's pop fly in the sun, and it dropped for a single. Centerfielder Merwin Jacobson followed with a two-run triple off the wall in left center. The Cardinals tied the game at 2–2 in the sixth on a Southworth homer and back-to-back doubles by Les Bell and Bob O'Farrell. But Haines ran into trouble in the eighth inning, giving up three runs on five singles.[19]

St. Louis turned the tables the following day and thumped Brooklyn, 11–5. Art Reinhart started and earned the win despite a mediocre performance. He did more damage with his bat than his arm. The Cardinals broke out with five runs in the fifth inning off Brooklyn hurler Jess Petty to snap a 2–2 tie. Reinhart drove in three with a bases-loaded triple and added an RBI single in the eighth. The Cardinals weren't the only team dealing with pitchers who enjoyed too much night life. The next day, Dodger manager Wilbert Robinson suspended Petty and fined him $100 for breaking training rules. He apparently was out late the night before his start as well as the night after absorbing his fifth straight loss.[20]

The Dodgers wrapped up the series on July 16 by beating the Redbirds, 8–7. For the first time in a Cardinal uniform, Grover Cleveland Alexander had a tough outing. In five innings of work, he allowed eight hits and seven runs. Trailing 7–2 in the sixth, St. Louis mounted a furious comeback against Brooklyn's Burleigh Grimes. Billy Southworth doubled home one run, and Wattie Holm scored Southworth with a single. St. Louis tallied another run in the seventh, and in the eighth, Jake Flowers' base hit brought in Les Bell. Blades' run-scoring single knotted the score at 7–7. The Cardinals' shaky defense let them down in the ninth. Flowers' throw pulled Bottomley off the bag, allowing Chick Fewster to reach base. He advanced to third on Jack Fournier's single and scored on a sacrifice fly. Hornsby led off the bottom of the ninth and took a called strike three on a 3–2 count. Frustrated by his 0 for 5 day at the plate, he protested to Peter McLaughlin that the pitch was outside, but the umpire stood by his call. At the end of the day, the Cardinals, given their erratic play, had to feel fortunate to continue their hold on third place. They trailed Cincinnati by 3½ games and Pittsburgh by 1½; however, they were only ½ game in front of the Cubs and one game in front of fifth-place Brooklyn.[21]

The cloud that seemed to envelop the Cards lifted as everything broke their way on July 17. Cincinnati, Pittsburgh, and Chicago all lost as the Cardinals trounced the seventh-place Philadelphia Phillies, 13–5. Flint Rhem regained his early-season form, at least for the first five innings, allowing only one hit and one run while earning his first victory in a month. The Cards had built the lead to 5–1 before erupting for seven runs in the sixth. Rhem led off the inning with a single, the first of six consecutive hits. He came up again with two outs and laced a two-run double to cap the scoring. St. Louis banged out 19 hits in total. Wattie Holm led the hit parade with four, and Jim Bottomley added three more. Les Bell drove home four runs with a pair of doubles. It was his 11th consecutive game with a hit.[22] During that span, he slugged at a blistering .511 clip, scoring ten runs and batting in ten.

Perhaps stifling mid-90s temperatures limited the Sunday, July 18, crowd to a rather sparse 10,000, but they were treated to a dramatic 9–7 win by the Cardinals. St. Louis, led by Jim Bottomley's three-run homer in the third, jumped on Phillies starter Hal Carlson for five runs in three innings and seemed headed for another rout. The hard-hitting Phillies, buoyed by the unlikely bat of relief pitcher Wayland Dean, had other ideas. Dean rapped a two-run single off Jess Haines in the fourth inning and then lined a three-run home run into the rightfield pavilion in the sixth to give Philadelphia a 7–6 lead and knock Haines out of the game. Billy Southworth came through in the clutch in the seventh frame with a bloop double to plate the tying run. Relief pitcher Allan Sothoron's "dipping and swerving" spitball shut down Philadelphia over the last three innings to set the stage for more heroics from Southworth. With Rogers Hornsby on first via a base on balls from Dean, Billy the Kid blasted the ball out of the park onto Grand Boulevard for the walk-off win. Over the past six games, Southworth had 11 hits, including three doubles, one triple, and two home runs, making the June swap with New York look like a stroke of genius.

The win boosted the Cards to a second-place tie with Pittsburgh, only 1½ games behind the Reds.[23]

The Cardinals could not continue the momentum the following day, falling 4–3 to Philadelphia before a Ladies Day crowd of 10,000. Vic Keen started for the first time on the Cardinals' homestand and contributed a gutsy performance. He gave up two runs in the first inning, primarily due to faulty defense by Taylor Douthit, who lost an easy fly ball in the sun with a man on first and one out. The Cardinals tied the game in their half of the third on Jim Bottomley's 14th home run, which tied him for the league lead. It was a "freak" clout that fell behind a wire screen, which had been installed several weeks earlier to help prevent outfielders from colliding with the concrete wall. Sportsman's Park

Third baseman Les Bell's potent bat was a crucial part of the Cardinals' offensive attack (St. Louis Cardinals Hall of Fame and Museum).

ground rules stated any ball that lodged behind the screen was a home run. Sunny Jim added an RBI triple in the fifth to give St. Louis a 3–2 lead, which Keen protected until the ninth. The Phillies had runners on first and third and no outs, and Hornsby brought the infield in on the grass. Catcher Jimmie Wilson hit a grounder to Thevenow, who bobbled the ball momentarily, just long enough to let the tying run score. The Cardinals failed to score in the ninth, sending the game to extra innings. Johnny Mokan's fourth hit knocked in the winning run in the tenth for Philadelphia.[24]

The schedule makers lent St. Louis a helping hand by giving them two days off before the Giants arrived for a four-game set. The break gave the team time to lick some wounds and take stock. On the plus side, the Cardinal offense had surged during the home stand, batting a collective .331, and catcher Bob O'Farrell continued his strong defensive play. He threw out five of six base stealers in the last two games. On the negative side of the ledger, Rogers Hornsby's chronic back pain and the outbreak of boils sapped nearly all the power from his swing. A Giants pitcher told sportswriter W.B. Hanna of the *New York Herald Tribune*, "At the bat he doesn't look anything like the old Hornsby. You wouldn't think he was the same fellow." Roy Stockton wrote the Redbird manager had "no more punch in his swing than a girl would have." The writer thought it wise for Hornsby to sit out the Giant series so he would be available when the team hit the road on Sunday night. Equally disconcerting was the collapse of the pitching staff. Opposing hitters punished St. Louis hurlers with a .335 batting average. That more than anything accounted for the Cardinals' mediocre 9–8 record at home. If not for recent struggles by the Reds and Pirates, St. Louis' hopes for a pennant would be nearly out of reach.[25]

This was Heine Mueller's first trip to St. Louis since his trade to New York, and his legion of local fans proclaimed July 22 "Heine Mueller Day." After a delegation presented him with a watch and chain, a razor, and a cigarette case, the Giants celebrated with a 5–3 win over Grover Cleveland Alexander. Mueller led off the game with a double and scored when Jim Bottomley bobbled a ground ball. New York added a run in the fourth, but Billy Southworth and Les Bell hit back-to-back home runs in the bottom of the frame to knot the score. The game remained tied until the eighth, when pinch hitter Bill Terry launched an Alexander pitch out of the park onto Grand Boulevard. St. Louis came back after Southworth walked and reached second when Frankie Frisch dropped a perfect throw on an attempted steal. Les Bell doubled to drive home Southworth. With two outs in the top of the ninth, Bob O'Farrell made a rare mistake when he dropped a foul tip off Irish Meusel's bat. It would have been strike three and the end of the inning. Given a second chance, Meusel laced a double to left centerfield. Douthit's throw to second took a bad hop and hit Hornsby in the eye, knocking him to the ground. "It felt," he told a reporter, "like Jack Dempsey had hit me." He was removed from the game, and Specs Toporcer took his place. A tiring Alexander then gave up a walk and two singles to plate two Giant runs for the win.[26]

The next day, the swelling around Hornsby's eye had reduced enough that he was determined to play as long as, according to Dr. Hyland, "he could find his way around the field without a guide." No guide was needed as St. Louis cruised to an easy 6–1 win. It was Bill Sherdel's ninth win and the third time he defeated the Giants that season. Billy Southworth punished his former team again by driving in four runs.

Flint Rhem took the mound on Saturday, July 24. He pitched well for the first four innings, holding the Giants scoreless while St. Louis built a 3–0 lead. The Cardinals tallied two runs in the fourth when Bottomley led off with a triple. Billy Southworth followed with an "excuse me" check swing double down the third base line and scored on Tommy Thevenow's single. That was the last hurrah for the St. Louis offense. Jack Scott relieved Freddie Fitzsimmons and pitched five scoreless innings while New York chipped away against an increasingly ineffective Rhem. Ross Youngs opened the eighth with a bunt single and eventually scored on Irish Meusel's base hit. First baseman George "High Pockets" Kelly followed with a booming double to drive Meusel home and even the score. There things stood until the 11th. Kelly led off with his fourth hit of the game, and Travis Jackson followed suit. Everyone in the stadium knew a sacrifice bunt was coming, and Giants catcher Hugh McMullen bunted the ball right back to Rhem. He had an easy force play at third, but he hurried and unleashed what Roy Stockton called "one of the wildest, wooliest and most costly wild throws in the history of St. Louis baseball." The throw was high, hard, and outside, and Les Bell had no chance to make a play on it. The ball caromed off the grandstand wall into leftfield. Before Ray Blades could retrieve the ball, both runners had scored, and McMullen ended up at third base. With a 49–43 record, the Cardinals remained in third place, 3½ games behind the Pittsburgh Pirates who, by virtue of a double-header sweep in Brooklyn, moved in front of the Cincinnati Reds by .005 percentage points.[27]

Hornsby took himself out of the lineup for the July 25 contest, the last game of the home stand. He had returned to active duty too soon after his bout with the boils, and it was said that complications had set in. He was mired in a 1 for 13 slump and failed to get the ball out of the infield in five trips to the plate in Saturday's contest. He told the *Sporting News* that he had felt weak for several weeks and had dropped ten pounds since the carbuncle operation. He felt his play was a hindrance rather than a help to the team, so he inserted Jake Flowers at second base.[28]

Even without the Rajah in the lineup, the 25,000 "sweat-rolling fans" witnessed a contest that Martin Haley of the *Globe-Democrat* called one of the "most dramatic baseball struggles that ever sent a home crowd's emotions running rampant." To Roy Stockton, the Cardinals' thrilling 6–5 win would "rank with the great games played in St. Louis." It was a "baseball drama" that featured "crisis after crisis." Hornsby tabbed Jess Haines to start for St. Louis, while John McGraw sent 23-year-old Kent Greenfield to the mound for New York. The Cardinals drew first blood with a run in the first. The Giants came back with two in the second. St. Louis tied it with a run in its half of the frame. New York retook the lead with a run in the third, and the Cardinals tied it again in the fourth on Les Bell's home run, another "freak" blow that got stuck behind the netting in front of the rightfield wall. While right fielder Ross Youngs frantically tried to pull the ball free, Bell circled the bases.

Neither team scored from the fifth through the seventh innings, but the Giants took the lead in the eighth. St. Louis had a chance to tie things up in their half of the inning. Ray Blades was perched at first and tried to advance to second base on a sacrifice bunt, but umpire James Sweeney called Blades out. Incensed, Ray grabbed Sweeney by the back of his collar and spun him around so Blades could calmly articulate his case. Sweeney was having none of it and promptly banished Blades from the game. National League president John Heydler later fined Blades $50 and considered a suspension but decided against it because of the Cardinal outfielder's good record. Jess Haines likewise voiced his displeasure and joined Blades in the St. Louis clubhouse. The fans' ire was further enflamed that inning when Jim Bottomley scorched a low liner to rightfield. Ross Youngs made a diving catch, but most fans thought he trapped the ball. Sweeney, however, ruled it a catch. When the umpire took his position along the third base line at the start of the ninth, fans in that section peppered him with pop bottles, several coming within inches of hitting him. Sweeney, however, stood with his back to the stands and never flinched as the bottles flew by. The Cardinals did tie the game with a run in the bottom of the ninth. Les Bell led off with a triple to the centerfield wall and scored on Toporcer's pinch-hit single.

"Stupid fielding and overeagerness" helped the Giants take a 5–4 lead in the tenth, and when the first two St. Louis batters went down in the bottom of the inning, fans started heading for the exits. Billy Southworth brought them back to their seats when he lofted a no-doubt home run into the rightfield seats. Giants outfielder Ross Youngs never moved from his position or watched the ball land in the stands. Billy's timely wallop prompted the fans, in a fit of delirium, to shower the field with seat cushions and straw hats. Art Reinhart set the Giants down in order in the 11th but not without some sparkling defense from Wattie Holm and Taylor Douthit. Douthit made a desperate leaping grab of George Kelly's drive against the left centerfield fence to prevent what most likely would have been a triple. In the bottom of the inning, Douthit slapped a one-out base hit and raced to third on O'Farrell's hit-and-run single. When Tommy Thevenow came to bat, the New York outfielders moved in for a play at the plate. But Thevenow hit a drive that sailed over leftfielder Irish Meusel's head for the game-winning single. Fans poured onto the field to celebrate and crowded the Cardinals' dugout to congratulate the players. Roy Stockton wrote it "seemed like a world series."[29]

Lines of fans waited at the stadium exits to wish their heroes good luck as they embarked on a two-week road trip. Though St. Louis finished the home stand with 11 wins and 10 losses, they managed to pick up a full game and left town only 2½ games behind the Pirates and Reds. Despite facing another prolonged absence by Hornsby, a confident, energized ball club headed east.

Chapter 9

The Race Heats Up, July 27–September 2

A stifling heat wave hit St. Louis in early August. Temperatures on August 5–6 hovered around 98 degrees and topped 100 degrees on August 10. The scorching temps compounded the misery of the most severe drought in the region in years. Rainfall in St. Louis in July was the second lowest since 1871.[1]

The heat was not the only danger St. Louis residents faced. Escalating violence imperiled gangsters and law-abiding citizens alike. On August 19, a group of eight men sat in front of the Santa Fara Club, an Italian organization at Eighth and Biddle streets, when several shots were fired from a passing automobile. Three men, including New York contractor Adamo Girolamo, who arrived in St. Louis the day before, were hit. The police surmised the incident was a gang flareup, another bootleg war, or an assassination attempt directed at Girolamo. In an apparent retaliatory strike the next evening, unknown gunmen fired shots as they drove by three men only four blocks from the Santa Fara Club and in view of the Carr Street Police Station. None of the men was injured, but a stray bullet struck Celia De Blaze in the knee. Finally, on August 30, Joseph Schambra, a young bootlegger in St. Louis' downtown Italian quarter, was shot by an assailant seven times. He died from his wounds outside a relative's home at Ninth and Wash streets.[2]

Amidst the heat and violence, St. Louis residents could take refuge in the air-conditioned comfort of the fabulous new Ambassador Theater, the crown jewel of the Skouras Brothers theater chain. On August 25, a noon-time parade downtown kicked off the sneak preview for the grand opening of the 17-story theater at Seventh and Locust streets. City officials, delegations from the army, navy, marines and fire department, as well as the theater's "immaculate" ushers marched before thousands of cheering spectators. The following day, 3,000 guests enjoyed their first glimpse of the "palace wrought in marble and gold." They marveled at the golden ceilings with elaborate Oriental chandeliers that lit the 40-foot marble lobby and promenades. The domes that helped achieve the unique "hanging" ceiling in the auditorium were finished in silver leaf. The main dome above the stage was illuminated with hidden lighting which gave it a blue-sky effect with continuously moving clouds. Rich red mural draperies lined *the walls, and plush rugs covered the floors. One of the most striking features was the massive Wurlitzer organ which cost $115,000. Its 1,000 pipes varied in size from one inch in diameter to a full six feet wide.*[3]

The Cardinals would provide their own on-field theater as Sam Breadon accompanied the team on its important trek among the National League's eastern teams. The road trip began with another exhibition stop in Ohio for a game against the Massillon Agathons of the Ohio-Pennsylvania League. St. Louis made quick work of its opponent, pounding out 16 hits in a 14–3 rout. Taylor Douthit contributed a pair of triples.[4]

The Redbirds returned to the hitter's paradise known as Baker Bowl on July 27 to take on the Phillies. Rogers Hornsby selected Grover Cleveland Alexander to pitch the opener of the four-game series on his former stomping grounds. The Rajah originally wanted to use Victor Keen but decided in favor of Alexander to give Pete time to visit old friends. The Phillies treated Alexander rudely, touching him for 14 hits and five runs. Nevertheless, St. Louis bombarded Philadelphia pitchers for 14 hits of their own and pulled out a 9–5 victory. Billy Southworth, hitting in Hornsby's customary third slot, had three hits as did leadoff hitter Ray Blades. Bottomley, Douthit, and Les Bell contributed two hits apiece, Bell extending his hitting streak to 18 games and raising his average to a robust .355, second in the league.[5]

The two teams played a double header on July 28 to make up for a game rained out on June 7. Wayland Dean started the first tilt for the Phillies and struggled throughout the contest. He surrendered 14 hits and three walks but worked his way out of multiple jams and downed St. Louis 6–3. The game was tied 2–2 going into the sixth inning when Philadelphia jumped on Bill Sherdel for four runs, including a run-scoring single from Dean and a three-run homer from Cy Williams. St. Louis loaded the bases with one out in the top of the eighth, but Dean induced Wattie Holm to ground into a double play to squelch the threat. The Cards again filled the bases in the top of the ninth with no outs but again failed to make the Phillies pay. Bottomley struck out; Bell hit a short fly ball to right; and Douthit flied out to left to end the game.

In the nightcap, Victor Keen opposed righty Claude Willoughby, one of the rare pitchers who actually pitched better at Baker Bowl than on the road—though he was still a punching bag for National League hitters. His ERA at home was north of 5.00, and his Walks/Hits to Innings Pitched (WHIP) was a hefty 1.605. The Cardinals took note and pushed three runs across in the first inning. Willoughby walked three batters and gave up a run-scoring groundout by Southworth and RBI single to Douthit before manager Art Fletcher removed Willoughby and brought in Ray Pierce, whom Bob O'Farrell greeted with a run-scoring single. St. Louis stretched the lead to 5–1 with a run in the fourth and another in the seventh on a Southworth double and Jim Bottomley triple. The Phillies battled back with two in the bottom of the seventh and made things interesting in the ninth. Third baseman Clarence Huber walked to lead off the inning. Second baseman Bernie Friberg smashed a triple to the deepest part of centerfield. With the tying run on third and no outs, Keen dug deep to retire pinch-hitter Ray Grimes, shortstop Heinie Sand, and the dangerous Cy Williams on harmless infield taps to win his tenth game of the season.[6]

Rain washed out the July 29 game with the Phillies, a development the Cardinals welcomed because they were about to play five games in four days against the Giants. While the players enjoyed the brief respite from the pennant chase, James Gould of the *St. Louis Star* described another team effort to keep players on the straight and narrow. In particular, he mentioned, though he didn't name, a pitcher who had "developed a habit of—well, straying off the reservation. He's here today and gone tomorrow, as it were." This particular pitcher had become so set in his "straying habits" that the Cardinals assigned coach Otto Williams to shadow the player's every move. This strategy may have been drastic, but, Gould added, "stringent measures are sometimes necessary when a pennant is in prospect."[7]

The extra day of rest seemed to do wonders for St. Louis. They jumped out to a 4–0 lead over Freddie Fitzsimmons and the Giants and held on for a 5–2 win. Jake Flowers, manning second base in Hornsby's absence, slammed a two-run homer into the upper-deck of the Polo Grounds in the top of the third, and Les Bell hit his 12th home run into the same area in the fourth inning. If Flint Rhem was the pitcher Otto Williams shadowed, the stringent measure worked. He toyed with the Giants with a biting curve and dazzling fastball to pitch a complete game for his 13th win. The victory, coupled with the Pirates' loss, lifted St. Louis to 2½ games behind Pittsburgh.[8]

The Redbirds closed July with a double header in front of a sizable New York crowd of 30,000. St. Louis continued the momentum from the previous day, plating two runs in the first and four more in the third on a Ray Blades homer, a two-run single by Taylor Douthit, and an RBI single from Tommy Thevenow. Jess Haines, however, let the lead slip away. He gave up three runs, including a leadoff home run to Travis Jackson in the bottom of the third. No further scoring took place until the Giants tied the game in the bottom of the sixth. Frankie Frisch drove home three runs with a bases-loaded double to knock Haines out of the game. Frisch struck again in the bottom of the seventh with a two-run single off Allen Sothoron. Cardinal hitters failed to mount a comeback against reliever Jack Scott, and New York took the game 8–6 and ended Les Bell's 21-game hitting streak. Hornsby sent Art Reinhart to the mound for game two, and he shut down New York for six innings, though everything fell apart in the seventh. New York bunched five hits and an intentional walk to score six runs. Ross Young's three-run home run off the right-field foul pole was the big blow. The Cards mustered only six hits in the 6–1 loss and fell to four games behind the Pirates.[9]

St. Louis dropped its third game in a row to New York on a drab, rainy Sunday afternoon before 20,000 fans. Jake Flowers injured his thumb on Saturday and was unable to play, so Hornsby inserted Specs Toporcer at second base. With Flowers on the bench and the club flailing, the Rajah was sorely tempted to suit up, but

Sam Breadon promptly rejected the idea. Once again, the Cards took an early lead on Jim Bottomley's 15th home run in the fourth inning. The lead, however, was brief. The Giants came right back in their half of the inning to score four runs off Grover Cleveland Alexander after two men were out. Heine Mueller hurt his former mates with a two-run single, and Travis Jackson added a two-run homer. The score did not change until the eighth inning, when George Kelly swatted another home run with two men on base to put the game out of reach. The Cards, wrote Martin Haley of the *Globe-Democrat*, were outclassed. "They plainly showed the effects of their double defeat yesterday. The dash that characterized their play of early innings of Saturday's game was gone."[10]

Hornsby's restlessness no doubt skyrocketed when the Redbirds lost 4–2 on Monday, August 2. St. Louis sportswriters condemned the team's poor showing. Roy Stockton asserted that the team without Hornsby was "only a second-division ball club," lacking "punch and staying qualities." James Gould bluntly accused the Cardinals of playing like schoolboys. Yet again, St. Louis took an early 2–0 lead on Bob O'Farrell's homer in the second inning. Vic Keen dominated New York for the first five scoreless innings, surrendering only two hits, though the game took a drastic turn in the sixth. Ross Youngs was perched on second base with two outs, and Keen had a 1–2 count on leftfielder Ty Tyson. The next pitch was high and tight and struck Tyson in the head. The ultrasensitive pitcher rushed to the plate to help Tyson to his feet. While the Giants' team doctor tended to Tyson, the visibly upset Keen nervously walked around. The New York outfielder remained in the game, though the St. Louis hurler was clearly rattled. George Kelly laced his next pitch into left to score Youngs. Heine Mueller drove a Keen pitch to deep centerfield, but Taylor Douthit hauled it in for the third out.

Keen still had not recovered his composure in the bottom of the seventh. Shoddy fielding heightened his problems. Travis Jackson led off with a single and advanced to second when Southworth fumbled the ball. He moved to third on Irish Meusel's infield single and scored when Frankie Frisch singled to right. Another Southworth bobble allowed the runners to reach second and third. Trying to stem the tide, Hornsby removed Keen in favor of Bill Sherdel. With two outs, Tyson hit a "feeble little roller" that evaded Specs Toporcer to allow the go-ahead runs to cross the plate. A fuming Roy Stockton claimed, "a man who cannot stop a ball like that in such a pinch does not belong in the big leagues." St. Louis threatened in the top of the eighth with singles by Thevenow and Hafey. With one out, a baserunning blunder by Thevenow cost the Cardinals dearly. Toporcer hit a low line drive to center. Thevenow had lost track of the number of outs and had already rounded third when Ty Tyson snared the ball and ran to second for the unassisted double play. Jack Scott retired the Cardinals in the ninth to save the 4–2 victory.[11]

The Cardinals limped across the East River for a six-game series with the Dodgers. Rogers Hornsby was absolutely determined to rejoin the lineup for the first time since July 24, despite Dr. Hyland urging him to continue to rest. "I have become nervous on the bench," Hornsby declared, "and I do not intend to remain idle much longer. The club needs me. I do not wish to appear in a boastful mood when I say that, but it is true. I was willing to rest so long as the club was winning or at least playing .500 baseball, but I will not remain a bench manager if my club continues to lose. The welfare of my club counts more now than my own physical condition."

Hornsby's return provided an immediate spark as the Cardinals ended their four-game losing streak with an 8–4 win. In his first at bat, he singled off the right field wall and scored on Jim Bottomley's double, though the Rajah told Roy Stockton, "I thought I was going to pass out when I scored from first on that double." Pitcher Bill Sherdel held the Dodgers in check with his array of off-speed stuff to earn his tenth win of the season. Thomas Holmes of the *Brooklyn Daily Eagle* claimed Sherdel "starts his slow ball delivery on Saturday morning and it reaches the home plate on the following Wednesday afternoon. Beg pardon, that's his fast one. His floater occupies two days longer in transit." But Wee Willie did as much damage with his bat as he did on the mound. He went three for four with a double, triple, and home run. He scored two runs and knocked in three.[12]

The next day, the Cardinal manager got in some batting practice and decided to play again, though he was in rough shape. He was fatigued from his efforts in the previous game, wore a bandage on his right hand after getting spiked when he tagged a runner, and had a bandage on his left ear after having a boil cut out. Those handicaps didn't affect his hitting in the Cardinals' 11–9 victory. Hornsby had three hits, as did Billy Southworth, Les Bell, and Bob O'Farrell. St. Louis built a 5–0 lead on a two-run single by Thevenow in the second and Southworth's three-run, inside-the-park homer in the fourth. Flint Rhem breezed through the first four innings, but three Cardinal errors in the fifth allowed the Dodgers to score seven runs. The Redbirds scored a run in the seventh and tied the game in the ninth on a Southworth double and Hornsby's triple. In the top of the tenth, St. Louis broke out for four runs, three scoring on Jim Bottomley's bases-loaded double. In the bottom of the inning, Hornsby brought in Jess Haines to finish the game. The Dodgers, however, made things interesting. Thirty-eight-year-old Hall of Famer Zack Wheat hit a home run over the rightfield wall. As he rounded the bases, he collapsed at second base after dislocating his ankle, but he managed to get to his feet and hobbled to home plate. Brooklyn tallied another run and had runners at first and third with two outs, when Hornsby turned to Grover Cleveland Alexander, who ended the threat after Les Bell made a nice catch down the leftfield foul line.[13]

The reenergized Cardinals continued their winning ways with a 7–3 victory on August 6. Art Reinhart got the starting assignment and pitched a solid game. His only blemish was Babe Herman's three-run home run in the third inning. Reinhart started the Cardinals comeback with an RBI triple in the fourth. In the fifth, St. Louis knocked Brooklyn starter Doug McWeeny out of the game. Southworth singled, Hornsby followed with a double, and Les Bell singled both runners home. A Douthit single and O'Farrell walk loaded the bases for Tommy Thevenow, who came through with a base hit to score two runners and put the Cards in the lead. St. Louis added two additional runs in the seventh on an O'Farrell double and another Reinhart RBI.

The Cards stretched their winning streak to five with a double header sweep on August 7. Bill Hallahan got his third start of the year and gave up only three hits in 4⅔ innings, though he seemed to consider the strike zone a passing acquaintance. He walked five batters in the fifth inning alone and seven overall. Herman Bell came on in relief in the fifth and turned in yeoman work. He gave up only one hit and no runs in 4⅓ innings to earn his sixth win of the season. Billy Southworth continued his torrid hitting with four hits, two runs, and two runs batted in. Game two was all about the ageless wonder Grover Cleveland Alexander, who scattered four hits in a 3–0 complete game shutout. The sweep, coupled with a double header loss by Pittsburgh, pulled the Cardinals within 2½ games of the Pirates and only ½ game behind the faltering Reds.[14]

St. Louis completed the six-game sweep of the Dodgers on August 8 with a 3–2 win in ten innings and jumped in front of Cincinnati, which lost four of five to the Giants. Bill Sherdel started his second game of the series and engaged in a nip-and-tuck duel with Jess Barnes. Brooklyn tallied single runs in the first and second innings, but Rogers Hornsby started a two-run rally in the fourth frame with a double. He scored on Bottomley's single, and Sunny Jim eventually crossed the plate on a hit from Bob O'Farrell. Sherdel and Barnes pitched scoreless ball thereafter, though Brooklyn nearly plated two runs in the eighth. With a runner on base, Babe Herman lofted a Sherdel pitch down the rightfield line, but a stiff breeze blowing from leftfield to right carried the ball foul "by a couple of Scotch inches." In the tenth inning, Hornsby smoked another double to center to score Ray Blades from second base, and Sherdel closed out the game to win his fifth straight against Brooklyn and 11th victory overall.

After the game, Sam Breadon departed for St. Louis but not before he and Hornsby discussed two exhibition games scheduled on Thursday, August 12, in Erie, Pennsylvania, and Friday, August 13, in Springfield, Ohio. Now that St. Louis was in the thick of the pennant chase and would be closing out a strenuous road trip, the Rajah, Coach Killefer, and several players requested that the games be cancelled. The *Globe-Democrat* reported that even Sam Breadon frowned upon the extra activity and had Travelling Secretary Clarence Lloyd reach out to the executives of the two clubs to work out a settlement. The team, meanwhile, headed to Boston for a three-game battle with the seventh-place Braves.[15]

Despite Boston's lowly place in the standings, the Braves were no pushover. Prior to the Cards' arrival, the club had won seven of 12 games against the other top teams in the league in Chicago, Cincinnati, and Pittsburgh and shut out the Pirates in both games of an August 7 twin bill. Their spirited play and dominant pitching continued in the first game of the St. Louis series. Cardinal hitters managed only five hits off Braves starter Larry Benton, who cruised to an easy 5–0 win over Vic Keen.

Perhaps the Parson's arm bothered him again because Hornsby uncharacteristically yanked Keen in the first inning after surrendering four hits and two runs. Former Cardinal Jack Smith and St. Louis native Andy High paced the Boston attack with three hits apiece.[16]

St. Louis rebounded with back-to-back wins on Tuesday and Wednesday. Flint Rhem regained his early season form in game two, though he was matched for eight innings by Boston hurler Harold Goldsmith. With the score tied 1–1 going into the ninth inning, Hornsby led off with a line single to center. Boston manager and shortstop Dave Bancroft immediately pulled Goldsmith to bring in southpaw George Mogridge to pitch to left-handed slugger Jim Bottomley. Hornsby signaled for the Card first baseman to bunt. Bottomley failed on his first attempt. He feigned another bunt to draw Braves third baseman Andy High in close and then slapped a bouncer over High's head. Les Bell followed with a long single to left to score Hornsby. Tommy Thevenow singled home another run for a 3–1 lead. Hornsby's brilliant fielding play on a grounder behind second base saved a run in the bottom of the ninth and enabled Rhem to secure his 14th victory. The Redbirds closed out their East Coast swing with Jess Haines making his first start since July 31. He was worth the wait for he turned in his best performance of the season, blanking Boston on five hits, 2–0. St. Louis had multiple scoring chances but could not break through against Johnny Wertz until Bob O'Farrell slammed a two-run double with two outs in the eighth inning.[17]

Hornsby was jubilant after the win. The Cards finished the road trip winning 11 of 17 games and climbed to within two games of the Pirates. He told Roy Stockton, "We have shown that we can beat the other fellow on his own lot and we're due to have a winning streak in our own park…. I wouldn't be surprised if we piled up 10 or 12 in a row." He praised the team's ability to bounce back after dropping four straight in New York, claiming, "We feel that we have the stuff and when we lose a game we go right after the next one."[18]

Though pleased with the team's play on the field, Hornsby was not thrilled that St. Louis was unable to cancel the exhibition games in Erie and Springfield. When he and the rest of the squad learned on Tuesday morning that the games were still on, they were "not the least bit backward in voicing their disgust." With a growing list of walking wounded, the players felt they were entitled to some rest to face the pennant grind in front of them. Hornsby, of course, was still recovering from his bout with boils and a wounded hand, while Jake Flowers missed time with an injured thumb, Tommy Thevenow was hobbling on an injured ankle, and Les Bell missed the final Boston game with a bad cold and a 102-degree fever. To top things off, it was revealed Bottomley, too, had been suffering from an outbreak of boils as well as a contusion received in Wednesday's game. While chasing a foul ball, he collided with a corner of the concrete Cardinal dugout, knocking him senseless for a few minutes. The *Post-Dispatch* reported that when Sunny Jim revived, he sighed and said, "Oh, I'm all right, but I just don't want to go to Erie." Livid over what he viewed as interference by Breadon and Rickey to make a few extra bucks, Hornsby decided he would do the bare minimum to meet the club's contractual obligations. He sent a skeleton crew to play the exhibition games, while he, Bob O'Farrell, the bulk of the pitching staff, and bruised and battered Jim Bottomley returned directly to St. Louis.[19]

During the ensuing homestand, Hornsby and Breadon clashed over what the Cardinals' star perceived as unwanted "meddling" by Rickey and Breadon. The spat over the exhibition games was raised again, but Sam raised the temperature even more when he questioned Hornsby about his betting on the horses. The player-manager "let out more than a mouthful" in response to the owner's invasion of his personal affairs. The argument then drifted to Rickey's encroachment upon the manager's territory. Branch occasionally invaded Hornsby's domain in the clubhouse, or he would lean over the railing near the St. Louis dugout and dispense batting tips to the players. In addition, word reached Breadon that several players had imbibed too much on the road trip. Hornsby didn't deny the claim, nor did it seem to bother him because the team had performed well. However, he immediately suspected the teetotalling Rickey had federal Prohibition agents spying on boozing ballplayers and the bootleggers who catered to them. Hornsby argued Rickey's actions undermined his authority and hurt the team's morale. While spewing his second "loud verbal explosion," the Rajah issued an ultimatum that either he or Rickey would have to go before the next season. Breadon resented Hornsby's gruff tirade as well as his invasion of the owner's territory, and their relationship grew ever frostier from this point on.[20]

The chill within the front office did not affect the team on the field as the pennant race heated up. The Cubs invaded Sportsman's Park on August 14 to kick off the Cardinals' final homestand of the season, a grueling 21-game slate in 19 consecutive days. A crowd of some 17,000—the largest Saturday gathering of the season—watched Grover Cleveland Alexander retire 14 of 15 Chicago batters through five scoreless innings. St. Louis, meanwhile, forged a 2–0 lead on Hornsby's RBI single in the first and O'Farrell's sacrifice fly in the fourth. Chicago mounted a comeback in the sixth frame. The key play was a missed opportunity to complete a double play on a groundball by Sparky Adams that would have ended the inning. Adams proceeded to steal second base and scored when Alexander hurried a throw to first, which got by Bottomley and allowed Cliff Heathcote to race all the way to third. Riggs Stephenson then hit a slow roller toward Thevenow, which took a crazy hop over his head into leftfield to tie the game. The Cubs took the lead in the seventh on a looping single by pitcher Sheriff Blake, and that was enough. Blake gave up only one hit over the last five innings to disappoint the hometown fans.[21]

A Sunday crowd of 20,000 enjoyed a reversal of fortunes as St. Louis pounded Cubs starter Charlie Root, one of the tougher pitchers in the league, for six runs. Jim Bottomley opened the Cardinal scoring with a two-run home run in the first, one of three hits on the day. The Redbirds knocked Root out of the game in the fourth after a single, a Les Bell homer, and two doubles. Flint Rhem held the Cubs hitless for the first five innings before giving up a leadoff home run to catcher Mike Gonzales in the sixth. He also surrendered a home run to Hack Wilson in the ninth but otherwise was in complete control to earn his 15th win of the season.

Bottomley foiled the Cubs again the following day in a 5–4 victory. Jess Haines started and surrendered solo home runs to Cliff Heathcote in the third and Hack Wilson in the fourth. The Cards stormed back, plating four runs in the fifth to take the lead. Billy Southworth drove two runs home with a bases-loaded single. With St. Louis runners on second and third, Cubs manager Joe McCarthy played the percentages. He intentionally walked Hornsby and brought in lefty Percy Jones to face Jim Bottomley. Sunny Jim spoiled McCarthy's strategy by drawing a walk to force in a run. In the eighth, Hack Wilson tied the score with his second long ball off Haines, but St. Louis pulled the game out in the ninth inning. McCarthy again played the percentages and ordered portsider George Milstead to walk Hornsby, loading the bases so that he could face the lefty-swinging Cardinal first baseman. Once again, Sunny Jim wrecked McCarthy's plans by pouncing on Milstead's first pitch for the game-winning single. Bottomley's heroics pulled St. Louis to within 1½ games of the idle Pirates and demonstrated that he had overcome his long batting slump. He had raised his average to .289 and was driving in runs at a steady clip, leading the league with 93 RBI's when the Cubs left town.[22]

The Dodgers charged into St. Louis, determined to avenge the six-game sweep they suffered in Brooklyn. Their fortunes, however, fared no better. The Cardinals sent Bill Sherdel to the mound after a ten-day layoff to square off against Doug McWeeny on an overcast, drizzly afternoon. St. Louis took a 3–0 lead in the first inning on Billy Southworth's 13th home run, an RBI triple by Les Bell, and run-scoring single by Taylor Douthit. The Cardinals seemed headed for an easy win, but the Dodgers fought back. In the second inning, centerfielder Gus Felix slammed a triple off the leftfield fence and scored on a groundout. Unfortunately, the injury bug struck again. Ray Blades made a valiant effort to catch Felix's drive. He climbed a chicken-wire fence along the outfield wall but caught a spike in the fence and badly wrenched his knee. He limped off the field and was replaced by Wattie Holm. The injury sidelined Blades, except for a single pinch-hitting appearance, for the rest of the season. The Dodgers finally got to Sherdel in the third, scoring three runs and sending their nemesis to an early shower. Brooklyn extended their lead to 7–3 with a run in the fifth and two more in the sixth off reliever Herman Bell. The Cardinal offense came alive in the seventh inning. Thevenow and Holm had run-scoring singles before Billy Southworth launched a three-run clout that bounced off the right-field pavilion roof onto Grand Boulevard. With a slim 8–7 lead, Hornsby brought in Grover Cleveland Alexander, who proceeded to shut down the Dodgers over the final two innings. The Cardinals now stood only one game behind the Pirates.[23]

St. Louis stretched its dominance over the Dodgers to nine consecutive wins with 6–2 victories on August 18 and 19. Art Reinhart relied on brilliant Cardinal fielding to scatter eight hits on the 18th. Bob O'Farrell, with a solo home run and RBI double, Taylor Douthit, with a two-run single, and Jim Bottomley, with three hits including a run-scoring double, furnished all the offense Reinhart needed. Hornsby sent Bill Sherdel back to the mound for the series finale, despite being shelled in the game on Tuesday. Like Reinhart the day before, Wee Willie scattered eight hits in the complete game victory, his sixth win over the Dodgers. Cardinal hitters rapped out 14 base hits, including three by Hornsby. The red-hot Redbirds had won 13 of their last 15 and, with a Pittsburgh split of a double header, had at long last climbed into a virtual tie for first place.[24]

The next day the *Post-Dispatch* observed the "pennant bee has stung St. Louis fans again for the first time since 1922." That morning, several hundred were in line—some waiting two hours—to purchase tickets for the weekend games with the Giants and for the double header that would kick off the crucial series against the Pirates the following Sunday. The newspaper had dubbed the upcoming Pittsburgh contests the "Little World's Series" because fans realized "the winner of the National League pennant probably will be decided."[25]

The Cardinals kicked off the series with John McGraw's Giants with another 6–2 win. The Giants took a 2–0 lead in the fourth with four singles off Flint Rhem, but St. Louis rebounded with three runs in its half of the inning. Southworth and Hornsby started with back-to-back singles, and Southworth scored when Heine Mueller's throw to third base went into the Cardinal dugout. Taylor Douthit singled home another run and then came around on a single by Thevenow. Rhem worked out of a New York threat in the seventh, and then McGraw and the Giants, according to Roy Stockton, "surrendered." Chick Davies took the mound, which "was the same as waving the white flag." Subpar Giants fielding allowed the Cardinals to put the game away with three unearned runs in the seventh, two scoring on a Billy Southworth double. Rhem finished the game to secure his 16th victory and help St. Louis take a ½ game lead over the Pirates and a one-game cushion over Cincinnati. The three teams were separated by only .009 percentage points.[26]

More than 20,000 fans filed into Sportsman's Park on Saturday, August 21, hoping to see St. Louis win its seventh straight game. What they didn't know is that the Giants' season, already in turmoil from holdouts, trades, erratic play, and internal bickering, reached a crescendo after Friday's game. An infuriated John McGraw berated the New Yorkers for their lackluster effort. He directed most of his fury at team captain and star second baseman Frankie Frisch because he missed a sign in the fourth inning and was out of position on a hit-and-run single by Tommy Thevenow that cost the Giants a run. McGraw also chastised Frisch for failing to cover first base on a groundball in the seventh inning, botching a chance for a double play and leading to three unearned St. Louis runs. The Giants' skipper promised to make changes, including moving Frisch to third base. McGraw said Frisch, as team captain, "never satisfied me in that place … but I kept him there hoping he would make the grade." The hypercritical McGraw was not an easy man to play for. He rarely had an encouraging word for his players and always blamed them if something didn't work. Centerfielder Edd Roush of the Reds disliked McGraw so much that he initially refused to join the Giants after he was traded in 1927. Bob O'Farrell likewise had a low opinion of the manager. O'Farrell was traded to New York in 1928, and he recalled that McGraw was "getting kind of old and childish by the time I joined the team. Quite honestly, I didn't like him."

After McGraw's latest tirade, Frisch decided he had had enough. Without informing the team, he packed his bags and took a train back to New York. McGraw fined his AWOL star $500 and named shortstop Travis Jackson the new team captain. The *Globe-Democrat* guessed Frisch's "impromptu retirement will lead to his permanent departure from the Giants in a trade this winter." No one at the time could have guessed that trade would send Frisch to St. Louis in a blockbuster deal.[27]

Back on the playing field, "Ol' Pete" Alexander faced a makeshift Giants lineup that included George Kelly moving from first to second base, Bill Terry at first base, and 17-year-old Mel Ott making his first major league start on his way to a Hall of Fame career. Minus Frisch, wrote Ik Shuman of the *New York Times*, the Giants were a "partially demoralized aggregation ... lacking in some of the spirit which Frisch gave the team." Shuman's assessment was spot on. New York mustered only four singles and one double against Alexander, who breezed to a 3–1 complete-game victory. The Cardinals clustered four of their six hits in the second to score all three runs off Jimmy Ring. Bottomley led off the inning with a single and crossed the plate on Les Bell's triple to the wall in right center. O'Farrell knocked in Bell with a base hit, and he came around to score on a looping single to right by Alexander. Despite the win, the Cardinals lost ground to Pittsburgh, which swept a double header against Philadelphia.[28]

The Redbirds continued to take advantage of the down-and-out Giants with a 4–2 victory in front of a Sunday crowd of 26,000. The Giants would have won the game, penned New York sportswriter Will Murphy, "if Mr. McGraw's charges were able to field approximately as well as the third freshman team at George Washington High School." George Kelly, subbing for Frisch, botched a double play ball in the bottom of the first that allowed a run to score, and a two-out error by Giants pitcher Virgil Barnes paved the way for Les Bell's two-run double in the third. Bell added a solo home run in the eighth to seal the victory. Jess Haines again silenced New York batters, giving up five hits to improve his record to ten wins against only two losses.[29]

Boston was next on St. Louis' schedule. Most fans expected the Cards to steamroll over the seventh-place Braves, but some bumps in the road slowed down the soaring Redbirds. Rain washed out the August 24 game, which would be made up as part of a double header the following day. A weekday record crowd of more than 23,000 fans flocked into Sportsman's Park to witness the twin bill. In game one, St. Louis ran into a buzzsaw in pitcher Larry Benton. The Boston hurler had shutout the Cards on the recently concluded road trip, and he again dominated the Mound City nine. Though he walked five batters, Benton limited St. Louis to only four hits and one run. That single run seemed to be all the support Bill Sherdel needed. He pitched six shutout innings before Boston scored the tying run in the seventh on a drag bunt along the first base line. The Braves scored what proved to be the game-winning run in the eighth on Eddie Brown's RBI single.

Game two was another nailbiter. Vic Keen continued his ineffective pitching. He gave up a first-inning homer to Jack Smith and was knocked out of the game in the second inning, when Boston scored three runs. Hornsby summoned Art Reinhart in relief, who gave up a single run in the third inning as Boston stretched its lead to 5–0. The fans grew restive at the prospect of a sweep by the lowly Braves, but the Cardinals stormed back with four runs in the fourth. Southworth plated the first run on a sacrifice fly. Hornsby then doubled home two runners and scored on Bottomley's two-bagger. Reinhart held the Braves in check until St. Louis took the lead in the eighth. Hornsby drew a base on balls to lead off. Bottomley bunted him over, and he scored on Les Bell's line drive to center. Douthit followed with a surprise bunt single down the third base line. Bob O'Farrell stepped up to the plate and whistled a line drive to leftfield to knock in Douthit with the go-ahead run, sending the crowd into a frenzy. The Braves threatened with one out in the ninth. Bancroft walked and raced to third on Doc Gautreau's single to center. Hornsby went with experience rather than playing the percentages and brought in Alexander to face left-handed swinging Jimmy Welsh. Pete induced Welsh to hit a groundball to Hornsby, who pegged a throw to O'Farrell to nip Bancroft at home, and got shortstop Eddie Moore to ground harmlessly to Thevenow to save the ballgame. At the end of the day, St. Louis and Cincinnati, which had won ten consecutive games, had identical 70–51 records and were in a virtual tie for first place with Pittsburgh, though the Pirates were ahead by .004 percentage points.[30]

St. Louis regained a slim lead in the standings on August 25 with a 4–3 victory over the Braves in 11 innings. Flint Rhem started and clung to a 3–2 lead going into the ninth. He ran into some trouble when Boston placed runners on second and third with one out. For the third time in two days, Hornsby called for Grover Cleveland Alexander to shut down the Braves. Though he allowed a sacrifice fly that tied the game, Ol' Pete held the Braves scoreless in the tenth and 11th frames. Tommy Thevenow started the Cards' rally by lining a double to left, one of his four hits on the day. Alexander came to bat, and everyone in the ballpark expected him to bunt. Pete crossed everyone up by swinging away and popped a base hit into rightfield. The Braves walked Wattie Holm intentionally to fill the bases. Chick Hafey pinch hit for Southworth to face lefty George Mogridge and came through with a Texas League single that dropped just inside the leftfield foul line. The razor-thin margins and constantly shuffling pennant chase prompted the *Sporting News* to exclaim, "We've simply gone mad on decimals!"[31]

The cellar-dwelling Philadelphia Phillies followed Boston into Sportsman's Park for a three-game set. After the tough struggle with the Braves, the St. Louis players knew they could not take a victory over the last-place Phillies for granted. Nevertheless, the Phillies stole the first game, 3–2, behind the pitching of Wayland Dean. His complete game victory was all the more remarkable given that he learned that morning that his wife had passed away in Arizona. The Phillies, however, were so shorthanded that Dean decided to take the mound. St. Louis peppered him for 13 hits, though failed numerous times to strike a telling blow. Pop Haines pitched a solid game, but Philadelphia grouped their hits to scratch out three runs. Johnny Mokan's fluke triple—Wattie Holm tripped chasing the fly ball and the ball "bounced crookedly" down the foul line—set up the game-winning run in the eighth inning. The loss dropped the Cardinals out of first place, the fourth time in four days that the lead had changed hands.[32]

St. Louis lost the second game to Philadelphia, 9–7. The *Philadelphia Inquirer* noted the two combatants "staged a circus exhibition this afternoon, but the Cardinals were the better clowns." It was no exaggeration. Martin Haley of the *Globe-Democrat* considered it the worst defensive game St. Louis played in three weeks and the poorest pitching performance in two weeks. Vic Keen took the mound and was shelled again for eight hits and five runs in 4⅓ innings. Trailing 5–3 going into the bottom of the fifth, St. Louis took the lead on Bottomley's RBI single and a two-run single by Taylor Douthit. In the top of the sixth, however, Philadelphia pushed four runs across against Bill Sherdel, aided by Wattie Holm and Les Bell errors. St. Louis fell to third place as a result. Roy Stockton painted a melodramatically morose picture: "The pallbearers began to form rapidly on the right and the lugubrious tones of the funeral dirge ... arose from the Sportsman's Park stands.... All the great deeds of the recent past were forgotten and the cash customers prepared to bury the pennant hopes."[33]

The gloom carried over into the series finale on August 28. During batting practice, Bob O'Farrell rifled a line drive that hit Syl Johnson's pitching hand and broke a finger, ending the season for the "unluckiest man in baseball." The mood did not improve any after the Phillies rapped four hits off Art Reinhart in the second inning to take a 3–0 lead. Reinhart, however, held Philadelphia scoreless for the remainder of the game while St. Louis mounted a comeback in the third inning. Thevenow led off with a double and moved to third, courtesy of an error on Reinhart's grounder. Southworth singled to bring Thevenow home. Phillies pitcher Ray Pierce proceeded to walk the next three batters to force in two runs to tie the score. Bob O'Farrell then tripled to left centerfield to drive Bottomley, Bell, and Douthit across home plate. Thevenow continued his hot hitting by slapping a two-run triple in the seventh as the Cardinals salvaged a 9–3 victory to keep pace with the Pirates and Reds.[34]

O'Farrell's crucial blow had Hornsby touting his catcher as the National League's most valuable player. He told the *Post-Dispatch* that O'Farrell had "done more for us than any other player.... You know he's caught more games than any other catcher in either league. All the pitchers want him there. There's no better catcher in baseball."[35] Still, the Rajah feared O'Farrell might wear down playing such a demanding position every day, so St. Louis finally claimed a veteran catcher to help ease the burden. Frank "Pancho" Snyder, who once played six years with the Cardinals, was another victim of the New York Giants' floundering season. He had been idle for the past two months with injuries to both hands after a fight with Pirates coach Eddie Onslew before the Giants waived the erstwhile pugilist. Reports he was sufficiently healed to return to action spurred the Cardinals to swoop in and claim the former Giant.

The experiment, however, never got off the ground. Snyder arrived in St. Louis and, before agreeing to play, requested that Breadon grant the catcher his unconditional release at the close of the season, out of consideration for his long service in the major leagues. "That's the most outrageous proposal I have ever heard of," howled Breadon. "We paid $4000 for Snyder and are bound by no rule in baseball to enter such an agreement with any player, no matter how long he has served." The instant Snyder made the request, the Cards' owner decided, "I would rather not have a player of that disposition with the club. I thought Snyder would be glad to join a team that has a chance to win a pennant, especially in view of the fact that the club from which we obtained him may not finish as high as fourth, but Snyder has proved that he was not enthused over his change in residence and cared more for his future status in baseball than for his immediate presence on a pennant contending team." Consequently, O'Farrell continued to carry the burden of everyday catching duties.[36]

Catcher Bob O'Farrell's outstanding defense and timely hitting earned him the National League's Most Valuable Player award in 1926 (St. Louis Mercantile Library at the University of Missouri-St. Louis).

Sunday, August 29, marked the start of the season's most eagerly anticipated series. The Pittsburgh Pirates came to town .004 percentage points ahead of Cincinnati and one full game in front of St. Louis. Most observers believed this five-game set would determine who claimed the league title, and the entire Midwest was caught up in the frenzy. Scalpers hawked choice seats for an outrageous $15. Telephones at the Cardinals' box office rang non-stop with ticket requests. Railroads offered special excursion rates to transport fans from

Kansas City, Omaha, Oklahoma, Texas, and Indiana. One avid fan drove all the way from Buffalo, New York, and stood in line from 7:30 a.m. to get a reserved seat only to have the ticket window close just before he put his money down. A *Post-Dispatch* editorial claimed the "Mississippi Valley is aflame.... Thanks to the Cardinals the Mississippi Valley is having a grand psychological spree. Some of us are only slightly jingled, others are uproariously tight, but everybody whose soul is alive at all is sharing in this delirium." In anticipation of the huge crowd, Sam Breadon and Branch Rickey added 7,000 seats—including roped-off areas along the left and rightfield foul lines.[37]

The Pirates, though they held first place, were a team in turmoil. Several injured players performed poorly and were benched, fined, or suspended, causing some bruised egos. The center of the storm revolved around the presence of team vice-president and former manager Fred Clarke on the bench. Several players resented Clarke's acerbic comments and believed he undermined the authority of current manager Bill McKechnie. On August 7, between games of a double header with Boston in which the Pirates were shutout twice, Clarke advised McKechnie that long-time centerfielder and team captain Max Carey should be removed from the lineup because he had been in a brutal slump. Outfielder Carson Bigbee overheard Clarke's comment and passed them on to his good friend Carey. The two called a secret player meeting to demand that Clarke be banned from the dugout because they "only needed one boss." Only six players sided with Carey; nevertheless, Carey, pitcher Babe Adams, and Bigbee presented their demand to McKechnie, who, in turn, passed it on to Clarke, a longtime friend of Pirates owner Barney Dreyfuss. The elder Dreyfuss was in Europe at the time, but Sam Dreyfuss, Barney's son and team treasurer, told the entire squad the next day that "any attempt at an insurrection of players must be put down at its inception." Bigbee and Adams were released, and Carey was placed on waivers and subsequently claimed by Boston. Adams and Carey had been heroes to many Pirate fans, and the move outraged those loyal rooters. They booed the team throughout its homestand.[38]

Despite threatening skies, a multitude of Cardinal fans packed their way into Sportsman's Park for the first game of the series. The gates opened at 9:00 a.m., and by 10:30 the unreserved seats in the bleachers, pavilion, and upper grandstand were filled. Standing-room space in the aisles and runways were soon occupied as well. All told, 36,000 nervous, excited, and raucous fans—just shy of the attendance record set in the June double header with the Cubs—viewed one of the more dramatic contests of the year. The Cardinals jumped out to a two-run lead in the first inning on Les Bell's two-out double off Vic Aldridge, prompting a shower of straw hats onto the field from overjoyed fans. A sudden and heavy shower of the normal kind interrupted the game in the bottom of the second. The stadium grounds crew managed to drag the tarpaulin to the edge of the infield but could not pull it any further after the torrential downpour soaked the tarp, which stuck to the outfield grass. They struggled for some time and finally abandoned the effort. Hornsby, some Cardinal players, and even some fans lent a hand to move the heavy canvas covering, though they quickly recognized it was futile and retreated to the dugout, which was soon surrounded by a throng of hero-worshipping fans. Mounted police had to move in to disperse the impromptu gathering.

After the rain abated, the grounds crew, directed by none other than Cardinal owner Sam Breadon, worked for more than an hour to get the infield, which had become a "sea of mud," in reasonable shape. Play finally resumed at 4:20, which undoubtedly pleased Breadon, who wanted to get the game in to collect the $40,000 gate, the best ever for a Cardinals game. The Pirates, on the other hand, were in no hurry, given the threat of more rain and the fact that they trailed by two runs. They used a variety of delaying tactics while Cardinal players and fans verbally abused them to speed things up to get an official game in the books. Pirate catcher Earl Smith became the principal villain, especially after umpire Barry McCormick had to roust him out of the dugout to start the bottom of the third. The teams squeezed in another half inning before another deluge interrupted the game in the bottom of the fourth. Hundreds of fans left the ballpark, thinking the game would be called. After a half hour, however, the clouds parted, and play resumed around 5:00. After four scoreless innings, Pittsburgh finally broke through against Grover Cleveland Alexander in the fifth. Clyde Barnhart led off with a single. George Grantham hit a tap to the right of the pitcher's mound, but the wet baseball skidded under Alexander's glove and Grantham reached base safely. After a bunt moved the two runners to second and third, Alexander got Earl Smith to pop out to Hornsby and appeared on the verge of working out of the jam. However, Pirate pitcher Vic Aldridge laced Alexander's first pitch down the third base line for a two-run single. For the rest of the game, Aldridge and Alexander put goose eggs up on the scoreboard with the help of some outstanding defense on both sides. Kiki Cuyler made a perfect throw to catch Hornsby trying to stretch a blast into a triple. Wattie Holm made a leaping, fingertip catch in the eighth to rob Pie Traynor of an extra base hit and potentially save two Pirates from scoring. The encroaching darkness prompted the umpires to finally halt play after ten innings and nearly five hours.[39]

Because the teams could not complete the regularly scheduled double header on Sunday, they were forced to play double headers on Monday and Tuesday. A record weekday crowd of more than 29,000 watched Bill McKechnie and Hornsby send their aces—Ray Kremer and Flint Rhem respectively—to the mound for the first Monday contest. Unfortunately, the home team gave the crowd little to cheer about. Rhem pitched a solid game. He allowed eight hits and only two earned runs in eight innings. It wasn't good enough to match Kremer's outstanding outing. The Cardinals managed only two meek singles and succumbed 3–0 to the Pirates right-hander. St. Louis turned the tables in the second game, topping Pittsburgh 5–3 behind a complete game by Jess Haines. Hornsby inserted Taylor Douthit into the leadoff spot for the first time, and he came through with a double, his 19th stolen base, and two runs scored. Jim Bottomley drove home two runs with a base hit in the fifth, and Les

Bell added a solo homer in the eighth inning to seal the victory. Both hits prompted the frenzied crowd to halt play by decorating the playing field with an assortment of straw hats.[40]

The Tuesday double header drew a large rabid throng of 23,000. Thousands more congregated in downtown St. Louis at soft drink parlors, appliance stores, anywhere within earshot of the WIL radio broadcast to follow the game. The Cardinals made them all happy with a sweep. St. Louis regained its batting eye and battered Pirates starter Lee Meadows for 12 hits and six runs in game one. Les Bell drove a Meadows pitch into the stands for a two-run homer in the third. As he rounded the bases, the fans once more flung hordes of straw hats onto the diamond. The four umpires—rather than the usual three, another sign of the importance of the series—apparently grew tired of the repeated interruptions. They discussed the matter with Pirate captain Pie Traynor and Hornsby and concluded nothing could be done about it. Chick Hafey contributed an RBI single and a solo home run, and Bill Sherdel humbled the hard-hitting Pirate lineup, scattering seven hits, for his 13th win.

The multiple twin bills put Hornsby in a bind regarding his pitching rotation. He had already used his frontline hurlers in the series, and he needed someone to pitch the second game. In a move that surprised everyone, he bypassed Herman Bell or Art Reinhart and tabbed little-used Allen Sothoron, who had not started a game in months. It was an inspired choice, though the game got off to an ominous start. Sothoron walked Paul Waner to lead off the game. The next batter, shortstop Hal Rhyne worked the count full before the veteran spitballer curved the next pitch on the inside corner, which Rhyne took while Waner took off from first, both thinking the pitch was ball four. Home plate umpire Barry McCormick, however, called it strike three and O'Farrell threw a laser to Thevenow for a strike-em-out, throw-em-out double play. Sothoron sailed through the next two innings before giving up a run in the fourth. A single and Sothoron's wild throw on a Cuyler bunt put runners on second and third with no outs. The tense crowd feared the worst with the heart of Pittsburgh's order coming to bat. Sothoron, however, got Traynor to foul out to Bottomley. Barnhart walked to fill the bases, and then George Grantham lifted a sacrifice fly for the Pirates only run. The spitballer settled down through the remainder of the game, allowing only three hits to the slugging Pirates. In the meantime, Johnny "Jug Handle" Morrison had St. Louis hitters flailing at his wicked curveball until they pushed two runs across in the seventh on RBI singles from Chick Hafey and Tommy Thevenow.

When Sothoron retired Glenn Wright on a pop up to Jim Bottomley to clinch the improbable win, fans streamed out of the stands onto the diamond to get a "look at this Moses from the bull pen who had led the Cardinals into first place and delivered the thrust that knocked down the proud Pittsburgh Pirates to third position." Cardinal players were no less jubilant. Each of them pushed their way through the swirling mass of humanity to hug Sothoron and slap him on the back for his epic performance.[41]

On September 1, James Gould of the *St. Louis Star* wrote, "yesterday will stand out as the red-letter day of the year." "The city can hardly realize," he added, "that September has arrived and their representatives in the oldest of all baseball leagues are actually at the top with a splendid chance of staying there until, on September 26, the season is officially closed."

The Cardinals concluded the series and homestand with their fourth consecutive victory over the Pirates. The Wednesday afternoon crowd of 25,000 cheered non-stop throughout St. Louis' 5–2 triumph. They cheered Art Reinhart, who pitched a complete game, scattering six hits and improving his record to 8–4. They cheered Billy Southworth, who took away five potential Pittsburgh hits in "one of the greatest displays of outfielding that ever has been staged in Sportsman's Park." And they cheered Rogers Hornsby, who slammed a triple and a home run off Pirates ace Ray Kremer. The Pirates, desperate to halt the Cards' streak, turned to Kremer after only one day's rest. The strategy worked for a while. He blanked St. Louis for the first five innings, but he finally tired in the sixth and seventh frames when the Redbirds tallied all five runs. The "little world's series" was everything the Cardinals hoped it would be. St. Louis knocked off the defending champion Pirates four straight to claim a firm, though slim, hold on first place. The clicking of the turnstiles—the series set a four-day attendance record of more than 113,000—and the raucous cheering of those fans was music to Breadon's ears.[42]

St. Louis went 15–5 on the homestand and 22–8 during the month of August to climb to the top of the heap in the National League, one game in front of the Reds and two in front of the discouraged Pirates. Even though the remainder of the season would be played on the road, the Cardinals felt good about their chances. Other than Ray Blades and Syl Johnson, the team was in good shape physically. The boils that plagued Hornsby and Bottomley had finally disappeared. The mound staff, except Vic Keen, had provided solid, if not spectacular, performances, and lastly, the offense was getting contributions from everyone up and down the lineup.

CHAPTER 10

The "Home" Stretch, September 3–September 30

Just after the Cardinals left town on the final road trip of the season, the eagerly anticipated Greater St. Louis Exposition opened its gates on September 4. The excitement had been building throughout the summer. More than 20,000 onlookers attended the formal dedication and groundbreaking in Forest Park on June 27. The Chamber of Commerce launched a "Tellafriend" campaign on August 1, imploring every organization and resident to do all they could to bring at least one million visitors to the Exposition.[1]

An afternoon parade kicked off the September 4 festivities. The procession reached "Exposition City" at Forest Park and passed through the elaborate main entrance formed by four large polychrome towers between eagle-tipped colonnades. The throng continued its march along the Presidents' Promenade, lined on both sides with busts of U.S. presidents, to Liberty Plaza, the circular area in the center of the 45-acre grounds, where Mayor Miller and two dignitaries from the Chamber of Commerce gave the obligatory opening speeches. At 7:00, factory and train whistles throughout the city blared, and the firing of 13 "bombs" on the grounds preceded the official turning on of the lights. Visitors strolled among some 600 booths displaying industrial and commercial products from nearly 250 St. Louis firms. Anheuser-Busch's booth included "Volstead-time products," and the firm also brought its famous 3,000-pound Royal Italian white bull from the Iowa State Fair. St. Louis public schools presented industrial arts work by its students, and the U.S. Army Air Service exhibit proved to be one of the more popular, with models of various planes and dirigibles, four types of airplane motors, and bombs ranging in weight from 100 to 2,000 pounds. An automobile show displayed the new 1927 models and an array of acts, including a display of horsemanship by 125 Russian Cossacks, a lavish musical revue, concerts, and vaudeville shows, entertained the crowd.[2]

Persistent rain reduced attendance figures; thus, exposition organizers extended the event another week in the hopes of clearing a profit beyond the $100,000 cost. Customers watched a dirigible from Scott Field land at the exposition grounds, a German Shepherd dog show, and a gymnastics exhibition by the St. Louis Turnvereins. The rain continued into the third week, and when the

*Exposition concluded, the results were disappointing. The event fell $30,000 short of meeting expenses and drew just over 300,000 visitors.*³

While the Exposition proved to be underwhelming, police were overwhelmed by the violent bootleg war, which escalated throughout September. On September 2, Joseph Manzella and Caesar Cipriano—a leader of the East Side Mob—visited Frank Agrusa at St. Louis Baptist Hospital. Agrusa, Cipriano's brother-in-law, was one of the three men seriously wounded in the opening salvo of the conflict in front of the Santa Fara Club on August 19. As Cipriano and Manzella were leaving in their car, a black automobile sped by and the occupants unleashed a barrage of bullets that fatally wounded both. The police suspected this incident was in retaliation for the August 29 murder of reputed bootlegger Joseph Schambra.⁴

The following day, unknown assailants shot and killed Pete Webbe, a notorious member of the Cuckoo gang. Weeks later, police found Joseph Consiglio slumped over the steering wheel of his car with four bullet wounds to the head. Consiglio had operated a confectionary in a neighborhood "infested by Cuckoo gangsters" and, according to police, sold whiskey, alcohol, and stolen cars in addition to candy. The police had no proof, but it was assumed Consiglio's murder was connected to the ongoing bootleg war that involved two rival factions within the Cuckoo gang. On September 23, what police described as the "bloodiest gang fight St. Louis has ever witnessed" occurred when four men walked into the Submarine Bar and Café, located in a basement on the corner of Fourteenth and Locust streets, and opened fire. In the ensuing melee, one person was killed and five were wounded; however, the police concluded, based on the blood that "literally flooded the floor and bespattered the walls," several more were injured but managed to leave before police arrived. The authorities believed the fray was in retaliation for Consiglio's murder.⁵

Hornsby's squad skipped town with injuries of its own. Minus outfielder Ray Blades and pitcher Syl Johnson, the team made its way to Chicago to make up two rained-out contests. Blades remained in St. Louis to deal with his injured knee, while Johnson returned to his home in Portland, Oregon. Syl recalled in an interview more than 50 years later that Hornsby told him before he left that, if St. Louis won the pennant, he would receive the same share everyone else got—a promise the St. Louis manager kept.⁶

Though the team was down two players, it was accompanied by a new companion as it trekked across National League ballparks: radio. Fueling the feverish excitement of Cardinals fans, stations KMOX and WIL began broadcasting road games for the first time. As the next few weeks passed, garages, drug stores, pool halls, furniture stores, hardware stores, and any other establishment with radio equipment became a magnet for baseball fans. Loudspeakers were placed strategically on streets around St. Louis—four on Olive Street alone between Sixth Street and

Broadway—so that fans could experience the euphoric highs and agonizing lows of the pennant race. The crowds at these locations grew steadily, becoming "a menace to pedestrians, as well as automobile traffic." Exhibitors at the Exposition likewise made elaborate preparations that allowed thousands of visitors to follow the Cardinals' fortunes.

According to the *Globe-Democrat*, the growing throngs of listeners "indicate that fans are learning to enjoy the play-by-play accounts as given by the radio announcers." Baseball fever, it went on, "is rampant over the countryside and one of the chief causes is the daily broadcasting of the play. A huge, unseen audience, many times larger than the fans who gather in the baseball park, has been hanging with intense interest to the account of every play." An instructor at the Jacksonville, Illinois, School for the Deaf wrote out game updates so the students could follow the exciting race. KMOX received numerous telegrams from communities throughout Missouri and Illinois noting that business in those towns came to a standstill during game broadcasts. Johnston City, Illinois, reported one-half of its 7,000 inhabitants congregated at local stores to listen to the action. Thanks to the new technology, thousands of small towns now had baseball "virtually at their doorstep," helping to create "the greatest following of fans in St. Louis baseball history."[7]

Radio coverage started with the September 2 double-header against the rival Cubs, whose 69–58 record put them just 5½ games behind St. Louis. The upstarts were determined to make some noise in the pennant chase as were the 32,000 fans who filled Wrigley Field. St. Louis, however, gave a severe jolt to Chicago's title hopes by taking both ends of the twin bill. Grover Cleveland Alexander started game one and gave the home team fans very little reason to cheer. He held his former teammates hitless until the sixth frame and limited them to three hits total in the 2–0 whitewashing. The Cardinals strung three extra-base hits together—a double by Alexander, a triple by Douthit, and a double by Southworth—to score both runs in the third and hand Cubs starter Charlie Root a tough-luck loss. The hostile crowd razzed Alexander mercilessly during the game, but when it was over, they gave their former hero an ovation as he walked off the field.

Flint Rhem and the Redbirds cruised to a 9–1 win in game two. They raked three Chicago pitchers for 13 hits, with Southworth and O'Farrell chipping in three apiece. Hornsby hit his 11th home run and drove home three teammates. "There is no objection hereabouts to the Cards winning a pennant," wrote Irving Vaughan of the *Chicago Tribune*, "but it is distressing to see a lot of Cubs transformed into so many goats, and that's what the Hornsby magicians did to them." The sweep, coupled with a rainout of the Pirates–Reds game at Cincinnati, pushed the Cards' advantage to two full games over the Reds.[8]

A showdown series at Redland Field was next on the schedule. Despite the Reds nipping at the Cardinals' heels for first place, James Gould of the *St. Louis Star* noticed an odd mindset among Cincinnati fans. Less than 14,000 boosters attended the "death grapple" between the league leaders. "There is no flag-talk around the streets or in the lobbies of the hotels," he noted, "fandom apparently not having much faith in their team, is strangely apathetic." That certainly wasn't the case with St. Louis rooters. Gould complained these "'little world series' are becoming quite a strain. So much depends on each battle the Cardinals wage that the personal observer takes but little enjoyment in the game, even if the Birds win. When they lose, gloom gathers and there is no possible balm of Gilead until the bell rings for the game the next day."[9]

Gloom certainly gathered among Cardinals fans after the Reds took the first game of the series, 4–2. With Edd Roush on third and Wally Pipp on first in the bottom of the first, Cincinnati attempted a double steal. Roush was caught in a rundown' but Les Bell's throw hit Roush in the head, and the ball rolled to the backstop, allowing Roush and Pipp to score. St. Louis came back to tie the game in the second on Chick Hafey's single, O'Farrell's triple, and Tommy Thevenow's sacrifice fly. The Reds pushed single runs across the plate against Jess Haines in the fifth and sixth innings, but the St. Louis offense could not solve Reds starter Carl Mays, who worked out of two jams with key strikeouts of Jim Bottomley and Thevenow.[10]

Cincinnati surged into first place by .0026 percentage points the next day with a 5–0 shutout over the Redbirds, the first time the Reds were in first place since July 23. The Reds rattled Bill Sherdel for four runs in the first. Hornsby's trouble with pop flies came back to haunt the Cardinals. Leadoff hitter Billy Zitzman hit a looper toward second, and Hornsby, per Roy Stockton, "ranged around like a ship without a rudder," tripped over his own spikes, dropped the ball, hit the back of his head on the ground, and knocked himself out. He revived after several minutes, but his error paved the way for all the runs the Reds would need on this day. Reds ace Pete Donohue, who had been shelled in his previous six starts, returned to form and surrendered only five hits. Back in St. Louis, the Missouri Theater staged a "graphic portrayal" of the game. The theater arranged for the immense electric scoreboard belonging to Washington University to be placed on the stage. The results of each play were "immediately transferred into action on the electric scoreboard, which will record every strike, ball or hit just as it occurs in the Cincinnati park." Lights indicated the player at bat and whether he hit safely or was thrown out. Other than the comic relief offered by Hornsby's pop fly misadventure, the theater's customers were undoubtedly not amused at the horror show unfolding in Cincinnati.[11]

Undeterred by the reverses of the past two days, a mass of nearly 2,000 Cardinal fans swarmed into Cincinnati on specially chartered trains that arrived early Sunday morning. The unruly boosters made no friends in Ohio, disrupting the city's slumber as they paraded through the streets, shouting and ringing cowbells on their way to the Cardinals' hotel to serenade Hornsby and the team. The Cardinal manager didn't seem to mind. "It's a great turnout," he told the *Globe-Democrat*. "The old town certainly is in back of us and I hope we can repay the fans by regaining the lead this afternoon. St. Louis deserves to be on top after this demonstration of loyalty." Stirred by the Reds' retaking first place, a sizable flock of Cincinnati faithful added to the festivities with their own bands, parades, flags, and banners. Included among the raucous crowd of more than 32,000 was a contingent of Redbird boosters from Madison, Indiana, who trekked to Cincinnati to present an assortment of gifts to the town's celebrated native son, Cardinal shortstop Tommy Thevenow. The mass of humanity at Redland Field filled temporary field seats installed in front of the first and third base stands, and fans stood fifty deep in overflow seats cordoned off by rope in front of the outfield wall. It was the largest crowd to attend a game in Cincinnati since the 1919 World's Series.[12]

Hornsby was set to start Art Reinhart on the mound but changed his mind after Ol' Pete Alexander approached the manager in the hotel lobby the night before and asked for the assignment, even though he would be pitching on only two days' rest. Alexander justified the move by defeating the Reds 7–3. He gave up only two hits in the first five innings while the Cardinals built a 6–0 lead and then eased up in the latter stages of the game. Herman Wecke of the *Post-Dispatch* believed "it is doubtful if Alexander ever pitched better baseball in his career than he has for the Cardinals in the past three weeks." Since August 17, he had appeared in eight games and was credited with five wins and a minuscule 1.26 earned run average. Tommy Thevenow repaid his hometown rooters and fueled the Cardinal victory by knocking out three hits and driving in the first two runs of the game with a second inning double. The Redbird offense was further aided by an oversight on the part of the Reds. For some unexplained reason, no ground rules were adopted concerning balls hit into the overflow crowd in left and right fields. Les Bell took advantage in the fourth inning when he hit a drive that bounced into the crowd. Bell stopped at second, thinking he had a ground rule double, but the umpires waved him on for a home run because no rules had been set prior to the game. With the win, St. Louis once again leapfrogged into first place.[13]

The Cardinals suffered through a "rough and rocky" train ride to Pittsburgh for a Labor Day double header. The locomotive pulled into Pittsburgh at 3:00 a.m., but for some reason, the players couldn't disembark for several hours. While they tried to catch some much-needed sleep, the train on the adjacent track was "whistling and snorting," causing a good deal of "plain and fancy swearing" by the St. Louis squad. When the team finally reached their hotel, hoping for a chance to clean up, their rooms were not yet available. The players were able to eat some breakfast and rest in the hotel lobby before heading to the ballpark for the 10:30 contest.

The Pirates' tumble in the standings continued after the disastrous August series in St. Louis. They lost three of four to the Cubs in Chicago but hoped they could turn things around at home. Despite the exhausting morning, the Cardinals blew past Pittsburgh in the first game, 8–1, much to the enjoyment of the few hundred St. Louis fans who extended their journey from Cincinnati. Flint Rhem went the distance to claim his 18th win of the season. He allowed only four hits, though he had bouts of wildness, walking six. Douthit, O'Farrell, and Hafey paced the Cardinal attack with two hits apiece. Chick Hafey, who assumed the regular leftfield spot in Ray Blades' absence, provided the key blow with a bases-clearing double in the five-run fifth.

In the night cap, Hornsby hoped lightning would strike twice as he sent Allen Sothoron to the mound to face Ray Kremer, who looked to redeem himself after the shellacking he absorbed in St. Louis. The Cards jumped to a 2–0 lead in the third inning on Billy Southworth's 15th homer. The Pirates struck back in the fourth when rookie second baseman Joe Cronin tripled home Pie Traynor and then scored on Sothoron's wild pitch. Both pitchers settled down thereafter until Pittsburgh mounted a rally in the seventh. Catcher Earl Smith led off with a single. Ray Kremer bunted and reached base safely when both Sothoron and Bottomley fell trying to field the ball. Paul Waner followed with another bunt single, and then Kiki Cuyler singled home the go-ahead runs. Kremer easily set down the Redbirds in the last two innings for his 17th win of the year. The Reds split their double header with the Cubs, and St. Louis maintained its .005 lead over Cincinnati.[14]

Another important turning point occurred during the Labor Day twin bill. Early in the season, owner Sam Breadon had arranged for St. Louis to play four exhibition games to fill open dates on September 9 and 10th in Syracuse and Buffalo, another in New Haven, Connecticut, on Sunday, September 12, and the final on Monday, September 20, in Springfield, Massachusetts. Hornsby's disdain for the contests was well known, and he urged Breadon to do what he could to cancel them. Sam tried, but the owners of the minor league clubs insisted St. Louis hold up its end of the deals because the Cardinals were a hot ticket now that they were in the thick of a grueling pennant race. Between games of the Pittsburgh double header, Breadon came into the clubhouse and informed Hornsby the Cards would have to honor the scheduled exhibitions.

The tension between Breadon and Hornsby had festered for weeks, and the latest announcement pushed Hornsby beyond the boiling point. His recollection of the event in his autobiography, *My War with Baseball*, is shaky on some details. For instance, Hornsby indicates St. Louis lost the first game of the double header, 1–0, when Sothoron, one of his "top pitchers," made a throwing error. In fact, St. Louis won the first game, and Sothoron was far from being one of the Cardinals' top pitchers that season. He went on to claim Breadon barged into the clubhouse and, in front of the entire team, belligerently told Hornsby that the Cardinals were going to play those exhibition games. The manager replied, "Hell, that's all right with me. We get a total of three thousand dollars for three games and take the chance of getting some players hurt on those minor-league fields. But if you want to take a chance of kicking away a half million dollars for winning the pennant for these silly exhibition games, then I'm not going to play all my regulars."[15]

The rough-hewed Texan admitted years later that "I suppose I spoke more bluntly than usual" and concluded the conversation by suggesting Breadon "make an utterly impossible disposition of all such contests" and to "get the hell out of my clubhouse!" It may be many Americans' dream to tell off the boss, but it's usually not a prudent course of action. That certainly was the case here. Breadon, a proud Irishman, stormed away determined that Hornsby was finished as manager no matter how the rest of the season played out. Years later, Breadon recalled, "I came to the decision that if I was president, my chief must work with me. If he didn't, either he or I must get out, and I wasn't ready to leave the club." Bob O'Farrell's recollection of the confrontation was as hazy as Hornsby's, but he and the other players who witnessed their manager's outburst realized what it meant, saying among themselves, "That's the end of Rogers Hornsby here."[16]

While that storm brewed, the Cardinals polished off the Pirates, 8–0, the following day in front of a disgruntled, sarcastic crowd. Bill Sherdel scattered nine singles, while Cardinal hitters battered Pirates starter Vic Aldridge for 12 hits and eight runs. Taylor Douthit and Chick Hafey belted out three hits each, with Hafey's output including a double and a triple, and Hornsby drove home three runs in the rout. St. Louis extended its lead to two games over Cincinnati, which lost to Chicago, and the Pirates slipped to 4½ back, just in front of the surging Cubs.

Cincinnati followed the Cardinals into Pittsburgh for a five-game series, including two double headers. Unless the Pirates made a "good showing" against the Reds, wrote Charles Doyle of the *Pittsburgh Gazette Times*, "their flag chances will be just about gone for the present season." As for the Cardinals, Hornsby was careful not to make the mistake of being overconfident as the team would face the "bottom feeder" teams in the east. "There'll be no letting up," he told Roy Stockton. "We are in great shape as far as our pitching is concerned. We realize the importance of every game and whenever a pitcher shows signs of weakening, we'll jerk him out of there and throw another hurler into the game. We've a great pitching staff and we're going to use it down the stretch."[17]

Hornsby kept a good part of that pitching staff behind as the remaining Cardinal roster headed to Syracuse. In the meantime, the Cardinal manager made a quick side trip to visit John "Bonesetter" Reese in Youngstown, Ohio. Though he had no formal medical training, Reese gained national notoriety treating muscle and tendon strains. His clients included such luminaries as then-presidential candidate Theodore Roosevelt, Supreme Court Chief Justice Charles Evan Hughes, former British prime minister David Lloyd George, and comedian Will Rogers. But his work with baseball players, such as Hall of Famers Honus Wagner, Ty Cobb, Cy Young, Grover Cleveland Alexander, Walter Johnson, and John McGraw, cemented his reputation as a miracle worker. Hornsby's back continued to detract from his accustomed hitting prowess—his batting average was 100 points lower than his 1925 figure, and his power production was well off his usual pace—and he decided to see what Reese could do to literally straighten him out. The Bonesetter worked on Rogers' spine and snapped something back in place. Hornsby told the *Post-Dispatch* that he felt a little better "though his back was sore after being under the bonesetter's vise-like grip."[18]

Once he returned to Pittsburgh, Hornsby as well as Alexander, O'Farrell, Rhem, Keen, and Sothoron immediately boarded a train to New York to spend the next two days scouting the probable American League champion Yankees. Meanwhile, the pared-down Cardinal squad topped Syracuse, 7–4, in the first exhibition, scoring all seven runs in the first inning. Acting manager Bill Killefer, no doubt under orders from Hornsby, then removed Les Bell, Jim Bottomley, Billy Southworth, and Tommy Thevenow from the game, much to the dismay of the paying customers. The weary warriors received a welcome respite when the September 9 exhibition in Buffalo was rained out.

The full roster gathered in Boston for a weekend series with the Braves. The Cardinals couldn't help feeling, despite Hornsby's warning, a trifle overconfident. During the two "idle" days, St. Louis' lead had stretched to three full games when the Reds imploded in a September 8 double header against the Pirates, losing both games. Furthermore, the Redbirds had defeated the Braves 14 of 18 times, and Boston reinforced its hold on seventh and/or eighth place by compiling a miserable 8–20 record in August and losing five of nine thus far in September. But the Braves refused to play doormat for the Cardinals. In game one, Boston rattled Grover Cleveland Alexander for 15 hits in 6⅔ innings enroute to an 11–3 drubbing. Tommy Thevenow had an especially rough day, committing three errors in the seventh frame that fueled Boston's six-run outburst. James Gould of the *St. Louis Star* deadpanned, "Alex [Grover Cleveland Alexander] couldn't hold 'em and neither could Tom." The Reds and Pirates split a double header, cushioning the damage from the Redbirds' setback. Hornsby told the *Globe-Democrat* that what he found "most pleasing" about the loss "was the way it was sustained. I don't mind losing when I'm soundly licked. It's the games we should win and don't that hurt. There was nothing doubtful about today's loss. They beat us good while they were at it and we have no excuses to offer, but we'll show them something tomorrow."[19]

St. Louis did show the Braves something the next day—at least for the first game of the twin bill. Jess Haines pitched a masterful, four-hit shutout. The Cardinal offense matched the Braves' meager output but were able to string together back-to-back doubles by Southworth and Hornsby and an error to plate two runs in the third inning, which was all the support Haines needed for his 12th win of the year.

The Braves evened things with a 4–3 victory in the nightcap. St. Louis jumped out to a 2–0 lead in the first on a Southworth double, an RBI single by Hornsby, and another run-scoring single by Les Bell. Boston came back with two runs of their own against Flint Rhem, and the score remained tied until Hornsby put St. Louis ahead in the sixth with a base hit. Boston answered again with a run in its half of the sixth on an RBI triple by Eddie Moore and scored the winning run in the eighth after Douthit misplayed Andy High's base hit to center. The ball took an odd hop past the Cardinal centerfielder and rolled deep into the outfield. By the time Douthit retrieved the ball, High was standing on third base and scored on a sacrifice fly. Cincinnati shaved the Cards' lead to two games with a win over the Pirates, who fell 3½ games behind St. Louis.[20]

Sunday, September 12, would have been an open date for the Cardinals because of Boston's Blue Laws, but, as Roy Stockton commented, the "Cardinal money changers fooled 'em and instead of having a day of rest, the Cardinals will play an exhibition game for a few dollars." Hornsby, O'Farrell, and several starting pitchers remained in Boston, while the rest of the team ventured to Connecticut to play the New Haven Profs of the Eastern League. St. Louis came out on top 13–10 as Toporcer, Douthit, and Jim Bottomley all had three hits each. Bottomley's blows included two triples. It was just as well Hornsby didn't make the trip because he would have suffered an apoplectic fit when Chick Hafey injured a finger on his left hand. It was the second time Hafey was hurt on the New Haven field during an exhibition game, fracturing an ankle in 1924. His 1926 injury was not as serious, but it was bad enough that he missed the final Boston game on September 13.[21]

Hornsby realized his young team was bending under the strain of the nail-biting pennant race, and prior to the series finale, he urged his squad to forget about the tension because they had the courage and will to bring home the title. He sent Bill Sherdel to the mound to face John Wertz, who pitched well the last time the Cardinals were in Boston. Hornsby's men took his message to heart and started fast. Southworth slapped a one-out single in the first. Hornsby followed with a double, and then Bottomley singled both runners home. The nerves, however, began to build. St. Louis had the bases loaded in the second with no outs but failed to score. In the third, Bottomley led off with a triple, and his teammates stranded him on third base. The Cardinals extended their lead to 4–1 when Taylor Douthit slugged a two-run, inside-the-park homer in the fourth, and things seemed in control as Sherdel had given up only two hits through five innings. However, Boston fought back with two runs on four hits in the sixth. A walk, hit batsman, and single knotted the score in the eighth and knocked Sherdel out of the game.

Hornsby turned to Alexander to quiet Boston's bats, and Ol' Pete did so through the next five innings. St. Louis' hitters fared just as poorly against Larry Benton, who relieved Wertz in the eighth and didn't give up a hit for four innings. The Cardinals had a golden opportunity to break the game open in the 12th when they again loaded the bases with no outs. On a full count, Hornsby hit a bouncer straight back to Benton, who started a 1–2–3 double play. St. Louis still had runners on second and third and the dangerous Jim Bottomley at the plate, but he too bounced back to Benton to end the inning. The Braves' pitcher stopped the Cardinals in the 13th and 14th innings before bad breaks caught up to Alexander in the bottom of the 14th. With one out, a grounder to Hornsby took a bad hop at the last second and bounced over his shoulder. Benton bunted the runner to second, and former Cardinal Jimmy Cooney slapped a single to right field. Southworth made a desperate heave to home plate, but it was a split second too late to get the runner. The agony of the team and Cardinal fans alike was magnified as Cincinnati won its fifth straight game to pull dead even with St. Louis in the standings.[22]

The Redbirds' stumble did not dampen their fans' enthusiasm. Since the start of the month, fans had deluged Sam Breadon with phone calls asking about World Series tickets to the point that he had his phone service discontinued. Finally, on the evening of September 12, Breadon announced distribution plans for World Series tickets. No one could purchase more than two tickets for each game. Box seats would cost $6.60 (including tax), reserved grandstand seats $5.50, general admission seats $3.30, and bleachers $1.10. In the morning mail on September 14, the Cardinal offices at Sportsman's Park received roughly 20,000 ticket requests. Breadon arranged to have four city detectives guard the cashier's checks and money orders contained therein, valued at several hundred thousand dollars. The paperwork was kept in a vacant store on Grand Boulevard, adjacent to the ballpark. It only took two days before ticket requests surpassed the capacity of Sportsman's Park.[23]

As the Cardinals headed to Philadelphia for a six-game series against the Phillies, Hornsby lamented the team's poor showing against the Braves. "We gave away two games in Boston," he told Roy Stockton. "When you have the bases filled twice with none out and don't score, and a man leads off with a triple and you can't get him home, you're giving away the game." The Cardinal manager took another swipe at Sam Breadon and the exhibition schedule, claiming the result might have been different if Hafey had been able to play, but he reassured fans the team would weather the storm. "Don't worry about us crackin.' You didn't see anybody crack in the field yesterday and you won't." Stockton was dubious. The St. Louis offense had scored in only six of the 41 innings against Boston. This, he asserted, was "not [a] championship attack and unless the team regains its batting eye against the Phillies, disaster will have to overtake the Reds or they will forge to the front." The Philadelphia series "will go a long way toward telling whether St. Louis is to have a pennant or whether the 1926 season is going to [be] one of the saddest collapses in the history of pennant fights."[24]

The Redbirds rolled into Philadelphia in second place. The Reds won their sixth straight by defeating Brooklyn on the Cardinals' travel day to take a half-game lead. Nevertheless, the Cards took care of business, regaining their batting eyes and then some in Baker Bowl. Hornsby handed the ball to Jess Haines for the first game, who responded by pitching a complete game victory. He worked out of multiple trouble spots as he scattered 11 hits and walked three, but Philadelphia scored only two runs off the veteran knuckleball pitcher. The offense, meanwhile, roused out of its lethargy in a steady 13-hit, nine-run attack. Every batter in the St. Louis lineup, including Chick Hafey who was back in action, had at least one hit. The team bunched together six hits to score four runs in the fourth and added four more in the eighth. Southworth paced the attack with three hits, while Douthit and Thevenow each drove in three runs.[25]

Wednesday's offensive outburst was just the beginning as the Phillies and Cards played a double header on September 16. In the opener, St. Louis blasted Philadelphia, 23–3. In the third inning, the Redbirds clubbed five Phillie pitchers for 12 runs on seven singles, two doubles, three walks, and two errors. They added four runs in the fifth inning, two on a double from Chick Hafey, and another four tallies in the sixth, two on another Hafey two-bagger. Overall, St. Louis pounded out 22 hits. Bottomley drove in four, and Hafey had five RBI's. Taylor Douthit had an effective game as the leadoff batter. In addition to his two base hits, he walked four times, stole two bases, and scored five runs. Flint Rhem earned his 19th win of the season, though he only pitched four innings. Herman Bell pitched five shutout innings in relief. St. Louis bats didn't let up in the nightcap. They added another 19 hits to the ledger in another rout, this time by a 10–2 score. St. Louis led 3–0 when the Cards erupted for six runs in the sixth frame to salt the game away. Douthit continued his hot hitting with three more hits, a feat matched by Southworth, Hornsby, and Hafey. Leading the way, however, was none other than pitcher Art Reinhart, who contributed four hits to his own cause. On the mound, the southpaw went the distance, allowing Philadelphia two runs on seven hits. The sweep again pulled St. Louis into a first-place tie with the streaking Reds, who had won eight in a row.[26]

The second game featured a humorous moment. The contest was delayed for several minutes as umpire Bill Klem tossed Phillies catcher Jimmie Wilson and manager Art Fletcher from the game in the fifth inning—Wilson for his vigorous dispute of Klem's strike zone calls and Fletcher for arguing and "making faces" from the third base coaching box. Shortly after Wilson and Fletcher reached the clubhouse, situated in the farthest confines of centerfield (the Polo Grounds in New York was the only other major league ballpark with that layout), Klem noticed some commotion in the bleacher seats. The umpire realized the fans were laughing uproariously and pointing toward Baker Bowl's archaic scoreboard, which included a slate section on which the scoreboard boy would print the names of the Phillies' pitcher and catcher battery in chalk. But what attracted the fans' attention was that someone erased the battery names and drew an excellent likeness of a catfish, writing "Catfish Klem" beneath the illustration. Some derisively thought the umpire's face resembled a catfish, and the dignified umpire despised that nickname. He was sure Fletcher was the culprit and wired National League president Heydler after the game to report the incident. Heydler suspended Fletcher for the rest of the season and fined Wilson $50. While Fletcher served his suspension, Phillies owner William F. Baker fired the contentious manager, an unjust punishment because Wilson was responsible for the insulting drawing. The Philadelphia catcher received an additional punishment beyond the $50 fine when Baker named Wilson to pilot the hapless Phillies for the rest of the season.[27]

During the series, several members of the Cardinals did some trash talking, mocking the Phillies for their woeful play. Hornsby told them to stop. "Don't do anything to get them sore at us," he warned, "Get one of these tailenders riled, and they play their heads off against you. Let 'em alone, and they stay dead."[28]

That's exactly what happened, though Hornsby viewed the threatening rain clouds on Friday, September 17, with alarm. This was the Redbirds' final road trip of the season, and with an already full schedule ahead, it would be extremely difficult, if not impossible, to make up a rained-out game, which might cost St. Louis the pennant. Such was his fear that he tried—and failed—to convince the Phillies to move the double header on Saturday to Friday. If rain postponed the Friday game, Hornsby was ready to ask the Phillies to agree to play three games on Saturday. Fortunately, that drastic move wasn't necessary. Hornsby desperately wanted the Cardinals to get off to a quick lead just in case the game was called after an official five innings. The team didn't disappoint. St. Louis blistered Phillies pitcher Claude Willoughby for four runs in the first and never looked back. Douthit slammed the first pitch of the game off the rightfield wall for a double and scored on Southworth's RBI single. Two batters later, Jim Bottomley launched a three-run home run, his first in over a month. The Cardinals kept up a steady offensive assault in the 10–1 rout, punctuated by Tommy Thevenow's first home run of the season in the ninth inning. It was a tainted blow, however. Thevenow hit a line drive down the leftfield line. Outfielder Freddy Leach retrieved the ball but twisted his left knee in the process and collapsed. He was unable to throw the ball back to the infield, and Thevenow scampered around the bases. Leach was injured badly enough that his teammates carried him off the field. Bill Sherdel cruised to his 15th win of the year, and the Cardinals took a one-game lead over the Reds, who lost a heartbreaker to the Giants when Frank Frisch slugged a walk-off homer in the 10th inning.[29]

The weather gods cooperated again for the September 18 twin bill. Flint Rhem took the mound in game one. The Redbirds scored a run in the first and two runs in the third, sixth, and seventh innings against Wayland Dean. Bottomley capped off the scoring in the seventh with his second home run in as many days. Rhem pitched around home runs by Cy Williams and Johnny Mokan to earn his 20th win of the season. Ol' Pete Alexander started for St. Louis in game two against Phillies ace Hal Carlson and once again found himself involved in a nip-and-tuck pitchers' duel. Alexander aided his cause with an RBI single in the third, and he maintained that 1–0 lead until the sixth. Second baseman Bernie Friberg led off with a single, and Carlson followed with a double to left center. Shortstop Heinie Sand then hit a slow roller to Thevenow. In his haste to catch Friberg at home, Thevenow threw wildly and both Friberg and Carlson scored. Douthit's sacrifice fly in the eighth tied the score, but the Phillies scored the winning run off Art Reinhart in the bottom of the ninth. With two outs and a runner on second, pinch hitter Denny Sothern hit a sharp single to center. Douthit pegged a throw to catcher Ernie Vick that seemed to be in time to nab the runner at home, but the ball took a short hop and Vick juggled the throw just enough to allow the runner to score. Despite the disappointing ending, St. Louis maintained its lead over Cincinnati, as the Giants nipped the Reds again by a 5–4 score.[30]

The Cardinals kicked off the final week of the season with a single game against the Giants on September 19. Some 35,000 fans showed up at the Polo Grounds and rather than clamoring for the Giants to continue to play the spoiler's role in the pennant chase, a large portion cheered on the Mound City nine. St. Louis took a two-run lead in the second on O'Farrell's run-scoring single and an error by third baseman Fred Lindstrom. The Giants retaliated in their half of the inning with three runs off Jess Haines, one scoring on a Travis Jackson double. Jackson struck again in the fourth with a two-run bomb off Haines to extend the lead to 5–2. St. Louis battled back with three runs in the fifth to tie the score. With one out, Douthit and Southworth singled to start the rally. Hornsby doubled home one run, and Bottomley and Les Bell contributed RBI singles. Bill Sherdel came on in relief and pitched a scoreless fifth. The Giants, however, strung together three singles in the sixth to take a 6–5 lead. The game came down to the eighth inning. Chick Hafey roped a double off the leftfield wall to lead off the frame. Bob

Southpaw Bill Sherdel used his repertoire of off-speed pitches to win 16 games in 1926 and frustrate the mighty New York Yankees during the World Series (St. Louis Mercantile Library at the University of Missouri-St. Louis).

O'Farrell followed with a single to leftfield. The youthful Hafey, determined to carry the tying run across the plate, ignored Coach Killefer's sign to hold at third. Leftfielder and former Cardinal Heinie Mueller came in fast, fielded O'Farrell's hit cleanly, and uncorked a perfect throw to New York catcher Hugh McMullen to easily cut down Hafey. The baserunning blunder was costly because the next batter, Tommy Thevenow, hit a fly ball to left that would have been deep enough to score Hafey had he held at third. The loss shaved St. Louis' lead to a scant one game over the Reds. James Gould of the *St. Louis Star* "used to think it would be great 'covering' a winner." The Cardinals, he acknowledged, were winners, "but their lead is, at best, a precarious one and the struggle has become a nerve-wracking one. Whatever the old days were, when the Cards were losing with ease and nonchalance, at least, they were much more comfortable and much less wearing on the constitution."[31]

The non-stop tension of the title chase likewise wore on Hornsby's troops, and Monday, September 20, would have been a most welcome day of rest. But Breadon had scheduled one final meaningless exhibition game against the Springfield, Massachusetts, Ponies of the Eastern League. The skeleton crew Hornsby sent to Springfield put in a listless performance and dropped the contest by a 5–3 score. The *Post-Dispatch* reported that the only life the Cardinals showed came in the fourth inning when an announcement was made that the Boston Braves had defeated Cincinnati 4–3 in the first game of a double header. At that point, the players "became jubilant and began to frisk about like colts tossing baseballs into the air and running [around] like kids, so happy were they. Their pep didn't last long and toward the end their only objective was to hurry the game along."[32] Their pep no doubt returned later in the day when they learned Boston topped the Reds 3–0 in the nightcap. The sweep dropped the Reds another full game behind St. Louis. "One week ago," enthused Martin Haley of the *Globe-Democrat*, "Boston would have been voted the most unpopular town in the world by all St. Louis baseball fans." After sweeping the twin bill from the Reds, however, Beantown's ballers were now beloved by those same fans. "If Boston's Braves dragged the Cardinal pennant hopes through the dust a week ago, they threw Cincinnati's chances into the Charles River today, with sand bags attached."[33]

With their confidence soaring, the Cardinals invaded Ebbets Field on Tuesday, September 21, to take on the Dodgers. Hornsby tapped Bill Sherdel to start, despite the fact that he was suffering from a severe cold and had pitched a complete game the Friday before as well as three more innings in the Sunday game against New York. Wee Willie's success against Brooklyn—he had defeated them six times during the season—convinced the Rajah that the southpaw was the one for the job. Sherdel made Hornsby look like a genius for the first seven innings. He took a 1–0 lead into the eighth, when the hurler made a catastrophic error. Brooklyn catcher Hank DeBerry led off the inning with a single. With pitcher Jesse Petty coming to the plate, the entire stadium knew a bunt was coming. Petty did the Cardinals a tremendous favor by bunting the ball directly back to Sherdel. A double play seemed a certainty with the slow-footed DeBerry chugging toward second base, but Bill put as much mustard as he could manage on the throw, and it skipped away from Tommy Thevenow covering the bag. Flustered, Sherdel gave up a single to Dick Cox to load the bases with no outs. The momentum shifting, Hornsby lifted Sherdel and brought in Grover Cleveland Alexander, who had bailed out the Cardinals numerous times since his arrival in June. On this occasion, however, Alexander could not save the day. He gave up two-run singles to former Pirate Max Carey and shortstop Johnny Butler to put St. Louis in a 4–1 hole. The Cards fought back in the ninth. Hornsby doubled home Douthit and advanced to third on Carey's error. Jim Bottomley came to bat and blasted a line drive headed for rightfield, but first baseman Babe Herman snagged the vicious blow and tried to double Hornsby off third. His throw got past the third baseman and Hornsby scored to narrow the deficit to a single run, but the threat ended there, and St. Louis suffered its third consecutive defeat. Fortunately, the Reds were floundering even more. They succumbed again to the Braves for their fifth straight loss; thus, there was no change in the standings.[34]

St. Louis exacted its revenge the next day, trouncing the Dodgers 15–7. Hornsby dispensed with the usual pre-game meeting to not clutter his players' minds with the usual strategizing. Sportswriter Martin Haley wasn't sure if Hornsby's tactic helped, but whatever it was that changed the Redbirds "from a tight bundle of quivering nerves to a free swinging horde, loose as draft beer in the old prewar garden days, did a good job of it." The Cardinals hammered three Brooklyn pitchers for 17 hits with starter Jess Barnes surrendering eight hits and eight runs in 1⅔ innings. Everyone in the lineup, except for Chick Hafey, contributed to the barrage. Les Bell belted three triples and a double; Billy Southworth lashed out a single, double, and triple; Jim Bottomley had a single, double, home run, and four RBI's; and Tommy Thevenow chipped in with a run-scoring single and his second inside-the-park homer within a week. Pitcher Art Reinhart was hardly at his best—Brooklyn raked him for 11 hits and six earned runs—but he didn't need to be as St. Louis gained a half game on the idle Reds and inched another step closer to the pennant. If the Reds, by some miracle, captured the National League flag, mused Roy Stockton, it would be "the greatest tragedy in the history of baseball and it would take months to drag all the bodies out of the Mississippi River."[35]

One of the 5,000 bodies who witnessed the game at Ebbets Field was a "sartorially perfect young man in the middle thirties with a cane thrown rakishly over the crooked arm." The well-dressed individual sauntered up to the Brooklyn press gate and, in a conspiratorial whisper, told the gate keeper that he was St. Louis Mayor Victor Miller, who was travelling incognito so as not to cause too much of a disruption. He wanted to attend the game but hoped to sit back in the stands, which would allow him to slip out of the ballpark unceremoniously about the sixth inning to return to St. Louis for an important engagement. The credulous gate keeper said, "That's all right, Mayor, come right on in." About 15 minutes later, Cardinal traveling secretary Clarence Lloyd approached the same gate keeper and asked nonchalantly how things were going, whereupon the gate keeper immediately divulged his secret about the important visitor. His suspicions aroused, Lloyd asked to be shown the self-proclaimed Mayor. When pointed out, Lloyd exclaimed, "Why, that fellow's an imposter." The gate keeper wanted to immediately oust the perpetrator from the premises, but Lloyd, said, "Naw, let him stay. Anybody who can get away with that line deserves a reward." The *Globe-Democrat* applauded the imposter's nerve, which outdid the era's most famous gatecrasher, James "One-Eye" Connolly.[36]

Few events could have distracted the attention of the sporting world from the baseball race, but the much-ballyhooed boxing title match between heavyweight champion Jack Dempsey and challenger Gene Tunney commanded that level of interest. In fact, the Cardinals–New York Giants contest scheduled for Thursday, September 23, was pushed back to Friday so that players and fans of both teams could travel to Philadelphia to witness the epic battle. More than 120,000 enthusiasts filled Sesquicentennial Municipal Stadium to watch the event and millions more tuned in on the radio to listen as Tunney dominated Dempsey in a steady rain and seized the championship belt in a unanimous decision.[37]

With the distraction of the title bout in the rearview mirror, Hornsby took steps to avoid any other distractions that might affect his young team's focus. He arranged to have the scorekeeper at the Polo Grounds not post updates of the Reds–Phillies contest on the scoreboard until the Cards' game was decided one way or the other. He sent a well-rested Flint Rhem to the mound to square off against curveballer Hugh McQuillan. Rhem did not have his best stuff, and the Giants tallied three runs in the first after two men had been retired. Frankie Frisch and George Kelly singled, and then Bill Terry tagged the Cardinal righthander for a three-run homer. At this point, Hornsby relented and allowed the scoreboard to post the result that Philadelphia had beaten the Reds in the first game of a twin bill. That good news lifted the team's spirits and woke up their bats. Les Bell led off the second inning with a double and moved to third on a wild pitch. O'Farrell's infield single brought Bell home, and Tommy Thevenow followed with a double. Hornsby sent Specs Toporcer to bat for Rhem, and he came through with a two-run double to center. Two batters later, Billy Southworth put St. Louis in the lead with an impressive upper-deck blast to plate two runs. Years later, Billy the Kid recalled as he neared first base that coach Otto Williams was "jumping up and down like a madman, jabbering and pointing to the right field stands." The clout "was the timeliest home run I ever hit, and to have it against the Giants, with McGraw snarling his defiance from the bench, made it doubly thrilling and satisfying." Bill Sherdel replaced Rhem on the mound and held the Giants to one run over the last eight innings to secure the victory and the Cardinals' first-ever National League pennant.[38]

Thousands of Cardinal fans congregated at various locations throughout St. Louis to listen to the ballgame, and the crowd grew even larger when news spread that Cincinnati had lost and the Cards could clinch the title with a win. As ominous storm clouds gathered overhead, an air of electric anticipation coursed through the multitude when the last of the ninth inning began with St. Louis in front 6–4. The crowd roared after each of the first two outs, and when Tommy Thevenow threw out the final Giant batter, bedlam ensued. The 30,000 people at the St. Louis Exposition triumphantly screamed in unison as 21 "bombs" exploded, and fireworks—including a flaming silhouette of Rogers Hornsby—were ignited. More bombs were set off at City Hall, only to be lost in the cacophony of cheers, blaring car horns, jangling cowbells, and shrieking factory and train whistles. Downtown traffic was hopelessly snarled, as an estimated 100,000 rooters paraded the streets. Telephone switchboards were overwhelmed with some 128,000 phone calls in one hour, the most in the city's history. For hours, confetti streamed down from nearly every office window and turned downtown into a wintry wonderland. A torrential downpour and the intermittent showers that followed, along with thousands of tramping feet, turned the confetti into a pulpy mush. The rain scattered the revelers for a time, but the boisterous partying renewed after the dinner

10. The "Home" Stretch, September 3–September 30   143

Pandemonium erupts in downtown St. Louis along Olive Street after the Cardinals clinch the National League pennant (Missouri Historical Society, St. Louis).

hour and carried on well into the morning. The city had not seen such unbridled joy since the end of World War I in 1918.[39]

In stark contrast, Branch Rickey celebrated the Cardinals' pennant-clinching win quietly at home. Though truly pleased with the club's success, he could not help but feel a certain amount of regret that he was not at the helm of the club he constructed.[40]

When a weary but overjoyed Hornsby learned of the partying in St. Louis, he was visibly moved. "I am glad I did not know before tonight how seriously the fans were following our every move and what joy would be occasioned by our victory," he told the *Globe-Democrat*. "If I had known, the strain would have been so much greater. It is wonderful to know that our efforts are so deeply appreciated and still more wonderful to know that our work has brought such happiness to St. Louis. Until tonight I did not realize what a pennant would mean, and certainly I am the happiest man in the world that my team has succeeded in causing so much joy." He went on to praise his players' spirit and ability. "They are the finest set of players I was ever associated with," he concluded, and "I am both proud and happy to be their manager." He ordered the team to forget training rules for the night, telling them, "You have done a great thing and you have been under a terrific strain. Now relax. You more than deserve a night off."[41]

With the pennant won, the Cardinals essentially took the next day off as well. Roy Stockton commented the players, free of the strain, "appeared suddenly to have knocked 10 years off their age." For the final game against the Giants, Hornsby sent Vic Keen to the mound, his first start in more than a month. He also kept several starters—himself, Billy Southworth, and Bob O'Farrell—out of the ballgame while the others in the lineup merely went through the motions, just wanting to end the game quickly. They got their wish. It took the Giants one hour and 14 minutes to demolish St. Louis 12–2. Keen continued his late-season struggles, giving up 12 hits and six runs in six innings. Ed Clough, heretofore relegated to pitching in exhibition games, made his first appearance of the season for St. Louis and gave up six runs in only two innings of work. On the other side, Giants pitcher Jack Scott pitched a complete game and went four for four at the plate with a home run and five RBI's.

Before the glorious season concluded, one more game had to be played against the downcast Reds. Hornsby, Jim Bottomley, Bob O'Farrell, and most of the pitchers remained in New York while the rest of the team took the train to Cincinnati. Some 17,000 fans turned out to watch the Reds nip St. Louis 2–1. Herman Bell and Bill Hallahan shut out the Reds through eight innings, but in the bottom of the ninth, Cincinnati pushed two runs across on a single and two doubles, giving Pete Donohue his 20th win of the season. Immediately after the game, the Cardinals got back on the train for the return journey to New York and reunited with their teammates on September 27. They had been away from New York for 46 hours, 41 of which were spent on the train.[42]

As the newly crowned National League champions rested and prepared to face off against the mighty New York Yankees in the World Series, Rogers Hornsby reflected on the season's ups and downs. "Yes, it was a hard race," he told reporters, "and at times it looked bad for us. We never doubted the final result.... We may not be a great team, but no one can say that we are not a game team."[43]

The Cardinals' offensive attack fueled the team's unwavering confidence. St. Louis led the National League in home runs (90), total bases (2234), runs scored (817), and slugging percentage (.415). They finished second in team batting (.286), on base percentage (.348), and doubles (259). Though Jim Bottomley's batting average (.299) was a dramatic drop from previous seasons, he finished second in home runs (19) and doubles (40), and his 120 RBI's led the league. With his back and boil issues, Hornsby also suffered through a "down" year in comparison to his 1925 Triple Crown performance but still batted .317 with 11 home runs and 93 RBI's. Others picked up the slack. Les Bell put together a career year with a .325 batting average (ninth in the league), 17 home runs (fourth in the league), and 100 RBI's (third in the league). Taylor Douthit provided a spark with a .308 batting average, .375 on base percentage, and 23 steals. Before his injury, Ray Blades enjoyed a solid season from the leadoff spot with a .305 batting average and .409 on base percentage. Mid-season acquisition Billy Southworth was key to the Cardinals' pennant drive. In 99 games with St. Louis, he batted .317 with 11 home runs and 69 RBI's, many of them in clutch situations. Tommy Thevenow batted only .256 but delivered one clutch hit after another, and Bob O'Farrell, despite catching more games than any other backstop, chipped in with a .293 batting average and 68 RBI's.

It was O'Farrell's defense that sparked chatter about his MVP chances. He led the league with 146 games caught, 43 more than Zack Taylor of Boston. He threw out 51 percent of would-be base stealers, was charged with only four passed balls, and was among the league leaders with a .983 fielding percentage. Overall, the Cards were middle of the pack defensively, though there were some notable performances beyond O'Farrell's. Tommy Thevenow committed the third most errors among NL shortstops with 45, but his extraordinary range was borne out by his league-leading 1,013 fielding chances (105 more than the runner up), 597 assists (102 more than the runner up and four short of Glenn Wright's major league record), and 371 putouts. Among those who patrolled the green expanses, Taylor Douthit led all National League outfielders with 20 errors, but he also led in chances, putouts, and range factor.

Cardinal pitching—considered the team's Achilles heel at the start of the season—held up well, especially after Grover Cleveland Alexander came on board. The staff tied for third in earned run average (3.67) and finished first in complete games (90) and second in WHIP at 1.301. Flint Rhem tied for the league lead with 20 wins, while Bill Sherdel posted 16 victories, and Jess Haines fashioned a 13–4 record. Victor Keen tailed off badly at season's end, thanks to a sore arm, but he provided a much-needed lift early in the year as the team struggled to find its footing. However, Alexander's arrival tipped the balance in the Cardinals' favor. His deceptive 9–7 won/loss record would have been much better if not for some miserly run support. Despite his reputation as an unreliable boozer, he answered every call Rogers Hornsby made. Ol' Pete completed 11 of his 16 starts and saved two others. He put together a sparkling 2.91 ERA, and his 1.108 WHIP paced the league. But, Roy Stockton wrote in the *Sporting News*, this "pitching genius did more for the Cardinals than cold statistics ever will tell." He "represented the difference between a good pitching staff and a championship pitching staff" because he instilled confidence in the other pitchers just when they most needed a "bracing influence."[44]

The Cardinals did enjoy a bit of luck on the injury front. Bumps, bruises, boils, and sore arms plagued the club all season, but the only players to miss significant time were Hornsby, Syl Johnson, and Ray Blades who played in only 107 games because of his season-ending knee injury in July. Overall, St. Louis used a total of 28 players during the entire season, the fewest of any team in the league. The Giants and Phillies, in comparison, cycled through a string of 55 players. Hornsby missed 22 games with his various afflictions and played many at less than full strength. Though his performance suffered, his grit and determination provided inspirational leadership and a role model for the rest of the squad, giving his players the confidence and resolve they needed to rise above their own maladies to help the team.[45] The Redbirds would need every bit of that confidence and luck against the vaunted New York Yankees.

CHAPTER 11

Reaching the Mountaintop, October 1–14

The World Series was not the only event to draw large crowds in St. Louis during the fall of 1926. On October 1, a capacity audience at the Capitol Theater, Sixth and Chestnut streets, paid up to $2 per ticket to be treated to a demonstration of Warner Brothers' Vitaphone and experienced the thrill of viewing the first "talking movies" in the city. The "talking" part of the program consisted of an introductory speech from Will H. Hays, president of the Motion Picture Producers and Distributors of America, a performance by the New York Philharmonic Society, and other musical numbers, including selections on the ukelele and steel guitar by Roy Smeck, the "Wizard of the Strings." The feature movie, "Don Juan" starring John Barrymore, was accompanied by synchronized music. Enthralled customers declared the Vitaphone a "sensation."[1]

A more traditional spectacle also vied for the attention of St. Louis residents. For 47 years, the annual Veiled Prophet Parade and Ball had been the apex of the social calendar for St. Louis' elites. The Veiled Prophet, so named in an 1817 work by Irish poet Thomas Moore, was a historical figure who led an anti-Islamic revolt in the eighth century. Rather than fomenting a revolt, the St. Louis figure was a symbol used by a group of wealthy White men to suppress labor unrest within the city. After police and militia stamped out a widespread strike in 1877, the elite formed a secret organization, the Mysterious Order of the Veiled Prophet, to celebrate their exalted social status and reassert their control of the city. The Veiled Prophet, styled in KKK-like robes, presided over the first Mardi Gras-esque parade on October 8, 1878, to commemorate the end of the strike. The floats, depicting the story of human progress, wound their way through St. Louis' working-class neighborhoods, not-so-subtly reminding White and Black laborers who was really in charge. A grand ball capped off the event, culminating in the crowning of a debutante as the Queen of Love and Beauty. The organization's whites-only policy drew the ire of civil rights activists in the 1960s and 1970s, and the Veiled Prophet diversified its membership and expanded its philanthropic activities in response to the pressure. But its historical baggage was too hard to discard. The event was rebranded several times. Today, the parade is called "America's Birthday Parade."[2]

The event's class and racial overtones, however, were far from the minds of those attending the 1926 event. Bright red Cardinal banners mingled with the traditional Veiled Prophet colors of purple, gold, and scarlet that festooned the city. A record-setting crowd—swelled by World Series spectators—witnessed the October 5 parade that featured floats with Moon Mullins, Mutt and Jeff, Krazy Kat, Barney Google, Jiggs and Maggie from Bringing Up Father, and other comic strip characters. Some 5,000 attended the formal ball the following night at the silver and orchid-lined Coliseum. The solemn ceremony concluded when the Veiled Prophet crowned Martha Love as the new Queen of Love and Beauty.[3]

The ongoing feud for control of the bootleg market between the Cuckoo gang and Italian gunmen was a far cry from love and beauty. For the past eight months, the battle between the two rivals resulted in 13 funerals, 18 wounded victims, and 14 "bullet-riddled automobiles." Chief of Police Joseph Gerk had had enough. On October 7, he warned the "gangsters and Italian gunmen must get out of St. Louis if we have to shoot them out." A specially detailed squad of police detectives put the plan into action the night before. They spotted a carload of known gangsters, and during the ensuing car chase and gunfight, the detectives wounded one offender and shot and killed 19-year-old Joe Bommarito, a "notorious police character." "These Italians, armed to the teeth, were out for slaughter when our men jumped them," Gerk claimed, "I have nothing but praise for my men for hanging on to them until they settled accounts." Despite the police's best efforts, the warfare continued. The Italians planned East Side raids in retaliation for the Cuckoos placing "spotters" to shoot at Italian enemies near their homes.[4]

The upcoming struggle between the Cardinals and the Yankees lacked the physical violence of the bootlegging feud, but it was no less fierce. New York had rebounded from a dismal seventh-place finish in 1925 to capture the American League crown. Behind the "Murderer's Row" slugging of Babe Ruth, Bob Meusel, Lou Gehrig, Earle Combs, and rookie Tony Lazzeri, the Yankees surged out of the gate to easily outpace the rest of the field. By August 6, New York had a 70–36 record, 11 games in front of the Cleveland Indians. Yankee fans thought the team could coast the rest of the way to claim the flag. Cleveland was not ready to concede anything and continued to pressure the Yankees, who began a late-season slide. The Bronx Bombers, however, never relinquished their lead, clinching the pennant on September 25 with a double header sweep of the Browns in St. Louis.[5]

Despite their end-of-season struggles, the Yankees presented a formidable lineup. They easily paced the American League in runs, home runs, runs batted in, and slugging percentage. Babe Ruth, of course, led the way. His 47 home runs far outdistanced runner up Al Simmons' 19. In fact, the Sultan of Swat outhomered every American League team except the Browns and Athletics. Ruth, Lazzeri, and Gehrig finished first, second, and sixth in RBI's, while Ruth, Gehrig, and Combs finished in the top four in runs scored. The veteran trio of lefty Herb Pennock (23 wins), Urban Shocker (19 wins), and Waite Hoyt (16 wins) headlined a sturdy pitching staff. The combination of Yankee experience and explosiveness prompted oddsmakers to make the Cardinals a 15–1 underdog. Yankee manager, and former Cards skipper, Miller Huggins oozed confidence. "We have a more experienced team and more experienced pitchers," he surmised, "and all the boys are cocky and ready to go. There is no doubt in their minds, or in mine, that the Yankees will win." Babe Ruth was even more to the point. "We'll beat 'em," he said, "There will be nothing to it."[6]

The two squads presented interesting contrasts regarding team building and roster makeup. With the game's top gate attraction in Babe Ruth, the Yankees had the wherewithal to pay exorbitant prices for top minor league players. For example, they paid $50,000 to acquire Tony Lazzeri from the Pacific Coast League. The threadbare Cardinals, on the other hand, relied upon Rickey's farm system to nurture young, untested talent as cheaply as possible. Author Paul Doutrich noted the two also reflected "American society's 'roaring' as well as its reactionary character." The Yankees represented sophisticated, cosmopolitan urban America and its ethnic and religious heterogeneity. Babe Ruth personified the excesses of the decade, and most members of the team were first- or second-generation immigrants from urban centers. Tony Lazzeri, in particular, became a hero to Italian Americans across the country. In contrast, the Cardinals, situated on the far western "frontier" of major league baseball, embodied the more rustic small town, rural America peopled primarily by White, Anglo-Saxon Protestants. The fiercely independent and rugged Rogers Hornsby and the pious Branch Rickey personified more traditional societal values.[7]

Days before the much-anticipated contest, Hornsby received word from an uncle that his mother's health was failing fast. "You could not possibly reach here to see her alive," the telegram read, "Her dying wish is that you remain for the series." Later that day, he learned his mother passed away. Grief stricken, he remained in his hotel room for several hours with his wife, Jeannette. After a good deal of anguished internal debate, he decided he would leave the team in Bill Killefer's hands and go to Texas, but relatives urged him to honor his mother's wishes. Instead, Jeannette made plans to make the trip. The relatives, however, wired back: "Stay with Rogers. He needs you. All is done here." Hornsby emerged from his room early in the evening and issued an emotionally wracked statement that he would remain with the team and attend his mother's funeral once the World Series had ended. The loss of his mother understandably changed his view of what should have been the pinnacle of his storied career. "The glory of this, my life's ambition, has passed," he told Killefer. "The thrill has gone. I will be playing, stirred only by my mother's thoughts of me. I hope my mother will look down upon me and say that I have done the right thing."[8]

A drab, gray sky matched the somber mood of the Cardinal skipper as he and his squad arrived at Yankee Stadium for Game One on October 2. When he introduced himself to the New York City policeman stationed outside the players' entrance, the dubious cop, thinking the group was trying to sneak into the ballpark, questioned, "Is that so? Run along now.... You can't stand here." Before the man in blue chased the Cardinals away, Yankee slugger Lou Gehrig arrived and vouched that the men were indeed that day's opponents. Having finally gained entrance to the clubhouse, Hornsby selected Bill Sherdel to take the mound. Southpaws had given the hard-hitting Yankees fits for years, and the Rajah felt Sherdel's slow ball repertoire was "poison to sluggers." Miller Huggins countered with crafty southpaw Herb Pennock. More than 60,000 fans filled Yankee Stadium. As the Cardinals, sporting their new gray road uniforms with the "two cocky birds, flaming Cardinals, rampant on a black bat across the bosoms of the shirts," filtered onto the field to warm up, the fans—either out of sympathy for Hornsby's burden or rooting for the underdog—gave them an ovation equaling that given the hometown heroes.[9]

The crowd was easily the largest to attend a Cardinals game, and the players were awestruck by the sea of humanity. Les Bell recalled that he was so nervous that he started shaking. Sherdel, about to start the most important game of his career, calmed down the young third baseman. He put his arm around Bell's shoulders and said, "Hey Les, I'll tell you what to do."

"What's that, Bill?"
"You count 'em upstairs and I'll count 'em downstairs, and we'll see how much money we're gonna make today."[10]

A radio network of 21 stations—including KSD of St. Louis—broadcast the game to 15 million fans across the nation, an amazing achievement in the still early days of the industry and a key to forming a national radio network. Some 10,000 fans crowded around radios and strategically placed loudspeakers in downtown St. Louis to listen to WEAF's Graham McNamee describe the action. One sardonic fan moved from his position at Eleventh and Olive streets to a spot in the 600 block on Olive because "he wanted to get a little closer to the third-base line."

McNamee was a frustrated opera singer who got involved with radio purely out of curiosity and with baseball by accident. He was coaching another announcer during the 1923 World Series, but the would-be protégé decided he wasn't cut out for the job and left in the fourth inning of Game Three, leaving McNamee to broadcast the rest of the series. Though he was inexperienced, he had a melodious baritone voice and an intuitive sense that played to the strengths of the new medium. He knew listeners didn't want long lulls in the broadcasts, so he resorted to "general description" to "make the quieter times vivid." He had the knack to make listeners thousands of miles away feel as if they were at the game "watching the movements of the game, the color, and flags; the pop-bottles thrown in the air; the straw hats demolished." He sometimes confused players or played fast and loose with the facts. After a particularly egregious broadcast, sportswriter Ring Lardner quipped, "I don't know which game to write about—the one I saw today, or the one I heard Graham McNamee announce as I sat next to him at the Polo Grounds." However, St.

Louis fans admitted after Game One that McNamee gave the Cardinals a "square deal" in his account of the game.[11]

St. Louis got off to a good start. Douthit smashed a double past Babe Ruth and advanced to third on Southworth's grounder to second baseman Tony Lazerri. The sympathetic fans warmly greeted Rogers Hornsby when he came to bat, but the Rajah failed to drive Douthit home, tapping out to Pennock. Jim Bottomley gave Cardinal fans a thrill when he looped a single to left to put St. Louis in front. The Yankees, however, benefited from Sherdel's case of nerves in the bottom of the inning. The normally reliable southpaw missed the corners and walked Combs, Ruth, and Meusel to load the bases with one out. Sherdel admitted after the game he tried to put too much stuff on his pitches. The menacing Lou Gehrig came to bat, and Sherdel seemed to work out of the jam by getting him to ground a tailor-made double play ball to Thevenow. The Cardinals got the force at second, but Gehrig hustled to beat Hornsby's relay to first, scoring Combs and tying the game.

Babe Ruth alleviated the tension by the seat of his pants in the third inning. With shortstop Mark Koenig on first, Ruth, apparently at the direction of manager Miller Huggins, laid down a bunt. Bob O'Farrell pounced on the ball and rifled a throw to Thevenow to force Koenig. Bob Meusel then hit a grounder back to Sherdel. The Babe charged toward second base and slid hard into the bag, while Sherdel tossed Meusel out at first. Ruth rose in "palpable distress." Yankee trainer Doc Woods sprinted from the dugout while the sellout crowd held its breath, fearing the slugger injured his sore ankle. It soon became clear the only injury was to Ruth's dignity. He had torn his pants while sliding. Woods sewed a piece of cloth cut from the infield tarpaulin onto Ruth's pants. While Woods operated on Babe's uniform, the star slugger modestly faced the grandstand crowd the "color of a nice red brick house" according to Graham McNamee.

The wardrobe malfunction provided some comic relief to what several sportswriters considered a "dull though well-played affair." The game remained knotted through five innings. Per James Harrison of the *New York Times*, Pennock cut down the Cardinal lineup "with the monotony of a threshing machine," while Sherdel regained his composure and pitched a fine game. The Yankees finally broke through in the bottom of the sixth. Ruth led off with a single to left. Meusel bunted him over to second, and Gehrig drove him home with a single. That slim one-run lead was all Pennock needed. The single he gave up to Jim Bottomley in the top of the ninth was the Redbirds' first hit since the first inning. It took Pennock only 101 pitches, 66 for strikes, to tame the Cardinal bats. The 2–1 setback failed to diminish Hornsby's optimism. "Our confidence is unshaken and the team came out of its first Series skirmish in great style," he told the *Post-Dispatch*. "There may be a different tale to tell tomorrow."[12]

Though disappointed with the result, fans in St. Louis received a visual treat the next day to supplement the radio broadcast. Fox News filmed the game and had the footage flown to Chicago immediately after the game ended. From there, a special train rushed the film to St. Louis for a showing at the Missouri Ambassador and Grand Central theaters.[13]

A warm, sunny afternoon welcomed a World Series record crowd of 63,600 for Game Two. The opposing managers selected two aging and well-rested hurlers to toe the pitching rubber. Huggins chose 35-year-old Urban Shocker, a former stalwart with the St. Louis Browns and a master of the spitball, while Hornsby opted for 39-year-old Grover Cleveland Alexander. Ol' Pete was one of the few St. Louis players with World Series experience, though it was 11 years earlier with the Philadelphia Phillies. St. Louis squandered a scoring opportunity against Shocker in the first inning. With two outs, Hornsby slammed a double into the rightfield corner for his first hit of the Series, but he was stranded when Bottomley grounded to short. In the Yankee first, Alexander walked leadoff hitter Earl Combs, the only free pass Pete would issue. New York shortstop Mark Koenig slapped a liner that deflected off Alexander's glove. Tommy Thevenow, reacting quickly, made a great pickup, flipped the ball to Hornsby, who relayed it to Bottomley for a sparkling double play. Alexander then fanned Ruth on three pitches to end the frame.

The Yankees struck first in the second inning. Bob Meusel started the rally with a leadoff single. Lou Gehrig advanced Meusel to second on a grounder back to the pitcher and then prized rookie Tony Lazzeri came to bat and did what he did best—drive in runs. He drove in an incredible 222 runs for the Salt Lake City Bees of the Pacific Coast League in 1925 and followed that with 117 RBIs with the Yankees during the 1926 season. He came through again in Game Two with a base hit to leftfield. The Yankees tested Chick Hafey's arm and waved Meusel home. Hafey unleashed a throw that had a chance to beat Meusel to the plate, but Alexander inexplicably cut off the throw, allowing the Yankees to score the first run. Alexander admitted later he couldn't hear O'Farrell above the crowd noise and thought the catcher yelled to cut off the throw. Either way, he also confessed he was out of position and should have backed up O'Farrell instead. Third baseman Joe Dugan looped a base hit to right, and Lazzeri raced to third. Alexander struck out catcher Hank Severeid for the second out and nearly worked out of the scrape. With two strikes on Urban Shocker, the Yankees attempted a double steal. O'Farrell pegged a throw to Thevenow, who trapped Lazzeri between third and home. During the ensuing rundown, Alexander made his second mistake. He inserted himself into the play and made a wild throw that skipped past Les Bell, allowing Lazzeri to scamper home. In his syndicated newspaper column, Brooklyn Dodger manager Wilbert Robinson criticized Alexander for not backing up the catcher. "I never let my pitchers take part in a run-up play," he wrote, "They aren't used to such plays, hardly ever make them right." St. Louis responded in the top of the third to knot the score. Douthit beat out a roller to deep short, and Southworth rapped a low liner to leftfield that Bob Meusel trapped for a single. Hornsby advanced both runners with a sacrifice bunt before Sunny Jim Bottomley slapped a single to right to score two runs.

Alexander went back to the mound in the bottom of the third and promptly gave up a leadoff single to Earle Combs, who would be the last Yankee baserunner of the game. "Alexander the Great" retired the next 21 batters. He had a little extra on his fastball, and his curve nipped the corners with great precision. Of his 112 total pitches, 79 were strikes. He struck out ten "Murderer's Row" hitters and allowed only one ball to reach a Cardinal outfielder. St. Louis hitters, however, weren't having much luck against Shocker. He retired 11 in a row before Bob O'Farrell led off the seventh inning with a double. When Tommy Thevenow came to the plate, the Yankees expected the Cardinal shortstop to bunt, but Thevenow crossed them up and slapped a single past third. The rally seemed to fizzle out as Alexander popped out and Douthit hit a short fly to left field, but with two outs, Billy the Kid Southworth lined Shocker's first pitch into the rightfield seats for a three-run homer. The crowd "let loose one of the greatest roars that ever rolled from a New York gathering." Southworth's decisive blow and Alexander's machine-like hurling clinched the game for the upstart Cardinals. St. Louis tacked on one more run in the ninth on another fluke inside-the-park home run by Tommy Thevenow. He lifted a fly ball down the rightfield line, toward an asymmetrical groove between the rightfield box seats and the old wooden bleachers dubbed "the bloody angle" by New York sportswriters. Ruth got a glove on the ball but dropped it when he went over the rails of the field boxes. When he righted himself, he couldn't locate the ball, frantically asking for the crowd's help as Thevenow raced around the bases. The Babe finally found his prey and heaved a throw to home plate, a beat too slow to nab the Cardinal shortstop. It was the final round tripper of Thevenow's major league career. After the game, the Bambino growled about the crowd's pro–St. Louis sympathies, "Not one of those birds in the bleachers would tell me where the ball was."[14]

The cast-offs whom the Cardinals scooped up in mid-season were the difference in the 6–2 victory. "We couldn't hit Alexander, that's all there is to it," said Miller Huggins after the game. "Alexander pitched an almost perfect game. He had everything on the ball, and we just couldn't connect." The *Sporting News* enthused the veteran hurler's "generalship and mastery were outstanding. His was the grace and finesse of the maestro with rhythmic baton." As for Southworth's clout, Babe Ruth declared, "I wasn't looking for that hit over my head. I know Southworth and I never figured he would have that much of a lick. Anyway, I couldn't have pulled in that drive with an eight foot ladder."[15]

The need to catch a train preempted any Cardinal celebration in the clubhouse. A fleet of limousines, escorted by motorcycle police, rushed the squad to Pennsylvania Station. The players didn't mind. They were going home after 33 days on the road and anticipated a royal welcome from their adoring fans. Denied a chance to celebrate their heroes when the Cardinals clinched the National League flag, St. Louis was determined not to let another chance pass when the team returned on Monday, October 4. Hornsby, however, insisted the festivities be brief so that the players could get some rest before Tuesday's game. Virtually the entire city was shut down. Mayor Miller ordered that all city offices close to allow municipal workers to greet the Cards' train when it arrived. Most other businesses followed suit, and all federal and circuit court trials were suspended the entire week.

Twelve bombs exploded on the levee to announce the train's arrival, but it turned out to be the Yankees' train they welcomed. The fans who gathered at Union Station also mistakenly assumed the train that just arrived carried their beloved Cardinals and started a raucous cheer, "which turned into something like a groan when they discovered their mistake." The Cardinals' train arrived ten minutes later, and as the players disembarked at the Washington Avenue station, the mob of delirious fans overwhelmed the police's futile efforts to maintain order. The Cardinal faithful subjected the players to nonstop handshakes, back slaps, and hugs. Women mussed Rogers Hornsby's hair and tried to kiss him. The jostling crowd knocked the hat off Jeanette Hornsby's head and brought tears to her eyes and those of Hornsby's son, Billy.

The police finally carved out enough space for Mayor Miller to make a brief speech and present each player with a $100 white gold wristwatch with their names and "National League Champions" inscribed on them. Hornsby received a much grander prize—a new Lincoln sedan from the fans. The players were ushered to a line of waiting cars, and the Hornsbys brought up the rear of the motorcade that slowly snaked its way through a red sea of more than 100,000 fans who swamped the downtown streets. Full-throated cheers, blaring horns, and every manner of noisemaker drowned out the marching band, and a shower of confetti rained down from buildings lining the parade route. Overexuberant fans jumped on the cars' running boards, hoods, and roofs to ride along with their heroes. Sam Breadon rode in the lead car and told Jack Grosse, chairman of the reception committee, "I know there was a terrific enthusiasm among the fans, but not one of us ever imagined that we'd see anything like this." By the time Hornsby got home, his brand-new automobile was badly scratched. The partying continued well into the night while the exhausted ball players tried to get some rest. The *Globe-Democrat* reported all other celebrations, including Armistice Day and the clinching of the National League pennant, "paled beside the scenes of the triumphal procession of the men who put St. Louis on the baseball map."[16]

St. Louisans who weren't indulging in the revelry lined up outside Sportsman's Park as early as 11:00 p.m. to purchase bleacher or pavilion seats for Game Three. By midnight, roughly 1,000 people braved rain and the night chill for the chance to get a ticket to the city's first World Series game in 38 years. Six hours later, lines surrounding the park were two and sometimes three and four deep. Sam Breadon was ecstatic at the feverish excitement. In late September, he planned to capitalize on the anticipated crowds by adding an extra 2,000 box seats, which would come within three feet of the first and third base foul lines and another 3,000 temporary seats in left and center fields, which would reduce the distance from home plate to 325 feet and 400 feet respectively. Sam abandoned the field seats plan after speaking with Commissioner Landis, explaining the series "might be won by a fluke home run, and we don't want to risk the championship by putting seats in the outfield, regardless of the money loss involved. The championship is more important." The fans who couldn't get tickets most likely disagreed with Breadon, but by the time the game started at 1:30, a record crowd of nearly 38,000 filled Sportsman's Park. Hundreds more occupied rooftops beyond the outfield walls to catch a glimpse of the action. Those who could not get tickets listened to the play-by-play account of Porter Brown through KMOX. "The radio," noted a *Globe-Democrat* editorial, "has turned the whole town into 'bleachers,' in fact, has made the whole nation a vast ball park, wherein the great majority of the fans are jubilant over the Cardinals' victories."[17]

Jess Haines, one of Hornsby's hotter pitchers down the stretch, took the mound and proceeded to hurl one of his best games of the season. Though his control was spotty, he made pitches when most needed to shut down the struggling Yankee attack on five hits and no runs in the Cards 4–0 victory. It was only the fourth time the Yankees had been shut out that season. Rain interrupted action with one out in the top of the fourth, but after a 30-minute delay, Haines went back to work and needed only five pitches to get out of the inning. He repeated the feat in the fifth. After the game, Grover Cleveland Alexander told the *Post-Dispatch* that Haines "had as much stuff as I have ever seen him possess during all his years in the National League." "It was," he added, "a sensational exhibition, one that will not be forgotten by St. Louis fans."[18]

Pops, never much of a threat as a hitter, also delivered with the bat. In the bottom of the third, he reached on an infield hit. Taylor Douthit walked, and Billy Southworth bunted the runners to second and third. While perched on third base, Haines was dreaming of winning a $500 watch the newspapers were going to award the Cardinal player who scored the team's first run. He figured his chances were pretty good with only one out and Rogers Hornsby and Jim Bottomley coming to bat. Lady Luck, however, did not smile on Jess on this occasion. He watched helplessly as Hornsby fouled out to the catcher and Bottomley hit a line drive to the centerfielder, stranding him on third. Les Bell claimed the prize in the fourth inning. He led off with a single and came around to score on Mark Koenig's wild throw to Gehrig at first base, which prevented a potential inning-ending double play. Bell said every time he showed the watch to Haines, the pitcher grumbled, "Yeah, that ought to be mine." Jess must have channeled his frustration and anger at losing out on the proverbial pot of gold because, in that same inning, he amazed his teammates and fans alike when he drove Dutch Ruether's first pitch into the rightfield seats for a two-run homer. It was his first home run since 1920.[19]

Babe Ruth was having a tough series against Cardinal pitching. Through the first three games, he was batting a meager .200 on two harmless singles. He had no home runs or runs batted in. After Haines' whitewash of New York, an obviously frustrated Ruth stormed, "I can't see the Cardinals as a ball club, no matter if they did lick us today. There are at least two better clubs in the National League—Pittsburgh and Cincinnati. The Cardinals have been lucky, that's all, by getting a lot of

Babe Ruth (left) and Rogers Hornsby at Sportsman's Park during the 1926 World Series, one of the classic showdowns in baseball history (Missouri Historical Society, St. Louis).

flukey hits. We are not licked yet. Tomorrow is another day. When we start hitting it will be a different story."[20]

Game Four was indeed a different story, and Ruth made the story all about himself in front of another record crowd of 38,825. He blasted three home runs, scored four runs, and drove in four runs, setting six World Series records in the Yankees' 10–5 rout. Twenty-game winner Flint Rhem was Ruth's initial sacrificial lamb. To this point, St. Louis pitchers experienced a good deal of success feeding the Babe a steady diet of off-speed pitches. The young, headstrong Rhem struck out the first two Yankee batters on biting curveballs but decided to challenge the slugger with a fastball. Ruth knocked the first pitch out of the ballpark for a 1–0 Yankee lead. Hornsby's RBI single in the bottom half of the inning tied the game, until Ruth came to bat in the third. This time, Rhem tried to fool the Babe with an off-speed offering. It made no difference. Ruth blasted the pitch over the rightfield pavilion roof onto Grand Boulevard. The ball bounced across the street and shattered the showroom window of the Wells Motor Company. The company made the best of a bad situation to generate a little publicity. The next day it posted a sign reading, "This window broken by Babe Ruth" and rewarded Ruth with a Chevy sedan.

New York touched Rhem for another run in the fourth inning. Tony Lazzeri walked with one out. Third baseman Joe Dugan then lofted a fly ball into short left-center. Taylor Douthit and Chick Hafey both gave chase and collided, allowing the ball to drop safely. Both were knocked unconscious, and by the time Les Bell retrieved the baseball, Lazzeri had scored, and Dugan was perched on second base. Yankee and Cardinal players as well as team doctor Robert Hyland ran to check on the prostrate outfielders. A whiff of smelling salts, a dose of cold water, and "frenzied towel-swinging" revived them. Though badly shaken, both stayed in the ball game. Douthit was tested immediately when catcher Hank Severeid laced a base hit to center. Douthit charged the ball and pegged a perfect throw to O'Farrell to beat Dugan to the plate.

St. Louis fought back in its half of the fourth against Yankee starter Waite Hoyt. Chick Hafey singled up the middle and advanced to second when Koenig fumbled O'Farrell's grounder. Tommy Thevenow continued his hot hitting by lining a double down the rightfield line, driving Hafey across home plate. Hornsby sent Specs Toporcer to pinch hit for Rhem, and he responded with a sacrifice fly to center to score O'Farrell. Taylor Douthit slashed a double off the rightfield wall to knock in Thevenow and give St. Louis its first lead of the game. The fans in the "madhouse" stands erupted in a scream that lasted two to three minutes. They got even louder when Billy Southworth followed with a base hit to leftfield. Douthit attempted to score, but Ruth uncorked a perfect throw to cut down the Cardinal centerfielder, ending the rally and quieting the partisan crowd.

Art Reinhart took the mound for St. Louis in the top of the fifth. The lefty had not pitched in two weeks, and the lay-off clearly affected his hurling. He faced five batters and all five reached base. Combs walked and scored on Koenig's bloop double to right. Reinhart then walked Ruth, Meusel, and Gehrig, forcing in another run before Hornsby lifted him for Herman Bell. The Yankees pushed two more runs home on a sacrifice fly and groundout, scoring four runs on only one hit to pull in front 7–4. In the sixth inning, Ruth extended New York's lead to 9–4 by blasting a Herman Bell fastball into the seats in straightaway centerfield for his third homer. Ruth was the first player to reach that lonely section of Sportsman's Park. "If the bleachers hadn't been there," Les Bell said years later, "I think that ball would have torn down the YMCA building across the street." Appreciating the magnitude of the Babe's feat, fans gave him "the finest ovation that St. Louis has ever given a visiting athlete."

Adding to the Ruth legend was the story involving Johnny Sylvester, a seriously ill 11-year-old from Essex Falls, New Jersey. Sylvester had hoped to attend a World Series game but couldn't because of his illness, which differed from one newspaper account to the other. His father telegraphed a friend in St. Louis and arranged to get two baseballs autographed by several players from both teams. When the balls arrived at the Sylvester home, there reportedly was also a note from Ruth promising to hit a home run for Johnny. The story goes that Johnny listened to the game on the radio, and his condition improved with each of the Babe's homers. The veracity of the story is highly questionable, but it became a staple within the myth surrounding the Bambino.

While Ruth's exploits may have cured Johnny Sylvester, they made Rogers Hornsby positively ill. He ripped the team's miserable pitching effort. "There's only one thing to be said about the game yesterday," he told the *Post-Dispatch*, "and that is that you can't expect to win a game that is as badly pitched as this one was.... Not once was Ruth pitched to properly and that's the story of the game." Ruth wasn't the only one to benefit from faulty pitching. The Yankee lineup, roused by the Babe's power display, raked Cardinal pitchers for 14 hits. To make matters worse, St. Louis hurlers issued ten walks, engineering what the *St. Louis Star* called the "Parade of the Wooden Soldiers." The Cardinal offense had Hoyt on the ropes much of the game. They banged out 14 hits, but the crafty hurler benefited from the cushion provided by his teammates and survived by walking only one and using timely strikeouts to escape several jams.[21]

If the Cardinal clubhouse was like a morgue, the Yankees' clubhouse was understandably more boisterous. Amid the laughing and back-slapping, Ruth started whistling "Bye-Bye Blackbird" and soon the entire team joined in. When someone told Ruth his third home run set a Sportsman's Park record, traveling nearly 500 feet, Babe broke into a wide grin and exclaimed, "Boy, that was a darling." Though the Series was now even at two games apiece, momentum had shifted to the Yankees. With ace pitcher Herb Pennock set to take the mound for Game Five and the team's offensive woes forgotten, Miller Huggins asserted, "I look to see the boys keep the hitting up in the next two or three games. If they do we can't miss winning the championship."[22]

Yet another record crowd of 39,552 customers packed Sportsman's Park to see the pivotal Game Five rematch between Herb Pennock and Bill Sherdel. The Cardinals were without Taylor Douthit because of the shoulder injury suffered in the collision with Chick Hafey the day before. Hornsby was forced to insert Wattie Holm, his final outfielder, in Douthit's place (for some reason no outfielder was signed to take Ray Blades' place on the roster). Despite the loss of Douthit's premier defense and speed at the top of the lineup, St. Louis took a 1–0 lead in the fourth when Bottomley's line drive got through Ruth for a double. He came around to score on Les Bell's single up the middle.

The Redbirds' luck turned in the top of the sixth. William F. Allen of the *Post-Dispatch* blamed the "treacherous, deceitful South Wind, blowing easy fly balls like tricky balloons out of the reach of Cardinal fielders." Herb Pennock led off and lifted a lazy fly ball to leftfield. Chick Hafey broke in on the ball but realized too late that the wind was carrying it over his head. He fell trying to reverse his steps, and what should have been an easy out fell safely for a double. Hafey's vision problems most likely were just as responsible as the wind for the play. Several years later Hafey claimed he "was groping for the ball like a man in a fog" the entire Series. St. Louis nearly nipped the threat in the bud. O'Farrell whipped a throw to Thevenow at second that clearly beat Pennock back to the bag. Thevenow tagged Pennock and umpire George Hildebrand called Pennock out but reversed the call when Thevenow dropped the ball. Earle Combs then drew a walk, and Mark Koenig followed with a base hit to left. Pennock just beat Hafey's throw home to score the tying run. Babe Ruth stepped to the plate with two runners on base and no outs. Sherdel challenged Ruth and won, striking out the home run king. Gehrig walked to load the bases, only to have the wind jinx the Yankees. The dangerous Tony Lazzeri lifted a high drive to rightfield, only to have the wind push the ball back to Billy Southworth, whose back scraped the wall when he made the catch.

The Cardinals regained the lead in the seventh when Les Bell scorched a double down the third base line and scored on Bob O'Farrell's third hit of the day. However, the wind and the baseball gods again turned against the Cardinals in the top of the ninth. Lou Gehrig hit a pop fly behind third base. Thevenow drifted over to make the routine play, but the wind pushed the ball toward the foul line just beyond the shortstop's reach, and Gehrig made it to second base. Lazzeri bunted safely, moving Gehrig to third. Pinch hitter Ben Paschal looped a single to open space in left center to tie the game. Pennock retired the Cardinals in order in the ninth to send the game into extra innings. Mark Koenig lined a single to left to lead off the tenth. Babe Ruth stepped up and to the disbelief of the crowd twice fouled off bunt attempts. Sherdel had Ruth in the hole but uncorked a wild pitch, allowing Koenig to advance. With first base open, Sherdel gave Ruth nothing to hit and Babe trotted to first on the free pass. Bob Meusel bunted successfully, and Tony Lazzeri's sacrifice fly sent Koenig home with the go-ahead run. In the bottom of the frame, Pennock gave up a one-out single to Thevenow but easily retired the next two batters to again best the Cardinals and again hand Sherdel a hard-luck defeat.[23]

The stunned crowd silently filed out of the stadium, in stark contrast to its non-stop cheering up to the bitter end. The Cardinals' clubhouse was in an equally morose mood. A tearful Bill Sherdel was inconsolable despite his teammates' best efforts to lift his spirits. He declared the 3–2 loss the most bitter in his entire career. Rogers Hornsby praised his pitcher but lashed out at the rest of the team and Hafey in particular. "I had a fine bunch of ball players out there this afternoon," he spouted loud enough for everyone to hear. "Back of the greatest pitching possible they slip and skid and hesitate when they should be on their toes all the time, working their heads off."[24]

Both teams rushed to catch trains for the return trip to New York. The Yankees were jubilant. They freely admitted "the baseball gods, if there are any, and the breaks, which all baseball players know there are" allowed them to steal a win. Now they were heading home, only one game away from the title. Another reason they were so giddy is that they wouldn't have to face Sherdel again in the Series. "I can't hit those soft ones," Ruth chimed, "and Sherdel is one fellow who will not give you any kind of a good ball to work on." With their backs to the wall, the Cardinals were fully aware of the daunting task that awaited them. Hornsby held a team meeting as the train sped eastward and backtracked from his stinging criticism after the Game Five loss. He did not chastise the players and offered no alibis for the outcome other than the breaks went against them. Instead, he thanked the squad for its determined work and expressed confidence they would come through in the days ahead.[25]

After the Cardinal train arrived in New York in a then-record 22 hours and 40 minutes, a sunny but cool day limited the Game Six crowd to only 48,615 paying customers, a far cry from the expected 65,000. Miller Huggins played a hunch and chose Bob Shawkey to face the Cards rather than Urban Shocker, who fell to St. Louis and Grover Cleveland Alexander in Game Two. Shawkey had turned in some stellar relief work in Games Two and Three. In 3⅔ innings, not one Cardinal reached base against Shawkey's fastball/curveball repertoire. Before the game, Hornsby called his troops together and told them, "If we don't do it today there ain't no more series.... Go out there and fight your heads off and don't concede a thing. Knock the ball down the pitcher's throat." St. Louis did just that and came out of the gates swinging, proving at the outset that Huggins' hunch was misguided. Wattie Holm, again playing in place of Taylor Douthit, led off the game with a single. Hornsby walked and Jim Bottomley sliced a double down the leftfield line, driving in the first run. Les Bell drove a ball over third baseman "Jumpin' Joe" Dugan's head to plate Hornsby and Bottomley and give St. Louis a three-run lead. St. Louis tacked on another run against Shawkey in the fifth frame when Holm singled home Thevenow.

The Cardinals put the game out of reach when they exploded for five runs in the seventh. Thevenow singled and moved to second when Tony Lazzeri dropped a throw on Alexander's bunt. Holm tried to sacrifice the runners over but forced Thevenow at third. Billy Southworth drove Shawkey's pitch to left center, which Meusel lost in the sun, Alexander scoring on the double. Miller Huggins brought in Urban Shocker to blunt the Redbird attack. Shocker was furious that Huggins had passed him over for Shawkey, and when Huggins made the call to the bullpen, Shocker "gave vent to his feelings" on the telephone. Apparently, his anger affected his pitching. Hornsby greeted him with a two-run single, and two batters later, Les Bell lofted Shocker's offering into the leftfield bleachers. The Cardinals capped the scoring with a run in the ninth on Southworth's triple and Hornsby's RBI groundout. Overall, St. Louis pounded three Yankee pitchers for 13 hits and ten runs. Les Bell had three hits and four RBI's, tying Ruth's World Series record. Holm, Southworth, Bottomley, and Thevenow joined the hit parade with two apiece.

Grover Cleveland Alexander's performance on the mound was not as spectacular as it was in Game Two, but it didn't need to be. The "poor old wreck, the Chicago castoff who was sold down the river at the waiver price" as Graham McNamee described him, bore down when needed and in a workmanlike fashion scattered eight New York hits. His pinpoint control was deadly; only 29 of his 104 total pitches were out of the strike zone. He walked Babe Ruth once, but in his three other trips to the plate, the Yankee slugger failed to get the ball out of the infield. After the ballgame, Alexander said the cold weather was his only worry. "I had no trouble with

Ruth at any time. Of course, I didn't give him a good one to hit. That would have been foolish."[26]

The Yankees were gloomy after the 10–2 trouncing, but Miller Huggins remained confident. "The players are ready for the fight of their lives now," he bristled, "It don't seem possible that we can take two on the chin in a row." And in his syndicated ghost-written column, Babe Ruth warned the Yankees "are strongest when there's something at stake. Tomorrow there will be plenty at stake. Watch us go out and win." The Cardinals' confidence likewise was sky-high. On his way to the clubhouse, Specs Toporcer yelled, "We got 'em on the run. They can't beat us now, not with Haines ready again and the team hitting the way it is." Hornsby was equally optimistic, though he hedged his bet, telling Alexander to be ready the next day in case he was needed in relief. Ol' Pete responded, "All right, Rog. But I'll tell you, I'm not going to warm up in the bullpen. I've got just so many throws left in this arm. I'll take my warmup pitches on the mound." With that, the stage was set for one of the classic showdowns in major league history.[27]

October 10 was dark, dreary, and cold with a steady drizzle. It seemed likely Game Seven would have to be called and played another day. However, Judge Landis called and told the team, "Get your asses out there boys. We're going to play."[28] The dismal weather diminished the crowd again. Only 38,093 gathered in the gloom at Yankee Stadium; yet the overall attendance set a record, besting the previous World Series total by more than 27,000.

In the bottom of the third, Ruth hit a soaring blast into the right centerfield bleachers to give New York a 1–0 lead. That clout, Hornsby insisted later, "was just what was needed to put the scrap and fight into our men." The Cardinals answered in the top of the fourth, assisted by some shoddy Yankee defense. With one out, Jim Bottomley singled to leftfield. Les Bell grounded sharply to Mark Koenig, who fumbled a potential double-play ball for his fourth error of the Series.[29] Chick Hafey blooped a single into short left to load the bases. Bob O'Farrell hit a lazy fly ball to left centerfield. Bob Meusel, who possessed the more powerful throwing arm, called off centerfielder Earle Combs and got in position to make a throw in case Bottomley tried to score. To the disbelief of the stunned crowd, Meusel dropped the ball, allowing Bottomley to score the tying run. Hornsby believed Meusel was so concerned with getting off a good throw that he took his eye off the ball just enough to let it bounce out of his glove. Tommy Thevenow came to bat and once more came through in the clutch. He hit a looping single off the end of his bat to right center to score two more runs.

The Yankees responded with a threat in their half of the inning. Gehrig coaxed a leadoff walk. Lazzeri skied a Haines pitch to deep right centerfield, which Wattie Holm hauled in. Joe Dugan's grounder back to Haines advanced Gehrig to second base. With two outs, catcher Hank Severeid hit a vicious line drive that seemed a sure thing to cut into the Cardinal lead, but Tommy Thevenow leaped high to snare the ball and snuff out the potential rally. Graham McNamee, "the thunder of the gods, the voice of fate, the oracle of the ages," was nearly apoplectic as he described Thevenow's stellar play for his radio audience: "Oh boy! Oh boy! I hope to tell you Thevenow made a catch! Holy cat! Oh what a catch of Severeid's liner. It was 10 feet up if it was an inch, and it started to go by shortstop. Thevenow—I now know, I suspected it before, but I now know that he wears springs in the bottom of his shoes. He went up in the air four feet. He was up so high it took him about 10 seconds to drop! ...there'll never be another catch like that ... the best infield play of the series ... bar none."

New York crept closer in the sixth. After Thevenow ranged far to his left to rob Gehrig of a single and Lazzeri struck out, Joe Dugan singled. Severeid came to bat and this time lined Haines' pitch over Thevenow's head. Rather than playing it safe, leftfielder Chick Hafey tried and failed to make a shoestring catch. The ball got by him, and Dugan raced around the bases to cut St. Louis' lead to 3–2.[30]

Herb Pennock took the mound in relief of starter Waite Hoyt and set the Cardinals down in the top of the fateful seventh inning. Combs led off the bottom of the frame with a single and advanced to second on Koenig's sacrifice. With first base open, Hornsby ordered Haines to walk Ruth intentionally. The Redbird manager's strategy nearly worked. Meusel hit a ground ball to Les Bell, who flipped the ball to Hornsby to force Ruth at second. The Rajah's relay to first, however, was too late to complete the double play. Haines had pitched a courageous game to that point, working in and out of trouble, but after getting two strikes on Lou Gehrig, he suddenly lost his control. He "floated three bad balls up to the plate, and another high one, around [Gehrig's] neck" to load the bases. O'Farrell noticed there was blood on the ball after some of Pops' pitches, and with the hurler's recent bout of wildness, O'Farrell went out to ask what was wrong. Haines had rubbed the skin off his right index finger throwing knuckleballs, making it difficult to spot his most effective pitch. Concerned, O'Farrell called Hornsby and the rest of the infielders to gather around Haines to decide what to do. Pops gamely said he could continue pitching, but Hornsby knew the veteran righthander was done for the day. With the crowd roaring, Hornsby motioned to the Cardinal bullpen in deep leftfield. Flint Rhem and Bill Sherdel were well rested and available, but the St. Louis manager wanted Grover Cleveland Alexander to face the hard-hitting Tony Lazzeri.[31]

Branch Rickey listened to the game from his St. Louis home—at least until his radio stopped working in the fourth inning at which point the frantic general manager rushed over to his next-door neighbor's house to listen to the rest of the game. When he heard Hornsby had brought in Alexander to pitch, he approved, telling his wife, Jane, "Alexander will take it nice and easy and get impatient Lazzeri out."[32]

Nearly every detail of what followed has been debated over the years as the event attained near mythical status. The most contested point focuses on the level of Alexander's sobriety. A persistent story is that Ol' Pete tied one on the night before. Bob O'Farrell believed Alexander didn't intend to drink after his Game Six victory, but "friends" got hold of him and bought multiple drinks. However, Alexander, his wife, Aimee, and Hornsby denied Pete was drunk. Les Bell denounced the story as "a lot of bunk … no man could have done what Alec did if he was drunk or even a little soggy." How Alexander spent his time in the bullpen was also disputed. Many claimed Pete was sleeping off a hangover while Flint Rhem claimed he and Alexander shared a bottle. Bill Sherdel maintained Pete spent most of the game talking to Herb Pennock in the nearby Yankee bullpen.[33]

Even the length of time of Alexander's stroll to the mound has fluctuated. James Harrison of the *New York Times* wrote there was a "breathless pause" as the nearly 40,000 fans "peered anxiously through the gray mist" toward the bullpen. Around the corner of the stands came Alexander in his oversized Cardinal sweater and cap set "rakishly on the corner of his head." He strode across the outfield "like a man who was going nowhere in particular and was in no hurry to get there." Alexander claimed in his ghost-written column that he took his time because he wanted to conserve every bit of energy for the coming battle. After the fact, he related he knew he would be facing an anxious rookie in Lazzeri, and he wanted to let the tension mount.

Hornsby trotted out to meet Alexander to assess the pitcher's condition and to fill him in on the situation. According to Roy Stockton of the *Post-Dispatch*, Hornsby said, "The bases are filled, Alex, but there's two out and Lazzeri's coming up. Do you feel all right?" Alexander replied, "Sure, I feel fine. Three on, eh? Well, there's no place to put Lazzeri, is there, with the sacks all loaded up? I'll just have to give him nothing but a lot of hell, won't I?"[34]

When the veteran hurler got to the mound, he threw a few practice pitches, hitched up his pants, casually scanned the crowd, and then went to work on the Yankee second baseman. Days later, Alexander told Roy Stockton, "Lazzeri was the batter in the pinch and that's the bird I felt sorry for. He had to make a base hit and all I had to do was throw 'em where he couldn't reach 'em." When asked about the signals catcher Bob O'Farrell used to call pitches, Alexander the Great shrugged, "Oh, I don't bother about signs with Old Bob O'Farrell working. He don't pay no attention to me and I don't pay no attention to him…. I just pitch whatever I happen to want to pitch and I know Bob will get 'em all."

The batterymates and Hornsby did discuss how to pitch to Lazzeri, raising another point of contention. O'Farrell recalled they decided to pitch him low and away. Third baseman Les Bell insisted all the Cardinal infielders were on the mound when Alexander said he would start with an inside fastball to the Yankee rookie. Hornsby objected, but Pete replied that if Lazzeri swung at the pitch, he would most likely hit it off the handle or, if he made solid contact, the ball would go foul. Then he would aim for the outside corner with a breaking pitch. Hornsby shrugged and supposedly said, "Who am I to tell you how to pitch?" O'Farrell's account seems the most likely, given that Bell was not actually part of the conversation on the mound. Moreover, it is unlikely Hornsby would allow Alexander, even with his exceptional accuracy, to jeopardize a championship by pitching to Lazzeri's strength.

There's also disagreement regarding the number of pitches Alexander made as well as the sequence of balls and strikes. O'Farrell claims there were three, but most accounts assert there were four. The first was a fastball that Lazzeri took inside for a ball. The second offering was a curveball that caught the outside corner for strike one. Alexander's third pitch was an inside fastball. Lazzeri brought the entire crowd to its feet when he drove a long fly ball down the leftfield line. Except for a well-positioned few, the stomachs of the entire Cardinal team must have sunk as they watched the ball soar toward the seats. Much to their relief, it hooked foul.[35]

Accounts vary about how close Lazzeri's clout came to being a grand slam. Some say it went foul by a matter of inches while others say it strayed a good ten feet. Alexander claimed he knew Lazzeri couldn't do anything but pull the pitch foul. Bob O'Farrell's recollection was a little different. Alexander was supposed to brush Lazzeri back. The pitch, however, was not high and tight enough, and Lazzeri drilled the ball down the line. From his vantage point, O'Farrell knew the ball would be foul, but he used a little body English—a reverse Carlton Fisk maneuver from the 1975 World Series—to help it along just in case. O'Farrell rushed out to the mound and asked, "I thought we were going to pitch him low and outside?" Alexander assured his batterymate, "He'll never get another one like that!" He went into his fluid motion and unleashed a curveball that was low and away. Lazerri swung and missed badly for strike three. This is the only strikeout mentioned on a plaque at baseball's Hall of Fame in Cooperstown. On the way to the dugout, Alexander's teammates hugged him and clapped him on the back, which the well-worn veteran accepted with a wry smile on his face.[36]

Pennock hurled a scoreless eighth, and Alexander did the same. The Cardinals went down in order in the top of the ninth, and Ol' Pete shuffled back to the mound to finish the game. Earle Combs and Mark Koenig both grounded out to third baseman Les Bell, bringing none other than Babe Ruth, the game's most feared hitter, to the plate. Alexander pitched carefully and just missed the corner on a full-count pitch. Frustrated at umpire George Hildebrand's call, Alexander asked what was wrong with the pitch. Hildebrand replied that it missed being a strike by inches. "For that much," Alexander fumed, "you might have given an old sonofagun like me a break." The umpire refused to budge, and Ruth took first with his fourth walk of the game and 11th of the Series. With the dangerous Bob Meusel at bat, Ruth surprised everyone by taking off for second on a steal attempt. Alexander heard the whistle of the ball go by as Bob O'Farrell rifled a perfect throw to Hornsby at second base to easily beat Ruth to the bag. Hornsby caught the ball and held his glove out, allowing Ruth to slide into it for the final out. In his autobiography, Rogers said slapping the tag on Ruth to end the game and win the championship was "my biggest thrill in all baseball."[37]

To Grover Cleveland Alexander, that play was "one of the grandest sights in my life." Beyond his own personal gratification, the epic clashes between Ol' Pete and the Yankees during the 1926 World Series assumed a deeper societal meaning. One study asserts the small-town pitcher from Nebraska was not a part of modernizing America, achieving his greatest fame during an era that was receding into the background. By 1926, he "was an old man on the way down.... He was a rumpled, 'any bar will do' drinker.'" During the World Series, he "stood as an individual, a man out of time, in an era of increasing professionalism, standardization, and mass production." Yet during that one week in October, he recaptured his former magic and temporarily halted the inexorable march of modernity. As he walked off the field, he "gave pastoral America a last champion for the decade."[38]

As for the king of the young, strong, brash, modern Yankees, Ruth absorbed a good deal of criticism for attempting what many considered a dumb, risky play. But others defended his strategic thinking. He told Bob O'Farrell a year later that he felt Alexander had forgotten he was on first and that he could get a good jump to get into scoring position. The way Alexander was pitching, he reasoned, it was better to be able to score on a single base hit because the Yankees would never get two hits in a row.[39]

The Cardinals rushed into the clubhouse to unleash their pent-up joy. They laughed, cheered, and yelled; bats, caps, gloves, and uniform shirts were tossed in the air. Grover Cleveland Alexander received most of the good-natured jostling from his comrades in arms. He pleaded with them, "Have a heart. I've got to pitch again. I haven't retired." Mostly he just grinned during the chaos, silently enjoying his personal and professional redemption. Considered by Cub manager Joe McCarthy a team cancer, Alexander was run out of Chicago only to latch onto a young, pennant-hungry ball club and lead it to a world championship. Doing so, he delivered one of the greatest pitching performances in World Series history. Tommy Thevenow, who batted .417 and made numerous spectacular plays in the field, was also singled out for praise. Hornsby proclaimed, "I want to tell everybody that Tommy Thevenow is the best shortstop in baseball. There are no 'ifs' or 'buts' on this."

Commissioner Landis was one of the first to congratulate Hornsby in the clubhouse, risking a shower (no indication if it was of the alcoholic variety) from the celebrating players. "Was there ever a greater series?" he asked. Yankee president Jacob Ruppert, National League president John Heydler, New York Giants manager John McGraw, and a half dozen other National League luminaries followed the commissioner to offer their congratulations to the Rajah.[40] Conspicuous by his absence was Sam Breadon.

Hornsby tagged Babe Ruth to end the series at 3:20 p.m. Central Standard Time. At that moment in St. Louis, there was a "city-wide detonation. It was as if dynamite had been planted in a hundred scattered spots and all touched off at the same instant." During the boisterous partying, reported the *St. Louis Star*, Olive Street "became Crazy Canyon, and Washington avenue was worse." The deafening noise enveloped the entire city for nine hours. Thirty men were taken to the hospital "in a more or less alcoholic condition," and 30 more were treated for injuries from auto accidents. Unfortunately, two lives were lost during the celebrations. One boy died

Rogers Hornsby tagging Babe Ruth out at second base to win the World Series. This was the proudest moment of Hornsby's illustrious baseball career (National Baseball Hall of Fame and Museum, Cooperstown, NY).

after he was hit by a car, and a 17-year-old died from a fractured skull. He was clinging to the running board of a sedan when he was knocked off by a passing streetcar.[41]

The celebration among Branch Rickey's family was more muted. Once the game ended, the architect of the newly crowned world champions shouted, "What a corking victory!" and embraced Jane. After reflecting on the personal and professional implications of the Cardinal victory, Branch told his neighbor, "Gene, you can't possibly realize what this means to me ... to the club. Not only vindication of all I've dreamed of and fought for, but it means capital to reinvest and spend for expansion and scouting and large training camps and more teams for developing the finest players."[42]

Cardinal fans were more interested in celebrating the here and now rather than looking down the road, and they had one more celebration in store for their conquering heroes at Sportsman's Park on Tuesday, October 12. Several players, travel weary and drained from the strain of the World Series, wanted to avoid the rigors of yet another chaotic demonstration of the fans' affection. They departed directly for their homes from New York or other points along the route west. Rogers Hornsby accompanied the remaining 15 players to St. Louis, though he planned to skip the festivities and leave for Texas to attend his mother's funeral. The reception committee, led by City Register Jack Grosse, feared that a repeat of the overly exuberant scene from the previous week might result in harm to the players, so they hoped to

Fans rejoicing in downtown St. Louis after the Cardinals clinched the World Series title (St. Louis Cardinals Hall of Fame and Museum).

have them escorted as inconspicuously as possible to their homes and then taken to Sportsman's Park later that evening. Those hopes were quickly dashed when another horde of adoring fans greeted the train as it pulled into Union Station at 5:10 p.m. Hornsby waited while the rest of the squad got off the train, hoping the crowd would thin out before he boarded a train bound for Texas. But that hope was forlorn. When he disembarked, a throng of admirers followed him as he dodged across tracks and through coaches of standing trains. Finally, the visibly irritated and nervous Hornsby got to the waiting train and slumped into a compartment.

As their manager made his mad dash to safety, most of the other Cardinal players refused to participate in any festivities and fought their way through the crowd on their way to their homes or hotel rooms. The reception committee managed to convince Grover Cleveland Alexander and Billy Southworth to join them at a banquet held at the Buckingham Hotel. With only two guests of honor, the caterers distributed the surplus food to the police detailed to guard the players, who relished the unexpected bounty. Southworth agreed to help the reception committee shore up the meager number of players who would attend the celebration that evening. Within an hour, he persuaded Tommy Thevenow, Bob O'Farrell, Jim Bottomley, Ray Blades, Victor Keen, Art Reinhart, Wattie Holm, and Coach Otto Williams to join the party.

The *St. Louis Star* called what ensued "the most unique celebration in the history of baseball." The crowd began gathering outside the stadium as early as 4:00 p.m. Thousands were in line when the gates opened two hours later. By 8:00, some 30,000 to 40,000 fans—men and women, young and old—filled the grandstand and pavilion, and a sizable crowd occupied the darkened bleachers in leftfield. The only light in that area was the glow from their cigarettes. While the fans awaited the players' arrival, they amused themselves by singing "Hail, Hail, the Gang's All Here" and other popular ditties before they immersed themselves in a cauldron of noise, which reached ear-splitting levels when the Cardinals' contingent appeared at 8:15.

At that moment, all hell broke loose, like a rock concert run amok. Thousands of feverish fans swarmed over the grandstand railings onto the field, despite the frantic efforts of 200 policemen to hold them back. The swirling mob surrounded the players as they struggled to reach the portable bandstand erected near the pitcher's mound. Several fans eluded police to climb upon the stand to pose with the players, sparking fears the rickety structure might collapse. Two young women crowded around Alexander, who "finally appeased their curiosity by bestowing kisses on them, while the crowd howled its approval." Police Chief Gerk and Jack Grosse appealed to the crowd to move back, but their voices were completely drowned out in the din. Southworth and Thevenow were pushed to the microphone to make some remarks. A *Post-Dispatch* reporter stood six inches away from Southworth and could not hear a word he said. After almost an hour of the cacophonous confusion, Mayor Miller turned off the bandstand lights for five minutes. The players slipped away in the darkness, and when the lights came back on, the crowd was told that the players had left and the celebration was over. The sheepish crowd filed toward the exits, but once out on Grand Boulevard, the more diehard fans resumed their merry making for several hours. Alexander told the *Globe-Democrat*, "I'm glad to be home, glad to have been one of those honored by such a demonstration. I lost my hat and my coat getting out of the park, but it was worth it."[43]

Once the initial uproar subsided, the players scattered to their winter dwellings to spend their $5,594.50 winners' shares and enjoy (or endure) being wined and dined at a stream of banquets in their honor. However, the team and its fans could not bask in the glow of a World Series championship for long. Long-simmering animosities erupted during the offseason and rocked the baseball world to its core.

Chapter 12

A Messy Divorce, October–December 1926

Reveling in a World Series championship, St. Louisans could be excused for believing the future looked rosy. Dr. Ernest Alexanderson, chief engineer with General Electric and the Radio Corporation of America, provided an intriguing glimpse into the future at a mid–December gathering of the St. Louis section of the American Institute of Electrical Engineers. He described a projector in G.E.'s Schenectady, New York, laboratory that could transmit moving images onto a screen. The new contraption, television, Dr. Alexanderson said, "is regarded by many scientists as absurd and impossible. But the same was said not so many years ago of trans–Atlantic telephony, which now is a practical reality." The St. Louis Star gushed, "Imagine, if you can, a radio receiving set which will transmit to a screen in your home pictures of objects in motion at that very moment hundreds of miles away! What a boon to the baseball fan! He would be able not only to hear the returns of world series games, but see the players in action in his home." The possibilities seemed endless the Star mused. "Business affairs could be transacted over the ether, with the principals in full sight of each other, though they actually may be 1,000 miles apart. Perhaps it may even be possible for traveling husbands to tune into their home stations and keep a watchful eye on fickle wives." Dr. Alexanderson could not predict when television would be commercially viable, but he was confident the day wasn't too far off. The people of St. Louis, however, would have to wait two more decades before the city's first commercial television station, KSD-TV, went into operation.[1]

Even St. Louis' underworld gave the city cause for hope. After a ten-month feud in which more than a dozen was killed and 14 more wounded, the Cuckoo gang and their Italian rivals agreed to a truce in late November. Mutual acquaintances from New York, Chicago, and Detroit brought representatives from the warring factions together for a three-day gathering at the St. Louis Hotel. The two sides apparently decided it was more profitable, going into the holiday season, to stop the attacks and resolve their differences concerning extortion payments from Italian merchants and Cuckoo interference in the Italians' bootlegging operations. A leader of the Italian gang informed Chief of Detectives Robert Kaiser about the agreement. Kaiser was happy but doubtful the peace would hold and told the

12. A Messy Divorce, October–December 1926   169

Italian the police would be ready. "We have just bought two gas guns costing $700 each, with which to handle gangsters. We are going to be ready for you fellows and we will kill every gangster who thinks he can rule St. Louis." In response, the Italian smiled and said, "Chief, I'll give you $1,000 for one of those guns." Kaiser and the police were spared from having to use the newly purchased guns as the truce held for several months until hostilities resumed in June 1927.[2]

Within the Cardinal ranks, however, the immediate future was not so serene. As early as the World Series, the *St. Louis Star* reported rampant speculation among fans regarding Hornsby's status for 1927. "Not that anything untoward is in the offing," the *Star* surmised, but Hornsby's contract was set to expire at the end of next season and fans wondered "what may happen next spring when Hornsby has his little talk about finances for 1927 and other years." James Gould of the *Star* added fuel to the fire before Game Six when he revealed there was dissension among the team's "higher-ups." Some, he noted, were given or taking credit for the team's success. Gould gave Branch Rickey credit for accumulating much of the talent on the roster, but to "just one man—and one man only—should be given the palm for bringing the pennant to St. Louis. His name is Rogers Hornsby." The Texan's spirit, sacrifice for the good of the team, and handling of his players turned the tide. "It is not too much to say," Gould concluded, "that without Hornsby—the manager, and not so much the player, this year—the Cardinals would not have won the 1926 flag."[3]

Hornsby didn't have the chance to enjoy the accolades. On the train back to St. Louis—barely 24 hours after capturing the city's first championship in 38 years—Sam Breadon called Bill Killefer into his private car and asked if he would consider managing the Cardinals in 1927. The Rajah's loyal friend and coach flatly refused the offer and informed Hornsby. Already stewing over the argument about exhibition games during the season and Breadon's refusal to visit the Cardinal clubhouse to congratulate him and the team for clinching the World Series, the Texan's festering resentment surely must have erupted into outright fury. He did not, however, confront the team owner on that return trip. Perhaps Hornsby was caught off guard by the swiftness of Breadon's efforts to oust him as manager or he was too fixated on getting back to Texas for his beloved mother's funeral. In either case, he skipped the post–World Series celebration in St. Louis and immediately headed home. When his mother was laid to rest, Rogers' normally stoic demeanor crumbled and gave way to unabashed grief, tears flowing freely.

On the long train ride back to St. Louis, the emotionally exhausted Hornsby undoubtedly pondered his future. He had to be satisfied with his accomplishments. With six batting titles, Hornsby was the most feared slugger in the National League, and he had just led the Cardinals to a championship. St. Louis baseball fans adored him, and as the team's second largest stockholder, he felt secure he would finish his career with the Cardinals, despite Breadon's overture to Killefer. But unresolved issues gnawed at him. Above all, there was his contract situation. When Breadon hired him to lead the team the year before, Rogers did not ask for a pay increase on his $30,000 contract, believing he had to prove himself as manager before reaping any financial rewards. Now that he had piloted the Cardinals to the title, he was determined to be fairly compensated for his double-duty work. And as the second largest stockholder, Hornsby also wanted to be added to the team's business operations at Branch Rickey's expense. This move would protect his position with the club while simultaneously eliminating Rickey's interference in on-field affairs, an accusation Rickey strongly denied.[4]

Sam Breadon was also thinking of the future and had his own grudges to address. He still smarted from Hornsby's verbal thrashing in September, and he resolutely vowed that he would show his manager who was really in charge. After reaching St. Louis, Sam left immediately for a six-week stay in Florida. Though he was supposed to be on vacation, he also conducted some business. In late October, he announced he had selected Avon Park for the next Cardinals spring training site. The city's central location as well as guarantees of $15,000 and the opportunity to play on a new field in a 2,200-seat stadium no doubt swayed Breadon's decision but wresting a modicum of power away from Hornsby was likely another factor.

Breadon stewed over other issues. While most Cardinal players respected Hornsby's grit as a player and his laissez-faire policies as manager, not everyone was enamored with his biting criticisms of their play. One newspaper account, for example, concerned Taylor Douthit, who had emerged as a dangerous leadoff hitter and ball-hawking centerfielder. Hornsby constantly gave the rookie instruction or chastised him for on-field mistakes, making Douthit feel as if he was being persecuted. Chick Hafey, who received more than his fair share of Hornsby's verbal abuse, also seemed to chafe under the manager's direction. Lastly, in August, Billy Southworth had settled a player feud that was dividing the team into two camps, though the exact nature of the discord was not revealed. The grumbling that went on in the clubhouse during the season was enough to make Breadon think Hornsby was losing control of the ball club.[5]

The Rajah's gambling was another problem. Breadon may have been aware of rumors that Hornsby had expanded his betting to include baseball and that he had either won $100,000 in September betting on the ponies and baseball games or suffered such steep losses that St. Louis bookies refused to take his bets unless he paid cash. It was also said that he gave away the car adoring fans gifted him to a bookie to pay off a gambling debt. There were even allegations that other Cardinal players were placing bets on the pennant race, raising suspicions that the Reds and Phillies had eased up against St. Louis in several games in September.[6]

At roughly the same time Breadon made his Avon Park decision, New York newspapers resurrected rumors that Hornsby would be traded to the Giants for Frankie Frisch. It was well known Giants manager John McGraw had long coveted Hornsby, but McGraw had consistently refused to include Frisch as part of any swap. With the mid-season squabbling between McGraw and his star infielder, New

York sportswriters believed the Giants were now open to dealing Frisch. The rumors gained even more traction as details about Hornsby's discontent with Breadon and Rickey emerged. *Globe-Democrat* sports editor Glen Wallar and the *Sporting News* acknowledged the difficulties between Breadon, Rickey, and Hornsby but refused to give the rumors any credence. With St. Louis having just won a World Series, the *Sporting News* concluded, Hornsby's popularity was at its peak and a trade "would prove the death knell of the St. Louis National League team."[7] For his part, Hornsby denied any knowledge of an impending deal and asserted he did not expect any trade to be made, nor did he want to leave St. Louis. Despite the friction, the *Sporting News* believed a Hornsby-Frisch swap was "about as imminent as the millennium. But it makes a roaring fire in the Hot Stove League."[8]

The situation remained in limbo throughout November. Hornsby reiterated his desire to remain in St. Louis and whether he did so was a matter for he and Breadon to discuss in private. However, he added, there "are certain things about the club that I want to take up with Mr. Breadon. I have invested heavily in the club. I am the second largest stockholder, Mr. Breadon being the only man who owns more stock than I do. Naturally having invested financially to such an extent, I am interested in protecting my investment." From Florida, Breadon responded, "Hornsby is logical and fair and I am confident that everything will be arranged to the satisfaction of all parties concerned when I return to St. Louis early in December. I want Rogers to continue to manage the team."[9]

The two held a brief, cordial meeting on December 2, though it resolved nothing. They met again on December 6, and Hornsby informed Sam he wanted his current player-only contract, which had one year remaining, torn up and a new three-year contract that compensated him for his dual role. Breadon countered that such a deal was beyond the club's financial capabilities and instead offered a one-year contract. Hornsby responded he wouldn't consider anything less than three years. Both sides contended that the length of Hornsby's contract was the only topic of discussion and that no specific salary figures were mentioned, though the press guessed Hornsby wanted something in the range of $50,000 per year. Nor was anything said about Hornsby being named vice-president or about Breadon's or Rickey's interference with the Rajah's managerial duties. The meeting ended with both sides digging in their heels, and Breadon declared there would be no further conferences until after the annual National League meeting in New York on December 14.[10]

Breadon was adamant in his desire to unload his superstar second baseman and years later admitted he was afraid Hornsby would accept his offer for a one-year deal! Despite his own difficulties with the irascible Texan, Rickey tried to smooth things over, urging Breadon, "If you two can work something out, I can handle Hornsby." But Sam couldn't be dissuaded. When he arrived in New York, he met with Giants owner Charles Stoneham and manager John McGraw and negotiated a tentative deal in case negotiations with Hornsby fizzled. McGraw recounted that Breadon initially wanted Frankie Frisch and future Hall of Famer Bill Terry for

Hornsby, but the Giants' manager refused to include both, so Breadon said he would take a pitcher instead of Terry. Once the league meetings got underway, Breadon repeated his managerial offer to Bill Killefer, who told Breadon, "There is not enough money in the world to make me take the job that Rogers Hornsby held last year." When the press broke the news, Breadon initially denied an offer had been made but later recanted and admitted he approached Killefer "to be prepared for any eventuality." Later, Sam disingenuously denied that a trade for Hornsby was in the works. "I realize that Hornsby is a great asset," Sam intoned, "and I still expect everything to be arranged to the satisfaction of all concerned." Even National League president John Heydler wasn't excited about the rift between the league's top player and the Cardinals. He met with Breadon about the situation, though nothing came of the brief exchange.[11]

Breadon was even more adamant when he reached Chicago for the joint major league meeting. "This talk about Hornsby being traded to another club is a lot of bunk," he raged. "While we haven't agreed as yet on terms of a contract, you can bet on seeing Hornsby as the manager of our club."[12]

The Breadon-Hornsby meeting scheduled for Monday, December 20, took on all the hallmarks of a final, knock-down, drag-out showdown. Roy Stockton argued both sides had made mistakes and needed to make concessions, but given the intransigence of the parties involved, that was unlikely. The big issue, Stockton wrote, is if "St. Louis is to be put in danger of being thrust back into the also-ran class." The controversy had already cost the team. Bill Killefer, much to the irritation of Sam Breadon, agreed to take a coaching position with the Browns. If Hornsby had been signed to a contract two weeks earlier, Killefer would not have considered leaving the Cardinals. He, however, did not want to be swept up in the animosity between Hornsby and Breadon and could not afford to wait until the issue was finally resolved. Despite losing such a key contributor to the team's success, Stockton held out hope that it wasn't "too late to prevent other damage from being done."[13]

Branch Rickey could have been part of that "other damage." He was in his office with future National League president Warren Giles, who at the time was president of the Cardinals' minor league club in Syracuse, when Breadon and Hornsby met behind closed doors. According to the *Sporting News*, it was a meeting that "consumed but 15 torrid minutes." Rickey heard the angry voices coming from Breadon's office and told Giles, "My fate could be settled right now." Hornsby did most of the talking. He once again asserted a multi-year contract was fair considering he had led the team to a championship without any bump in pay. Breadon retorted that the dividends the manager would receive from the improved value of his Cardinal stock constituted a bonus. Hornsby dismissed that line of reasoning, declaring he assumed a certain amount of risk when purchasing the shares of stock but took the chance because he was confident of making good as the team's manager. Any profit he made from the stock was completely separate from the contract negotiations. Breadon again offered a one-year $50,000 deal, the richest salary in National

League history, then insisted the contract include a clause in which Hornsby promised to stop his rampant gambling and association with known bookmakers. At that, Hornsby erupted and exclaimed his betting was "nobody's damn business." He demanded to be traded if a deal couldn't be reached.[14]

When the negotiations reached that impasse, Hornsby stormed out of Breadon's office and slammed the door behind him. Sam poured himself a drink and tried to call Charles Stoneham in New York. It took several hours before the Giants' owner could be reached, but Breadon said, "You've wanted Hornsby for some time. You can have him now for Frisch and [pitcher Jimmy] Ring." Sam pressed Stoneham for a decision, not giving him time to consult with McGraw, and the deal was done. Breadon then called Hornsby at home, tersely told him he'd been traded, and then abruptly hung up.[15] Hornsby told sportswriter James Gould, "My whole baseball world had crumbled." Though rumors of a deal had circulated for weeks, Hornsby said the only inkling he had that a trade was possible came at the end of the meeting when Breadon approached him and shook his "rather unwilling hand and said: 'Well, good-by. Good luck to you.'" Rogers responded, "The same to you."[16]

News of the first true blockbuster deal in Major League Baseball history stunned all of St. Louis. Breadon was fully aware of the storm that was coming. He told the *Sporting News*, "I expect to catch hell for the next few months. Yes sir, I'm in for it—I'm going to get the devil proper!" He was right, but the extent and vehemence of the backlash shocked him. Mark Steinberg, a member of the team's board of directors, called the deal an "insult to the fans of St. Louis and to the members of the board of directors, who were not consulted before the deal." A *Post-Dispatch* editorial skewered the trade because all St. Louis received was "a fading second baseman and an aging pitcher." The deal once more showed baseball fans that "what they regard as a rosily romantic sport is just hard-boiled business to the heroes who engage in it." Neither Breadon nor Hornsby exhibited "one glimmer of love of the game or evidence of willingness to make sacrifices in the name of sportsmanship and sentiment. How baseball retains its popularity in the face of all the sordid and disagreeable happenings which have disfigured it in the last few years is a subject of wonder."[17]

Fans and sportswriters accused Breadon of selling out to the Giants, and the *Star*'s James Gould vowed never to cover another Cardinals game at Sportsman's Park, a promise he kept for nearly ten years. The day after the trade was announced, Breadon walked into the Hotel Jefferson for lunch. He remembered it as "the worst moment of my life. No one said a word to me. Friends I had known for years turned their back on me. I ate alone—and in silence." The St. Louis Chamber of Commerce telegraphed Commissioner Landis that the swap was "a terrible blow" and would "have a disastrous effect upon the loyalty of baseball fans and will injure the game immensely." The Chamber appealed to Landis to negate the deal and settle the dispute between Hornsby and Breadon. The Commissioner, however, declined to act because changing managers was a team and not a league matter. Landis said that if he intervened in one case, he'd have to get involved in all of them. Irate fans threatened to boycott Breadon's auto dealership and decorated his home and office with black crepe paper. He received several death threats and so many abusive phone calls at home that he had his phone disconnected.[18]

Breadon stood his ground and blamed a "small group of flatterers and fair weather friends, who gave Rogers Hornsby too big an opinion of himself" for the trade. Because of these "would-be personal managers," said Breadon, Hornsby had "grown to think that he is bigger than the Cardinals, or anyone in the club." For some time, the Rajah had made comments about Branch Rickey and upper management in general that rankled Breadon, but Sam said nothing because he so desperately wanted to win the pennant. On the train to St. Louis after the World Series, Breadon told Hornsby that he wanted to see a change in attitude, but by December, Sam saw no evidence of that. The contract squabble was simply the last straw. "No matter how good a ball player may be, or a manager," Breadon insisted, "he must take orders and do his part toward keeping harmony in the organization." "We had a good baseball team with Hornsby," Sam added, "and we will have a good one without him."[19]

The day after the stunning trade, Commissioner Landis helped divert the attention of baseball fans nationwide when he released information pertaining to a game-fixing scandal involving two baseball immortals—Ty Cobb and Tris Speaker. Dutch Leonard, a former Detroit pitcher blamed the two superstar players for railroading him out of major league baseball in 1925. From his California farm, Leonard nursed a bitter grudge against Cobb and Speaker and made his move during the 1926 season to exact his revenge. Dutch turned over letters to American League president Ban Johnson that purportedly implicated the two superstars in a scheme to throw a Detroit–Cleveland game late in the 1919 season.

Fearing Leonard would go public with the explosive news and spark a repeat of the Black Sox scandal, Johnson and Tigers owner Frank Navin arranged to buy the pitcher's silence. Johnson kept the letters under his hat until a secret meeting with American League owners on September 9. The owners voted to forward the damning letters to Commissioner Landis. Johnson then met secretly with Cobb and Speaker and divulged all he knew. Despite their protestations of innocence, Johnson told both they were through as players and should retire rather than irreparably damaging their reputations, and they grudgingly complied. Johnson thought the matter was closed, but Landis conducted his own investigation, culminating with a formal hearing on December 20. Cobb and Speaker again proclaimed their innocence and demanded that Landis release all the documents and testimony to the public, which the Commissioner did on December 21. The bombshell revelation made headlines across the country. Landis exploited the situation to exact some revenge in his power struggle with bitter rival Ban Johnson. Weeks after the public disclosure, Landis exonerated both ballplayers and reinstated them to active status.[20]

While tongues wagged during the Cobb–Speaker affair, Sam Breadon tried

12. A Messy Divorce, October–December 1926

to calm some of the fans' outrage over the Hornsby trade. A week after the deal, Breadon named Bob O'Farrell the new player-manager. O'Farrell was well liked by Cardinal players and rooters, and his brilliant play behind the plate in 1926 earned him the National League's Most Valuable Player award weeks earlier, the first ever by a catcher. Though the hiring was a popular move, many fans refused to forgive Breadon for the breakup with Hornsby and held it against him for decades. Sam even considered selling the team after the 1934 season because, according to John Wray of the *Post-Dispatch*, he still felt like "something of a pariah in his own baseball bailiwick."[21]

Epilogue:
The Brain Trust Revisited

Hornsby's trade to the Giants did not sever his tangled connections to St. Louis. The most consequential was the fact that he owned 1,167 shares of stock in the Cardinals while he was the property of another team. National League president John Heydler viewed the situation as an obvious conflict of interest and said Hornsby couldn't play for the Giants as long as he held onto the shares. The Rajah had no qualms about selling them, but he felt he was entitled to a big payday and was determined to wring every possible dollar from Sam Breadon in the transaction. Hornsby had purchased the stock at $43 per share in 1925. Immediately after St. Louis won the World Series, Hornsby estimated his shares were worth anywhere from $300 to $600 each, but by the time negotiations began, he asked for what he thought was a reasonable $105 per share.

Breadon refused and countered with an offer of $85. Bitterness between the two prevented a settlement, and the affair dragged on through spring training. Hornsby went about his business with his new team seemingly unaffected by the ongoing wrangling. Heydler, however, was anxious to resolve the problem before the 1927 season started. The Giants went so far as to threaten to obtain a court injunction to stop the National League from enforcing Heydler's ruling.

Anxious to avoid a messy legal squabble, a frustrated Heydler convened a meeting of National League representatives on April 8 in Pittsburgh. He told the gathering that he hoped an amicable agreement would have been easy but Hornsby had hired a lawyer and "instead of the thing becoming better, it has grown steadily so bad, that with all the efforts I have made over the long distance, personally and otherwise, trying to bring about a settlement, I have come to this time practically to report that nothing so far has been done." For his part, Sam Breadon resolutely refused to pay the Rajah's demands. "I might add to this," he continued, "that Hornsby is absolutely dead-broke, hasn't a dime, owes thousands of dollars in St. Louis and he needs money badly."[1]

During the eight-hour session, the club officials finally convinced Breadon to agree to a price of $100 per share for Hornsby's holdings. The Rajah, however, rejected the offer and held firm at $105. League representatives adjourned after voting 7–1 to uphold Heydler's ruling barring Hornsby from playing for New York. The crisis was resolved the following morning when Hornsby and Heydler met with Giants owner Charles Stoneham and John McGraw in New York. Rogers agreed to sell his stock for $100,000 plus $12,000 to cover legal expenses. Breadon paid $86,000 of that total, while the seven other National League clubs chipped in $2,000 apiece and the Giants covered the legal costs. "I am glad it is over," Hornsby chirped, "I can now put my mind on the game, and I look forward to a great season."[2]

While this scenario resulted in a windfall for Hornsby, financial matters other than baseball occupied his mind and pocketbook. He was being sued by his first wife's former attorney for unpaid fees incurred during Rogers' messy divorce proceedings dating back to 1923, and he still owed the bank some $22,000 plus interest on the money he borrowed to purchase Cardinals stock in 1925. To top things off, Kentucky bookmaker Frank Moore filed a lawsuit in January 1927, claiming Hornsby owed him more than $70,000 for bets he placed on Rogers' behalf in January and February 1926 and for personal loans Moore made to Hornsby and his wife, Jeannette. Moore met Hornsby in Cincinnati in May 1925, and the two became close friends. According to the bookie, Hornsby visited him any time the Cardinals were in Cincinnati and began calling him to place bets whenever the Cardinals were on the road. Hornsby had two phones installed in his St. Louis home so that Jeannette could also get in on the action. Moore and his wife often traveled to St. Louis for visits, and Hornsby invited the couple to spring training in 1926, going so far as to pay the Moore's hotel expenses on those occasions.

Moore painted a dire portrait of Rogers' gambling problem. He said Hornsby frittered away his entire 1926 salary in one month and that he placed bets every day. Hornsby denied he owed the bookie a dime and swore he had never made bets through him. Rogers did admit, however, that he had received racing "tips" from Moore. With spring training looming, the judge overseeing the suit delayed proceedings until the fall term. In the end, a Missouri jury did not find Hornsby liable for any debts to Moore, but the Rajah's admission concerning out-of-control gambling certainly tarnished his reputation.[3]

Though the irritable Texan changed uniforms, he didn't change his stripes. His truculent feuding with teammates and baseball management continued, which explains his nomadic major league existence after he left the Cardinals. In 1927, John McGraw named Hornsby team captain, and most baseball aficionados expected he would succeed McGraw as manager. But Hornsby's repeated clashes with several Giants players and owner Charles Stoneham muddied those plans. According to a New York newspaper, eight players signed a petition demanding Stoneham get rid of Hornsby. Much to their relief, Stoneham did just that and shipped Hornsby to the Boston Braves. It didn't take long for Rogers to wear out his welcome there, before he was traded to the Cubs prior to the 1929 season. In Chicago, he enjoyed a spectacular campaign, leading the Cubs to the National League pennant before they fell to the Philadelphia Athletics in the World Series.

That was essentially his last hurrah. A bone spur in his heel and a broken ankle ruined his 1930 season. Rumors that Hornsby was at odds with manager Joe McCarthy and several Cubs teammates added to his misery. With the Cubs only 2½ games behind St. Louis, owner William Wrigley made a surprising move. Believing McCarthy had lost control of his players, Wrigley named Hornsby manager for the remaining four games and going into the 1931 season. Rogers personally had a productive year in 1931—batting .331 with 94 RBIs—and the team fought valiantly despite a good deal of grumbling about Hornsby's training rules and managerial criticisms. Yet the Cubs finished third, 17 games behind pennant-winning St. Louis. The following season, the Cubs were barely hovering over the .500 mark in early August, when team president William K. Veeck abruptly dismissed Hornsby as manager.

The two had squabbled recently over the handling of the team, and Rogers' gambling again raised its ugly head. For the past three seasons, Hornsby had borrowed considerable sums of money from several Cubs players to cover gambling losses. With Rogers relieved of his duties, Veeck worked out an installment plan for Hornsby to repay his debts from the money the Cubs still owed on his contract. Commissioner Landis investigated the matter. Hornsby and other Cubs players denied the borrowed money was used for gambling nor were they involved in a horseracing pool. A skeptical Landis decided not to press the issue but complained to J.G. Taylor Spink of the *Sporting News* that Hornsby's "betting has gotten him into one scrape after another, cost him a fortune and several jobs, and still he hasn't enough sense to stop it." Included in the losses his betting cost him was a share of the 1932 World Series money. With Charlie Grimm installed as the new manager, the Cubs caught fire and captured the National League pennant. Prior to the start of the World Series, the Cubs' players met to decide how to apportion their share of the series proceeds. They voted to give Hornsby nothing.[4]

After the bitter and ignominious parting in Chicago, Rogers made a surprising return to the Cardinals for the 1933 season. Years later, Branch Rickey wrote he took Hornsby back because his "condition morally, socially and financially at that time was bad, very bad. The boy really needed a friend." Sam Breadon agreed to take back his former sparring partner for less sentimental reasons, believing Hornsby's bat could help the team in the upcoming season. The experiment lasted 46 games. Though Rogers did well in a pinch-hitting role, Rickey waived the aging ballplayer so that he might catch on as manager of the Browns. But, as author Mike Mitchell wrote in *Mr. Rickey's Redbirds*, Hornsby's years with the Browns "followed a familiar arc; he played sparingly, managed controversially, and was fired abruptly when his betting behavior became an issue too large to ignore."[5]

In contrast, Branch Rickey and Sam Breadon maintained their ambivalent relationship while the arc for the Cardinals after the Hornsby trade continued its upward trajectory. Despite down years from several starters and key injuries to others, the Redbirds won three more games in 1927 than during the previous championship season yet finished second to Pittsburgh, a scant 1½ games behind. Frankie Frisch put together a spectacular campaign and made Breadon look like a genius.

The "Fordham Flash" hit .337, scored 112 runs, and stole a league-leading 48 bases. He also led all National League second basemen in fielding percentage, chances, putouts, assists, and double plays. Jim Bottomley slugged his way to a .303 average, 15 triples, 19 home runs and 124 runs batted in, while Chick Hafey, who underwent off-season surgery for his sinus problem, blossomed with a .329 average and 18 home runs in only 346 at bats.

The mound crew relied on the stalwart pitching of Jesse Haines, Grover Cleveland Alexander, and Bill Sherdel, who won 24, 21, and 17 games respectively. Beyond those three, however, the pitching staff was unimpressive. Jimmy Ring, the other piece of the Hornsby trade, failed to win a single game for St. Louis. Flint Rhem's production slipped to ten wins and a 4.41 earned run average. Art Reinhart slumped to win only five games, and Vic Keen won twice before his career essentially ended in June, when he hit Pirates shortstop Glenn Wright in the face with a pitch. The high-strung, distraught pitcher rushed to the prostrate Wright and tried to help him but was so agitated that teammates grabbed him and took him to the dugout. Wright was unconscious for 32 hours but was back in the lineup after six weeks. Though greatly relieved he didn't seriously hurt Wright, Vic, according to the Pirate shortstop, "was finished. He wasn't much good after that."[6]

On the offensive side, Ray Blades was never the same dynamic ball player after he injured his knee during the 1926 season. In December, he underwent surgery on the badly torn ligaments, but the operation robbed him of his speed and power. He played in only 61 games, and though his batting average was a productive .317, he hit a mere two home runs and stole only three bases. Les Bell's production likewise declined precipitously due to a shoulder injury; he hit .259, nine home runs and 65 RBIs. Additionally, Taylor Douthit had a subpar season. His batting average dropped more than 40 points, and he stole only six bases. Bob O'Farrell suffered with shoulder and thumb ailments during the season, limiting him to 61 games. Even more devastating, Tommy Thevenow fractured his ankle sliding into second base in June. O'Farrell believed the Cardinals' inability to find an effective replacement cost St. Louis a second consecutive pennant.[7]

Though the Redbirds just missed returning to the World Series, Frisch's outstanding performance vindicated Breadon's trade of Hornsby. Emboldened, the Cardinal owner was never again "afraid to dispose of a player, regardless of his ability or popularity." "I knew." he related, "after that year that what the fans want is a winner, and that a popular player is quickly forgotten by one who is equally popular."[8]

Breadon also learned not to be afraid to change managers. Despite the Cards' near-miss in the standings, Breadon fired Bob O'Farrell as manager and replaced him with assistant coach and former Pirates manager Bill McKechnie. Breadon blamed O'Farrell's double duties as catcher and manager for the injuries that short circuited his season and the team's pennant hopes. "To spoil a great catcher like O'Farrell," Breadon lamented, "is an expensive way of obtaining a manager and for that reason, after a conference with Bob, I decided to make a change." Breadon and

Branch Rickey must have felt O'Farrell was so spoiled that they traded him to the Giants in 1928. O'Farrell's removal was just one part of a managerial merry-go-round (six managers in a six-year stretch!) that would have made George Steinbrenner proud. Even with the mayhem of a revolving door of on-field leaders, the Cardinals capitalized on its bountiful farm system to continue its magic, winning four pennants and two Worlds Series during that span.[9]

In the late 1930s, however, several factors strained the relationship between Breadon and Rickey, the maestro who orchestrated the farm system, to the breaking point. Sam sold his automobile business and devoted all his time to the Cardinals. Determined to expand his imprint on the club, he dismissed several Rickey hires, splitting the organization into two camps. Furthermore, in 1938, Commissioner Landis finally clamped down on what he considered unethical activities within Rickey's farm system and "freed" 74 Cardinal minor leaguers. Sam's meek acceptance of Landis' decision stung Rickey, who felt he and his precious system deserved a more forceful defense from the owner.

Breadon's penny pinching further complicated matters. He instituted wage cuts for all front office personnel and, after the Cardinals endured a pennant drought of seven years from 1935 to 1941, Breadon wondered if Rickey was worth his hefty salary. The tension got to the point that Rickey told Breadon, "Sam, I will dig ditches at a dollar a day rather than work for you one minute beyond the expiration of my contract." Breadon beat Branch to the punch. Sam told the board of directors, including Rickey, at a February 1941 meeting that he would not renew Rickey's contract after the 1942 season. Even though St. Louis won another pennant and another World Series title in 1942—with a lineup stocked with players who rose through the Cardinal farm system—Branch left for Brooklyn, where he laid the groundwork for another baseball dynasty with the Dodgers.[10]

St. Louis' win over the Yankees in the 1942 World Series was a fitting bookend to the final split among the 1926 Cardinals' brain trust. Given the volatile mixture of inflated egos and excessive pride that permeated the interaction between Sam Breadon, Branch Rickey, and Rogers Hornsby, it was not surprising the triumvirate fractured as early as it did. But none of that mattered to long-suffering St. Louis fans during the magical summer of that first championship season.

Chapter Notes

Abbreviations

HOF—Major League Baseball Hall of Fame, Cooperstown, New York
SABR—Society of American Baseball Research
SLGD—*St. Louis Globe-Democrat*
SLPD—*St. Louis Post-Dispatch*

Preface

1. Paul E. Doutrich, *The Cardinals and the Yankees, 1926: A Classic Season and St. Louis in Seven* (Jefferson, NC: McFarland, 2011).

Introduction

1. Peter Golenbock, *The Spirit of St. Louis: A History of the St. Louis Cardinals and Browns* (New York: Avon, 2000), 4–9; Alfred H. Spink, *The National Game: A History of Baseball, America's Leading Outdoor Sport* (St. Louis: National Game Publishing Co., 1910), 36, 38; Alfred H. Spink, "Jeremiah Fruin," *The St. Louis Baseball Reader*, Richard Peterson, ed. (Columbia: University of Missouri Press, 2006), 47–50; Joan M. Thomas, "Of Prominent Men and Baseball Fields: A History of Ballparks in St. Louis," *Gateway* 25 (Winter 2004–05), 36–37; "Out Door Sports," *Daily Missouri Republican*, March 7, 1861.
2. "The Baseball Season," *SLPD*, April 24, 1875.
3. Jon David Cash, *Before They Were Cardinals: Major League Baseball in Nineteenth-Century St. Louis* (Columbia: University of Missouri Press, 2002), 11–49; Edward Achorn, *The Summer of Beer and Whiskey: How Brewers, Barkeeps, Rowdies, Immigrants, and a Wild Pennant Fight Made Baseball America's Game* (New York: Public Affairs, 2014), 10–11; Joan M. Thomas, *St. Louis' Big League Ballparks* (Charleston, SC: Arcadia, 2004), 33.
4. Cash, *Before They Were Cardinals*, 55–61; Achorn, *The Summer of Beer and Whiskey*, 7–14.
5. Achorn, *The Summer of Beer and Whiskey*, 1–3.
6. *Ibid.*, 1–4, 13–17; Cash, *Before They Were Cardinals*, 61–64; Jon David Cash, "Chris Von der Ahe, the American Association versus National League: Cultural War and the Rise of Major-League Baseball," *Missouri Historical Review* 109 (October 2014), 41–47.
7. Cash, *Before They Were Cardinals*, 64–178.
8. Roger D. Launius, *Seasons in the Sun: The Story of Big League Baseball in Missouri* (Columbia: University of Missouri Press, 2002), 2–13; Golenbock, *The Spirit of St. Louis*, 9–55; Bryan Soderholm-Difatte, *America's Game: A History of Major League Baseball Through World War II* (Lanham, MD: Rowman & Littlefield, 2018), 251; Jon David Cash, *Boom and Bust in St. Louis: A Cardinals History, 1885 to the Present* (Jefferson, NC: McFarland, 2020), 16; Cash, *Before They Were Cardinals*, 178–200.

Chapter 1

1. Susan Currell, *American Culture in the 1920s* (Edinburgh: Edinburgh University Press, 2009), 1–5.
2. Paul V. Murphy, *The New Era: American Thought and Culture in the 1920s* (Lanham, MD: Rowman & Littlefield, 2012), 12.
3. Niall Palmer, *The Twenties in America: Politics and History* (Edinburgh: Edinburgh University Press, 2006), 110–112; Ronald Allen Goldberg, *America in the Twenties* (Syracuse: Syracuse University Press, 2003), 83–91, 122–130; Bryson, *One Summer: America, 1927* (New York: Doubleday, 2013), 66.
4. Palmer, *The Twenties in America*, 124–125; Bryson, *One Summer*, 68–69; W.J. Rorabaugh, *Prohibition: A Concise History* (New York: Oxford University Press, 2018), 77; Goldberg, *America in the Twenties*, 92–95; Nathan Miller, *New World Coming: The 1920s and the Making of Modern America* (New York: Scribner, 2003), 253–259.
5. Currell, *American Culture in the 1920s*, 103–105.
6. *Ibid.*, 127–133; Palmer, *The Twenties in America*, 53–57.
7. Bryson, *One Summer: America, 1927*, 27–30; Miller, *New World Coming*, 329–340; Michael K. Bohn, *Heroes and Ballyhoo: How the Golden Age of the 1920s Transformed American Sports* (Washington, D.C.: Potomac, 2009), 1–7; Palmer, *The Twenties in America*, 126.

8. Bryson, *One Summer: America, 1927*, 68–69; Miller, *New World Coming*, 63–65; Murphy, *The New Era*, 45–71.

9. Palmer, *The Twenties in America*, 117–124; Currell, *American Culture in the 1920s*, 15–21; Miller, *New World Coming*, 228–235; Murphy, *The New Era*, 194–198; William A. Sunday, *The Sawdust Trail: Billy Sunday in His Own Words* (Iowa City: University of Iowa Press, 2005), vii–viii; Daniel Okrent, *Last Call: The Rise and Fall of Prohibition* (New York: Scribner, 2010), 96–97.

10. Palmer, *The Twenties in America*, 40–43; Goldberg, *America in the Twenties*, 101–107, 110–115; Miller, *New World Coming*, 143–145; Murphy, *The New Era*, 117–121.

11. Mike Mitchell, *Mr. Rickey's Redbirds: Baseball, Beer, Scandals & Celebrations in St. Louis* (By the author, 2020), 131–136; Palmer, *The Twenties in America*, 7–10; Bryson, *One Summer: America, 1927*, 162–169; Miller, *New World Coming*, 296–316; Okrent, *Last Call*, 373.

12. *SLPD*, April 18, 1926.

13. The most in-depth modern treatment of St. Louis' history is James Neal Primm, *Lion of the Valley: St. Louis, Missouri, 1764–1980*, 3rd edition (St. Louis: Missouri Historical Society Press, 1998).

14. Gary Ross Mormino, *Immigrants on the Hill: Italian-Americans in St. Louis, 1882–1982* (Urbana: University of Illinois Press, 1986), 11–18, 21; Bonnie Stepenoff, *The Dead End Kids of St. Louis: Homeless Boys and the People Who Tried to Save Them* (Columbia: University of Missouri Press, 2010), 14; Primm, *Lion of the Valley*, 143–144, 164, 338–339, 432–433; William Barnaby Faherty, S.J., *The St. Louis Irish: An Unmatched Celtic Community* (St. Louis: Missouri Historical Society Press, 2001); Joseph Heathcott and Angela Dietz, *Capturing the City: Photographs from the Streets of St. Louis, 1900–1930* (St. Louis: Missouri Historical Society Press, 2016), 11–12.

15. Mormino, *Immigrants on the Hill*, 5, 39–100; idem., "The Playing Fields of St. Louis: Italian Immigrants and Sports, 1925–1941," *Journal of Sports History* 9 (Summer 1982), 5–6; Stepenoff, *The Dead End Kids of St. Louis*, 86–88; Primm, *Lion of the Valley*, 417–418.

16. Katharine T. Corbett and Mary E. Seematter, "No Crystal Star: Black St. Louis, 1920–1940," *Gateway Heritage* 8 (Fall 1987), 9; "Whites Win in Negro Restriction Suit," *SLGD*, July 16, 1926. While the original case was being appealed, more Black families moved into the neighborhood, prompting another lawsuit. Again, the presiding judge ruled the restrictive covenant was legal. See "Ouster Suit Is Filed Against Residents on Cote Brilliante Ave.," *St. Louis Argus*, October 8, 1926.

17. Mormino, *Immigrants on the Hill*, 19–21; Primm, *Lion of the Valley*, 410–416; George Lipsitz, *The Sidewalks of St. Louis: Places, People, and Politics in an American City* (Columbia: University of Missouri Press, 1991), 34–36; Ann Morris, ed., *Lift Every Voice and Sing: St. Louis African Americans in the Twentieth Century* (Columbia: University of Missouri Press, 1999), 3–5; Keona K. Ervin, *Gateway to Equality: Black Women and the Struggle for Economic Justice in St. Louis* (Lexington: University Press of Kentucky, 2017), 11–13; Robbi Courtaway, *Wetter Than the Mississippi: Prohibition in St. Louis and Beyond* (St. Louis: Reedy Press, 2008), 238–241; Corbett, "No Crystal Star," 12; Heathcott and Dietz, *Capturing the City*, 13–15; Calvin Riley and Nini Harris, *Black St. Louis: 1764 to the New Millenium* (St. Louis: Reedy Press, 2023), 60–70.

18. Eric Sandweiss, *St. Louis: The Evolution of an American Urban Landscape* (Philadelphia: Temple University Press, 2001), 185, 191–212; Primm, *Lion of the Valley*, 347–349.

19. Primm, *Lion of the Valley*, 422.

20. Ibid., 396–410, 422–424; William Barnaby Faherty, S.J., *Saint Louis—A Concise History* (St. Louis: Print/Graphics, 1989), 100–101; "Year's Progress in Making a Better St. Louis with Money Authorized by Big Bond Issue," *SLPD*, January 10, 1926; "Less Building in St. Louis in 1926 Than in 1925, Real Estate Exchange Reports," *SLPD*, January 2, 1927.

21. "Shoe Industry of St. Louis Has Grown Steadily Until Today It Leads the World," *Know St. Loui 8* (January 3, 1926), 1, 3, 5–6, 12; Courtaway, *Wetter Than the Mississippi*, 1; Primm, *Lion of the Valley*, 436; Walter B. Weisenberger, "St. Louis Closes Year of Wealth and Happiness and Is Ready for 1927" and John A. Bush, "St. Louis 1926 Shoe Output $250,000,000," *SLPD*, January 2, 1927; *Polk-Gould St. Louis Directory* 56 (St. Louis: Polk-Gould Directory Co., 1927), 9–10.

22. Primm, *Lion of the Valley*, 340, 447–450, 474–477; Courteway, *Wetter Than the Mississippi*, 10–11; *St. Louis Star*, June 19, 1926.

23. *SLGD*, July 11, 1926; *Polk-Gould St. Louis Directory* 56 (1927), 15, 3274; Mormino, "The Playing Fields of St. Louis," 6–14; idem, *Immigrants on the Hill*, 195–197.

24. Courtaway, *Wetter Than the Mississippi*, 37, 64–65.

25. Okrent, *Last Call*, 249–251; William Knoedelseder, *Bitter Brew: The Rise and Fall of Anheuser-Busch and America's King of Beer* (New York: HarperCollins, 2012), 25–31; Peter Hernon and Terry Ganey, *Under the Influence: The Unauthorized Story of the Anheuser-Busch Dynasty* (New York: Simon & Schuster, 1991), 132–134; Courtaway, *Wetter Than the Mississippi*, 68–69; "Anheuser-Busch, Inc., Will Make Yeast," *SLPD*, February 10, 1926.

26. Martha Bensley Bruere, *Does Prohibition Work? A Study of the Operation of the Eighteenth Amendment Made by the National Federation of Settlements, Assisted by Social Workers in Different Parts of the United States* (New York: Harper & Brothers, 1927), 128; *The National Prohibition Law: Hearings Before The Subcommittee of the Committee on the Judiciary United States Senate, 69th Congress, 1st Session, April 5 to 24, 1926* (Washington, D.C.: Government Printing Office, 1926), Vol. 1, p. 15; Mitchell, *Mr. Rickey's Redbirds*, 136; Mormino,

Immigrants on the Hill, 126–135; Courtaway, *Wetter Than the Mississippi*, 33–40, 52, 106–111, 124–130, 224, 242–244.

27. Stepenoff, *The Dead End Kids of St. Louis*, 86–88, 93–103; Mormino, *Immigrants on the Hill*, 138–140; Courteway, *Wetter Than the Mississippi*, 45–46, 156–186; Daniel Waugh, *Egan's Rats: The Untold Story of the Prohibition-Era Gang That Ruled St. Louis* (Nashville: Cumberland House, 2007), 125–171; Daniel Waugh, *The Gangs of St. Louis: Men of Respect* (Charleston, SC: The History Press, 2010).

28. Courteway, *Wetter Than the Mississippi*, 272–277, 292.

29. Mitchell Nathanson, *A People's History of Baseball* (Urbana: University of Illinois Press, 2012), xi–xii.

30. Paul Adomites, et al., eds., *The Golden Age of Baseball* (Lincolnwood, IL: Publications International, 2003), 20.

31. David George Surdam and Michael J. Haupert, *The Age of Ruth and Landis: The Economics of Baseball During the Roaring Twenties* (Lincoln: University of Nebraska Press, 2018), 40–72; G. Edward White, *Creating the National Pastime: Baseball Transforms Itself, 1903–1953* (Princeton: Princeton University Press, 1996), 84–105; Charles C. Alexander, *Our Game: An American Baseball History* (New York: Henry Holt, 1991), 123–134; Harold Seymour, *Baseball: The Golden Age* (New York: Oxford University Press, 1971), 372–391.

32. Robert F. Burk, *Much More Than a Game: Players, Owners, & American Baseball Since 1921* (Chapel Hill: University of North Carolina Press, 2001), 3–28; Seymour, *Baseball: The Golden Age*, 343–347, 357–358; White, *Creating the National Pastime*, 206–227; Surdam and Haupert, *The Age of Ruth and Landis*, 73–100; Jules Tygiel, *Past Time: Baseball as History* (New York: Oxford University Press, 2000), 65–66, 71–73.

33. White, *Creating the National Pastime*, xi–xii, 4–5.

34. Richard C. Crepeau, *Baseball: America's Diamond Mind, 1919–1941* (Orlando: University Presses of Florida, 1980), 24–46, 55–63; Christopher H. Evans, "Baseball as Civil Religion: The Genesis of an American Creation Story," *The Faith of 50 Million: Baseball, Religion, and American Culture*, Christopher H. Evans and William R. Herzog II, eds. (Louisville: Westminster John Knox Press, 2002), 14, 26–31.

35. Owners "grandfathered" in 17 pitchers, allowing them to continue using the spit ball.

36. William Curran, *Big Sticks: The Batting Revolution of the Twenties* (New York: William Morrow, 1990), 11–17; Alexander, *Our Game*, 136–140; Seymour, *Baseball: The Golden Age*, 423–427; Crepeau, *Baseball: America's Diamond Mind*, 73–101; Surdam and Haupert, *Age of Ruth and Landis*, 136–145; Adomites, *The Golden Age of Baseball*, 9–30; Bill James, *The New Bill James Historical Baseball Abstract* (New York: The Free Press, 2001), 120–122.

37. John P. Rossi, *Baseball and American Culture: A History* (Lanham, MD: Rowman & Littlefield, 2018), 113; Fred Lieb, *Baseball as I Have Known It* (New York: Coward, McCann & Geoghegan, 1977), 162; James A. Cox, *The Lively Ball: Baseball in the Roaring Twenties* (Alexandria, VA: Redefinition, 1989), 63–76.

Chapter 2

1. "Auxiliary Committee of Legion Condemns Miller's Statement," *SLGD*, December 8, 1921; "Victor Miller's Candidacy," Editorial, *SLPD*, January 7, 1925; "Miller Makes First Announcement of Candidacy for Mayor," *SLGD*, January 7, 1925; "Victor J. Miller Dies, Ex-Mayor of St. Louis," *SLPD*, January 6, 1955; Victor Miller Obituary, *SLGD*, January 7, 1955.

2. Golenbock, *The Spirit of St. Louis*, 88–90; *Sporting News*, October 7, 1926.

3. Mark Armour, "Sam Breadon: Relentless Owner," *Sportsman's Park in St. Louis: Home of the Browns and Cardinals at Grand and Dodier*, Gregory H. Wolf, ed. (Phoenix: Society for American Baseball Research, 2017), 36; Mitchell, *Mr. Rickey's Redbirds*, 178–79; Bob Broeg, "Breadon's Legacy Doesn't Deserve Rumor of Card Strike in '47," *Baseball Magazine*, July 1997: 14–17, in HOF "Sam Breadon" Clipping File; Ellis J. Veech, "Sam Breadon and the New Cardinal Set-Up," *Baseball Magazine*, February 1948, in HOF "Sam Breadon" Clipping File; Daniel M. Daniel, "Sam Breadon Left Indelible Imprint on Baseball Operation," *Baseball Magazine*, July 1949, in HOF "Sam Breadon" Clipping File; J. Roy Stockton, "Singing Sam the Cut-Rate Man," *The Saturday Evening Post*, February 22, 1947, in HOF "Sam Breadon" Clipping File.

4. Armour, "Sam Breadon," 36; John Snyder, *Cardinals Journal: Year by Year & Day by Day with the St. Louis Cardinals Since 1882* (Cincinnati: Emmis Books, 2006), 164, 178–79; Lee Lowenfish, *Branch Rickey: Baseball's Ferocious Gentleman* (Lincoln: University of Nebraska Press, 2007), 119–21; Steve Steinberg, *Baseball in St. Louis, 1900–1925* (Charleston, SC: Arcadia, 2004), 91–92; Mitchell, *Mr. Rickey's Redbirds*, 177–80.

5. Frederick G. Lieb, *The St. Louis Cardinals: The Story of a Great Baseball Club*, Writing Baseball Series Edition (Carbondale: Southern Illinois University Press, 2001), 73–78; Mitchell, *Mr. Rickey's Redbirds*, 180; Marion F. Parker, "Transfer of Cardinals to Sportsman's Park Is Announced by Breadon," *SLGB*, June 25, 1920; J.B. Sheridan, "Cardinal Ball Park, Regarded as Model in 1892, Given Up as Unfit for Sport in 1920," *SLGB*, July 11, 1920.

6. Ed Wheatley, *The St. Louis Cardinals: Everything You Need to Know!* (St. Louis: Reedy Press, 2023), 39.

7. Harold Seymour, *Baseball: The Golden Age*, 401–16; Murray Polner, *Branch Rickey: A Biography*, rev. ed. (Jefferson, NC: McFarland, 2007), 18–19; J. Roy Stockton, "A Brain Comes to Brooklyn,"

The Saturday Evening Post, February 13, 1943, in HOF "Branch Rickey, 1960–1979_01" Clipping File; Lowenfish, *Branch Rickey*, 14–22.

8. Lowenfish, *Branch Rickey*, 25–32; Polner, *Branch Rickey*, 56–60; "Branch Rickey's 'Baseball Autobiography,'" Arthur Mann Papers, Library of Congress, Box 8, folder 8.

9. Mitchell, *Mr. Rickey's Redbirds*, 71; Richard J. Puerzer, "Engineering Baseball: Branch Rickey's Innovative Approach to Baseball Management," *Nine: A Journal of Baseball History & Culture*, 12 (Fall 2003): 72–87; Polner, *Branch Rickey*, 60–68; John B. Sheridan, "Back of the Home Plate," *Sporting News*, June 11, 1925.

10. Golenbock, *The Spirit of St. Louis*, 67–68.

11. Steinberg, *Baseball in St. Louis*, 85; Cash, *Boom and Bust in St. Louis*, 52–53; Polner, *Branch Rickey*, 72–76.

12. Bob Broeg, *Bob Broeg's Redbirds: A Century of Cardinals' Baseball*, rev. ed. (St. Louis: River City, 1987), 23–24; Mitchell, *Mr. Rickey's Redbirds*, 181; Jonathan D'Amore, *Rogers Hornsby: A Biography* (Westport, CT: Greenwood, 2004), 31; Jimmy Breslin, *Branch Rickey* (New York: Viking, 2011), 47; Lowenfish, *Branch Rickey*, 121–24; Polner, *Branch Rickey*, 76–78; James Rygelski and Robert L. Tiemann, *10 Rings: Stories of the St. Louis Cardinals World Championships* (St. Louis: Reedy Press, 2011), 9.

13. Golenbock, *The Spirit of St. Louis*, 83–88; Lieb, *The St. Louis Cardinals*, 81–90; Seymour, *Baseball: The Golden Age*, 400–16; Mitchell, *Mr. Rickey's Redbirds*, 182–84; Crepeau, *Baseball: America's Diamond Mind*, 108–9; Roger I. Abrams, *Legal Bases: Baseball and the Law* (Philadelphia: Temple University Press, 1998), 97–101; Mitchell, *Mr. Rickey's Redbirds*, 175–77; J.G. Taylor Spink, *Judge Landis and Twenty-Five Years of Baseball* (New York: Thomas Y. Crowell, 1947), 144, 192; Alexander, *Our Game*, 146–47; Peter Morris, *A Game of Inches: The Stories Behind the Innovations That Shaped Baseball* (Chicago: Ivan R. Dee, 2010), 348–56; Soderholm-Difatte, *America's Game*, 259–60, 284–87; James J. Morgan, "Pastoral America's Last Stand: Grover Cleveland Alexander Takes the Mound During the 1926 World Series" (M.A. Thesis, University of Nebraska, 2017), 36–42.

14. Bob Broeg, "Cardinal Managers: From Huggins to Herzog," *Road Trips: SABR Convention Journal Articles*, Jim Charlton, ed., 116. Originally in *St. Louis's Favorite Sport*, Convention Brochure of the 22nd National SABR convention, 1992, 13–20.

15. Paul Warburton, "Offense? Try Hornsby," *The Baseball Research Journal* 28 (1999), 4.

16. In December 2020, Major League Baseball elevated seven distinct leagues from the Negro Leagues to "Major League" status and began counting single season and career statistics among Major League leaders.

17. Seymour, *Baseball: The Golden Age*, 448; Robert W. Cohen, *The 50 Greatest Players in St. Louis Cardinals History* (Lanham, MD: Scarecrow, 2013), 15–19.

18. A contrasting view of Hornsby can be found in Howard Green, "A Tale of Two Hornsbys: A Sweetheart Back Home," *Baseball Research Journal*, 2001.

19. Charles C. Alexander, *Rogers Hornsby: A Biography* (New York: Henry Holt, 1995), 3–7, 97–98; Steinberg, *Baseball in St. Louis*, 121; Snyder, *Cardinals Journal*, 159; Alexander, *Our Game*, 145–46; Jim Hunstein, *1, 2, 6, 9…& Rogers: The Cardinals' Retired Numbers and the Men Who Wore Them* (St. Louis: Stellar Press, 2004), 1–2; James, *The New Bill James Historical Baseball Abstract*, 485–486, 592.

20. Alexander, *Rogers Hornsby*, 6–7; Mitchell, *Mr. Rickey's Redbirds*, 184–85; D'Amore, *Rogers Hornsby*, 41–42; Jimmy Powers, *Baseball Personalities (the Most Colorful Figures of All Time)* (New York: Rudolph Field, 1949), 174; Rogers Hornsby and Bill Surface, *My War with Baseball* (New York: Coward-McCann, 1962), 24–25; Daniel E. Ginsburg, *The Fix Is In: A History of Baseball Gambling and Game Fixing Scandals* (Jefferson, NC: McFarland, 1995), 213–15; Spink, *Judge Landis*, 85–86; Roger I. Abrams, *The Dark Side of the Diamond: Gambling, Violence, Drugs and Alcoholism in the National Pastime* (Burlington, MA: Rounder, 2007), 35–101.

21. D'Amore, *Rogers Hornsby*, 3–12; Alexander, *Rogers Hornsby*, 9–29; Hornsby, *My War with Baseball*, 34–40; J. Roy Stockton, "Rogers Hornsby," *SLPD Sunday Magazine*, January 3, 1926, 110.

22. D'Amore, *Rogers Hornsby*, 21–22; Alexander, *Rogers Hornsby*, 43–48; "Rickey Declares Hornsby Did Not Speak to Players," *SLPD*, July 17, 1918; "Hornsby Fined $50 for Umpire Baiting," *SLPD*, August 27, 1926; Lowenfish, *Branch Rickey*, 98–99.

23. J. Roy Stockton, "Hornsby, the Man, a Blunt, Cussin,' Undiplomatic Square-Shooter," *SLPD*, October 3, 1926.

24. Clarence F. Lloyd, "Hornsby Gets Offer from Ship Builders to Jump Cardinals," *The St. Louis Star*, July 9, 1918; Alexander, *Rogers Hornsby*, 37, 42, 44–49, 64, 69–70.

25. *Bob Broeg's Redbirds*, 33; D'Amore, *Rogers Hornsby*, 37.

26. Golenbock, *The Spirit of St. Louis*, 96; Lieb, *The St. Louis Cardinals*, 99–100; Alexander, *Rogers Hornsby*, 74–81; D'Amore, *Rogers Hornsby*, 45–47; Harry F. Pierce, "Rogers Hornsby May Be Traded by Rickey in Shakeup of Team," *St. Louis Star*, September 10, 1923; Snyder, *Cardinals Journal*, 195.

27. Martin J. Haley, "Rickey Not Worried by Hornsby Go," *SLGD*, September 12, 1926.

28. Surdam and Haupert, *Age of Ruth and Landis*, 160–63; "Rogers Hornsby May Wear Cubs Uniform," *Muncie Evening Press*, September 27, 1923; Alexander, *Rogers Hornsby*, 80–84; Lowenfish, *Branch Rickey*, 145–48.

29. Lowenfish, *Branch Rickey*, 145–48; Mitchell, *Mr. Rickey's Redbirds*, 186–89; Arthur Mann, *Branch Rickey: American in Action* (Boston: Houghton Mifflin, 1957), 122–124; Golenbock, *The*

Spirit of St. Louis, 97; Joseph F. Holland, "Hornsby, Suspended and Fined $500, Will Not Be Sold or Traded, Owner of Cardinals Declares," *SLPD*, September 27, 1923; Joseph F. Holland, "Hornsby Snarl Will Be Ironed Out, Cards' President Believes," *SLPD*, September 28, 1923; "Rickey's Statement in Hornsby Case" and "Hornsby Disciplined Because Morale of the Club Hurt, Rickey Statement Says," *SLPD*, September 30, 1923.

30. *Sporting News*, October 7, 1926.

31. Alexander, *Rogers Hornsby*, 99–102; Golenbock, *The Spirit of St. Louis*, 97–99; D'Amore, *Rogers Hornsby*, 50–52; Hornsby, *My War with Baseball*, 42–44; Jack Sher, "Rogers Hornsby: The Mighty the Rajah," *Sport*, July 1949; Polner, *Branch Rickey*, 84–87.

32. J. Roy Stockton, "Hornsby, the Man, a Blunt, Cussin,' Undiplomatic Square-Shooter," *SLPD*, October 3, 1926.

33. Broeg, "Cardinal Managers: From Huggins to Herzog," *Sporting News*, April 8, 1926.

34. Cash, *Boom and Bust in St. Louis*, 56–57; Alexander, *Rogers Hornsby*, 50–51; Snyder, *Cardinals Journal*, 205–206; Mitchell, *Mr. Rickey's Redbirds*, 190–91; Donald Honig, "Yesterday" as told by Les Bell, *Sports Illustrated* 49 (October 9, 1978), 128–30; "Hornsby Says Harmony, Courage and Determination Won Flag," *SLPD*, September 27, 1926. See also, Donald Honig, *The October Heroes: Great World Series Games Remembered by the Men Who Played Them* (New York: Simon & Schuster, 1979), 91.

Chapter 3

1. "Man Drowns in Whisky Mash in Shed at Home," *SLPD*, February 3, 1926.

2. "Prohibition Unknown Here, Dr. Starkloff Tells Senator Edge," *SLGD*, April 6, 1926; "Aldermen Vote, 22–4, to Repeal or Modify Dry Laws," *SLGD*, April 9, 1926.

3. Golenbock, *The Spirit of St. Louis*, 4–55; Achorn, *The Summer of Beer and Whiskey*; Cash, *Boom and Bust in St. Louis*, xx.

4. Martin J. Haley, "Improved Ball Park May Prove Charm Necessary to Bring Pennant Here," *SLGD*, January 1, 1926; Scott Ferkovich, "Sportsman's Park," *Sportsman's Park in St. Louis: Home of the Browns and Cardinals at Grand and Dodier*, Gregory H. Wolf, ed. (Phoenix: Society for American Baseball Research, 2017), 4–5.

5. J. Roy Stockton, "St. Louis Prospects for a Pennant Are Brightest in Years," *SLPD*, January 17, 1926.

6. "Hornsby Has Own Ideas on Training," *Sporting News*, January 21, 1926.

7. Cohen, *The 50 Greatest Players in St. Louis Cardinals History*, 149–150; Doutrich, *The Cardinals and the Yankees, 1926*, 33–35; Gregory H. Wolf, "Jesse Haines," SABR Biography Project (https://sabr.org/bioproj/person/afeb716c).

8. Broeg, *Bob Broeg's Redbirds*, 35.

9. Thomas Holmes, "Flint Rhem Believes That 'Master Minds' Do Not Aid Pitchers," *Brooklyn Daily Eagle*, June 15, 1926.

10. "Flint Rhem on Hold List," *SLPD*, February 24, 1926; *SLPD*, February 26, 1926; William J. McGoogan, "Full Squad to Gather Sunday at San Antonio," *SLPD*, February 27, 1926; William J. McGoogan, "Keen and Rhem Pitch Shutout Game Against San Antonio Club," *SLPD*, March 22, 1926; Doutrich, *The Cardinals and the Yankees, 1926*, 64; Nancy Snell Griffith, "Flint Rhem," SABR Biography Project (https://sabr.org/bioproj/person/97c73ab1).

11. Broeg, *Bob Broeg's Redbirds*, 29; Gregory H. Wolf, "Bill Sherdel," SABR Biography Project (https://sabr.org/bioproj/person/bill-sherdel/).

12. Bulger indicated this particular game would decide the Pacific Coast League championship, but neither Oakland nor Portland seriously challenged for the league championship in 1923 or 1924. See Bozeman Bulger, "Duster Mails' Return to Major Club Brings New Color to Game," reprinted in *Moline* [IL] *Daily Dispatch*, August 27, 1925.

13. Ronald T. Waldo, *Baseball's Roaring Twenties: A Decade of Legends, Characters, and Diamond Adventures* (Lanham, MD: Rowman & Littlefield, 2017), 42–45, 129–131; Bulger, "Duster Mails' Return to Major Club Brings New Color to Game."

14. William J. Moir, ed., *Past and Present of Hardin County Iowa* (Indianapolis: B.F. Bowen & Company, 1911), 284–286; James M. Gould, "Cards Figured in 24 Shut-Outs, Won Only Three in 1918," *St. Louis Star*, February 27, 1919; "Shaughnessy Found Reinhart for Cards," [Kingston, Ontario, Canada] *Daily British Whig*, November 7, 1925; Duane Winn, "Rogers Hornsby in 1932," *The National Pastime* 23 (2003).

15. Gregory H. Wolf, "Bill Hallahan," SABR Biography Project (https://sabr.org/bioproj/person/bill-hallahan).

16. Joseph F. Holland, "Eddie Dyer, Making His First Big League Start, Blanks Cubs, 3–0," *SLPD*, September 10, 1923; Warren Corbett, "Eddie Dyer," SABR Biography Project (https://sabr.org/bioproj/person/eddie-dyer/).

17. Matthew Clifford, "A Phil Named Syl," *The National Pastime: From Swampoodle to South Philly* (Philadelphia, 2013). Accessed https://sabr.org/journal/article/a-phil-named-syl/ (April 22, 2023).

18. Martin J. Haley, "Hornsby Elated Over Deal that Made Keen a Cardinal," *SLGD*, December 12, 1925; William McGoogan, "Keen and Rhem Pitch Shutout Game Against San Antonio Club," *SLPD*, March 22, 1926; Marty Payne, "Vic Keen," SABR Biography Project (https://sabr.org/bioproj/person/vic-keen/); Doutrich, *The Cardinals and the Yankees, 1926*, 63–65.

19. James M. Gould, "Mails and Hallahan Will Handle Hurling for Hornsby's Team," *St. Louis Star*, March 11, 1926; "Herman Bell, Who Hurled for Cards and Giants, Dies," *Sporting News*, June 15,

1949; Dent McSkimming, "Recruit Right-Hander Holds Braves to Six Safeties in 18 Innings," *SLPD*, July 20, 1924.

20. Charles F. Faber, "Allen Sothoron," SABR Biography Project (https://sabr.org/bioproj/person/allen-sothoron); Charels F. Faber and Richard B. Faber, *Spitballers: The Last Legal Hurlers of the Wet One* (Jefferson, NC: McFarland, 2006), 145–50.

21. Doutrich, *The Cardinals and the Yankees, 1926*, 65–66; Joseph Wancho, "Bob O'Farrell," SABR Biography Project (https://sabr.org/bioproj/person/e701600d); Lawrence S. Ritter, *The Glory of Their Times: The Story of the Early Days of Baseball Told by the Men Who Played It* (New York: Macmillan, 1966), 235, 240–242; Eugene Murdock, *Baseball Players and Their Times: Oral Histories of the Game, 1920–1940* (Westport, CT: Meckler, 1991), 62.

22. "Penn Football Squad Doubled," *Wilmington Morning News*, September 28, 1918; "Two Penn Stars in Big Leagues," *Philadelphia Evening Public Ledger*, July 13, 1921.

23. Harry F. Pierce, "Ernie Vick Holds Unique Record in Gridiron Pastime," *St. Louis Star*, February 9, 1922; *SLPD*, September 13, 1924.

24. Chilly Doyle, "Chilly Sauce," *Pittsburgh Post-Gazette*, April 15, 1926.

25. Doutrich, *The Cardinals and the Yankees, 1926*, 111–112; Bill Johnson, "Jim Bottomley," SABR Biography Project (https://sabr.org/bioproj/person/ea08fc60); Cohen, *The 50 Greatest Players in St. Louis Cardinals History*, 81–82; Bob Broeg, "Bottomley Funeral Tomorrow; Career of Redbird Star," *SLPD*, December 13, 1959, in HOF "Jim Bottomley" Clipping File.

26. L.H. Addington, "Ability Speaks for Thevenow," *Sporting News*, October 21, 1926; "Texas Goes Back on Famous Native Son," *Sporting News*, March 25, 1926; William J. McGoogan, "Hornsby Picks Team for First Spring Contest," *SLPD*, February 28, 1926; Warren Corbett, "Tommy Thevenow," SABR Biography Project (https://sabr.org/bioproj/person/6b3dc76b); "Shaughnessy Found Reinhart for Cards," [Kingston, Ontario, Canada] *Daily British Whig*, November 7, 1925; James M. Gould, "Balance of Cardinals Will Join Squad of Batterymen Tomorrow," *St. Louis Star*, February 27, 1926; Doutrich, *The Cardinals and the Yankees, 1926*, 18–21.

27. Broeg, *Bob Broeg's Redbirds*, 36; unidentified newspaper clipping, October 1928, in HOF "Les Bell" Clipping File; [Harrisburg, PA] *The Evening News*, June 3, 1920; "Detroit Scout Gets Two Stars," *Harrisburg Telegraph*, July 9, 1921; "Twilight League Stars Show Good Averages; Many Players on List," *Harrisburg Telegraph*, July 21, 1921; [Harrisburg, PA] *The Evening News*, August 2, 1921; "Cards Get Hurler and Shortstop from Lansing," *SLPD*, August 2, 1922; "Lester Bell Purchased by St. Louis Cardinals," [Harrisburg, PA] *The Evening News*, August 7, 1922; Joseph F. Holland, "Recruit Lester Bell's Timely Hit Ends Cardinals' Losing Streak," *SLPD*, September 26, 1923; 'Rogers Hornsby Praises Les Bell," *San Francisco Bulletin*, October 2, 1923; "Cardinals Get Star Milwaukee Infielder," *St. Louis Star*, May 6, 1924; Doutrich, *The Cardinals and the Yankees, 1926*, 97–98.

28. David A. Goss, "Major-League Players Who Wore Glasses," *The Baseball Research Journal* (2008), accessed at https://sabr.org/journals/2008-baseball-research-journal/; David E. Skelton, "'Specs' Toporcer," SABR Biography Project (https://sabr.org/bioproj/person/specs-toporcer/); Seymour, *Baseball: The Golden Age*, 449.

29. John J. Watkins, "Jake Flowers," SABR Biography Project (https://sabr.org/biogproj/person/jake-flowers); "Caliber of Peninsula Ball Surprises Diamond Veteran," *The Baltimore Sun*, August 6, 1922.

30. Russell Wolinsky, "Ray Blades," SABR Biography Project (https://sabr.org/bioproj/person/92a8ae6f); Mike Lynch, "Austin McHenry," SABR Biography Project (https://sabr.org/bioproj/person/austin-mchenry/).

31. Cohen, *The 50 Greatest Players in St. Louis Cardinals History*, 127–129; Greg Erion, "Chick Hafey," SABR Biography Project (https://sabr.org/bioproj/person/96ae4951); Goss, "Major-League Players Who Wore Glasses"; Broeg, *Bob Broeg's Redbirds*, 30.

32. Lieb, *The St. Louis Cardinals*, 93; Waldo, *Baseball's Roaring Twenties*, 45–48; Thomas Holmes, "Cardinals Make It Two Straight by Scoring Ten Runs with Two Men Out," *Brooklyn Daily Eagle*, August 6, 1926; William J. McGoogan, "Struggle for Jobs in Hornsby's Outfield Opens at San Antonio," *SLPD*, March 5, 1926; William J. McGoogan, "Heine Mueller, with His Head Up, Is Fighting for Regular Job," *SLPD*, March 9, 1926.

33. John J. Watkins, "Taylor Douthit," SABR Biography Project (https://sabr.org/bioproj/person/cf023577); *Sioux City Journal*, December 28, 1925; *Tacoma Daily Ledger*, December 7, 1925.

34. "Holm, Former Iowa Man, Is Batting .321," *Quad City Times*, August 4, 1924; "Holm, Banned in 'Big Ten' To St. Louis," *Iowa City Press-Citizen*, January 24, 1923; Ford Sawyer, "Baseball Birthday Sketches," *Boston Globe*, December 28, 1924.

Chapter 4

1. Lonnie Wheeler, *The Bona Fide Legend of Cool Papa Bell: Speed, Grace, and the Negro Leagues* (New York: Abrams Press, 2020), 33, 43–48; William F. McNeil, *Cool Papa and Double Duties: The All-Time Greats of the Negro Leagues* (Jefferson, NC: McFarland, 2001), 115–117; Joel Walsh, "Shining Stars: The Negro Leagues in St. Louis," *Gateway* 25 (Winter 2004–05), 12–19; Scott Jarman Levy, "Tricky Ball: 'Cool Papa' Bell and Life in the Negro Leagues," *Gateway Heritage* 9 (Spring 1989), 26–35.

2. "Local Baseball News of Interest," *St. Louis

Argus, March 26, 1926; "Stars and Monarchs Play Five Exhibition Games at Star's Park Starting Sat.," *St. Louis Argus*, April 9, 1926; "St. Louis Stars Lose All Games to Monarchs," *St. Louis Argus*, May 7, 1926.

3. Team and individual statistics accessed through baseball-reference.com and seamheads.com.

4. Martin J. Haley, "Diet a La Hornsby Gave Club Road Power," *SLGD*, August 15, 1926.

5. Ibid.; *Sporting News*, February 11, 1926; https://sabr.org/spring-training-database.

6. William J. McGoogan, "Hornsby's Determination to Instill Winning Habit Responsible for Victory," *SLPD*, March 20, 1926; D'Amore, *Rogers Hornsby*, 55–57.

7. Roy Stockton, "St. Louis Prospects for a Pennant Are Brightest in Years," *SLPD*, January 17, 1926.

8. William J. McGoogan, "Cardinal Advance Squad Reaches Texas Camp and Starts Spring Training," *SLPD*, February 22, 1926.

9. William J. McGoogan, "Rogers Hornsby Lays Down Law for Cardinals," *SLPD*, March 2, 1926; Lieb, *St. Louis Cardinals*, 109–110.

10. William J. McGoogan, "Hornsby Ready to Start His First Full Season as Pilot, Outlines Baseball Policies," *SLPD*, March 21, 1926; Doutrich, *The Cardinals and the Yankees*, 17, 22.

11. James M. Gould, "Heine Mueller Is Hit on Head by Foul Ball in Cardinal Workout," *St. Louis Star*, March 2, 1926.

12. "Cardinals Not Fast Enough for Home Duty—Run Too Easily," *SLPD*, January 8, 1926; "New Cardinal and Brown Uniforms on Display at Sport Shop," *SLGD*, April 4, 1926; Gary Kodner and Oliver Kodner, *St. Louis Cardinals Uniforms & Logos: An Illustrated History, 1882–2016* (St. Louis Cardinals Hall of Fame and Museum, 2016), 38–39.

13. *SLPD*, March 7, 1926; *SLPD*, March 10, 1926; "William J. McGoogan, "Pitching of Hallahan and Mails Features Cardinal Victory," *SLPD*, March 12, 1926; William J. McGoogan, "Hornsby Tackles Task of Picking 11 Hurlers from the 18 Men in Texas Camp," *SLPD*, March 16, 1926; William J. McGoogan, "Cards to Play Houston Today and Tomorrow," *SLPD*, March 18, 1926; *SLPD*, March 19, 1926; William J. McGoogan, "Hornsby Ready to Start His First Full Season as Pilot, Outlines Baseball Policies," *SLPD*, March 21, 1926; "Texas Goes Back on Famous Native Son," *Sporting News*, March 25, 1926.

14. Martin J. Haley, "Cards Call Off Third Straight Contest Because of Rain," *SLGD*, March 19, 1926 idem., "Cardinals Beat Houston, 9–4, in Spite of Continued Rain," *SLGD*, March 20, 1926; idem, "Cardinals Lose Fourth game in Five Days Owing to Rain," *SLGD*, March 21, 1926; William J. McGoogan, "Hornsby's Determination to Instill Winning Habit Responsible for Victory," *SLPD*, March 20, 1926; "No Game Too Cheap in Hornsby's Code," *Sporting News*, April 8, 1926.

15. William McGoogan, "Keen and Rhem Pitch Shutout Game Against San Antonio Club," *SLPD*, March 22, 1926.

16. https://historyinnewbraunfels.com/history/; 1845 to 1929 | New Braunfels, TX—Official Website (nbtexas.org).

17. William J. McGoogan, "Huntzinger's Curve as Good as Any in National League, Manager Hornsby Declares," *SLPD*, March 23, 1926; Martin J. Haley, "Hornsby's Homer Features Defeat of Des Moines, 9 to 3," *SLGD*, March 23, 1926.

18. William J. McGoogan, "Sherdel Second Cardinal Pitcher to Hurl Nine Innings," *SLPD*, March 25, 1926; McGoogan, "Cardinals Make 21 Safeties and Trounce Fort Worth Club, 16 to 7," *SLPD*, March 28, 1926.

19. "Bill Hallahan Is Master of Sox in Great 2–0 Victory," *St. Louis Star*, March 30, 1926; "No Game Too Cheap in Hornsby's Code," *Sporting News*, April 8, 1926; "Wintry Weather in Texas Gives Cards Two-Day Vacation," *St. Louis Star*, March 31, 1926.

20. William J. McGoogan, "Rhem Holds Dallas to 5 Hits, Hurling Second 9-Inning Game in 8 Days," *SLPD*, April 4, 1926; Martin J. Haley, "Cardinals Beat Dallas, 3 to 1," *SLGD*, April 4, 1926. Statistics bear out Hornsby's view of the less lively baseball. Batting production in the major leagues nosedived in 1926. Homeruns declined by 31 percent in the National League and 20 percent in the American League. See Curran, *Big Sticks*, 213–214.

21. Martin J. Haley, "Cardinals Defeat Dallas, 6–4," *SLGD*, April 5, 1926; "Hornsbymen Expect to Add Shreveport to List of Victims," *St. Louis Star*, April 5, 1926.

22. *SLGD*, April 6, 1926; "Texas Leaguers, in Hitting Mood, Slap Cardinal Pitchers," *St. Louis Star*, April 6, 1926.

23. "Full House Given Old-Time Wallop by Billy Sunday," *SLPD*, April 6, 1926; "Billy Sunday Packs Moolah Temple with Orthodox Sermon," *SLGD*, April 6, 1926; Okrent, *Last Call*, 96–97.

24. Martin J. Haley, "Cards Down Springfield, Mo., 16–2, in Final Road Training Game," *SLGD*, April 9, 1926; Lowenfish, *Branch Rickey*, 155–158.

25. William J. McGoogan, "Cardinals Should Finish One, Two, Three, in Race for the Pennant, Hornsby Says," *SLPD*, April 4, 1926; McGoogan, "Cardinals in Fine Condition for Opening of Pennant Race," *SLPD*, April 9, 1926; Martin J. Haley, "Cards to End Road Training Session at Springfield, Mo., Today," *SLGD*, April 8, 1926.

26. "Why Not Ball Stadium," *Sporting News*, April 8, 1926.

27. "Sportsman's Park Ready for Spring Series Opener," *SLPD*, April 9, 1926; Martin J. Haley, "Cardinals and Browns Open Spring Series This Afternoon," *SLGD*, April 10, 1926; Ferkovich, "Sportsman's Park," 5.

28. J. Roy Stockton, "Browns Beat Cardinals, 4–2; Hornsby Hits Home Run," *SLPD*, April 11, 1926; Martin J. Haley, "Hornsby Hits Homer in 4th, but Fouls Out with Bases Loaded in 9th to End Rally," *SLGD*, April 11, 1926.

29. "American League Refuses to Sanction Pitchers' Use of Resin," *SLPD*, February 10, 1926; "Gould's Gossip," *St. Louis Star*, April 12, 1926; Doutrich, *The Cardinals and the Yankees*, 85–86; Morris, *A Game of Inches*, 309–312. American League pitchers could not use the resin bag until 1931 when new league president Will Harridge allowed it.

30. J. Roy Stockton, "Strategy Gives Browns Victory In Spring Series Final," *SLPD*, April 13, 1926; "Browns Defeat Cardinals, 3–2, in Final Clash of City Series," *SLGD*, April 13, 1926.

31. *Sporting News*, March 18, 1926; Martin J. Haley, "Cardinals and Browns Open Spring Series This Afternoon," *SLGD*, April 10, 1926; John B. Foster, "Team Today as Good as Giants and Pittsburgh," *SLPD*, April 8, 1926.

Chapter 5

1. A. Scott Berg, *Lindbergh* (New York: G.P. Putnam's Sons, 1998), 62–89; Bryson, *One Summer*, 37–45; Doutrich, *The Cardinals and the Yankees*, 37–39; "Air Mail Linking City with South American Points Soon Predicted," *SLGD*, April 16, 1926; *St. Louis Star*, April 15, 1926; *St. Louis Star*, November 4, 1926; *SLPD*, September 17, 1926; *SLPD*, November 4, 1926.

2. Doutrich, *The Cardinals and the Yankees, 1926*, 31–32; Angelo J. Louisa, *The Pirates Unraveled: Pittsburgh's 1926 Season* (Jefferson, NC: McFarland, 2015), 91–102; Herman Wecke, "Carey, Pirates' Spark Plug, Will Not Face Cardinals Today," *SLPD*, April 13, 1926; Wecke, "Cards Show Tremendous Punch in Beating World Champions," *SLPD*, April 14, 1926; Martin J. Haley, "Rhem Holds Bucs Scoreless Until Sixth, When St. Louis Defense Hits Toboggan, Buc Hurler's Brilliance Saves Day," *SLGD*, April 14, 1926.

3. James M. Gould, "Keen and Meadows Scheduled to Hurl in Today's Battle," *St. Louis Star*, April 15, 1926; Martin J. Haley, "Pitcher Haines Hurt as Pirates Swamp Cardinals, 10 to 3," *SLGD*, April 15, 1926; Herman Wecke, "Cards Get 16 Runners on Base But Lose to Pirates, 10 to 3," *SLPD*, April 15, 1926; *Pittsburgh Post-Gazette*, April 15, 1926.

4. John J. Sheridan, "Keen Hurls Superbly and Cardinals Shut Out Pirates, 2 to 0," *SLGD*, April 16, 1926; James M. Gould, "Former Cub Hurler Turns in Splendid Bit of Mound Work," *St. Louis Star*, April 16, 1926; Herman Wecke, "Vic Keen Blanks the Pirates and Cardinals Win Again, 2 to 0," *SLPD*, April 16, 1926.

5. James M. Gould, "Hornsby May Choose Flint Rhem to Work Against Chicagoans," *St. Louis Star*, April 17, 1926; Martin J. Haley, "Mueller's Single in Ninth Inning Brings Cardinals Victory, 3 to 2," *SLGD*, April 17, 1926; Herman Wecke, "Cardinals Uncover Badly Needed Right-Hand Pitching Strength," *SLPD*, April 17, 1926; Charles J. Doyle, "Enemy Takes Advantage of Bucco Slips to Win by 3–2," *Pittsburgh Post-Gazette*, April 17, 1926.

6. Glenn Stout, *The Cubs: The Complete Story of Chicago Cubs Baseball* (New York: Houghton Mifflin, 2007), 115–120; Frank Russo, *The Cooperstown Chronicles: Baseball's Colorful Characters, Unusual Lives, and Strange Demises* (Lanham, MD: Rowman & Littlefield, 2014), 59; Roberts Ehrgott, *Mr. Wrigley's Ball Club: Chicago & The Cubs During The Jazz Age* (Lincoln: University of Nebraska Press, 2013), 10, 22–25, 55–63; William F. McNeil, *Gabby Hartnett: The Life and Times of the Cubs' Greatest Catcher* (Jefferson, NC: McFarland, 2004), 60–94.

7. Herman Wecke, "Cards Down Cubs, 3–2, in Game Full of Thrills," *SLPD*, April 18, 1926; *Chicago Tribune*, April 18, 1926; Martin J. Haley, "Cardinals Triumph Over Cubs, 3 to 2, in First Game of Series," *SLGD*, April 18, 1926.

8. Martin J. Daley, "Cardinals Again Trim Cubs, 10 to 5, to Assume League Leadership," *SLGD*, April 19, 1926; Herman Wecke, "Fine Pitching Puts Cardinals at Top in Pennant Race," *SLPD*, April 19, 1926; Irving Vaughan, "Cards Rap Out 15 Hits Off Two Bruin Pitchers," *Chicago Tribune*, April 19, 1926.

9. "Cardinals Sell Smith to Braves; Had Served St. Louis Ten Years," *SLGD*, April 20, 1926.

10. Herman Wecke, "Cardinals 'Army' Game Fails, Cubs Win 14-Inning Contest, 5–4," *SLPD*, April 20, 1926; Martin J. Haley, "Cardinal Streak Broken When Cubs Win in Fourteen Innings, 5–4," *SLGD*, April 20, 1926.

11. "Cardinals Going at Top Speed in 'Hitting the Air,'" *SLGD*, April 20, 1926; Martin J. Daley, "Cubs Hammer Reinhart's Slants and Shut Out Cardinals, 7 to 0," *SLGD*, April 21, 1926; "Cardinals Are in Terre Haute Today," *SLGD*, April 21, 1926.

12. Lou Wollen, "Waner and Rhyne Benched for Bucs' Home Opener," *Pittsburgh Press*, April 21, 1926.

13. "Hafey's Homer in Tenth, with Hornsby On, Beats Pirates, 5 to 3," *SLGD*, April 23, 1926; Lou Wollen, "Pirates Show Improvement in Hitting in Home Opener," *Pittsburgh Press*, April 23, 1926; Charles J. Doyle, "31,000 See Pirates Drop Into Cellar," *Pittsburgh Post-Gazette*, April 23, 1926; Curt Smith, *Storied Stadiums: Baseball's History Through Its Ballparks* (New York: Carroll & Graf, 2001), 72–74; Philip J. Lowry, *Green Cathedrals: The Ultimate Celebration of All 271 Major League and Negro League Ballparks Past and Present* (New York: Addison-Wesley, 1992), 216; Ronald M. Selter, *Ballparks of the Deadball Era: A Comprehensive Study of Their Dimensions, Configurations and Effects on Batting, 1901–1919* (Jefferson, NC: McFarland & Company, Inc., 2008), 8.

14. Charles J. Doyle, "Pie Traynor's Home Run with Two on Gives Vic Aldridge Winning Margin," *Pittsburgh Post-Gazette*, April 24, 1926; "Johnson Holds Pirates to Six Hits, but Cardinals Lose, 3 to 2," *SLGD*, April 24, 1926.

15. Herman Wecke, "Cards Show Old Punch and Beat Pirates, 9–3," *SLPD*, April 25, 1926; "Cardinals

Hammer Pirate Hurlers to Capture Final Game, 9 to 3," *SLGD*, April 25, 1926; Charles J. Doyle, "Cards Beat Bucs in Series' Finale, 9 to 3," *Pittsburgh Post-Gazette*, April 25, 1926.

16. Doutrich, *The Cardinals and the Yankees*, 60–61; Ritter, *The Glory of Their Times*, 203–209; Gregory H. Wolf, ed., *Cincinnati's Crosley Field: A Gem in the Queen City* (Phoenix: Society for American Baseball Research, 2018), 1; Lon Garber, "Crosley Field," in *Cincinnati's Crosley Field*, Wolf, ed., 8–12; Smith, *Storied Stadiums*, 85–86.

17. "Lucas Pitches Effectively and Reds Shut Out Cardinals, 4 to 0," *SLGD*, April 26, 1926; Herman Wecke, "Keen, with Three Victories, to Hurl for Cards in Next Game," *SLPD*, April 27, 1926; Tom Swope, "Cards Crack in Home Stretch," *Cincinnati Post*, April 27, 1926; Ray J. Gillespie, "Hornsby Picks Keen to Oppose Luque in Third Redland Game," *St. Louis Star*, April 27, 1926.

18. "Ninth-Inning Drive Nets Cardinals 5 to 3 Victory Over Reds," *SLGD*, April 29, 1926; Herman Wecke, "Cards Play Reds in Frigid Weather; Keen on Mound," *SLPD*, April 28, 1926; "Notes of the Game," *Cincinnati Enquirer*, April 29, 1926.

19. "Errors by Mails and Thevenow Permit Cubs to Beat Cardinals, 6–5," *SLGD*, April 30, 1926; Irving Vaughan, "Adams Tosses Victory Away; Foes Return It," *Chicago Tribune*, April 30, 1926.

20. Irving Vaughan, "Ill Wind Blows Bruins Good in Uphill Battle," *Chicago Tribune*, May 1, 1926; "Cardinals Fall Before Bruins in Eleven-Inning Struggle, 10 to 9," *SLGD*, May 1, 1926; "Old Road Complex Stays with Cards," *Sporting News*, May 6, 1926.

21. Herman Wecke, "Cardinals Make 14 Hits But Lose to Chicago, 11 to 8," *SLPD*, May 2, 1926; "Cubs Score Five Runs in Eighth to Beat Cards Third Straight, 11–8," *SLGD*, May 2, 1926.

22. Herman Wecke, "Cardinals, at Home After Losing 7 of 10 on Road, Tackle Cincinnati Today," *SLPD*, May 3, 1926; Irving Vaughan, "Bruins Again Nose Out Foes in Ninth, 6 To 5," *Chicago Tribune*, May 3, 1926; "Cardinals Off in Lead, but Cubs Again Nose Them Out, 6 to 5." See John C. Skipper, *Wicked Curve: The Life and Troubled Times of Grover Cleveland Alexander* (Jefferson, NC: McFarland, 2006) for a thorough account of Alexander's life.

Chapter 6

1. "1000 at Dedication of New $2,500,000 Jewish Hospital," *SLGD*, May 17, 1926; "City Officials Break Ground for Courthouse," *St. Louis Star*, May 19, 1926; "New Courthouse to Be Loftiest Building in City," *SLPD*, June 20, 1926; Editorial, *SLGD*, May 22, 1926; "River Front Park and Auditorium Proposals Heard," *SLPD*, May 21, 1926; Editorial, *SLGD*, May 7, 1926.

2. Editorial, *SLPD*, May 18, 1926.

3. "Murder Witnesses Were Not Sought by Circuit Attorney," *SLGD*, May 14, 1926; "Gentry to Open Rutherford Murder Probe Tomorrow," *SLGD*, May 24, 1926; Editorial, "Fraud Against Justice," *SLGD*, May 28, 1926; "The Grand Jury Acts," *SLPD*, June 2, 1926; "Sidener Indicted for Compounding Felony and Fraud," *SLGD*, June 2, 1926; "Bender Freed After Jury Deliberates One Hour," *SLGD*, July 31, 1926; "Attorney Bender Is Acquitted in Rutherford Case," *SLPD*, July 31, 1926; "Sidener Cleared by Court Order in Rutherford Case," *SLPD*, September 29, 1926; "Sidener Acquitted by Order of Court for Lack of Proof," *SLGD*, September 30, 1926.

4. Editorial, *SLPD*, September 30, 1926.

5. Martin J. Haley, "Cardinals Drop Fifth Straight Game When Reds Win, 9 to 6," *SLGD*, May 4, 1926; Jack Ryder, "Reds Come Through to Win Over Cards in Sloppy Contest," *Cincinnati Enquirer*, May 4, 1926.

6. "Scribbled by Scribes," *Sporting News*, May 13, 1926; J. Roy Stockton, "Cards, Despite Five Straight Defeats, Are Tied with Pirates," *SLPD*, May 4, 1926; *SLGD*, May 5, 1926; Leo Doyle, "Sports Topics," *Baltimore The Evening Sun*, August 25, 1926.

7. J. Roy Stockton, "Cards, Despite Five Straight Defeats Are Tied with Pirates," *SLPD*, May 4, 1926.

8. J. Roy Stockton, "Herman Bell Pitches Cardinals to 3-to-2 Victory Over Reds," *SLPD*, May 5, 1926; Martin J. Haley, "Two Bells Enable Cards to Beat Reds, 3–2, and End Losing Streak," *SLGD*, May 5, 1926; Jack Ryder, "Ding Dong Bell Stops Reds to Walk After Third Inning," *Cincinnati Enquirer*, May 5, 1926.

9. Martin J. Haley, "Cardinals, Held to Five Scattered Hits, Lose to Reds, 6 to 1," *SLGD*, May 6, 1926; J. Roy Stockton, "Flint Rhem to Pitch Against League Leading Dodgers Today," *SLPD*, May 6, 1926; Clifford, "A Phil Named Syl."

10. Glenn Stout, *The Dodgers: 120 Years of Dodgers Baseball* (New York: Houghton Mifflin, 2004), 87–92; Greg Erion, "Babe Herman," SABR Biography Project (https://sabr.org/bioproj/person/babe-herman/).

11. Ritter, *The Glory of Their Times*, 207–208; Thomas Holmes, "Hot St. Louis Weather Figures to Get Vance in Shape," *Brooklyn Daily Eagle*, May 6, 1926; Charles F. Faber, "Dazzy Vance," SABR Biography Project (https://sabr.org/bioproj/person/dazzy-vance).

12. Martin J. Haley, "Cardinals Make Only Three Hits, but Win from Dodgers, 3 to 1," *SLGD*, May 7, 1926; J. Roy Stockton, "Sherdel to Pitch Against the Dodgers Today," *SLPD*, May 7, 1926; Thomas Holmes, "Robby Cannot Explain Why Dazzy Vance Is Still Off Form," *Brooklyn Daily Eagle*, May 7, 1926; Alexander, *Rogers Hornsby*, 110.

13. J. Roy Stockton, "Reinhart or Keen to Face Barnes Today," *SLPD*, May 8, 1926; Martin J. Haley, "Grimes Yields Five Hits and Robins Trounce Cardinals, 7 to 1," *SLGD*, May 8, 1926; Thomas Holmes, "Grimes Advances to Even Keel in Victories and Defeats," *Brooklyn Daily Eagle*, May 8, 1926.

14. J. Roy Stockton, "Herman's Homer Helps Robins Defeat Cards, 5–3," *SLPD*, May 9, 1926; Thomas Holmes, "Herman's Big Blow Saves First Place for Robins with Homer in Seventh," *Brooklyn Daily Eagle*, May 9, 1926; Martin J. Haley, "Dodgers Hit Reinhart Opportunely to Win from Cardinals, 5 to 3," *SLGD*, May 9, 1926; J. Roy Stockton, "Keen to Pitch Against Giants in First Game of Series Today," *SLPD*, May 10, 1926; Thomas Holmes, "Chicago Must Win Three Games to Assume Lead; St. Louis Is Squelched," *Brooklyn Daily Eagle*, May 10, 1926; Richard Vidmer, "Bob M'Graw Wins His 4th for Robins," *New York Times*, May 10, 1926.

15. Stout, *The Dodgers*, 87–92; Bob McGee, *The Greatest Ballpark Ever: Ebbets Field and the Story of the Brooklyn Dodgers* (New Brunswick, NJ: Rivergate Books, 2005), 105–107.

16. "Alderman Stand by Browns And Cards," *SLGD*, May 8, 1926; "Gould's Gossip," *St. Louis Star*, May 8, 1926; "KMOX to Broadcast Baseball Scores of St. Louis Teams," *SLGD*, May 11, 1926; Mitchell, *Mr. Rickey's Redbirds*, 226–227.

17. Charles C. Alexander, *John McGraw* (Lincoln: University of Nebraska Press, 1988), 271–273; Doutrich, *The Cardinals and the Yankees*, 62–63.

18. J. Roy Stockton, "Keen Beats the Giants for His Fourth Victory of Season," *SLPD*, May 11, 1926; Martin J. Haley, "Cardinals Concentrate Attack to Down Giants in Opener, 5 to 4," *SLGD*, May 11, 1926; Harry Cross, "Giants Hit Often, But Lose to Cards," *New York Times*, May 11, 1926; J. Roy Stockton, "Rhem Scores Fifth Victory, Thanks to Haines' Rescue Work," *SLPD*, May 12, 1926; Rud Rennie, "Giants Drop Fifth Straight, Losing to Cardinals by 6 to 5," *New York Herald Tribune*, May 12, 1926.

19. J. Roy Stockton, "Cardinals' Inability to Bunt Gives Giants 2–1 Victory," *SLPD*, May 13, 1926; Harry Cross, "Giants' 2 Homers Better Cards' One," *New York Times*, May 13, 1926; J. Roy Stockton, "Giants Pound 4 Hurlers for 18 Hits and Maul Cardinals, 12 to 1," *SLPD*, May 14, 1926; James M. Gould, "Jackson Is Hurt as Are Feelings of Card Hurlers," *St. Louis Star*, May 14, 1926; Harry Cross, "Giants Win, 12 to 1, But Lose Jackson," *New York Times*, May 14, 1926.

20. J. Roy Stockton, "Giants Pound 4 Hurlers for 18 Hits and Maul Cardinals, 12 to 1," *SLPD*, May 14, 1926; James M. Gould, "Jackson Is Hurt as Are Feelings of Card Hurlers," *St. Louis Star*, May 14, 1926.

21. Harold Kaese and R.G. Lynch, *The Milwaukee Braves: An Informal History of a Great Baseball Team in Boston and Milwaukee* (New York: G.P. Putnam's Sons, 1954), 187–200; J. Roy Stockton, "Cardinals Bat Genewich Hard and Defeat Braves, 12 to 7," *SLPD*, May 16, 1926; Martin J. Haley, "Cardinals Pound Genewich to Take Opener from Braves, 12 to 7," *SLGD*, May 16, 1926; Martin J. Haley, "Sixteen Hits for 33 Bases Enable Cardinals to Swamp Braves, 13–2," *SLGD*, May 17, 1926; Martin J. Haley, "Cardinals Again Total 16 Hits and Win Third Straight Game, 8 to 5," *SLGD*, May 18, 1926; J. Roy Stockton, "Huntzinger or Haines to Hurl For Cards Today," *SLPD*, May 18, 1926.

22. James M. Gould, "Series To Open Tomorrow With Fletcher's Phils," *St. Louis Star*, May 18, 1926.

23. Frederick G. Lieb and Stan Baumgartner, *The Philadelphia Phillies* (New York: G.P. Putnam's Sons, 1953), 156; David M. Jordan, *Occasional Glory: The History of the Philadelphia Phillies* (Jefferson, NC: McFarland, 2002), 58–65; J. Roy Stockton, "Rain At Philadelphia Interrupts Cardinals' Pennant March," *SLPD*, July 29, 1926; Cappy Gagnon, "Cy Williams," SABR Biography Project (https://sabr.org/bioproj/person/cy-williams/).

24. J. Roy Stockton, "Carlson Baffles Cards and Phils Take First Game, 6 to 2," *SLPD*, May 20, 1926; Martin J. Haley, "Hornsby, Spiked in Left Instep in Third Inning, Is Forced to Retire," *SLGD*, May 20, 1926; "Hal Carlson Hurls Phils to Victory," *Philadelphia Inquirer*, May 20, 1926; Martin J. Haley, "Cardinals Make Only Four Hits, but Win from Phillies, 4 to 1," *SLGD*, May 21, 1926.

25. "Knight Loses Tough Tilt To Vic. Keen," *Philadelphia Inquirer*, May 21, 1926; Martin J. Haley, "Cardinals Make Only Four Hits, but Win from Phillies, 4 to 1," *SLGD*, May 21, 1926; J. Roy Stockton, "Cards' Great Fielding and Timely Hitting Win for Victor Keen," *SLPD*, May 21, 1926; Martin J. Haley, "Cardinals Open Barrage Late in Game to Smother Phillies, 12 to 4," *SLGD*, May 22, 1926; Jack Alexander, "Hornsby Receives 1925 Player Award Today," *SLPD*, May 22, 1926; "Cards Hand Another Spanking to Phils," *Philadelphia Inquirer*, May 22, 1926.

26. "Hornsby, a $750 Rookie in 1915, Honored as Most Valuable Player," *SLPD*, May 23, 1926; J. Roy Stockton, "Cardinals Reach .500 Mark by Beating Phils, 9–2," *SLPD*, May 23, 1926; Martin J. Haley, "Sherdel Holds Phillies at Bay as Cardinals Triumph by 9 to 2 Score," *SLGD*, May 23, 1926.

27. J. Roy Stockton, "Cards Open Series with Reds Today," *SLPD*, May 24, 1926; Martin J. Haley, "Bases on Balls Prove Medium of Cardinals' Defeat by Phillies, 7 to 5," *SLGD*, May 24, 1926.

28. Mitchell Conrad Stinson, *Edd Roush: A Biography of the Cincinnati Reds Star* (Jefferson, NC: McFarland, 2010), 175–178; J. Roy Stockton, "Cards Score 11 Runs in Last 3 Innings and Beat Cincinnati, 11 to 6," *SLPD*, May 25, 1926; Martin J. Haley, "Cards Overcome Six-Run Lead to Down League-Leading Reds, 11–6," *SLGD*, May 25, 1926; Jack Ryder, "Six-Run Lead of Cincinnati Team Is Shot to High Heavens," *Cincinnati Enquirer*, May 25, 1926.

29. "Hit an Ardent Fan as Well as Ball on the Nose," *SLPD*, May 26, 1926; "Jim Bottomley in Court for Breaking Fan's Nose with Ball," *SLGD*, May 26, 1926. The State of Illinois enacted the nation's first "foul ball" legislation on September 24, 1992. It prevented fans injured by a foul ball from suing the stadium owner unless the injury resulted from a defective screen that was due to the owner's negligence or "willful and wanton" conduct of the owner, manager, coaches, or players.

See Ed Edmonds and Frank G. Houdek, *Baseball Meets the Law: A Chronology of Decisions, Statutes and Other Legal Events* (Jefferson, NC: McFarland, 2017), 145, and Robert Neymeyer, "Fans Strike Out with Foul Ball Litigation," *Sports and the Law: Major Legal Cases*, Charles E. Quirk, ed. (New York: Garland, 1996), 24–27.

30. J. Roy Stockton, "Cards Start Road Campaign After Today's Game with the Reds," *SLPD*, May 26, 1926; Martin J. Haley, "Cardinals Outhit and Outslugged, Score 9 to 7 Victory Over Reds," *SLGD*, May 26, 1926; Nick C. Wilson, *Early Latino Ballplayers in the United States* (Jefferson, NC: McFarland, 2005), 67–82, 97–98.

31. "Jim Bottomley's Home Run to Cost Cardinals $3500," *SLPD*, May 27, 1926; "Nose Broken by Bottomley's Homer, Gets $3500 Award," *SLPD*, May 27, 1926; "Fan Hit by Home Run Loses $15,000 Suit," *SLPD*, January 12, 1928; Waldo, *Baseball's Roaring Twenties*, 215–218.

32. Tom Swope, "Hendricks Calls Hurlers Together for More Serious Efforts," *Cincinnati Post*, May 26, 1926; James M. Gould, "Heine Mueller and Bob O'Farrell Hit Ball for Circuit," *St. Louis Star*, May 26, 1926; Jack Ryder, "Oh, Those Brutal Cardinals, How They Love Cincinnati," *Cincinnati Enquirer*, May 27, 1926; Martin J. Haley, "Cardinals Register Seven Runs in Eighth and Vanquish Reds, 8 to 5," *SLGD*, May 27, 1926.

Chapter 7

1. "75,000 Present When $3,000,000 Concordia Seminary Is Dedicated by Leaders of Lutheran Church," *St. Louis Star*, June 14, 1926; "16,000 Hear Papal Legate Sing Mass," *St. Louis Star*, June 29, 1926; "Thousands Cheer Papal Legate on Arrival Here," *SLGD*, June 29, 1926; "Throngs Jam Streets for Final Consecration Ceremonies," *SLGD*, June 30, 1926; "Flag Now Flies from Mast on New Skyscraper," *SLPD*, June 18, 1926.

2. Helen D. and Joseph E. Vollmar, "Caves, Tunnels and Other Holes … Under St. Louis," *Gateway Heritage* 8 (Fall 1987), 2; "Opening to Cave Still Was Under 2 Feet of Ashes," *St. Louis Star*, June 26, 1926; "Distillery Found in Cave Beneath Morgan Street," *SLPD*, June 26, 1926; "Agents Find Cave Distillery Under Morgan Street," *SLGD*, June 26, 1926; "Dry Director Ambushed and Shot in Neck," *SLGD*, June 8, 1926.

3. "Pugilist Shot to Death During Street Brawl," *SLPD*, June 14, 1926; "Police Hold Man Named by Victim," *SLGD*, June 14, 1926; "Saloon Keeper, Held in Pugilist's Death, Maintains Silence," *SLGD*, June 15, 1926.

4. "Cardinals Drop Two Bitterly Fought Games to Reds, 4–3 and 2–1," *SLGD*, May 28, 1926; Tom Swope, "Red Pitchers Hand Cardinals Double Defeat by Keeping Ball Over Plate in Pinches," *Cincinnati Post*, May 28, 1926; Jack Ryder, "Both Ends of Twin Bill Taken by Reds, 4 to 3 and 2 to 1," *Cincinnati Enquirer*, May 28, 1926.

5. "Cincinnati Makes Third Straight Conquest Over Cards a 12 to 4 Rout," *SLGD*, May 29, 1926; Jack Ryder, "Reds, Aided by Passes, Clout Out 12-to-4 Win Over Cards," *Cincinnati Enquirer*, May 29, 1926; "Hallahan Routed in Sixth," *St. Louis Star*, May 28, 1926.

6. "May's Effective Hurling Enables Reds to Trip Cardinals, 3 to 1," *SLGD*, May 30, 1926; "Jakie May, Making First Start, Humbles Cardinals, 3 to 1," *SLPD*, May 30, 1926.

7. "Rhem Limits Cubs to Seven Hits as Cardinals Score 5–2 Victory," *Chicago Tribune*, May 31, 1926; "Knot Holers Beat Bruins in Opener by Margin of 5–3," *St. Louis Star*, May 31, 1926; "Cardinals and Cubs Break Even in Rain-Soaked Double-Header," *SLGD*, June 1, 1926; James Crusinberry, "Cubs and Cards Fight Damp Draw, 5–3 and 8–8," *Chicago Tribune*, June 1, 1926.

8. James Crusinberry, "Cubs Hit 4 Homers to Beat Cards, 10–9," *Chicago Tribune*, June 2, 1926.

9. "Cardinals Take Odd Game of Series from Cubs, Winning, 14 to 6" and "Chick Hafey, Suffering from Eye Trouble, Returns to St. Louis," *SLGD*, June 3, 1926; "Injured Finger Will Keep Keen Out for 10 Days," *SLPD*, June 3, 1926; "Browns Not Quite So Helpless Now," *Sporting News*, June 10, 1926; Bob Broeg, "Hafey's Dilemma: Born Too Soon for Big Money," *SLPD*, July 8, 1973.

10. Lowry, *Green Cathedrals*, 207–208; Rich Westcott, *Philadelphia's Old Ballparks* (Philadelphia: Temple University Press, 1996), 27–42; "A Historical Sketch of Baker Bowl," philadelphiaathletics.org, retrieved April 7, 2024; Murdock, *Baseball Players and Their Times*, 121.

11. "Cards Beat Phils in First Game, 4–0, Rhem Gains 9th Victory," *SLPD*, June 5, 1926; "Cards Take Doubleheader and Reach First Division," *SLPD*, June 6, 1926; "Cards Seize Both Ends of Double-Header from Phils, 4–0 and 7–4," *SLGD*, June 6, 1926; S.O. Grauley, "Phillies Drop Two: Go Into Last Place," *Philadelphia Inquirer*, June 6, 1926.

12. Doutrich, *The Cardinals and the Yankees*, 70–71; "Rain Again Keeps Cards Idle; Team Goes to New York," *SLPD*, June 8, 1926.

13. Stew Thornley, "The Polo Grounds," SABR Biography Project (https://sabr.org/bioproj/park/polo-grounds-new-york); Ron Selter, "By the Numbers: The Five Polo Grounds Ballparks," in *The Polo Grounds: Essays and Memories of New York City's Historic Ballpark, 1880–1963*, Stew Thornley, ed. (Jefferson, NC: McFarland, 2019), 82–91; Lowry, *Green Cathedrals*, 195–196; Smith, *Storied Stadiums*, 106.

14. Will Wedge, "Rogers Hornsby Drives in 2 Runs as Red Birds Win," *St. Louis Star*, June 9, 1926; Will Wedge, "Red Birds Defeat New Yorkers for 5th Straight Win," *St. Louis Star*, June 10, 1926; "Cardinals Hammer Three Giant Pitchers Freely and Gain 4–2 Victory," *SLGD*, June 10, 1926; "Keen Beats the Giants for Cardinals' Sixth Straight Victory," *SLPD*, June 12, 1926; Harry Cross, "Giants Are Shaded by Rhem's Hurling," *New York Times*,

June 11, 1926; Harry Cross, "Cards Heap Runs on Passive Giants," *New York Times*, June 12, 1926; Will Murphy, "M'Graw Outfit Simply Rotten in Series Final," *New York Daily News*, June 12, 1926; Rud Rennie, "Flint Rhem Turns Back Giants by 3 to 2," *New York Herald Tribune*, June 11, 1926; Rud Rennie, "Cardinals Take Third Straight from Giants, 10-2," *New York Herald Tribune*, June 12, 1926.

15. "Keen Beats the Giants for Cardinals' Sixth Straight Victory," *SLPD*, June 12, 1926.

16. Bob McGee, *The Greatest Ballpark Ever*, 61-63; Smith, *Storied Stadiums*, 102-104; Lowry, *Green Cathedrals*, 117-118, Stout, *The Dodgers*, 50-51; Peter Golenbock, *Bums: An Oral History of the Brooklyn Dodgers* (New York: G.P. Putnam's Sons, 1984), 19, 25; John Zinn, "Ebbets Field," *Ebbets Field: Great, Historic, and Memorable Games from Brooklyn's Lost Ballpark*, Gregory H. Wolf, ed. (Phoenix: Society for American Baseball Research, 2023), 6.

17. "Cardinal Winning Streak Ends When Brooklyn Takes Opener, 8 to 5," *SLGD*, June 15, 1926.

18. "Southworth's Steadier Fielding Will Stabilize Outfield, Hornsby Says," *SLPD*, June 15, 1926; "Cardinals Trade 'Heinie' Mueller to New York for Billy Southworth," *SLGD*, June 15, 1926; Doutrich, *The Cardinals and the Yankees*, 72-73; "Both St. Louis Clubs Figure in Late Deals," *Sporting News*, June 17, 1926; "Rain in Brooklyn Halts Drive of the Climbing Cardinals," *SLPD*, June 16, 1926. In a post-season interview, Hornsby mistakenly claimed McGraw approached him during a series in which St. Louis won the first game but lost four in a row. That series, however, took place in late July/early August when Southworth had already been acquired. See "Hornsby Tells How He Happened to Get Alexander and Southworth," *SLPD*, September 28, 1926.

19. Jon Daly, "Billy Southworth," SABR Biography Project (https://sabr.org/bioproj/person/billy-southworth); Lieb, *The St. Louis Cardinals*, 110-111.

20. "Rain in Brooklyn Halts Drive of the Climbing Cardinals," *SLPD*, June 16, 1926; "Sherdel's Mound Mastery and Bottomley's Bat Beat Robins, 4 to 0," *SLGD*, June 16, 1926.

21. Lowry, *Green Cathedrals*, 110-111; William J. Craig, *A History of the Boston Braves: A Time Gone By* (Charleston, SC: The History Press, 2012), 39, 42; Bill Price, "Braves Field," *Baseball Research Journal*, 1978; Bob Ruzzo, "Braves Field: An Imperfect History of the Perfect Ballpark," *Baseball Research Journal* 41 (Fall 2012), 53-55; Ray Miller, "A Biography of Braves Field." *Braves Field: Memorable Moments at Boston's Lost Diamond*, Bill Nowlin and Bob Brady, eds. (Phoenix: Society for American Baseball Research, 2015), 3-6; Selter, *Ballparks of the Deadball Era*, 35-36.

22. "Cardinals Win First Game of Twin Bill with Braves, 4-2," *SLPD*, June 17, 1926; "Cardinals Take Double-Header from Braves, 4 to 2 and 6 to 2," *SLGD*, June 18, 1926.

23. "Cardinals Win First Game from Boston, 4-0," *SLPD*, June 19, 1926; James C. O'Leary, "Hornsby Satisfied with Cards' Place," *Boston Globe*, June 19, 1926; "Herman Bell Outhurls Joe Genewich," *St. Louis Star*, June 19, 1926; "Cards Win Two from Braves; Still One Game from Top," *SLPD*, June 20, 1926; "Haines and H. Bell Pitch Cardinals to Twin Victory Over Braves," *SLGD*, June 20, 1926; Wolf, "Jesse Haines," SABR Biography Project.

24. "Sherdel Allows Only Two Hits and Cardinals Shut Out Dodgers, 9 to 0," *SLGD*, June 21, 1926; Thomas Holmes, "Still Too Early to Pick Winner in Brooklyn-Boston Trade," *Brooklyn Daily Eagle*, June 21, 1926.

25. "Cards to Play in Pittsburgh Monday," *SLGD*, June 18, 1926; "Pitchers Roughly Handled as Cardinals Drop 13-11 Verdict to Bucs," *SLPD*, June 22, 1926; "Cards and Pirates Hold Slugging Match; Rhem Is Batted Out," *SLPD*, June 21, 1926; Charles J. Doyle, "Waner Leads Vicious Assault Against Six of Foe's Moundsmen," *Pittsburgh Post-Gazette*, June 22, 1926.

26. "Cards Greeted by Rooters at Union Station" and "Cardinals, 1 1-2 Games Out of Lead, Play Pirates Here Today," *SLPD*, June 22, 1926; Martin J. Haley, "Wright Poles Two Homers as Bucs Down Cards, 3-1, in First of Series," *SLGD*, June 23, 1926; Charles J. Doyle, "Meadows, Wright Beat Cardinals, 3-1," *Pittsburgh Gazette Times*, June 23, 1926.

27. J. Roy Stockton, "Cards Increase Pennant Chances by Claiming Alexander of Cubs," *SLPD*, June 23, 1926; "He's 39 and Still 'The Great,'" *Sporting News*, July 1, 1926.

28. James Crusinberry, "Alexander Suspended by Cubs," *Chicago Tribune*, June 16, 1926; Joe Foley, sports editor of *Chicago Journal*, "Alexander Deal Shock to Chicago," *SLPD*, June 23, 1926; Skipper, *Wicked Curve*, 100-103; Mitchell, *Mr. Rickey's Redbirds*, 207-212; Peter Golenbock, *Wrigleyville: A Magical History Tour of the Chicago Cubs* (New York: St. Martin's Press, 1996), 185-189, 191-193; Stout, *The Cubs*, 115-120; Ehrgott, *Mr. Wrigley's Ball Club*, 63-74; "An Idol Falls Off Cubs' Hero Throne," *Sporting News*, June 24, 1926.

29. Skipper, *Wicked Curve*, 103-105; Mitchell, *Mr. Rickey's Redbirds*, 212; Doutrich, *The Cardinals and the Yankees*, 75-76; J. Roy Stockton, "Cards Increase Pennant Chances by Claiming Alexander of Cubs," *SLPD*, June 23, 1926; D'Amore, *Rogers Hornsby*, 60-62; Bob Broeg, "O'Farrell's Memories Vivid of Redbirds' First Title," *SLPD*, January 25, 1976; Lowenfish, *Branch Rickey*, 160-161.

30. "Alexander Tells Killefer He Is Ready to Pitch," *SLPD*, June 23, 1926; Hornsby, *My War with Baseball*, 152; "Grover Alexander Helps Cards Fan Pennant Fire in St. Louis," *Sporting News*, July 1, 1926; Mel R. Freese, *The Glory Years of the St. Louis Cardinals. Volume 1: The World Championship Seasons* (St. Louis: Palmerston & Reed, 1999), 14-15.

31. J. Roy Stockton, "Thevenow, Haines and Hornsby Heroes as Cards Start Big Push," *SLPD*,

June 24, 1926; Martin J. Haley, "Hornsby's Homer with Three On and Haines' Hurling Beat Bucs, 6–2," *SLGD*, June 24, 1926; "Buccos Close Series Today," *Pittsburgh Press*, June 24, 1926.

32. Martin J. Haley, "Call to Train Stops Cardinal-Pirate Final in Ninth with Score 3–3," *SLGD*, June 25, 1926; Charles J. Doyle, "Bucs and Cards Play to 3–3 Deadlock," *Pittsburgh Gazette Times*, June 25, 1926.

33. Martin J. Haley, "Cards Defeat Cubs, 8–7, for Second Place," *SLGD*, June 27, 1926; J. Roy Stockton, "Cards in 2nd Place After Beating Cubs, 8–7," *SLPD*, June 27, 1926.

34. "Grover Alexander Helps Cards Fan Pennant Fire in St. Louis," *Sporting News*, July 1, 1926; J. Roy Stockton, "Alexander Makes Good Before Record Baseball Throng," *SLPD*, June 28, 1926; Martin J. Haley, "38,000 See Cardinals Break Even in Double Bill with Cubs," *SLGD*, June 28, 1926; Honig, *The October Heroes*, 185.

35. Golenbock, *Wrigleyville*, 194; Hornsby, *My War with Baseball*, 152; J. Roy Stockton, "Alexander Makes Good Before Record Baseball Throng," *SLPD*, June 28, 1926; Martin J. Haley, "38,000 See Cardinals Break Even in Double Bill with Cubs," *SLGD*, June 28, 1926; James Crusinberry, "Cubs Beaten by Cardinals, 3–2; Then Win, 5 to 0," *Chicago Tribune*, June 28, 1926.

36. "Alexander to Pitch Today," *SLPD*, June 27, 1926; J. Roy Stockton, "Alexander Makes Good Before Record Baseball Throng," *SLPD*, June 28, 1926; "Hats, Not Heads Broken, as Fans Throw Cushions," *SLPD*, June 28, 1926; Martin J. Haley, "38,000 See Cardinals Break Even in Double Bill with Cubs," *SLGD*, June 28, 1926; "Gould's Gossip," *St. Louis Star*, June 29, 1926.

37. Martin J. Haley, "Cubs Rout Keen and Score Eight Runs in Fifth to Thrash Cards, 11–3," *SLGD*, June 29, 1926; James Crusinberry, "Cubs Bat Out 16 Hits to Wallop Cardinals, 11–3," *Chicago Tribune*, June 29, 1926.

38. "Hornsby Undergoes Minor Operation; Hopes to Play Again Sunday," *SLPD*, June 29, 1926; "Hornsby Goes to Hospital as Team Departs for Road Trip," *SLGD*, June 29, 1926; *Sporting News*, July 1, 1926.

Chapter 8

1. "Suspect Slain, Pal Shot in Police Trap," *SLGD, July 2, 1926*, "St. Louis Gangsters Wanted for Murders Found on East Side," *SLPD*, July 2, 1926; "Police Here Carry War on Gangsters to Illinois Towns," *St. Louis Star*, July 2, 1926; "4 Arrested, 20,000 Gallons of Mash Seized in Dry Raid," *SLGD*, July 23, 1926.

2. "Old Olive Street Abodes of Riches and Culture Abdicate to Progress," *St. Louis Star*, July 19, 1926; "Actual Work of Widening Olive Street to Begin Soon," *SLPD*, July 16, 1926.

3. John J. Sheridan, "Cardinals Go to Pittsburgh for Series Against Pirates," *SLGD*, June 30, 1926.

4. John J. Sheridan, "Cardinals Defeat Pirates, 6–2, to Strengthen Hold on Second Place," *SLGD*, July 1, 1926; Charles J. Doyle, "Buccaneers Extend Losing Streak, 6–2," *Pittsburgh Gazette Times*, July 1, 1926; "Blades and Bell Clout Home Runs," *St. Louis Star*, June 30, 1926; "Ralph Davis Says," *Pittsburgh Press*, June 30, 1926.

5. John J. Sheridan, "Rhem Blows Up in Seventh and Pirates Defeat Cardinals, 7 to 3," *SLGD*, July 2, 1926; Charles J. Doyle, "Pirates End Losing Streak; Win, 7–3," *Pittsburgh Gazette Times*, July 2, 1926.

6. John J. Sheridan, "Pirates Withstand Cardinal's Belated Attack and Win, 3 to 2," *SLGD*, July 3, 1926; Charles J. Doyle, "Bucs Repeat Triumph Over Cards, 3–2," *Pittsburgh Gazette Times*, July 3, 1926; Jack Alexander, "Pirates Score Eight Runs in Inning; Herman Bell Routed," *SLPD*, July 3, 1926; "Knot-Holers Drop to Third Place," *St. Louis Star*, July 3, 1926.

7. "Hornsby Will Be on Bench Today, Directing Cards," *SLPD*, July 4, 1926; Martin J. Haley, "Cardinals Losing Streak Reaches Four Straight as Reds Win, 7 to 2," *SLGD*, July 5, 1926; Jack Ryder, "Redlegs Batter Down the Defenses of St. Louis Cardinals," *Cincinnati Enquirer*, July 5, 1926.

8. "Southworth's Home Run Gives Cardinals Even Break with Reds," *SLGD*, July 6, 1926; Herman Wecke, "Cards Rely on Vic Keen to Gain Even Break with Reds Today," *SLPD*, July 6, 1926; Jack Ryder, "League Leaders Split Twin Bill with St. Louis Team," *Cincinnati Enquirer*, July 6, 1926; Doutrich, *The Cardinals and the Yankees*, 95.

9. J. Roy Stockton, "Vic Keen Nursing Sore Arm; Sherdel Likely to Face Reds Today," *SLPD*, July 7, 1926; Martin J. Haley, "Alexander Weakens in Ninth and Reds Win in Eleventh, 5 to 2," *SLGD*, July 7, 1926.

10. Jack Ryder, "Reds Exhibit Eccentric Baseball and Are Downed Easily," *Cincinnati Enquirer*, July 8, 1926; J. Roy Stockton, "Cards Five Games Behind Reds After Leaders Take 3 Out of 4," *SLPD*, July 8, 1926; Martin J. Haley, "Reinhart Pitches Brilliantly as Cardinals Submerge Reds, 11 to 2," *SLGD*, July 8, 1926.

11. Jack Alexander, "Second Place in Sight as Cardinals Face Braves Today," *SLPD*, July 10, 1926; Martin J. Haley, "Cardinals Stamp Hornsby's Return with 2–1 Victory Over Braves," *SLGD*, July 10, 1926; "Double by O'Farrell Scores Deciding Run," *Boston Globe*, July 10, 1926.

12. J. Roy Stockton, "Cards Bat Hard and Trounce Braves, 18–6," *SLPD*, July 11, 1926; Martin J. Haley, "Cards Pound Brave Hurlers to Win, 18–6, and Climb Nearer Reds," *SLGD*, July 11, 1926.

13. J. Roy Stockton, "Cards Gain Half a Game on Reds by Breaking Even in Twin Bill," *SLPD*, July 12, 1926; Martin J. Haley, "Cards Win Opener of Twin Bill, but Drop Farcical Final, 19–5," *SLGD*, July 12, 1926.

14. J. Roy Stockton, "Cards Gain Half a Game on Reds by Breaking Even in Twin Bill," *SLPD*, July 12, 1926; "Gould's Gossip," *St. Louis Star*, July 14, 1926; "Flint Rhem, Fined $2,000, Quits Game,"

Atlanta Constitution, July 28, 1927, in HOF "Flint Rhem" Clipping File; Griffin, "Flint Rhem," SABR Biography Project; Golenbock, *Spirit of St. Louis,* 125.

15. Griffin, "Flint Rhem," SABR Biography Project; Golenbock, *Spirit of St. Louis,* 140–141; "'Imagine Me, of All People,' Wails Flint Rhem as He Tells of Booze Seduction," *Atlanta Constitution,* September 19, 1930, and Neil Russo, "Rhem Spoils 1930 Story—He Wasn't Kidnapped at All," *SLPD,* August 7, 1960, in HOF "Flint Rhem" Clipping File; John Thom, "The Kidnapping of Flint Rhem," *The National Pastime: A Review of Baseball History* 10 (1990), 79–82.

16. "Prosperity Reacts Against Cardinals," *Sporting News,* July 15, 1926; Freese, *The Glory Years of the St. Louis Cardinals,* 15–16.

17. J. Roy Stockton, "Cardinals Must Defeat Dodgers Today to Remain in Third Place," *SLPD,* July 13, 1926; Martin J. Haley, "Welsh's Home Run in Ninth Enables Braves to Defeat Cardinals, 8–6," *SLGD,* July 13, 1926.

18. J. Roy Stockton, "Cardinal Pitchers Battered for 37 Runs, 54 Hits in 3 Games," *SLPD,* July 14, 1926; "Tuberculosis Society to Stage 12th Annual Baseball Game Today," *SLGD,* July 14, 1926; Martin J. Haley, "Cardinals Beat Robins, 12–10, Despite Fournier's Three Home Runs," *SLGD,* July 14, 1926.

19. Martin J. Haley, "McWeeny Is Stingy in Pinches and Dodgers Repulse Cardinals, 5 to 2," *SLGD,* July 15, 1926; J. Roy Stockton, "Cardinals Can Jump to Second or Drop to Fifth Place Today," *SLPD,* July 15, 1926; "Tuberculosis Day Ball Game Draws 16,000 Attendance," *SLGD,* July 15, 1926.

20. J. Roy Stockton, "Dodgers Score 20 Runs in 3 Games, But Cards Win 2 Out of 3," *SLPD,* July 16, 1926; John J. Sheridan, "Cardinals, Aided by Reinhart's Arm and Bat, Wallop Dodgers, 11–5," *SLGD,* July 16, 1926; Thomas Holmes, "Robbie Nicks Jess Petty's Bankroll for One Hundred Iron Men," *Brooklyn Daily Eagle,* July 16, 1926.

21. J. Roy Stockton, "Cardinals, Despite Many Misfortunes, Still in Strategic Position," *SLPD,* July 17, 1926; Martin J. Haley, "Cardinals Shaded by Dodgers, 8–7, in Hectic, Drawnout Struggle," *SLGD,* July 17, 1926.

22. J. Roy Stockton, "Cards Whip Phils, 13–5; Rhem Returns to Form," *SLPD,* July 18, 1926; Martin J. Haley, "Cardinals Overwhelm Phillies, 13 to 5, and Gain on Leaders," *SLGD,* July 18, 1926.

23. J. Roy Stockton, "Sothoron's Pitching and Southworth's Homer Beat Phils, 9–7," *SLPD,* July 19, 1926; Martin J. Haley, "Southworth's Homer with Hornsby On in 9th Gives Cards 9–7 Victory," *SLGD,* July 19, 1926.

24. Martin J. Haley, "Cardinals' Weak Defense Aids Phils to Victory in 10 Innings, 4 to 3," *SLGD,* July 20, 1926; "Phillies Tie in Ninth Then Win in Tenth," *Philadelphia Inquirer,* July 20, 1926.

25. J. Roy Stockton, "Cards in Good Strategic Position, Despite Poor Record at Home," *SLPD,* July 20, 1926; James M. Gould, "Cards Will Have Plenty of 'Pep' When N.Y. Comes," *St. Louis Star,*

July 20, 1926; Herman Wecke, "Cards Hit .331 During Home Stay, But Hurlers Fail," *SLPD,* July 21, 1926; W.B. Hanna, "Briefs," *New York Herald Tribune,* August 23, 1926.

26. J. Roy Stockton, "Rogers Hornsby Will Try To Play Today, Despite Injured Eye," and Herman Wecke, "Southworth Hits Home Run To Celebrate Mueller Day," *SLPD,* July 23, 1926; Martin J. Haley, "Giants Score Twice with Two Out in Ninth to Beat Cardinals, 5–3," *SLGD,* July 23, 1926; IK Shuman, "Giants Beat Cards in the Ninth, 5–3," *New York Times,* July 23, 1926; Will Murphy, "Giants Nick Cards For First, 5–3," *New York Daily News,* July 23, 1926.

27. J. Roy Stockton, "Sherdel Baffles and Southworth Batters the New York Giants," *SLPD,* July 24, 1926; Martin J. Haley, "Sherdel Wins 3d Straight At-Home Victory as Cards Down Giants, 6–1," *SLGD,* July 24, 1926; IK Shuman, "Sherdel Humbles the Giants Again," *New York Times,* July 24, 1926; J. Roy Stockton, "Cardinals Drop 11-Inning Game to Giants, 5 to 3," *SLPD,* July 25, 1926; Martin J. Haley, "Rhem's Wild Heave in 11th Gives Giants 5–3 Victory Over Cards," *SLGD,* July 25, 1926; IK Shuman, "Giants Beat Cards in Eleventh, 5 To 3," *New York Times,* July 25, 1926; Will Murphy, "Rhem's Wild Toss Gives Giants Game," *New York Daily News,* July 25, 1926.

28. *Sporting News,* July 29, 1926.

29. J. Roy Stockton, "Confident Cards on Way East Only 2½ Games Behind Leaders," *SLPD,* July 26, 1926; Martin J. Haley, "Cards Down Giants in Eleventh, 6–5, in Nip-and-Tuck Battle," *SLGD,* July 26, 1926; IK Shuman, "2 Cardinal Homers Help Down Giants," *New York Times,* July 26, 1926; Will Murphy, "Cards Take Giants in Eleventh, 6–5," *New York Daily News,* July 26, 1926; W.B. Hanna, "Southworth Robs McGrawmen of Victory in Tenth with Homer," *New York Herald Tribune,* July 26, 1926.

Chapter 9

1. "Millions Lost by Drought in St. Louis Area," *St. Louis Star,* August 6, 1926; "Heat Wave Continues with No Relief in Sight," *SLPD,* August 11, 1926.

2. "Three Shot by Auto Gunmen," *SLGD,* August 20, 1926; "Gang Shooting Traced to Feud," *SLGD,* August 21, 1926; "Woman Shot by Auto Gunmen in Renewal of an Italian Feud," *SLGD,* August 22, 1926; "Bootlegger Shot to Death While Taking a Walk," *SLPD,* August 30, 1926.

3. "3000 Attend Formal Opening of Ambassador Theater, St. Louis' Newest Palace of Wonders," *SLGD,* August 26, 1926; "Magnificent New Ambassador Theater to Open Tomorrow," *St. Louis Star,* August 25, 1926; "3,000 Guests at Formal Opening of Ambassador," *St. Louis Star,* August 26, 1926; https://cinematreasures.org/theaters/2351/ (accessed April 4, 2024).

4. "Cards Win Exhibition Game, 14 to 3," *SLGD,* July 27, 1926.

Notes—Chapter 9

5. J. Roy Stockton, "Southworth's Single Scores Blades in Third; Alexander Hurls," *SLPD*, July 27, 1926; James M. Gould, "Southworth Gets 3 Straight Hits," *St. Louis Star*, July 27, 1926; Martin J. Haley, "Cards Open Eastern Invasion by Trouncing Lowly Phils, 9 to 5," *SLGD*, July 28, 1926.

6. J. Roy Stockton, "Williams' Home Run with Two on Beats Cards in First Game, 6–3," *SLPD*, July 28, 1926; James M. Gould, "Williams' Homer Beats Sherdel in Opening Game, 6–3," *St. Louis Star*, July 28, 1926; Martin J. Haley, "Cardinals Beat Phils, 5–4, After Losing First Game of Twin Bill, 6–3," *SLGD*, July 29, 1926.

7. "Gould's Gossip," *St. Louis Star*, July 29, 1926.

8. Martin J. Haley, "Rhem Holds Giants to Seven Hits, Cardinals Take Opener, 5 to 2," *SLGD*, July 31, 1926.

9. J. Roy Stockton, "With Six-Run Lead, Haines Fails, Giants Win First Game, 8–6," *SLPD*, July 31, 1926; Stockton, "Fighting Giants Twice Defeat Cardinals, 8–6 and 6–1," *SLPD*, August 1, 1926; James M. Gould, "Young Clouts Homer," *St. Louis Star*, July 31, 1926; Martin J. Haley, "Cardinal Flag Hopes Bumped as Giants Take Double-Header, 8–6, 6–1," *SLGD*, August 1, 1926.

10. Martin J. Haley, "Alexander Weakens and Cards Drop Third Straight to Giants, 7–2," *SLGD*, August 2, 1926; IK Shuman, "Giants Beat Cards for Third in Row," *New York Times*, August 2, 1926.

11. J. Roy Stockton, "Hornsby Likely to Resume His Place in Batting Order Tomorrow," *SLPD*, August 3, 1926; James M. Gould, "Cards Play Like School Boys and Drop 4th in Row," *St. Louis Star*, August 3, 1926; Martin J. Haley, "Cardinals Fail When Leading and Lose Fourth Straight, 4 to 2," *SLGD*, August 3, 1926; IK Shuman, "Giants Again Trim Cardinals, 4 To 2," *New York Times*, August 3, 1926; Will Murphy, "Giants Grab Another from Cardinals, 4 to 2," *New York Daily News*, August 3, 1926.

12. J. Roy Stockton, "Hornsby Returns to Game and Singles Off Wall First Time Up," *SLPD*, August 4, 1926; Martin J. Haley, "Hornsby to Appear in Practice Today Prior to Cards-Robins Tilt," *SLGD*, August 4, 1926; J. Roy Stockton, ""Hornsby, the Man, a Blunt, Cussin,' Undiplomatic Square-Shooter," *SLPD*, October 3, 1926; Martin J. Haley, "Sherdel Bats and Hurls Cards to 8–4 Victory Over Superbas," *SLGD*, August 5, 1926; Thomas Holmes, "Runs Scored with Two Out Have Proved Costly to Staggering Robins," *Brooklyn Daily Eagle*, August 5, 1926; Doutrich, *The Cardinals and the Yankees*, 106–107.

13. J. Roy Stockton, "Southworth Hits Home Run with O'Farrell and Rhem on Base," *SLPD*, August 5, 1926; Martin J. Haley, "Cardinal Bats Overcome Loose Fielding to Beat Brooklyn, 11 to 9," *SLGD*, August 6, 1926; Thomas Holmes, "Cardinals Make It Two Straight by Scoring Ten Runs with Two Men Out," *Brooklyn Daily Eagle*, August 6, 1926.

14. Martin J. Haley, "Reinhart's Fine Pitching, Cards' Timely Hitting Beat Robins, 7 to 3," *SLGD*, August 7, 1926; J. Roy Stockton, "Cardinals Defeat Robins Twice, 6–3 and 3–0," *SLPD*, August 8, 1926; Martin J. Haley, "Cards Trounce Robins Twice, 6–3, 3–0, and Draw Nearer Leaders," *SLGD*, August 8, 1926.

15. Martin J. Haley, "Cards Down Robins in Tenth, 3–2, and Move Into Second Place," *SLGD*, August 9, 1926.

16. Martin J. Haley, "Cardinals Get Only Five Hits off Benton and Lose to Braves, 5–0," *SLGD*, August 10, 1926; James M. Gould, "Jimmy Welsh and Bancroft Clout Three-Baggers," *St. Louis Star*, August 9, 1926.

17. Doutrich, *The Cardinals and the Yankees*, 109–110; Martin J. Haley, "Cardinals Score Twice in Ninth to Nose Out Braves, 3 to 1," *SLGD*, August 11, 1926; Haley, "Haines Holds Braves to Five Hits, Cardinals Take Series Final, 2–0," *SLGD*, August 12, 1926.

18. J. Roy Stockton, "Cards Climbed to Second Place, Gained 17 Points on Trip East," *SLPD*, August 12, 1926.

19. J. Roy Stockton, "Blades Triples and Scores on Hornsby's Long Sacrifice Fly," *SLPD*, August 10, 1926; J. Roy Stockton, "Cardinals Fill Bases on Braves in Fifth But Fail to Score," *SLPD*, August 11, 1926; *SLPD*, August 12, 1926; *SLGD*, August 10 and August 11, 1926; Doutrich, *The Cardinals and the Yankees*, 110; "Spirit of Cardinals Enhances Chances," *Sporting News*, August 19, 1926.

20. "Everything Not So Pleasant in Cardinal Official Family," *Sporting News*, October 28, 1926; "Hornsby Satisfied with St. Louis, But—," *Sporting News*, November 18, 1926; "Fanning with Farrington," Unidentified clipping, August 11, 1932, in HOF "Rogers Hornsby 4" Clipping File.

21. Martin J. Haley, "16,000 Persons See Cubs Nose Out Cardinals in Tense Battle, 3 to 2," *SLGD*, August 15, 1926; J. Roy Stockton, "Cards Beaten by Cubs, 3–2, Lose a Lap in Race," *SLPD*, August 15, 1926.

22. J. Roy Stockton, "Bottomley Upsets Cub Strategy and Cardinals Gain in Race," *SLPD*, August 17, 1926; Martin J. Haley, "Single by Bottomley in Ninth Gives Cardinals 5 to 4 Victory," *SLGD*, August 17, 1926; James J. Gould, "Knot-Holers Rally in 9th to Win," *St. Louis Star*, August 16, 1926; Doutrich, *The Cardinals and the Yankees*, 111.

23. J. Roy Stockton, "Cardinals Reduce Pirates' Lead to .014 by Beating Dodgers, 8–7," *SLPD*, August 18, 1926; Martin J. Haley, "Cards Nose Out Robins, 8–7, and Draw Within Game of First Place," *SLGD*, August 18, 1926; James M. Gould, *St. Louis Star*, August 17, 1926; Wolinsky, "Ray Blades" SABR Biography Project.

24. J. Roy Stockton, "Cardinal Punch and Fielding Carry Team Nearer First Place," *SLPD*, August 19, 1926; Martin J. Haley, "Cards Trounce Robins Again, 6–2, and Cut Pirates' Lead to Half Game," *SLGD*, August 19, 1926; J. Roy Stockton, "Cardinals, with 13 of Last 15 Games Won, Tackle Giants Today," *SLPD*, August 20, 1926; Martin

J. Haley, "Cards Trounce Robins Again, 6–2, and Cut Pirates' Lead to Half Game," *SLGD*, August 20, 1926.

25. "Pennant Fever Bug Bites St. Louis Fans," *SLPD*, August 20, 1926.

26. J. Roy Stockton, "Cardinals, 5 Points Behind Pirates, Can Go Into the Lead Today," *SLPD*, August 21, 1926; Martin J. Haley, "Cards Could Get 13-Point Lead Today," *SLGD*, August 21, 1926.

27. Doutrich, *The Cardinals and the Yankees*, 114; Alexander, *John McGraw*, 271–274; Murdock, *Baseball Players and Their Times*, 65; Norman L. Macht, *They Played the Game: Memories from 47 Major Leaguers* (Lincoln: University of Nebraska Press, 2019), 126; "Frisch Quits Giants and Goes Home," *SLGD*, August 22, 1926; "Frisch Quits Giants, Angered by M'Graw," *New York Times*, August 22, 1926.

28. J. Roy Stockton, "Cards Defeat Giants, 3–1, for Seven in Row," *SLPD*, August 22, 1926; Martin J. Haley, "Cards Beat Giants, 3–1, Before 18,000," *SLGD*, August 22, 1926; IK Shuman, "Makeshift Giants Fall Before Cards," *New York Times*, August 22, 1926; Will Murphy, "Cardinals Defeat Giants for Seventh Straight," *New York Daily News*, August 22, 1926.

29. J. Roy Stockton, "Cards Take Lead When Pirates Lose First Game to Robins, 7–3," *SLPD*, August 23, 1926; James M. Gould, "Haines Earns Tenth Decision and Birds Again Tie Corsairs," *St. Louis Star*, August 23, 1926; Will Murphy, "Cards Mop Up with Giants, 4 To 2," *New York Daily News*, August 23, 1926; Martin J. Haley," Braves Open Today with Cards, Now in Tie for First Place," *SLGD*, August 23, 1926.

30. Martin J. Haley, "Cards Break Even with Braves and Drop to Tie for Second Place," *SLGD*, August 25, 1926; J. Roy Stockton, "Cardinals Have Chance Today to Regain Lead They Lost Yesterday," *SLPD*, August 25, 1926.

31. J. Roy Stockton, "Cardinals in First Place by Four Points, Meet Phillies Today," *SLPD*, August 26, 1926; Martin J. Haley, "Cards Win, 4–3; Lead Again by Four Points," *SLGD*, August 26, 1926; "Fans Must Know Their Decimals to Follow National League Race," *Sporting News*, August 26, 1926.

32. Martin J. Haley, "Cards Drop Into Second Place Tie with Reds When Phils Win, 3–2," *SLGD*, August 27, 1926; J. Roy Stockton, "Cards Today Can Regain Lead; Now Tied with Reds in Second Place," *SLPD*, August 27, 1926.

33. J. Roy Stockton, "Two Defeats in Row Drop Hornsby's Men to Third Position," *SLPD*, August 28, 1926; Martin J. Haley, "Cardinals, Beaten by Phillies, 9 to 7, Drop to Third Place," *SLGD*, August 28, 1926; "Phils Drive Cards to Third Position," *Philadelphia Inquirer*, August 28, 1926.

34. James M. Gould, "Hornsby Nominates Art Reinhart to Hurl Series Final Against Quakers," *St. Louis Star*, August 28, 1926; "Cardinals Descend on Pierce, Sew Up Game in 3D Frame," *Philadelphia Inquirer*, August 29, 1926; Martin J. Haley,

"Cards and Pirates Clash in Double-Header This Afternoon in What May Decide Pennant Race," *SLGD*, August 29, 1926; J. Roy Stockton, "Cards Trim Phils, 9–3; Still at Leaders' Heels," *SLPD*, August 29, 1926.

35. Bob O'Farrell Biography, *SLPD*, August 27, 1926.

36. Cardinals Laying Some Golden Eggs," *Sporting News*, September 2, 1926; Louisa, *The Pirates Unraveled*, 120–121; "Cards Disagree with Snyder on Release Clause," *SLGD*, September 2, 1926. Ironically, Snyder did join the Cardinals for the 1927 season.

37. "Cards to Put 7000 More Seats on Sale for Sunday's Games," *SLGD*, August 24, 1926; "Many Cities to Send Crowds to See Cardinals," *SLPD*, August 27, 1926; Editorial, *SLPD*, August 28, 1926; Doutrich, *The Cardinals and the Yankees*, 115; "Cardinals Laying Some Golden Eggs," *Sporting News*, September 2, 1926.

38. *SLPD*, August 14, 1926; Doutrich, *The Cardinals and the Yankees*, 115–116; Louisa, *The Pirates Unraveled*, 121–165.

39. Martin J. Haley, "36,000 See Cardinals and Pirates Battle to 2–2 Tie in Sea of Mud," *SLGD*, August 30, 1926; "Rain Fales to Dampen Spirit of Gay Crowd at Cards-Pirates Game," *SLGD*, August 30, 1926; William F. Allen, "36,000 See the Cardinals and Pirates Open Series, Record Gate of $40,000," *SLPD*, August 30, 1926; "Balked Yesterday, Pirates and Cardinals Play Twin Bill Today," *Pittsburgh Press*, August 30, 1926.

40. Martin J. Haley, "Cards Can Go to First Place Again Today," *SLGD*, August 31, 1926; "Immense Crowd, Downhearted in Defeat, Wild in Victory," *SLGD*, August 31, 1926.

41. *St. Louis Star*, August 31, 1926; J. Roy Stockton, "Bell Hits Home Run and Cardinals Lead Pittsburgh by 5 to 1," *SLPD*, August 31, 1926; J. Roy Stockton, "Sothoron Steps from Bull Pen and Hurls Cards Into First Place," *SLPD*, September 1, 1926; James M. Gould, "St. Louis Takes 'Lead' in Sport 'Melodrama'" and "Birds Rally Behind Hurling of Sherdel and Allan Sothoron," *St. Louis Star*, September 1, 1926; Martin J. Haley, "Impregnable Pitching Aids Birds to Top," *SLGD*, September 1, 1926.

42. Jack Alexander, "Reinhart's Hurling and Southworth's Fielding Clinch Final Victory," *SLPD*, September 2, 1926; William F. Allen, "Greatest Rooting Spectacle in Local History Features Final Game with Pittsburgh," *SLPD*, September 2, 1926; Martin J. Haley, "Cards Win, 5–2, Now Full Game Ahead of Reds," *SLGD*, September 2, 1926.

Chapter 10

1. "More Than 20,000 Attend Dedication of St. Louis Exposition," *SLGD*, June 27, 1926; "Chamber to Launch a Campaign to Bring Million to Exposition," *SLGD*, July 12, 1926.

2. "Greater St. Louis Exposition Opens at Forest

Park Tonight," *SLGD*, September 4, 1926; "Brilliant Spectacle as Greater St. Louis Exposition Is Opened," *SLPD*, September 5, 1926; "Parade to Usher in Exposition's Official Opening," *St. Louis Star*, September 4, 1926.

3. "Exposition Opens Third Week; Many Special Days," *SLPD*, September 20, 1926; "Exposition Falls $30,000 Of Meeting Expenses," *SLPD*, September 27, 1926.

4. "Volley Fired at Pair from Speeding Auto," *SLGD*, September 3, 1926; "Gang Leader Is Killed in Bootlegger Feud Flareup," *SLPD*, September 3, 1926; "Police Baffled in Investigation of Cipriano Slaying," *SLGD*, September 4, 1926.

5. "Gangster Shot to Death on Street," *SLGD*, September 6, 1926; "3 Cuckoo Gangsters Held as Bootleg War Breaks Out Again," *SLGD*, September 9, 1926; "Another Cuckoo Gangster Shot As Feud Is Renewed," *SLPD*, September 9, 1926; "Two Suspects Held After County Pistol Battle of Gangsters," *SLGD*, September 17, 1926; "Italian Slain in Flareup of Rum War," *SLGD*, September 23, 1926; "Bootlegger Shot to Death in Auto, Slayer Escapes," *SLPD*, September 23, 1926; "One Slain, Five Wounded In Liquor War Battle," *SLGD*, September 24, 1926.

6. "Cards Leave Without Blades and Johnson," *SLGD*, September 2, 1926; "Greater St. Louis Exposition Opens at Forest Park Tonight," *SLGD*, September 4, 1926; Clifford, "A Phil Named Syl."

7. "KMOX to Broadcast Cards' Double-Header Today Play by Play," *SLGD*, September 2, 1926; "Early Birds Gobbled All of World Series Tickets, Says Breadon," *SLGD*, September 17, 1926; James J. Gould, "Cards Have Backs to Wall to Hold First Place," *St. Louis Star*, September 13, 1926; "Radio Creating Huge Following for Cardinals," *SLGD*, September 18, 1926; "Thousands Cock Ears and Hear KMOX Story of Cards Play by Play, *SLGD*, September 19, 1926; *SLGD* editorial, September 21, 1926.

8. J. Roy Stockton, "Cardinals Win First Game from Chicago, 2-0; Rhem Pitches in Second," *SLPD*, September 2, 1926; Martin J. Haley, "Cards Win, 2-0 and 9-1, to Take 13 Point Lead," *SLGD*, September 3, 1926; Irving Vaughan, "Cubs Bow to Cardinals Twice, 2-0, 9-1," *Chicago Tribune*, September 3, 1926; James M. Gould, "Haines May Oppose Mays in Opener of Cincy Series Today," *St. Louis Star*, September 3, 1926.

9. James M. Gould, "Too Straight Throw Gives Cincy Margin in First of Series," *St. Louis Star*, September 4, 1926.

10. James M. Gould, "Too Straight Throw Gives Cincy Margin in First of Series," *St. Louis Star*, September 4, 1926; J. Roy Stockton, "Cincinnati Gets Two Runs in First Inning, Cardinals Match Them in Second," *SLPD*, September 3, 1926; Martin J. Haley, "Cards Lose to Reds, 4-2, but Still Lead League by One Game," *SLGD*, September 4, 1926; J. Roy Stockton, "Cincinnati Bats Sherdel from Box in First Inning," *SLPD*, September 4, 1926.

11. J. Roy Stockton, "Cincinnati Bats Sherdel from Box in First Inning," *SLPD*, September 4, 1926; J. Roy Stockton, "Reds Blank Cards; Lead League by 3 Points," *SLPD*, September 5, 1926; Martin J. Haley, "Cards Blanked, 5 to 0, But Can Regain Lead by a Victory Today," *SLGD*, September 5, 1926; Jack Ryder, "Slashing Attack in Opener Lands Reds at Top of Ladder," *Cincinnati Enquirer*, September 5, 1926; "Portrayal of Cards-Reds Tilt at Missouri Theater," *SLGD*, September 4, 1926.

12. "Cardinal Excursionists 1900 Strong, Awaken Cincy at 6:30 A.M.," *SLGD*, September 6, 1926; Tom Swope, "Pair of Scratch Hits Help Bring Defeat to Luque," *Cincinnati Post*, September 6, 1926.

13. Doutrich, *The Cardinals and the Yankees*, 142; "Cardinals Inspired by Hornsby, Flash the Steel of Champions," *Sporting News*, September 9, 1926; Jack Ryder, "One Day Only Is Reds Hold on First Place," *Cincinnati Enquirer*, September 6, 1926; Herman Wecke, "Alexander, in Last 8 Games, Has Allowed Enemy Only 6 Runs," *SLPD*, September 6, 1926; Martin J. Haley, "Thevenow's Hitting Paces Attack as Cards Trounce Reds, 7-3, to Regain Lead," *SLGD*, September 6, 1926.

14. J. Roy Stockton, "Rhem Holds Pittsburgh to Four Hits; Cards Win Morning Game, 8-1" and "Pittsburgh Bats Sothoron from the Box to Win Afternoon Game, 4 to 2," *SLPD*, September 6, 1926; Martin J. Haley, "Sothoron Loses Own Game as Cards Break Even, but Still Lead," *SLGD*, September 7, 1926.

15. Hornsby, *My War With Baseball*, 106-107; Amore, *Rogers Hornsby*, 64-65; Alexander, *Rogers Hornsby*, 114; Lowenfish, *Branch Rickey*, 162-163; "Fanning with Farrington," Unidentified Newspaper Clipping, August 11, 1932, in HOF "Rogers Hornsby 4" Clipping File.

16. J. Roy Stockton, "Singing Sam, the Cut-Rate Man," *The Saturday Evening Post*, February 22, 1947, in HOF "Sam Breadon" Clipping File; Rogers Hornsby, as told to J. Roy Stockton, "How to Get Fired," *Look*, July 14, 1953, in HOF "Rogers Hornsby 14" Clipping File; Lieb, *The St. Louis Cardinals*, 126-127; Broeg, *Bob Broeg's Redbirds*, 40; Murdock, *Baseball Players and Their Times*, 57-59.

17. Martin J. Haley, "Cards Trim Pirates and Go East with 2-Game Advantage," *SLGD*, September 8, 1926; Charles J. Doyle, "Pirates Give Aldridge Poor Support and No Runs in 8-0 Knockout," *Pittsburgh Gazette Times*, September 8, 1926; J. Roy Stockton, "Cardinals, Leading by Two Games, Face Braves in Next Series," *SLPD*, September 8, 1926.

18. David W. Anderson, "Bonesetter Reese: Youngstown's Baseball Doctor," *Baseball Research Journal* (2001); "Hornsby Disavows Miracle Title, Shrinks from Fan Hero Worship," *Sporting News*, September 16, 1926; "Hornsby Says He Feels Better After Visit to Bonesetter," *SLPD*, September 8, 1926.

19. "Cards Leader And Veterans Watch Yanks" and "Cardinals Win Exhibition at Syracuse, 7-4," *SLPD*, September 9, 1926; Martin J. Haley, "Cards Get 3-Game Lead as Reds Lose 2," *SLGD*, Septem-

ber 9, 1926; Doutrich, *The Cardinals and the Yankees*, 147; James M. Gould, "Haines and Rhem to Oppose Boston Club in Today's Battles," *St. Louis Star*, September 11, 1926; Martin J. Haley, "Cards Have Chance to Gain Ground in Flag Race Today," *SLGD*, September 11, 1926; James C. O'Leary, "Braves, Playing Like Champions, Crush St. Louis as Reds and Pirates Divide Double Header," *Boston Globe*, September 11, 1926.

20. J. Roy Stockton, "Haines Allows Only Four Hits, Blanking Braves in Opener, 2 to 0" and "Cardinals Win First Game from Boston, 2–0; Rhem Pitches in Second," *SLPD*, September 11, 1926; J. Roy Stockton, "Cards' Lead Two Games After Split in Boston," *SLPD*, September 12, 1926; Martin J. Haley, "$50,000 Bonus for Rickey If Cards Win Pennant and World Series; First Game October 2," *SLGD*, September 12, 1926.

21. J. Roy Stockton, "Cardinals Win First Game from Boston, 2–0; Rhem Pitches in Second," *SLPD*, September 11, 1926; J. Roy Stockton, "Bottomley's Single and Douthit's Home Run Give Cardinals Four Scores," *SLPD*, September 13, 1926; Martin J. Haley, "Cards Oppose Boston Today 1 Game in Lead," *SLGD*, September 13, 1926; "Cards Take Exhibition Game, 13–10," *SLGD*, September 13, 1926; "Hafey, Injured in Exhibition, to Be Out for Several Days," *SLGD*, September 14, 1926.

22. J. Roy Stockton, "Bottomley's Single and Douthit's Home Run Give Cardinals Four Scores," *SLPD*, September 13, 1926; Martin J. Haley, "Reds Tie for Lead When Cards Falter and Lose to Boston," *SLGD*, September 14, 1926; Ford Sawyer, "Cooney's Solid Drive in 14th Topples Cards," *Boston Globe*, September 14, 1926; J. Roy Stockton, "Cardinals Must Show Real Courage Now in Fight for Pennant," *SLPD*, September 14, 1926.

23. "Tickets to World Series Will Be Put in Mail Tuesday," *SLGD*, September 26, 1926; "Reservations Now Taken for World Series If Cards Win," *SLGD*, September 13, 1926; "World Series Reservations Open Tuesday," *St. Louis Star*, September 13, 1926; "20,000 Request Series Seats in Morning Mail," *St. Louis Star*, September 14, 1926.

24. J. Roy Stockton, "Cardinals Must Show Real Courage Now in Fight for Pennant," *SLPD*, September 14, 1926; Doutrich, *The Cardinals and the Yankees*, 148.

25. J. Roy Stockton, "Cardinals Get Haines Four Runs, Philadelphia Scores One in the Third," *SLPD*, September 15, 1926; Martin J. Haley, "Cards, Winning Twice Today, Can Take Lead If Giants Beat Reds," *SLGD*, September 16, 1926; James C. Isaminger, "Haines Holds Phils When Men Reach Path," *Philadelphia Inquirer*, September 16, 1926.

26. J. Roy Stockton, "Cards Score 12 Runs in Inning and Capture First Game, 23 to 3" and "Cardinals Lead in Second Game After Defeating Philadelphia in First," *SLPD*, September 16, 1926.

27. Lieb and Baumgartner, *The Philadelphia Phillies*, 160–161; Waldo, *Baseball's Roaring Twenties*, 95–97; Martin J. Haley, "Double Victory Over Phillies Ties Cards with Reds for Lead," *SLGD*, September 17, 1926; James C. Isaminger, "Cards Grab Pair from Phillies and Tie Reds for National League Lead," *Philadelphia Inquirer*, September 17, 1926; "Fletcher Is Out for Rest of Year," *Philadelphia Inquirer*, September 18, 1926; Martin J. Haley, "Cards, Game in Lead, Play Double-Header with Phils Today," *SLGD*, September 18, 1926.

28. Lieb, *The St. Louis Cardinals*, 115–116.

29. "Hornsby Fails to Get Phils' Double-Header Moved Up to Today," *SLGD*, September 17, 1926; Martin J. Haley, "Cards, Game in Lead, Play Double-Header with Phils Today," *SLGD*, September 18, 1926; James M. Gould, "Alex and Haines to Pitch," *St. Louis Star*, September 18, 1926.

30. J. Roy Stockton, "Cards Break Even, Lead By Game and Half," *SLPD*, September 19, 1926; Martin J. Haley, "Cards on Top, Enter Final Week Today," *SLGD*, September 19, 1926.

31. J. Roy Stockton, "Reckless Baserunning Costs Cardinals Victory Over Giants," *SLPD*, September 20, 1926; Martin J. Haley, "Hafey Errs and Cards Lose, 6–5, to Giants, Dropping Half Game," *SLGD*, September 20, 1926; James M. Gould, "Mueller's Throw Is Deciding Factor in Polo Grounds Scrap," *St. Louis Star*, September 20, 1926.

32. "Cards in Blasé Mood Beaten by Springfield, 5–3," *SLPD*, September 21, 1926.

33. Martin J. Haley, "Boston, Despised Week Ago, Now Beloved by St. Louis Baseball Fans," *SLGD*, September 21, 1926.

34. J. Roy Stockton, "Cardinals Lead, 1 to 0, in Brooklyn Game; Cincinnati Loses Again," *SLPD*, September 21, 1926; Martin J. Haley, "Cards Can Virtually Cinch Flag If They Beat Dodgers Today," *SLGD*, September 22, 1926; James M. Gould, "Pennant Almost Ours If Cardinals Win Today," *St. Louis Star*, September 22, 1926.

35. Martin J. Haley, "Cards Defeat Robins, 15–7; 2 More Games Will Clinch Pennant," *SLGD*, September 23, 1926; J. Roy Stockton, "Haines and Sherdel Suffering from Colds, Alex May Work Saturday," *SLPD*, September 23, 1926.

36. "St. Louis 'Mayor' Sees Cards Win; Beats One-Eye Connolly's Line," *SLGD*, September 23, 1926; Waldo, *Baseball's Roaring Twenties*, 204–206.

37. "Cards-Giants' Game Postponed for Bout," *SLGD*, September 23, 1926.

38. J. Roy Stockton, "Cards Lead, 5–3, in the 4th; Pennant Theirs If They Win," *SLPD*, September 24, 1926; Martin J. Haley, "Victory Ends Months of Gruelling Toil," *SLGD*, September 25, 1926. Southworth quote from John Carmichael, ed., *My Greatest Day in Baseball: Forty-Seven Dramatic Stories by Forty-Seven Stars* (Lincoln: University of Nebraska Press, 1996), cited in Mitchell, *Mr. Rickey's Redbirds*, 217 and Golenbock, *The Spirit of St. Louis*, 107–108.

39. "Bedlam Loosed as Pennant-Mad Fans Celebrate," *SLPD*, September 25, 1926; "Surging Thousands of Revelers Cruise City Streets All Night Singing Praises of Cardinals," *St. Louis Star*, September 25, 1926; "Armistice Day Recalled By Wild Orgy" and "Exposition Converted Into Celebration

of Cardinals' Victory," *SLGD*, September 25, 1926; Robert L. Tiemann, *Immortal Moments in Cardinals History* (St. Louis: Reedy Press, 2016), 40–41; Jack Francis, "The Day the Cardinals Drove St. Louis Wild: Sept. 24, 1926," in *Cardinals Magazine* (September 1992), 32–34; Doutrich, *The Cardinals and the Yankees*, 149.

40. Lowenfish, *Branch Rickey*, 164.

41. "Hornsby Happiest Man in World Over Celebration in St. Louis" and "Hornsby Suspends Training Rules," *SLGD*, September 25, 1926.

42. Martin J. Haley, "Cards Take Things Easy in Last Game in East and Lose to Giants, 12–2," *SLGD*, September 26, 1926; Martin J. Haley, "Cardinals Put Up Great Battle, but Lose Final Game," *SLGD*, September 27, 1926; J. Roy Stockton, "Cards Favorites in World Series; Sherdel Likely Starter," *SLPD*, September 25, 1926; Martin J. Haley, "Cardinal Squad Ready for First Practice," *SLGD*, September 28, 1926.

43. "Confidence Enabled Cards to Win National League Pennant, Hornsby Asserts," *SLPD*, September 26, 1926.

44. J. Roy Stockton, "Alexander's Crafty Right Arm Rallies Cardinal Title Hopes," *Sporting News*, October 7, 1926.

45. Sid C. Keener, "Cards Used But 28 Players in Capturing Championship," *The Commercial Appeal*, November 14, 1926; Freese, *The Glory Years*, 7–8.

Chapter 11

1. Frances V. Feldkamp, "Vitaphone, Newest Movie Sensation, Introduced Here," *SLGD*, October 2, 1926; "Talking Pictures Seen and Heard," *SLPD*, October 2, 1926; Bristol French, "Vitaphone Movie Scores Triumph at Premier Here," *St. Louis Star*, October 2, 1926.

2. Karen McCaskey Goering, "Pageantry in St. Louis: The History of the Veiled Prophet Organization," *Gateway Heritage* 4 (Spring 1984), 2–16; Teens Make History Apprentices, "Behind the Veil: The Secret Society of St. Louis Elites," Missouri Historical Society, October 25, 2022, accessed at https://mohistory.org/blog/veiled-prophet/; Primm, *Lion of the Valley*, 394–395; Jo Allison, *Storied & Scandalous St. Louis: A History of Breweries, Baseball, Prejudice, and Protest* (Guilford, CT: Globe Pequot, 2021), 57, 221–223.

3. "Comic Strip Fellows to Be on Veiled Prophet Floats," *SLPD*, September 19, 1926; "Greatest Throngs in History See Veiled Prophet Parade," *SLGD*, October 6, 1926; "Veiled Prophet Parade Draws Record Crowd," *St. Louis Star*, October 6, 1926; "Martha Love Is Chosen Queen by Veiled Prophet as Gayety and Color Riot at Coliseum," *St. Louis Star*, October 7, 1926.

4. "Gunmen Must Leave or Get Shot, Says Gerk," *St. Louis Star*, October 7, 1926; "Gangster Slain, Pal and Officer Shot," *SLGD*, October 7, 1926; "Sicilians Plan East Side Raids as Cuckoos Exact Tribute in Blood," *St. Louis Star*, October 16, 1926.

5. Doutrich, *The Cardinals and the Yankees*, 119–127, 130–141.

6. "Yankees Are Confident of Winning Title," *SLGD*, September 28, 1926.

7. Paul E. Doutrich, "The 1926 World Series: A Reflection of the 'Roaring Twenties,'" *The Cooperstown Symposium on Baseball and American Culture, 2011–2012*, William M. Simons, ed. (Jefferson, NC: McFarland, 2013), 32–34; Benjamin G. Rader, *Baseball: A History of America's Game* (Urbana: University of Illinois Press, 2018), 137, 143–144; Rygelski, *10 Rings*, 7; Paul Votano, *Tony Lazzeri: A Baseball Biography* (Jefferson, NC: McFarland, 2005), 28–33.

8. Rygelski, *10 Rings*, 6; Martin J. Haley, "Mother Dead, Hornsby Will Play in Series," *SLGD*, September 30, 1926; Martin J. Haley, "Hornsby's Inestimable Grief Supplanted by Grim Determination," *SLGD*, October 1, 1926.

9. "Confidence Enabled Cards to Win National League Pennant, Hornsby Asserts," *SLPD*, September 26, 1926; "Thousands to Throng City for Series and Veiled Prophet Ball," *SLGD*, September 28, 1926; Martin J. Haley, "Cardinal Squad Ready for First Practice," *SLGD*, September 28, 1926; J. Roy Stockton, "Cardinals Get Ovation from New York Fans," *SLPD*, October 2, 1926.

10. Golenbock, *Spirit of St. Louis*, 108–109; Rygelski, *10 Rings*, 10.

11. "Radio Carries Story of Game to St. Louis Fans," *SLPD*, October 2, 1926; "Card Fans Jam Streets Getting Game by Radio," *SLPD*, October 3, 1926; Graham McNamee, *You're on the Air* (New York: Harper & Brothers, 1926), 5–19, 50–53; Cort Vitty, "Graham McNamee," SABR Biography Project (https://sabr.org.bioproj/person/graham-mcnamee/); Stan Isaacs, "Baseball's Radio Pioneers," *Newsday*, July 11, 1989; Mitchell, *Mr. Rickey's Redbirds*, 226–228; Doutrich, *The Cardinals and the Yankees*, 171; Doutrich, "The 1926 World Series," 38–39; Curt Smith, *Memories From the Microphone: A Century of Baseball Broadcasting* (Cooperstown, NY: National Baseball Hall of Fame and Museum, 2021), 24–27.

12. Doutrich, *The Cardinals and the Yankees*, 155–158; Mitchell, *Mr. Rickey's Redbirds*, 228–229; David S. Neft and Richard M. Cohen, *The World Series: Complete Play-by-Play of Every Game, 1903–1989* (New York: St. Martin's Press, 1990), 114; Snyder, *Cardinals Journal*, 213; Herman Wecke, "Yanks' Waiting Game Helps Defeat Sherdel; Both Hurlers Strong," *SLPD*, October 3, 1926; Heywood Broun, "Elusive Curves of New Yorker Upset Cardinals," *SLPD*, October 3, 1926; Martin J. Haley, "Yankees Nose Out Cards, 2–1, Before 61,658," *SLGD*, October 3, 1926; "Yankees Win, 2 to 1, While 63,000 Watch, 15,000,000 Listen In" and James R. Harrison, "63,000 See Yankees Beat Cardinals, 2–1; Pennock's Triumph," *New York Times*, October 3, 1926.

13. "World Series Movies to Be Exhibited Here Tomorrow Afternoon," *SLPD*, October 2, 1926.

14. Doutrich, *The Cardinals and the Yankees*, 159–162; Mitchell, *Mr. Rickey's Redbirds*, 230–231; Wilbert Robinson, "Old-Timers Get a Kick When Alec's Fadeway Buzzes Over the Slab" and Martin J. Haley, "Southworth's Homer, Alec's Hurling Even Series Before 63,600," *SLGD*, October 4, 1926; James H. Harrison, "65,000 See St. Louis Beat the Yankees, 6-2"; Alexander Is Hero," *New York Times*, October 4, 1926; James M. Gould, "Hornsby Says Three of His Hurlers Are Ready for Yankees," *St. Louis Star*, October 4, 1926; Herman Wecke, "Analysis of Alexander's Work Reveals He Became Stronger in Late Innings," *SLPD*, October 4, 1926; Lieb, *The St. Louis Cardinals*, 120; Harvey Frommer, *Remembering Yankee Stadium: An Oral and Narrative History of "The House That Ruth Built"* (Guilford, CT: Lyons Press, 2016), 9.

15. Vernon Van Ness, "Alexander Deserves Credit for Victory, Both Pilots Say," *SLGD*, October 4, 1926; "Cardinals Gay as Train Speeds on Toward Home," *St. Louis Star*, October 4, 1926; "Alexander's Crafty Right Arm Rallies Cardinal Title Hopes," *Sporting News*, October 7, 1926.

16. Morgan, "Pastoral America's Last Stand," 69–70; "Record Celebration Marks Home-Coming of St. Louis Team," *New York Times*, October 5, 1926; "Appeals to Fans to Give Up Seats at World's Series," *SLPD*, September 29, 1926; "Cards' Special Due at Washington Ave. at 4:15," *St. Louis Star*, October 4, 1926; "Frenzied Thousands Give Cards Most Thrilling Welcome Home in the History of St. Louis," *St. Louis Star*, October 5, 1926; "Tumultuous Thousands Welcome Cards" and "Sidelights on Parade of Red Birds," *SLGD*, October 5, 1926; "Noisy Fans Tell World St. Louis Is Proud of Cardinals," *SLPD*, October 5, 1926; Doutrich, *The Cardinals and the Yankees*, 162–163; Mitchell, *Mr. Rickey's Redbirds*, 231–234; Lowenfish, *Branch Rickey*, 165–166.

17. "Noisy Fans Tell World St. Louis Is Proud of Cardinals," *SLPD*, October 5, 1926; "Tickets to World Series Will Be Put in Mail Tuesday," *SLGD*, September 26, 1926; "World Series Games Here Without Seats in Outfield and Without Ground Rules," *SLPD*, September 27, 1926; "Thousands to Throng City for Series and Veiled Prophet Ball," *SLGD*, September 28, 1926; "Fans Dangling from Chimneys See Cards Win Over Yankees," *SLGD*, October 6, 1926; "All St. Louis One Big Ball Park as KMOX Takes Air" and "Whole Town Turned Into 'Bleachers,'" *SLGD*, October 6, 1926.

18. Herman Wecke, "Hornsby and Ruth, Kings of Swat, Bat .182 and .200 in First Three Contests" and "Haines Unbeatable and That's the Whole Story of Third Game, Says Alexander," *SLPD*, October 6, 1926.

19. D'Amore, *Rogers Hornsby*, 68; Doutrich, *The Cardinals and the Yankees*, 164; Unidentified clipping, September 14, 1936, in HOF "Les Bell" Clipping File; Golenbock, *The Spirit of St. Louis*, 110.

20. Charles W. Dunkley, "Stinging Defeat Galls Yanks; Ruth Whines Like a Babe," *SLGD*, October 6, 1926.

21. Mitchell, *Mr. Rickey's Redbirds*, 237–240; Doutrich, *The Cardinals and the Yankees*, 165–167; Golenbock, *The Spirit of St. Louis*, 110–111; Rygelski, *10 Rings*, 13–14; James R. Harrison, "Ruth Hits 3 Homers and Yanks Win, 10–5; Series Even Again," *New York Times*, October 7, 1926; "Parade of the Wooden Soldiers Is Enacted at Sportsman's Park for 38,825 Who Sought Baseball," *St. Louis Star*, October 7, 1926; "Pitching Wrong for Ruth Cost Game, Hornsby Says," *SLPD*, October 7, 1926.

22. Charles W. Dunkley, "Yanks Hilarious After Victory; Ruth Big Figure," *SLGD*, October 7, 1926.

23. William F. Allen, "South Wind the Villain of Yesterday's Defeat of Cardinals by Yankees," *SLPD*, October 8, 1926; F.C. Lane, "A Great Player's Heavy Handicap," unidentified magazine article, March 1933 in HOF "Chick Hafey" Clipping File; James R. Harrison, "Yanks Win in Tenth, 3 to 2; Lead Series; Koenig Is the Hero," *New York Times*, October 8, 1926; Doutrich, *The Cardinals and the Yankees*, 168–170; Mitchell, *Mr. Rickey's Redbirds*, 244–246; Lieb, *The St. Louis Cardinals*, 122–123; "Yanks Nose Out Cards, 3 to 2, in 10 Innings," *SLGD*, October 8, 1926.

24. "Yankees' Courage Won, Says Huggins," *New York Times*, October 8, 1926; Martin J. Haley, "Fighting Mad Cards Out for Victory Today," *SLGD*, October 9, 1926; Charles W. Dunkley, "Hafey Most to Blame for Loss, Says Hornsby," *SLGD*, October 8, 1926.

25. Henry I. Farrell, "Gotham Players Admit They Were Lucky To Triumph" and James M. Gould, "Cards Discuss Plans for Next Two Games at Meeting on Train," *St. Louis Star*, October 8, 1926.

26. James R. Harrison, "50,000 Chilled Fans See Cards Win, 10–2; Final Game Today" and "Series Even Again: St. Louis Wins, 10–2, as Nation Listens," *New York Times*, October 10, 1926; J. Roy Stockton, "Cardinals Even Up Series by Beating Yankees, 10–2," *SLPD*, October 10, 1926; Martin J. Haley, "Haines Faces Hoyt Today in Decisive Game," *SLGD*, October 10, 1926; Doutrich, *The Cardinals and the Yankees*, 173–175; "Hornsby Confident of Victory Today," *New York Times*, October 10, 1926.

27. "Hornsby Confident of Victory Today," and Babe Ruth, "Alex, That's All, Is the Way Babe Explains Defeat," *SLPD*, October 10, 1926; Donald Honig, "Yesterday," *Sports Illustrated*, 49 (October 9, 1978), 128.

28. Golenbock, *The Spirit of St. Louis*, 112.

29. Koenig had a tough World Series. His four errors paved the way for three unearned Cardinal runs. His work with the bat was equally woeful. He hit .125, struck out six times, and hit into three double plays. The *Sporting News* and New York newspapers labeled him the "goat" [*not* the "Greatest of All Time"!] of the Series.

30. "Radio Trumpets Millenium to Baseball Crowd," *SLPD*, October 11, 1926; "Play in Final Game as Told Over Radio" and James R. Harrison, "Cards Win World Series, Taking Final Game, 3 to 2; $1,207,864 Is Record Gate," *New York Times*,

October 11, 1926; Doutrich, *The Cardinals and the Yankees*, 175–179; Mitchell, *Mr. Rickey's Redbirds*, 248–250; Rygelski, *10 Rings*, 15–17.

31. James R. Harrison, "Cards Win World Series, Taking Final Game, 3 to 2; $1,207,864 Is Record Gate," *New York Times*, October 11, 1926; James M. Gould, "Grover Alexander Turns Back Lazzeri to Save Final Game," *St. Louis Star*, October 11, 1926; Murdock, *Baseball Players and Their Times*, 56.

32. Lowenfish, *Branch Rickey*, 168.

33. Ritter, *The Glory of Their Times*, 236; Golenbock, *The Spirit of St. Louis*, 113–115; Murdock, *Baseball Players and Their Times*, 56; Skipper, *Wicked Curve*, 117–120; Donald Honig, as told by Less Bell, "Yesterday," *Sports Illustrated* 49 (October 9, 1978); Morgan, "Pastoral America's Last Stand," 100–108; Bill Duncan, "Willie Sherdel Staunch Card Rooter," *Sporting News*, March 5, 1966, HOF "Bill Sherdel" Clipping File.

34. Hornsby, *My War with Baseball*, 193–195; Hornsby as told to J. Roy Stockton, "How to Get Fired," *Look*, July 14, 1953, in HOF "Rogers Hornsby 14" Clipping File.

35. J. Roy Stockton, "Alexander: The Cardinals' Million Dollar $4000 Beauty," *SLPD*, October 17, 1926; Honig, "Yesterday," *Sports Illustrated* 49 (October 9, 1978).

36. J. Roy Stockton, "Team's Fighting Spirit and Alexander's Great 39-Year-Old Arm Give World's Title to Cards," *SLPD*, October 11, 1926; Bob Broeg, "O'Farrell's Memories Vivid of Redbirds' First Title," *SLPD*, January 25, 1976; Bob Broeg, "O'Farrell: A Link to Golden '20's," *SLPD*, February 6, 1976; Ritter, *The Glory of Their Times*, 237; Morgan, "Pastoral America's Last Stand," 90; Murdock, *Baseball Players and Their Times*, 55–57.

37. Golenbock, *The Spirit of St. Louis*, 117; Hornsby, *My War with Baseball*, 192–196; Murdock, *Baseball Players and Their Times*, 55; Lieb, *The St. Louis Cardinals*, 124–125.

38. Morgan, "Pastoral America's Last Stand," 61–62, 91.

39. Golenbock, *The Spirit of St. Louis*, 117; Marty Appel, *Pinstripe Empire: The New York Yankees from Before the Babe to After the Boss* (New York: Bloomsbury, 2012), 149; Murdock, *Baseball Players and Their Times*, 55–56; Robert W. Creamer, *Babe: The Legend Comes to Life* (New York: Simon & Schuster, 1974), 305–307; Leigh Montville, *The Big Bam: The Life and Times of Babe Ruth* (New York: Doubleday, 2006), 235.

40. Brian Bell, "Mates Class Alexander as Ace of Aces," *SLGD*, October 11, 1926; "Joyful Cardinals Praise Alexander," *New York Times*, October 11, 1926.

41. "Fans in 9-Hour Rampage Give Vent to Noisy Joy Over Cardinals' Victory" and "Youth Is Killed; 30 Persons Hurt in Celebration," *SLPD*, October 11, 1926; "Hilarious Fans Paint Old Town Cardinal Red, Olive Street Is Turned Into 'Crazy Canyon,'" *St. Louis Star*, October 11, 1926; "St. Louis Goes Wild as Cardinals Take World Pennant in Sensational Victory," *SLGD*, October 11, 1926.

42. Polner, *Branch Rickey*, 87–88; Lowenfish, *Branch Rickey*, 169–70; Mann, *Branch Rickey*, 145.

43. "World Champions to Receive City's Welcome Tonight," *SLPD*, October 11, 1926; "Hail Cards! City to Greet Heroes Today," *SLGD*, October 11, 1926; "35,000 Over-Enthusiastic Fans Prevent Speeches of Cardinal Heroes in Welcoming Jubilee," *St. Louis Star*, October 12, 1926; "Crowd of 30,000 Makes Bedlam of Cards' Welcome," *SLPD*, October 12, 1926; "40,000 Jam Park to Welcome Cards," *SLGD*, October 12, 1926; "40,000 Roar Welcome to Cardinals," *Chicago Tribune*, October 12, 1926.

Chapter 12

1. "Movies by Wireless, Like Radio, Forecast," *SLPD*, December 14, 1926; "Radio Fans May Get Pictorial Action of World Series Games as Well as Verbal Description," *St. Louis Star*, December 14, 1926; James Forr, "Commercial Television Arrives in Missouri: The Birth of KSD-TV in St. Louis," *Missouri Historical Review*, 105 (July 2011), 233–244.

2. "Truce in Feud of Italian and Cuckoo Gangs," *SLPD*, November 23, 1926; "Peace Pact Is Signed by Rival Bootleg Gangs," *St. Louis Star*, November 23, 1926; "Blast Demolishes 3-Story Building, Gang War Is Seen," *St. Louis Star*, June 20, 1927; "Cuckoo Gang Suspected in Two Killings," *St. Louis Star*, August 11, 1927.

3. "Hornsby's Salary for Next Year Is Basis of Rumors," *St. Louis Star*, October 6, 1926; "Gould's Gossip," *St. Louis Star*, October 9, 1926.

4. Alexander, *Rogers Hornsby*, 121–124; D'Amore, *Rogers Hornsby*, 71–72; Hornsby, *My War with Baseball*, 28, 157–158; "Hornsby Satisfied with St. Louis, But—," *Sporting News*, November 18, 1926; "Hornsby's Job Tendered Him, Killefer Says," *St. Louis Star*, December 16, 1926; J. Roy Stockton, "Killefer Offered Hornsby's Place as Cardinals Boss," *SLPD*, December 16, 1926.

5. Mario Vricella, *The St. Louis Cardinals—The First Century: A Short History of the National League's Greatest Team* (New York: Vantage Press, 1992), 69–70; Unidentified clipping, October 25, 1928, in HOF "Taylor Douthit" Clipping File; "Chick Hafey, Wearing Glasses, Goes After Slugging Laurels," unidentified clipping, May 2, 1929, in HOF "Chick Hafey" Clipping File; Daly, "Billy Southworth," SABR Biography Project.

6. Alexander, *Rogers Hornsby*, 132–133; Dan Taylor, *Baseball at the Abyss: The Scandals of 1926, Babe Ruth, and the Unlikely Savior Who Rescued a Tarnished Game* (Lanham, MD: Rowman & Littlefield, 2023), 62.

7. "Avon Park Seems Certain Site for Champs' Training," *St. Louis Star*, October 27, 1926; "Everything Not So Pleasant in Cardinal Official Family," *Sporting News*, October 28, 1926; Glen L. Wallar, "Rogers Hornsby May Go to Giants in Trade for Frisch," *SLGD*, October 27, 1926.

8. "Hornsby Says He Has No Knowledge of Reported Deal," *St. Louis Star*, October 27, 1926; "Scribbled by Scribes" Column, *Sporting News*, November 4, 1926.

9. "Hornsby Satisfied with St. Louis, But—," *Sporting News*, November 18, 1926.

10. Ray J. Gillespie, "Breadon and Hornsby Not Likely to Confer Before N.L. Meeting," *St. Louis Star*, December 8, 1926; "Hornsby Demands Three-Year Contract to Again Lead Cards," *Sporting News*, December 9, 1926.

11. Golenbock, *Spirit of St. Louis*, 118; "Breadon Explains Offers to Killefer as Possible Leader," *SLGD*, December 18, 1926; "St. Louis Aroused Over Hornsby Deal," *New York Times*, December 22, 1926; James M. Gould, "Hornsby's Job Tendered Him, Killefer Says," *St. Louis Star*, December 16, 1926; J. Roy Stockton, "Killefer Offered Hornsby's Place As Cardinals Boss," *SLPD*, December 16, 1926; "'Hornsby Left No Alternative,' Says Breadon Discussing Trade," *Sporting News*, December 23, 1926; Mitchell, *Mr. Rickey's Redbirds*, 278; Mann, *Branch Rickey*, 147–148.

12. "Sam Breadon Says Hornsby Will Pilot Cardinals in 1927," *St. Louis Star*, December 17, 1926.

13. J. Roy Stockton, "Conference on Contract Tomorrow," *SLPD*, December 19, 1926.

14. "Hornsby Refuses $50,000 for One Cardinal Season," *SLPD*, December 20, 1926; Mitchell, *Mr. Rickey's Redbirds*, 275–277; Alexander, *Rogers Hornsby*, 125–126; Broeg, *Bob Broeg's Redbirds*, 40.

15. In his autobiography, Hornsby claimed Clarence Lloyd, the Cardinals travelling secretary, called with news of the trade because Breadon "didn't have the nerve to call." See Hornsby, *My War with Baseball*, 45, 158.

16. D'Amore, *Rogers Hornsby*, 77–78; James M. Gould, "Hornsby Fired by Breadon in 11-Word Notice," *St. Louis Star*, December 21, 1926; Polner, *Branch Rickey*, 89.

17. Editorial, *SLPD*, December 21, 1926.

18. Fran Zimniuch, *Going, Going, Gone! The Art of the Trade in Major League Baseball* (Lanham, MD: Taylor Trade, 2008), 60; Mitchell, *Mr. Rickey's Redbirds*, 277–278; Alexander, *Rogers Hornsby*, 127; Lieb, *The St. Louis Cardinals*, 127–128; "Commerce Chamber Protest of No Avail Against Release of Hornsby," *SLPD*, December 21, 1926; "St. Louis Aroused Over Hornsby Deal," *New York Times*, December 22, 1926; "Hornsby Trade Insult to Fans, Says Steinberg," *St. Louis Star*, December 21, 1926; "Breadon Tempers the Bad News, Also Feelings of St. Louis Fans," *Sporting News*, December 30, 1926.

19. "Breadon Blames Trade on Hornsby Flatterers," *St. Louis Star*, December 21, 1926.

20. Charles C. Alexander, *Ty Cobb* (New York: Oxford University Press, 1984), 185–194; Ginsburg, *The Fix Is In*, 196–218; Taylor, *Baseball at the Abyss*, 1–9, 21–27, 34–57.

21. "Breadon Tempers the Bad News, Also Feelings of St. Louis Fans," *Sporting News*, December 30, 1926; Mitchell, *Mr. Rickey's Redbirds*, 314.

Epilogue

1. Minutes of Meeting, April 8, 1927, HOF, National League Meetings, Minutes, Conferences, and Financial Ledgers Collection (BA Mss055), Box 6, folder 2.

2. "Giants to Ask Injunction to Keep Hornsby," *SLGD*, April 9, 1927; "Hornsby Is Barred, Giants to Seek Stay," *New York Times*, April 9, 1927; "Hornsby Ends Turmoil Over Stock by Selling at $64,000 Profit," *SLGD*, April 10, 1927; Alexander, *Rogers Hornsby*, 127–132; Mitchell, *Mr. Rickey's Redbirds*, 280–281; D'Amore, *Rogers Hornsby*, 79.

3. Mitchell, *Mr. Rickey's Redbirds*, 278–280; Alexander, *Rogers Hornsby*, 109, 132–133, 139–141; Ginsberg, *The Fix is In*, 213–215; Taylor, *Baseball at the Abyss*, 59–64.

4. "Players Ousted Rogers," Unidentified Clipping, 1928, in HOF "Rogers Hornsby 4" Clipping File; Cohen, *The 50 Greatest Players in St. Louis Cardinals History*, 19–20; Alexander, *Rogers Hornsby*, 129, 133–181; Mitchell, *Mr. Rickey's Redbirds*, 292–295; D'Amore, *Rogers Hornsby*, 93–115.

5. Branch Rickey to Arthur Mann, November 27, 1942, Branch Rickey Collection, Library of Congress, Box 18, folder 5; Alexander, *Rogers Hornsby*, 182–188; Mitchell, *Mr. Rickey's Redbirds*, 305.

6. Murdock, *Baseball Players and Their Times*, 244; J. Roy Stockton, "Wright Hit on Head, Retires from Game; Homer for Bottomley," *SLPD*, June 28, 1927; "Wright, Recovered, Leaves for Pittsburgh; May Play in Holiday Double-Header," *The Pittsburgh Post*, June 30, 1927.

7. Wolinsky, "Ray Blades," SABR Biography Project; "Tommy Thevenow Dies; On First Cardinal Champs," Unidentified Newspaper Clipping, August 7, 1957, in HOF "Thevenow" Clipping File; Corbett, "Tommy Thevenow," SABR Biography Project; Wancho, "Bob O'Farrell," SABR Biography Project.

8. Lowenfish, *Branch Rickey*, 180.

9. Broeg, "Cardinal Managers: From Huggins to Herzog"; Wancho, "Bob O'Farrell," SABR Biography Project.

10. Mel Jones' Comments on Branch Rickey, July 27, 1956, Arthur Mann Papers, Library of Congress, Box 7, folder 28; "Branch Rickey: An Autobiography," Arthur Mann Papers, Library of Congress, Box 8, folder 9; Lowenfish, *Branch Rickey*, 176–320; Mitchell, *Mr. Rickey's Redbirds*, 313–335; Armour, "Sam Breadon: Relentless Owner," 38.

Bibliography

Books, Articles, Published Sources

Abrams, Roger I. *The Dark Side of the Diamond: Gambling, Violence, Drugs and Alcoholism in the National Pastime.* Burlington, MA: Rounder, 2007.

Abrams, Roger I. *Legal Bases: Baseball and the Law.* Philadelphia: Temple University Press, 1998.

Achorn, Edward. *The Summer of Beer and Whiskey: How Brewers, Barkeeps, Rowdies, Immigrants, and a Wild Pennant Fight Made Baseball America's Game.* New York: Public Affairs, 2014.

Adomites, Paul, et al., eds. *The Golden Age of Baseball.* Lincolnwood, IL: Publications International, 2003.

Alexander, Charles C. *John McGraw.* Lincoln: University of Nebraska Press, 1988.

Alexander, Charles C. *Our Game: An American Baseball History.* New York: Henry Holt, 1991.

Alexander, Charles C. *Rogers Hornsby: A Biography.* New York: Henry Holt, 1995.

Alexander, Charles C. *Ty Cobb.* New York: Oxford University Press, 1984.

Allison, Jo. *Storied & Scandalous St. Louis: A History of Breweries, Baseball, Prejudice, and Protest.* Guilford, CT: Globe Pequot, 2021.

Anderson, David W. "Bonesetter Reese: Youngstown's Baseball Doctor." *Baseball Research Journal* (2001). https://sabr.org/journal/article/bonesetter-reese/.

Appel, Marty. *Pinstripe Empire: The New York Yankees from Before the Babe to After the Boss.* New York: Bloomsbury, 2012.

Armour, Mark. "Sam Breadon: Relentless Owner." *Sportsman's Park in St. Louis: Home of the Browns and Cardinals at Grand and Dodier*, Gregory H. Wolf, ed. Phoenix: Society for American Baseball Research, 2017, 36–40.

Berg, A. Scott. *Lindbergh.* New York: G.P. Putnam's Sons, 1998.

Bohn, Michael K. *Heroes and Ballyhoo: How the Golden Age of the 1920s Transformed American Sports.* Washington, D.C.: Potomac, 2009.

Breslin, Jimmy. *Branch Rickey.* New York: Viking, 2011.

Broeg, Bob. *Bob Broeg's Redbirds: A Century of Cardinals' Baseball.* Rev. ed. St. Louis: River City, 1987.

Broeg, Bob. "Cardinal Managers: From Huggins to Herzog." *Road Trips: SABR Convention Journal Articles.* Originally in *St. Louis's Favorite Sport*, Convention Brochure of the 22nd National SABR convention, 1992, 13–20.

Bruere, Martha Bensley. *Does Prohibition Work? A Study of the Operation of the Eighteenth Amendment Made by the National Federation of Settlements, Assisted by Social Workers in Different Parts of the United States.* New York: Harper & Brothers, 1927.

Bryson, Bill. *One Summer: America, 1927.* New York: Doubleday, 2013.

Burk, Robert F. *Much More Than a Game: Players, Owners, & American Baseball Since 1921.* Chapel Hill: University of North Carolina Press, 2001.

Carmichael, John, ed. *My Greatest Day in Baseball: Forty-Seven Dramatic Stories by Forty-Seven Stars.* Lincoln: University of Nebraska Press, 1996.

Cash, Jon David. *Before They Were Cardinals: Major League Baseball in Nineteenth-Century St. Louis.* Columbia: University of Missouri Press, 2002.

Cash, Jon David. *Boom and Bust in St. Louis: A Cardinals History, 1885 to the Present.* Jefferson, NC: McFarland, 2020.

Cash, Jon David. "Chris Von der Ahe, the American Association versus National League Cultural War, and the Rise of Major-League Baseball." *Missouri Historical Review* 109 (October 2014): 41–61.

Clifford, Matthew. "A Phil Named Syl." *The National Pastime: From Swampoodle to South Philly.* Philadelphia, 2013. Accessed April 22, 2023, https://sabr.org/journal/article/a-phil-named-syl/.

Cohen, Robert W. *The 50 Greatest Players in St. Louis Cardinals History.* Lanham, MD: Scarecrow, 2013.

Corbett, Katharine T., and Mary E. Seematter. "No Crystal Star: Black St. Louis, 1920–1940." *Gateway Heritage* 8 (Fall 1987): 8–15.

Corbett, Warren. "Eddie Dyer." SABR Biography Project, https://sabr.org/bioproj/person/eddie-dyer/.

Corbett, Warren. "Tommy Thevenow." SABR Biography Project, https://sabr.org/bioproj/person/tommy-thevenow/.

Courtaway, Robbi. *Wetter Than the Mississippi: Prohibition in St. Louis and Beyond.* St. Louis: Reedy Press, 2008.

Cox, James A. *The Lively Ball: Baseball in the Roaring Twenties.* Alexandria, VA: Redefinition, 1989.

Craig, William J. *A History of the Boston Braves: A Time Gone By.* Charleston, SC: The History Press, 2012.

Creamer, Robert W. *Babe: The Legend Comes to Life.* New York: Simon & Schuster, 1974.

Crepeau, Richard C. *Baseball: America's Diamond Mind, 1919–1941.* Orlando: University Presses of Florida, 1980.

Curran, William. *Big Sticks: The Batting Revolution of the Twenties.* New York: William Morrow, 1990.

Currell, Susan. *American Culture in the 1920s.* Edinburgh: Edinburgh University Press, 2009.

Daly, Jon. "Billy Southworth." SABR Biography Project, https://sabr.org/bioproj/person/billy-southworth/.

D'Amore, Jonathan. *Rogers Hornsby: A Biography.* Westport, CT: Greenwood Press, 2004.

Doutrich, Paul E. *The Cardinals and the Yankees, 1926: A Classic Season and St. Louis in Seven.* Jefferson, NC: McFarland, 2011.

Doutrich, Paul E. "The 1926 World Series: A Reflection of the 'Roaring Twenties.'" *The Cooperstown Symposium on Baseball and American Culture, 2011–2012.* William M. Simons, ed. Jefferson, NC: McFarland, 2013, 31–40.

Edmonds, Ed, and Frank G. Houdek. *Baseball Meets the Law: A Chronology of Decisions, Statutes and Other Legal Events.* Jefferson, NC: McFarland, 2017.

Ehrgott, Roberts. *Mr. Wrigley's Ball Club: Chicago & The Cubs During the Jazz Age.* Lincoln: University of Nebraska Press, 2013.

Erion, Greg. "Babe Herman." SABR Biography Project, https://sabr.org/bioproj/person/babe-herman/.

Erion, Greg. "Chick Hafey." SABR Biography Project, https://sabr.org/bioproj/person/96ae4951.

Ervin, Keona K. *Gateway to Equality: Black Women and the Struggle for Economic Justice in St. Louis.* Lexington: University Press of Kentucky, 2017.

Evans, Christopher H. "Baseball as Civil Religion: The Genesis of an American Creation Story." *The Faith of 50 Million: Baseball, Religion, and American Culture*, Christopher H. Evans and William R. Herzog II, eds. Louisville: Westminster John Knox Press, 2002.

Faber, Charles F. "Allen Sothoron," SABR Biography Project, https://sabr.org/bioproj/person/allen-sothoron.

Faber, Charles F. "Dazzy Vance." SABR Biography Project, https://sabr.org/bioproj/person/dazzy-vance.

Faber, Charles F., and Richard B. Faber. *Spitballers: The Last Legal Hurlers of the Wet One.* Jefferson, NC: McFarland, 2006.

Faherty, William Barnaby, S.J. *St. Louis—A Concise History.* St. Louis: Print/Graphics, 1989.

Faherty, William Barnaby, S.J. *The St. Louis Irish: An Unmatched Celtic Community.* St. Louis: Missouri Historical Society Press, 2001.

Ferkovich, Scott, "Sportsman's Park." *Sportsman's Park in St. Louis: Home of the Browns and Cardinals at Grand and Dodier.* Gregory H. Wolf, ed. Phoenix: Society for American Baseball Research, 2017, 4–11.

Fontane, Walter M. "Baseball to Bullets: The Rise and Fall of the Cuckoo Gang." *Gateway* 27 (2007): 20–31.

Forr, James. "Commercial Television Arrives in Missouri: The Birth of KSD-TV in St. Louis." *Missouri Historical Review* 105 (July 2011): 233–244.

Francis, Jack. "The Day the Cardinals Drove St. Louis Wild: Sept. 24, 1926." *Cardinals Magazine* 1 (September 1992): 32–34.

Freese, Mel R. *The Glory Years of the St. Louis Cardinals. Volume 1: The World Championship Seasons.* St. Louis: Palmerston & Reed, 1999.

Frommer, Harvey. *Remembering Yankee Stadium: An Oral and Narrative History of "The House That Ruth Built."* Guilford, CT: Lyons Press, 2016.

Gagnon, Cappy. "Cy Williams." SABR Biography Project, https://sabr.org/bioproj/person/cy-williams/.

Garber, Lon. "Crosley Field." *Cincinnati's Crosley Field: A Gem in the Queen City.* Gregory H. Wolf, ed. Phoenix: Society for American Baseball Research, 2018, 8–15.

Ginsburg, Daniel E. *The Fix Is In: A History of Baseball Gambling and Game Fixing Scandals.* Jefferson, NC: McFarland, 1995.

Goering, Karen McCaskey. "Pageantry in St. Louis: The History of the Veiled Prophet Organization." *Gateway Heritage* 4 (Spring 1984): 2–16.

Goldberg, Ronald Allen. *America in the Twenties.* Syracuse: Syracuse University Press, 2003.

Golenbock, Peter. *Bums: An Oral History of the Brooklyn Dodgers.* New York: G.P. Putnam's Sons, 1984.

Golenbock, Peter. *The Spirit of St. Louis: A History of the St. Louis Cardinals and Browns.* New York: Avon, 2000.

Golenbock, Peter. *Wrigleyville: A Magical History Tour of the Chicago Cubs.* New York: St. Martin's Press, 1996.

Goss, David A. "Major-League Players Who Wore Glasses." *The Baseball Research Journal* (2008). https://sabr.org/journals/2008-baseball-research-journal/.

Green, Howard. "A Tale of Two Hornsbys: A Sweetheart Back Home." *Baseball Research Journal* (2001). https://sabr.org/journal/article/a-tale-of-two-hornsbys/.

Griffith, Nancy Snell. "Flint Rhem." SABR Biography Project, https://sabr.org/bioproj/person/97c73ab1.

Heathcott, Joseph, and Angela Dietz. *Capturing the City: Photographs from the Streets of St. Louis, 1900–1930.* St. Louis: Missouri Historical Society Press, 2016.

Hernon, Peter, and Terry Ganey. *Under the Influence: The Unauthorized Story of the Anheuser-Busch Dynasty.* New York: Simon & Schuster, 1991.

Hochman, Benjamin. *The Big 50 St. Louis Cardinals: The Men and Moments That Made the St. Louis Cardinals.* Chicago: Triumph Books, 2018.

Honig, Donald. *The October Heroes: Great World Series Games Remembered by the Men Who Played Them.* New York: Simon & Schuster, 1979.

Honig, Donald, as told by Less Bell. "Yesterday." *Sports Illustrated* 49 (October 9, 1978): 128–130.

Hornsby, Rogers, and Bill Surface. *My War with Baseball.* New York: Coward-McCann, 1962.

Hunstein, Jim. *1, 2, 6, 9… & Rogers: The Cardinals' Retired Numbers and the Men Who Wore Them.* St. Louis: Stellar Press, 2004.

Isaacs, Stan. "Baseball's Radio Pioneers." *Newsday*, July 11, 1989.

James, Bill. *The New Bill James Historical Baseball Abstract.* New York: The Free Press, 2001.

Johnson, Bill. "Jim Bottomley." SABR Biography Project, https://sabr.org/bioproj/person/ea08fc60.

Jordan, David M. *Occasional Glory: The History of the Philadelphia Phillies.* Jefferson, NC: McFarland, 2002.

Kaese, Harold, and R.G. Lynch. *The Milwaukee Braves: An Informal History of a Great Baseball Team in Boston and Milwaukee.* New York: G.P. Putnam's Sons, 1954.

Knoedelseder, William. *Bitter Brew: The Rise and Fall of Anheuser-Busch and America's King of Beer.* New York: HarperCollins, 2012.

Kodner, Gary, and Oliver Kodner. *St. Louis Cardinals Uniforms & Logos: An Illustrated History, 1882–2016.* St. Louis Cardinals Hall of Fame and Museum, 2016.

Launius, Roger D. *Seasons in the Sun: The Story of Big League Baseball in Missouri.* Columbia: University of Missouri Press, 2002.

Levy, Scott Jarman. "Tricky Ball: 'Cool Papa' Bell and Life in the Negro Leagues." *Gateway Heritage* 9 (Spring 1989): 26–35.

Lieb, Fred. *Baseball as I Have Known It.* New York: Coward, McCann & Geoghegan, 1977.

Lieb, Frederick G. *The Pittsburgh Pirates.* New York: G.P. Putnam's Sons, 1948.

Lieb, Frederick G. *The St. Louis Cardinals: The Story of a Great Baseball Club.* Writing Baseball Series Edition. Carbondale: Southern Illinois University Press, 2001.

Lieb, Frederick G., and Stan Baumgartner. *The Philadelphia Phillies.* New York: G.P. Putnam's Sons, 1953.

Lipsitz, George. *The Sidewalks of St. Louis: Places, People, and Politics in an American City.* Columbia: University of Missouri Press, 1991.

Louisa, Angelo J. *The Pirates Unraveled: Pittsburgh's 1926 Season.* Jefferson, NC: McFarland, 2015.

Lowenfish, Lee. *Branch Rickey: Baseball's Ferocious Gentleman.* Lincoln: University of Nebraska Press, 2007.

Lowry, Philip J. *Green Cathedrals: The Ultimate Celebration of All 271 Major League and Negro League Ballparks Past and Present.* New York: Addison-Wesley, Inc., 1992.

Lynch, Mike. "Austin McHenry." SABR Biography Project, https://sabr.org/bioproj/person/austin-mchenry/.

Macht, Norman L. *They Played the Game: Memories From 47 Major Leaguers.* Lincoln: University of Nebraska Press, 2019.

Mann, Arthur. *Branch Rickey: American in Action.* Boston: Houghton Mifflin, 1957.

McGee, Bob. *The Greatest Ballpark Ever: Ebbets Field and the Story of the Brooklyn Dodgers.* New Brunswick, NJ: Rivergate Books, 2005.

McNamee, Graham. *You're on the Air.* New York: Harper & Brothers, 1926.

McNeil, William F. *Cool Papa and Double Duties: The All-Time Greats of the Negro Leagues.* Jefferson, NC: McFarland, 2001.

McNeil, William F. *Gabby Hartnett: The Life and Times of the Cubs' Greatest Catcher.* Jefferson, NC: McFarland, 2004.

Miller, Nathan. *New World Coming: The 1920s and the Making of Modern America.* New York: Scribner's, 2003.

Miller, Ray. "A Biography of Braves Field." *Braves Field: Memorable Moments at Boston's Lost Diamond.* Bill Nowlin and Bob Brady, eds. Phoenix: Society for American Baseball Research, 2015, 2–10.

Mitchell, Mike. *Mr. Rickey's Redbirds: Baseball, Beer, Scandals & Celebrations in St. Louis.* By the author, 2020.

Moir, William J., ed. *Past and Present of Hardin County, Iowa.* Indianapolis: B.F. Bowen & Company, 1911.

Montville, Leigh. *The Big Bam: The Life and Times of Babe Ruth.* New York: Doubleday, 2006.

Morgan, James J. "Pastoral America's Last Stand: Grover Cleveland Alexander Takes the Mound During the 1926 World Series." M.A. Thesis, University of Nebraska, 2017.

Mormino, Gary Ross. *Immigrants on the Hill: Italian-Americans in St. Louis, 1882–1982.* Urbana: University of Illinois Press, 1986.

Mormino, Gary Ross. "The Playing Fields of St. Louis: Italian Immigrants and Sports, 1925–1941." *Journal of Sports History* 9 (Summer 1982): 5–19.

Morris, Ann, ed. *Lift Every Voice and Sing: St. Louis African Americans in the Twentieth Century.* Columbia: University of Missouri Press, 1999.

Morris, Peter. *A Game of Inches: The Stories Behind the Innovations That Shaped Baseball.* Chicago: Ivan R. Dee, 2010.

Murdock, Eugene. *Baseball Players and Their Times: Oral Histories of the Game, 1920–1940.* Westport, CT: Meckler, 1991.

Murphy, Paul V. *The New Era: American Thought and Culture in the 1920s.* Lanham, MD: Rowman & Littlefield, 2012.

Nathanson, Mitchell. *A People's History of Baseball.* Urbana: University of Illinois Press, 2012.

Neft, David S., and Richard M. Cohen. *The World Series: Complete Play-by-Play of Every Game, 1903–1989*. New York: St. Martin's Press, 1990.

Neymeyer, Robert. "Fans Strike Out with Foul Ball Litigation." *Sports and the Law: Major Legal Cases*. Charles E. Quirk, ed. New York: Garland, 1996, 24–27.

Okrent, Daniel. *Last Call: The Rise and Fall of Prohibition*. New York: Scribner's, 2010.

Palmer, Niall. *The Twenties in America: Politics and History*. Edinburgh: Edinburgh University Press, 2006.

Payne, Marty. "Vic Keen." SABR Biography Project, https://sabr.org/bioproj/person/vic-keen/.

Peterson, Richard, ed. *The St. Louis Baseball Reader*. Columbia: University of Missouri Press, 2006.

Polk-Gould St. Louis Directory 56. St. Louis: Polk-Gould Directory Co., 1927.

Polner, Murray. *Branch Rickey: A Biography*. Rev. ed. Jefferson, NC: McFarland, 2007.

Powers, Jimmy. *Baseball Personalities (The Most Colorful Figures of All Time)*. New York: Rudolph Field, 1949.

Price, Bill. "Braves Field." *Baseball Research Journal* (1978).

Primm, James Neal. *Lion of the Valley: St. Louis, Missouri, 1764–1980*. 3rd edition. St. Louis: Missouri Historical Society Press, 1998.

Puerzer, Richard J. "Engineering Baseball: Branch Rickey's Innovative Approach to Baseball Management." *Nine: A Journal of Baseball History & Culture* 12 (Fall 2003): 72–87.

Rader, Benjamin G. *Baseball: A History of America's Game*. Urbana: University of Illinois Press, 2018.

Riley, Calvin, and Nini Harris. *Black St. Louis: 1764 to the New Millenium*. St. Louis: Reedy Press, 2023.

Ritter, Lawrence. *The Glory of Their Times: The Story of the Early Days of Baseball Told by the Men Who Played It*. New York: Macmillan, 1966.

Rorabaugh, W.J. *Prohibition: A Concise History*. Oxford University Press, 2018.

Rossi, John P. *Baseball and American Culture: A History*. Lanham, MD: Rowman & Littlefield, 2018.

Russo, Frank. *The Cooperstown Chronicles: Baseball's Colorful Characters, Unusual Lives, and Strange Demises*. Lanham, MD: Rowman & Littlefield, 2014.

Ruzzo, Bob. "Braves Field: An Imperfect History of the Perfect Ballpark." *Baseball Research Journal* 41 (Fall 2012): 50–60.

Rygelski, James, and Robert L. Tiemann. *10 Rings: Stories of the St. Louis Cardinals World Championships*. St. Louis: Reedy Press, 2011.

Sandweiss, Eric. *St. Louis: The Evolution of an American Urban Landscape*. Philadelphia: Temple University Press, 2001.

Selter, Ron. "By the Numbers: The Five Polo Grounds Ballparks." *The Polo Grounds: Essays and Memories of New York City's Historic Ballpark, 1880–1963*. Stew Thornley, ed. Jefferson, NC: McFarland, 2019, 69–91.

Selter, Ronald M. *Ballparks of the Deadball Era: A Comprehensive Study of Their Dimensions, Configurations and Effects on Batting, 1901–1919*. Jefferson, NC: McFarland, 2008.

Seymour, Harold. *Baseball: The Golden Age*. New York: Oxford University Press, 1971.

Shea, Stuart. *Calling the Game: Baseball Broadcasting from 1920 to the Present*. Phoenix: Society for American Baseball Research, 2015.

Sher, Jack. "Rogers Hornsby: The Mighty the Rajah." *Sport* (July 1949): 62–63.

Skelton, David E. "'Specs' Toporcer." SABR Biography Project, https://sabr.org/bioproj/person/specs-toporcer/.

Skipper, John C. *Wicked Curve: The Life and Troubled Times of Grover Cleveland Alexander*. Jefferson, NC: McFarland, 2006.

Smith, Curt. *Memories from the Microphone: A Century of Baseball Broadcasting*. Cooperstown, NY: National Baseball Hall of Fame and Museum, 2021.

Smith, Curt. *Storied Stadiums: Baseball's History Through Its Ballparks*. New York: Carroll & Graf, 2001.

Snyder, John. *Cardinals Journal: Year by Year & Day by Day with the St. Louis Cardinals Since 1882*. Cincinnati: Emmis Books, 2006.

Soderholm-Difatte, Bryan. *America's Game: A History of Major League Baseball Through World War II*. Lanham, MD: Rowman & Littlefield, 2018.

Spink, Alfred H. "Jeremiah Fruin." *The St. Louis Baseball Reader*. Richard Peterson, ed. Columbia: University of Missouri Press, 2006, 47–50.

Spink, Alfred H. *The National Game: A History of Baseball, America's Leading Outdoor Sport*. St. Louis: National Game Publishing Co., 1910.

Spink, J.G. Taylor. *Judge Landis and Twenty-Five Years of Baseball*. New York: Thomas Y. Crowell, 1947.

Steinberg, Steve. *Baseball in St. Louis, 1900–1925*. Charleston, SC: Arcadia, 2004.

Stepenoff, Bonnie. *The Dead End Kids of St. Louis: Homeless Boys and the People Who Tried to Save Them*. Columbia: University of Missouri Press, 2010.

Stinson, Mitchell Conrad. *Edd Roush: A Biography of the Cincinnati Reds Star*. Jefferson, NC: McFarland, 2010.

Stout, Glenn. *The Cubs: The Complete Story of Chicago Cubs Baseball*. New York: Houghton Mifflin, 2007.

Stout, Glenn. *The Dodgers: 120 Years of Dodgers Baseball*. New York: Houghton Mifflin, 2004.

Sunday, William A. *The Sawdust Trail: Billy Sunday in His Own Words*. Iowa City: University of Iowa Press, 2005.

Surdam, David George, and Michael J. Haupert. *The Age of Ruth and Landis: The Economics of Baseball during the Roaring Twenties*. Lincoln: University of Nebraska Press, 2018.

Taylor, Dan. *Baseball at the Abyss: The Scandals of 1926, Babe Ruth, and the Unlikely Savior Who Rescued a Tarnished Game*. Lanham, MD: Rowman & Littlefield, 2023.

Teens Make History Apprentices. "Behind the Veil: The Secret Society of St. Louis Elites." Missouri Historical Society, October 25, 2022. https://mohistory.org/blog/veiled-prophet/.

Thom, John. "The Kidnapping of Flint Rhem." *The National Pastime: A Review of Baseball History* 10 (1990): 79–82.

Thomas, Joan M. "Of Prominent Men and Baseball Fields: A History of Ballparks in St. Louis." *Gateway* 25 (Winter 2004–05): 34–45.

Thomas, Joan M. *St. Louis' Big League Ballparks*. Charleston, SC: Arcadia, 2004.

Thornley, Stew. "The Polo Grounds." SABR Biography Project, https://sabr.org/bioproj/park/polo-grounds-new-york.

Thornley, Stew, ed. *The Polo Grounds: Essays and Memories of New York City's Historic Ballpark, 1880–1963*. Jefferson, NC: McFarland, 2019.

Tiemann, Robert L. *Immortal Moments in Cardinals History*. St. Louis: Reedy Press, 2016.

Tygiel, Jules. *Past Time: Baseball as History*. New York: Oxford University Press, 2000.

Vitty, Cort. "Graham McNamee." SABR Biography Project, https://sabr.org.bioproj/person/graham-mcnamee/.

Vollmar, Helen D., and Joseph E. "Caves, Tunnels and Other Holes ... Under St. Louis." *Gateway Heritage* 8 (Fall 1987): 1–7.

Votano, Paul. *Tony Lazzeri: A Baseball Biography*. Jefferson, NC: McFarland, 2005.

Vricella, Mario. *The St. Louis Cardinals—The First Century: A Short History of the National League's Greatest Team*. New York: Vantage Press, 1992.

Waldo, Ronald T. *Baseball's Roaring Twenties: A Decade of Legends, Characters, and Diamond Adventures*. Lanham, MD: Rowman & Littlefield, 2017.

Walker, James R. *Crack of the Bat: A History of Baseball on the Radio*. Lincoln: University of Nebraska Press, 2015.

Walsh, Joel. "Shining Stars: The Negro Leagues in St. Louis." *Gateway* 25 (Winter 2004–05): 10–21.

Wancho, Joseph. "Bob O'Farrell." SABR Biography Project, https://sabr.org/bioproj/person/e701600d.

Warburton, Paul. "Offense? Try Hornsby." *The Baseball Research Journal* 28 (1999): 3–7.

Watkins, John J. "Jake Flowers." SABR Biography Project, https://sabr.org/biogproj/person/jake-flowers.

Watkins, John J. "Taylor Douthit." SABR Biography Project, https://sabr.org/bioproj/person/cf023577.

Waugh, Daniel. *Egan's Rats: The Untold Story of the Prohibition-Era Gang That Ruled St. Louis*. Nashville: Cumberland House, 2007.

Waugh, Daniel. *The Gangs of St. Louis: Men of Respect*. Charleston, SC: The History Press, 2010.

Westcott, Rich. *Philadelphia's Old Ballparks*. Philadelphia: Temple University Press, 1996.

Wheatley, Ed. *The St. Louis Cardinals: Everything You Need to Know!* St. Louis: Reedy Press, 2023.

Wheeler, Lonnie. *The Bona Fide Legend of Cool Papa Bell: Speed, Grace, and the Negro Leagues*. New York: Abrams Press, 2020.

White, G. Edward. *Creating the National Pastime: Baseball Transforms Itself, 1903–1953*. Princeton: Princeton University Press, 1996.

Wilson, Nick C. *Early Latino Ballplayers in the United States*. Jefferson, NC: McFarland, 2005.

Winn, Duane. "Rogers Hornsby in 1932." *The National Pastime* 23 (2003).

Wolf, Gregory H. "Bill Hallahan." SABR Biography Project https://sabr.org/bioproj/person/bill-hallahan.

Wolf, Gregory H. "Bill Sherdel." SABR Biography Project, https://sabr.org/bioproj/person/bill-sherdel/.

Wolf, Gregory H. "Jesse Haines." SABR Biography Project, https://sabr.org/bioproj/person/afeb716c.

Wolf, Gregory H., ed. *Cincinnati's Crosley Field: A Gem in the Queen City*. Phoenix: Society for American Baseball Research, 2018.

Wolf, Gregory H., ed. *Ebbets Field: Great, Historic, and Memorable Games from Brooklyn's Lost Ballpark*. Phoenix: Society for American Baseball Research, 2023.

Wolinsky, Russell. "Ray Blades." SABR Biography Project, https://sabr.org/bioproj/person/92a8ae6f.

Zimniuch, Fran. *Going, Going, Gone! The Art of the Trade in Major League Baseball*. Lanham, Taylor Trade, 2008.

Zinn, John. "Ebbets Field." *Ebbets Field: Great, Historic, and Memorable Games from Brooklyn's Lost Ballpark*. Gregory H. Wolf, ed. Phoenix: Society for American Baseball Research, 2023, 5–18.

Manuscript Collections

Arthur Mann Collection, Library of Congress
Branch Rickey Collection, Library of Congress
National League Meetings, Minutes, Conferences, and Financial Ledgers Collection (BA Mss 055), National Baseball Hall of Fame

Government Document

The National Prohibition Law: Hearings Before the Subcommittee of the Committee on the Judiciary United States Senate, 69th Congress, 1st Session, April 5 to 24, 1926. Vol. 1. Washington, D.C.: Government Printing Office, 1926.

Newspapers and Magazines

Atlanta Constitution
Baltimore Evening Sun
Boston Globe
Brooklyn Daily Eagle
Brooklyn Daily Times

Brooklyn Standard Union
Cardinals Magazine
Chicago Tribune
Cincinnati Enquirer
Cincinnati Post
Daily British Whig [Kingston, Ontario, Canada]
Daily Missouri Republican
The Evening News [Harrisburg, PA]
Harrisburg [PA] *Telegraph*
Iowa City Press-Citizen
Know St. Louis
Moline [IL] *Daily Dispatch*
Muncie Evening Press
New York Daily News
New York Herald Tribune
New York Times
Philadelphia Evening Public Ledger
Philadelphia Inquirer
Pittsburgh Gazette Times
Pittsburgh Post-Gazette
Pittsburgh Press
Quad City Times
St. Louis Argus
St. Louis Globe-Democrat
St. Louis Post-Dispatch
St. Louis Star
San Franciso Bulletin
Sioux City Journal
Sporting News
Tacoma Daily Ledger
Washington Post
Washington Times
Wilmington Morning News

Websites

baseball-almanac.com
baseball-reference.com
cinematreasures.org/theaters
historyinnewbraunfels.com/history
philadelphiaathletics.org/history/a-historical-sketch-of-baker-bowl
retrosheet.org
sabr.org/spring-training-database
seamheads.com/NegroLgs
statscrew.com

Index

Numbers in *bold italics* indicate pages with illustrations

Alexander, Grover Cleveland "Ol' Pete" 68, **92**, 95, 129, 131, 145, 151–152, 154, 159–160, 167, 179; acquired by St. Louis Cardinals 91–93; World Series Game Seven 161–164
Ambassador Theater 109–110
American Association 5
American society: modern vs traditional 8–9; nativist backlash 9; progress 7–8; prohibition 9; traditional 8–9
Anheuser-Busch Brewery 13, 127
Avon Park, Florida 170

Baker Bowl 86, 137
Ball, Phil 22, 24
Barrett, Charlie 37, 39–40, 42, 44
baseball: early history in St. Louis 3–5; gambling scandals 4, 15, 174; rule changes 15–18, 57–58
Bell, Herman 40, 156
Bell, Lester 44, 104–**105**, 144, 149, 154, 156, 159, 162, 179
Blades, Ray 46, 107, 117, 179
Boston Braves 75–76, 89–90, 100–103, 114–115, 119–120, 134–135
Bottomley, Jim 42–43, **78**, 115, 117, 144, 179; lawsuit 79–80
Braves Field 89–90
Breadon, Sam **20**, 25, 114, 136, 153, 164; early life 21; Branch Rickey conflict 178–180; Rogers Hornsby feud 116, 132–133, 169–176
Brooklyn Dodgers 72–73, 88–90, 103–104, 112–114, 117–118, 140–, 180

Carey, Max 60, 123
championship celebrations 142–143; 152–153; 164–167
Chicago Cubs 62–63, 66–68, 84–85, 92–93, 116–117, 129, 177–178
Cincinnati Reds 65–66, 70–71, 77–80, 83–84, 98–100, 129–131, 144
Clarke, Fred 123
Cobb, Ty 174
Combs, Earle 147
Comiskey, Charles 5
Cuckoo Gang 14, 97, 128, 147, 168–169; *see also* gangs

Dean, Wayland 120–121
Dempsey-Tunney Fight 141–142
Douthit, Taylor 47–**48**, 84, 144–145, 156–157, 170, 179
Dugan, Joe 151, 156
Dyer, Eddie 38–39

Ebbets Field 88
Egan's Rats 10; *see also* gangs
exhibition games 63, 86, 110, 114–116, 132–135, 139–140

farm system 24–25, 148, 180
Fisk, Carlton 163
Fletcher, Art 76, 137
Flowers, D'Arcy "Jake" 45–46
Forbes Field 64
Frisch, Frankie 111, 118–119, 170–171, 178–179
Fruin, Jeremiah 3

gangs 10, 14, 97, 109, 128, 147, 168–169; *see also* Cuckoo Gang; Egan's Rats; Green Ones (Green Onions); "Jellyroll" Hogan Gang
Gehrig, Lou 147, 149, 158, 161
Gerk, Joseph 147
Gould, James 74–75, 77, 96, 101, 111, 125–126, 139, 169, 173
Grand Avenue Park 4; *see also* Sportsman's Park
Greater St. Louis Exposition 69, 127–129, 142

Green Ones (Green Onions) 10, 14; *see also* gangs

Hafey, Charles "Chick" 46, 99, 139, 156; vision problems 85–86, 157, 170, 179
Haines, Jesse "Pops" 34–35, 154, 160–161, 179
Haley, Martin 34, 58, 71, 76, 99, 101, 107, 112, 140–141
Hallahan, Bill "Wild Bill" 38
Hayes, Irwin 79–80
Heydler, John 57, 77, 107, 137, 164, 172, 176–177
Holm, Roscoe "Wattie" 48, 157, 159
Hornsby, Jeannette 148, 153, 177
Hornsby, Rogers 26, **28**, 144, 153, **155**, **165**; Branch Rickey feud 29–31, 116, 170; contract dispute 169; early life and baseball career 27–29; end of baseball career 177–178; feuds with teammates 28–29, 177–178; gambling addiction 27, 170, 173, 177–178; injuries 71–72, 76, 95–96, 100, 105–107, 113, 130, 133, 177–178; mother's death 148; named Cardinals manager 31–32; Sam Breadon feud 116, 132–133, 169–177; spring training regimen 51–53; traded to New York Giants 170–175
Hoyt, Waite 148, 156–157, 161
Huggins, Miller 28, 148, 159–160
Huntzinger, Walter 39, 93
Hyland, Robert 73, 85–86, 96, 98–100, 106, 112, 156

"Jellyroll" Hogan Gang 14; *see also* gangs
Johnson, Ban 57, 174
Johnson, Sylvester "Syl" 39, 71, 121, 128

Index

Keen, Victor 39, 61, 112, 179
Killefer, Bill 40–41, 51, 93, 98, 134, 169, 172
Klem, Bill 137
"Knothole Gang" 24–25
Koenig, Mark 151, 158

Landis, Kenesaw Mountain 15, 26–27, 153, 160, 164, 173–174, 178, 180
Lardner, Ring 149
Lazzeri, Tony 147–148, 151, 158, 161–163
Leonard, Dutch 174
Lindbergh, Charles 17, 59
Lloyd, Clarence 141
Luque, Adolpho 65, 80

Mails, John Walter "Duster" 37, 54–55, 58, 66, 70–71
McCarthy, Joe 92–93, 95
McGraw, John 30–31, 39, 46, 74–75, 118–119, 142, 171, 177
McNamee, Graham 149–150, 159–161
Meusel, Bob 147, 159, 163
Miller, Victor 19–20, 141, 152–153
Moore, Frank 177
Motion Pictures 146, 150–151
Mueller, Clarence "Heine" 47, 67, 83, 106; traded to New York Giants 88

New Braunfels, Texas 54
New York Giants 74–75, 87–88, 106–108, 111–112, 118–119, 138–139, 141–144, 176–177
New York Yankees 147–164

O'Farrell, Bob 41, 103, 105, 121–*122*, 145, 161, 163, 175, 179–180

Pennock, Herb 147, 149–150, 157–158, 161

Philadelphia Phillies 76–77, 86–87, 104–105, 110–111, 120–121, 136–138
Pittsburgh Pirates 60–61, 63–65, 91, 93–94, 98; "Little World's Series" 122–126, 131–133
Polo Grounds 87
prohibition: St. Louis 13–14, 33, 82–83; United States 9

radio 8, 12, 15–16. 74, 128–129, 149, 154
Redland Field 65, 131
Reese, John "Bonesetter" 133
Reinhart, Art 37–38, 100, 113, 156
Rhem, Charles "Flint" 35–*36*, 155; alcoholism 101–102, 161, 179
Rickey, Branch 22–*24*, 25–26, 143, 161, 165; early life and education 22; managerial career 23–26, 29; professional baseball career 23; Rogers Hornsby feud 29–31, 116, 170, 172; Sam Breadon conflict 178–180
Ruth, Babe 17, 147–148, 150, 152, 154–*155*, 156–158, 163–*165*
Rutherford, William murder trial 69–70

St. Louis: African Americans 10–11, 50–51; air pollution 12; civic improvements 11–12, 69, 82, 97, 109–110; founding and growth 10; German immigration 10; Irish immigration 10; Italian immigration 10; Prohibition 13–14, 33, 82–83
St. Louis Brown Stockings *see* St. Louis Browns
St. Louis Browns 3–5, 22–23, 56, 178

St. Louis Stars 50–51
Shawkey, Bob 159
Sherdel, Bill "Wee Willie" 36, 113, *139*–140, 149, 157–158, 179
Shocker, Urban 148, 151–152, 159
Smith, Jack 48–49, 63
Snyder, Frank "Pancho" 121–122
Sothoron, Allen 40–41, 125, 132
Southworth, Billy "Billy the Kid" 75, 104, 142, 144, 152, 159; traded to St. Louis Cardinals 88–*89*
Speaker, Tris 174
Sportsman's Park 4, 22, 33, 56–*57*, 79, 153–154, 165–167; *see also* Grand Avenue Park
Steinberg, Mark 173
Stockton, Roy 28–29, 31, 100, 162, 172
Sunday, Billy 9, 55
Sylvester, Johnny 156–157

television 168
Thevenow, Tommy 43–*45*, 138, 145, 152, 160–161, 179
Toporcer, George "Specs" 44–45, 160

Uhrig's Cave 82–83

Vance, Dazzy 72
Veeck, William 178
Veiled Prophet 146–147
Vick, Henry "Ernie" 41–42
Von der Ahe, Chris 4–5, 20

Warwick, Firman "Bill" 41–42
Williams, Cy 76
Williams, Otto 111, 142
Wilson, Hack 62, 67
Wilson, Jimmie 137

www.ingramcontent.com/pod-product-compliance
Ingram Content Group UK Ltd.
Pitfield, Milton Keynes, MK11 3LW, UK
UKHW051850210426
5322IPUK00025B/639